W•MEN
IN THE
CHURCH

WOMEN
IN THE
CHURCH

AN ANALYSIS AND
APPLICATION OF
1 TIMOTHY 2:9–15

SECOND EDITION

EDITED BY
ANDREAS J. KÖSTENBERGER
AND THOMAS R. SCHREINER

Baker Academic

Grand Rapids, Michigan

Published by Baker Academic
a division of Baker Publishing Group
P.O. Box 6287, Grand Rapids, MI 49516-6287
www.bakeracademic.com

Printed in the United States of America

Library of Congress Cataloging-in-Publication Data
Women in the church : an analysis and application of 1 Timothy 2:9–15 / edited by Andreas J. Köstenberger and Thomas R. Schreiner.—2nd ed.
    p.   cm.
Includes bibliographical references and indexes.
ISBN 0-8010-2904-X (pbk.)
    1. Women in Christianity—Biblical teaching. 2. Bible. N.T. Timothy, 1st, II, 9–15—Criticism, interpretation, etc. I. Köstenberger, Andreas J., 1957– II. Schreiner, Thomas R.
BS2745.6.W65W65 2005
227′.8306—dc22
                                    2005009477

Contents

Contributors

Henry Scott Baldwin (Ph.D., Trinity Evangelical Divinity School) is associate professor of New Testament literature and language at Tyndale Theological Seminary, Amsterdam, Netherlands.

S. M. Baugh (Ph.D., University of California, Irvine) is professor of New Testament at Westminster Seminary California, Escondido, California.

Andreas J. Köstenberger (Ph.D., Trinity Evangelical Divinity School) is professor of New Testament and Greek and director of Ph.D./Th.M. studies at Southeastern Baptist Theological Seminary, Wake Forest, North Carolina.

Dorothy Kelley Patterson (Th.D., University of South Africa) is professor of theology in women's studies at Southwestern Baptist Theological Seminary, Fort Worth, Texas.

Thomas R. Schreiner (Ph.D., Fuller Theological Seminary) is professor of New Testament interpretation and associate dean for Scripture and interpretation at The Southern Baptist Theological Seminary, Louisville, Kentucky.

Robert W. Yarbrough (Ph.D., University of Aberdeen) is associate professor of New Testament and department chair at Trinity Evangelical Divinity School, Deerfield, Illinois.

PREFACE

Ten years after the publication of the first edition of *Women in the Church*, the debate over women's roles in the church is as fierce as it has ever been. Not that significant new biblical information has come to light—Scripture does not change, and no major new data have been discovered that have a bearing on the interpretation of 1 Timothy 2:9–15—but the larger culture continues to press on the church to recognize women as men's equals without any distinctions in function or role.

For this reason the witness to the teaching of Scripture borne by the present volume in our politically correct context with its largely egalitarian worldview continues to be both timely and needed. To enhance the work's usefulness, material judged to be less central to the overall argument of the book has been omitted, while a new chapter on application has been added. All included essays have been updated in light of recent developments in scholarship pertaining to the interpretation of 1 Timothy 2:9–15.

In the new streamlined format of the argument of *Women in the Church*, Steven Baugh continues to maintain that first-century Ephesus was not a feminist society, so that egalitarian attempts to construe the present passage as Paul's effort to counteract unruly women in this city in Asia Minor are without a proper foundation. The chapters by Henry Baldwin and Andreas Köstenberger on the meaning of αὐθεντέω and the Greek syntax of 1 Timothy 2:12 have held up well under ten years of critical scrutiny. They are included here again in an updated format.

The second half of the book is devoted to a thorough verse-by-verse commentary on 1 Timothy 2:9–15; principles guiding the interpretation of the present passage; and a new chapter on the application of its teachings by Dorothy Patterson. As a woman who has been involved in significant ministry for several decades, Dr. Patterson is highly qualified to comment on the passage's implications for women's roles in the church. She argues that women ought to exercise their God-given spiritual gifts within biblical parameters in obedience to God.

It is the desire of the editors and contributors to this volume that the teachings of Scripture on this vital topic will continue to be upheld and commended to all those who sincerely seek God's guidance. May women of any age who seek the Lord on how to serve him find a reliable word from God in the pages of this book. And may pastors whom God has put in charge of teaching his Word and of leading congregations in the truth be equipped to know and be encouraged to communicate biblical truth in this critical area.

To be sure, the tempter will continue to whisper into women's ears, "Has God really said . . . ?" But contrary to the devil's charge, the boundaries set by God are good, intending to enhance, rather than harm, women's fulfillment as they live out their God-given roles. It would clearly be unrealistic to expect a world that misconstrues equality as sameness and that seeks to erode any meaningful distinction between male and female (witness the push toward gay marriage) to embrace the biblical counsel on male-female roles and relationships.

But it should be different with those in the church. As the present volume makes clear, all the various elements affecting the interpretation of 1 Timothy 2:9–15 combine to suggest that it is not God's will for women to teach or have authority over men in the church, so that the offices of pastor-teacher as well as elder ought to be reserved for men. These elements are the first-century background, the meaning of αὐθεντέω and the Greek syntax of 1 Timothy 2:12, the interpretation of 1 Timothy 2:9–15 in its proper context, and proper principles of interpretation.

As you read this book, may God the Holy Spirit guide you to have not only a mind to understand but also the will to obey the teaching of the present passage, and may you find that personal fulfillment comes, not from rebelling against God's will, but from obeying it. *Soli Deo gloria.*

Andreas J. Köstenberger
Thomas R. Schreiner

ABBREVIATIONS

ABD	*Anchor Bible Dictionary*, ed. D. N. Freedman, 6 vols. (New York: Doubleday, 1992)
AJA	*American Journal of Archaeology*
ANRW	*Aufstieg und Niedergang der römischen Welt*, ed. H. Temporini and W. Haase (Berlin: de Gruyter, 1972–)
Ant.	*Jewish Antiquities*
BAGD	W. Bauer, W. F. Arndt, F. W. Gingrich, and F. W. Danker, *Greek-English Lexicon of the New Testament*, 2nd ed. (Chicago: University of Chicago Press, 1979)
BDAG	*A Greek-English Lexicon of the New Testament and Other Early Christian Literature*, rev. and ed. F. W. Danker, 3rd ed. (Chicago: University of Chicago Press, 2000)
BDF	F. Blass, A. Debrunner, and R. W. Funk, *A Greek Grammar of the New Testament and Other Early Christian Literature* (Chicago: University of Chicago Press, 1961)
BGU	*Ägyptische Urkunden aus den Königlichen/Staatlichen Museen zu Berlin, Griechische Urkunden* (Berlin, 1895–)
Bibl. hist.	*Bibliotheca historica*
BMC	*Catalogue of the Greek Coins in Ionia*, by B. V. Head, Catalogue of the Greek Coins in the British Museum 14 (1892; reprint, Bologna: Forni, 1964)
BZ	*Biblische Zeitschrift*
ClPhil	*Classical Philology*
Descr.	*Graeciae descriptión*
DGE	*Diccionario Griego-Español*, ed. F. Adrados (Madrid: Consejo Superior de Investigaciones Cientificas, Instituto Filologia, 1991)
Diod. Sic.	Diodorus Siculus

EQ	*Evangelical Quarterly*
G&R	*Greece & Rome*
Geogr.	*Geographica*
GRBS	*Greek, Roman and Byzantine Studies*
Hist.	*Historia*
HUCA	*Hebrew Union College Annual*
IBM	*The Collection of Ancient Greek Inscriptions in the British Museum,* ed. E. L. Hicks, part 3 (Oxford: Clarendon, 1890)
IvE	*Die Inschriften von Ephesos,* ed. H. Wankel et al., 8 vols. in 11 (Bonn: Habelt, 1979–84)
IvM	*Die Inschriften von Magnesia am Maeander,* ed. O. Kern (Berlin: Spemann, 1900)
IvPr	*Die Inschriften von Priene,* ed. C. J. Fredrich and F. Hiller von Gaertringen (Berlin: Reimer, 1906)
IvPrusias	*Die Inschriften von Prusias ad Hypium,* ed. W. Ameling (Bonn: Habelt, 1985)
JANESCU	*Journal of the Ancient Near Eastern Society of Columbia University*
JETS	*Journal of the Evangelical Theological Society*
JÖAI	*Jahreshefte des Österreichischen Archäologischen Instituts in Wien*
JRS	*Journal of Roman Studies*
JSNTSup	Journal for the Study of the New Testament: Supplement Series
KJV	King James Version
Kl. Pauly	*Der Kleine Pauly: Lexikon der Antike,* ed. K. Ziegler and W. Sontheimer, 5 vols. (Munich: Deutscher Taschenbuch, 1979)
Lampe	G. W. H. Lampe, ed., *Patristic Greek Lexicon* (Oxford: Clarendon, 1968)
LCL	Loeb Classical Library (Cambridge, MA: Harvard University Press)
Louw and Nida	J. P. Louw and E. A. Nida, eds., *Greek-English Lexicon of the New Testament Based on Semantic Domains,* 2nd ed., 2 vols. (New York: United Bible Societies, 1989)
LSJ	H. G. Liddell and R. Scott, *A Greek-English Lexicon,* rev. H. S. Jones (Oxford: Clarendon; New York: Oxford University Press, 1996)
Mayser	Edwin Mayser, *Grammatik der griechischen Papyri aus der Ptolemäerzeit,* Band 1 (Berlin: de Gruyter, 1970)
Mor.	*Moralia*
Moulton and Milligan	J. H. Moulton and G. Milligan, *The Vocabulary of the Greek New Testament: Illustrated from the Papyri and Other Non-literary Sources* (repr., Grand Rapids: Eerdmans, 1963)
NAB	New American Bible
NASB	New American Standard Bible
Neue Inschriften VIII	D. Knibbe and B. Iplikçioglu, "Neue Inschriften aus Ephesos VIII," *Jahreshefte des Österreichischen Archäologischen Instituts in Wien* 53 (1981–82): Hauptblatt, 87–150

Neue Inschriften IX	D. Knibbe and B. Iplikçioglu, "Neue Inschriften aus Ephesos IX," *Jahreshefte des Österreichischen Archäologischen Instituts in Wien* 55 (1984): Hauptblatt, 107–35
Neue Inschriften X	D. Knibbe and B. Iplikçioglu, "Neue Inschriften aus Ephesos X," *Jahreshefte des Österreichischen Archäologischen Instituts in Wien* 55 (1984): Hauptblatt, 137–49
Neue Inschriften XI	D. Knibbe, H. Engelmann, and B. Iplikçioglu, "Neue Inschriften aus Ephesos XI," *Jahreshefte des Österreichischen Archäologischen Instituts in Wien* 59 (1989): Beiblatt, 163–237
Neue Inschriften XII	D. Knibbe, H. Engelmann, and B. Iplikçioglu, "Neue Inschriften aus Ephesos XII," *Jahreshefte des Österreichischen Archäologischen Instituts in Wien* 62 (1993): Hauptblatt, 113–50
Neue Inschriften XIII	H. Engelmann, "Neue Inschriften aus Ephesos XIII," *Jahreshefte des Österreichischen Archäologischen Instituts in Wien* 69 (2000)
New Docs	*New Documents Illustrating Early Christianity*, ed. G. H. R. Horsley and S. R. Llewelyn (North Ryde, NSW, Australia: Ancient History Documentary Research Centre, Macquarie University, 1981–)
NIV	New International Version
NTS	*New Testament Studies*
OCD	*The Oxford Classical Dictionary*, ed. N. Hammond and H. Scullard, 2nd ed. (Oxford: Clarendon, 1970)
PFamTebt	*A Family Archive from Tebtunis*, ed. B. A. van Groningen (Lugdunum Batavorum [Leiden]: E. J. Brill, 1950)
PLond	*Greek Papyri in the British Museum*, vols. 1–2, ed. F. G. Kenyon (1893, 1898); vol. 3, ed. F. G. Kenyon and H. I. Bell (1907); vols. 4–5, ed. H. I. Bell (1910, 1917)
POxy	*The Oxyrhynchus Papyri*, ed. B. P. Grenfell, A. S. Hunt, et al. (1898–1972)
Preisigke	Friedrich Preisigke, *Wörterbuch der griechischen Papyrusurkunden* (Berlin: Erben, 1925)
PW	A. Pauly, G. Wissowa, and W. Kroll, eds., *Paulys Real Encyclopädie der classischen Altertumswissenschaft* (Stuttgart: Metzler, 1894–1963)
PWSup	G. Wissowa, W. Kroll, and K. Witte, *Paulys Real-Encyclopädie der classischen Altertumswissenschaft, Supplement* (Stuttgart: Metzler, 1903–78)
RAM	T. R. S. Broughton, "Roman Asia Minor," in *An Economic Survey of Ancient Rome*, ed. T. Frank, vol. 4 (Baltimore: Johns Hopkins University Press, 1938), 499–950
RRAM	David Magie, *Roman Rule in Asia Minor*, 2 vols. (Princeton, NJ: Princeton University Press, 1950)
RSV	Revised Standard Version
SBLDS	Society of Biblical Literature Dissertation Series
SBLSBS	SBL Sources for Biblical Studies
SEG	Supplementum epigraphicum graecum (1923–)

SEHHW	Mikhail Rostovtzeff, *The Social and Economic History of the Hellenistic World*, 3 vols. (Oxford: Clarendon, 1941)
Sel. Pap.	A. S. Hunt and C. C. Edgar, *Select Papyri*, 2 vols., LCL (Cambridge, MA: Harvard University Press; London: Heinemann, 1932–34)
SNTSMS	Society for New Testament Studies Monograph Series
Sophocles	E. A. Sophocles, *Greek Lexicon of the Roman and Byzantine Periods (from BC 146 to AD 1100)* (New York: Scribner, 1887)
ST	*Studia Theologica*
TDNT	*Theological Dictionary of the New Testament*, ed. G. Kittel and G. Friedrich, trans. G. W. Bromiley, 10 vols. (Grand Rapids: Eerdmans, 1964–76)
TLG	*Thesaurus Linguae Graecae*
TynBul	*Tyndale Bulletin*
Vit. soph.	*Vitae sophistarum*
WTJ	*Westminster Theological Journal*
ZNW	*Zeitschrift für die neutestamentliche Wissenschaft*
ZPE	*Zeitschrift für Papyrologie und Epigraphik*

I

A FOREIGN WORLD

Ephesus in the First Century

S. M. BAUGH

Some serious obstacles face anyone who investigates the sociohistorical background of 1 Timothy 2:12–15 in first-century Ephesus. Although there are some valuable standard resources for Asia Minor and we do possess a good amount of primary archaeological and epigraphical materials, our passage warrants a narrow inquiry into the social role of women in early Ephesus.[1] This rather focused issue is hampered by a lack of directly relevant scholarly research to guide us. While we do have a few valuable articles or sections in books, there is no comprehensive investigation into the social fabric of ancient Asia Minor or of Ephesus in our period and how women fit into it. We do have studies of Roman or of classical Greek women, but work in Asia Minor has not been done with the same amount of energy. And we must not make the tempting mistake of imputing the situation of Roman or of classical Greek women to first-century Ephesus; these were quite different eras and cultures with distinct traditions and social institutions. There are indeed similarities, but differences extending even between Ephesus

13

and its contemporaries like Smyrna or Pergamum could trip us up if we were not careful.

Let me briefly illustrate this last problem. In his book *Jewish Communities in Asia Minor,* Paul Trebilco has a chapter titled "The Prominence of Women in Asia Minor," in which he concludes that "at least some Jewish communities in Asia Minor gave an unusually prominent place to women."[2] To arrive at this conclusion on Jewish women, Trebilco makes a general argument for the prominent "leadership" role of women in Asia Minor in general.[3] This is where more detailed treatment of the evidence is required.

For instance, Trebilco reports that twenty-eight women of Asia Minor are attested as holding the municipal magistracy as *prytanis* (πρύτανις) from the first to the third centuries in eight cities of Asia Minor. While we are not explicitly told which cities these are, the unwary could conclude from this evidence that it represents a considerable number of *prytaneis* and that since Ephesus was a city of Asia Minor, it must have had a number of prominent female politicians in Paul's day.[4] But the prytany of Ephesus has its own unique history, which Trebilco's quick survey, understandably, does not describe. We will look more carefully at the Ephesian prytany below (see under *"Prytanis"*), but for now let me point out that no women served as *prytanis* in first-century Ephesus according to our extant primary sources, which provide the names of quite a few male *prytaneis* in this period.[5] Furthermore, the office of *prytanis* in Pauline Ephesus apparently had no political power but was changed after Augustus to a minor priesthood of Hestia Boulaia, held sometimes by unmarried girls probably in their early teen years or younger.

Hopefully this shows the need to read general treatments relating to the historical situation behind 1 Timothy 2 very carefully and only in conjunction with a more focused study of ancient Ephesus. Even this proposed project is complicated by the fact that evidence for late-second to mid-third century Ephesus itself must always be read in light of the severe economic and social upheavals happening at this time, not least of which was the sack of the temple of Artemis Ephesia in AD 262/63 by a marauding band of Goths, from which Ephesus never fully recovered.[6] In other words, third-century Ephesus was quite different from Paul and Timothy's city, and the evidence for this later period must be interpreted with this fact in view.

A final complication facing us in our own inquiry into the background of 1 Timothy 2:12–15 is a popular portrayal of first-century Ephesus—sometimes with apparent scholarly foundation—as a very singular feminist society. For example, we may still read that Ephesus was "a bastion and bulwark of women's rights"[7] in the midst of a uniformly unfeminist Greco-Roman world.[8] Its renowned state goddess, Artemis

Ephesia, is said to have been "a powerful female deity who elevated the status of women,"[9] "a symbol of Women's Liberation"[10] and of "matriarchy."[11] Her cult statue alone—"a multi-mammary grotesque"[12]—is said to attest to a society overshadowed by a runaway fertility cult serviced by multitudes of priestesses, indeed, sacred prostitutes, eunuchs, and hermaphrodites.[13] The Amazons (mythical female warriors), sometimes regarded as the founders of Ephesus, were symbolic of a general "sex reversal" in this city that engaged in anti-male cult practices.

What makes this portrait of ancient Ephesus important is that it often serves a popular egalitarian reading of 1 Timothy 2:9–15. For example, Richard and Catherine Kroeger have suggested:

> Such a pagan element, based upon sex hostility and reversal of gender roles, may well have found a place in a cult practice among the dissidents in the congregation at Ephesus. . . . If this is the case, the condemnation (i.e., 1 Tim. 2:12) is not directed against women participating in leadership but rather against a monopoly on religious power by women.[14]

Hence, in their opinion, Paul required only that *Ephesian* women not teach or exercise authority over men, since they were infected by an anomalous cultural outlook. His words do not relate to women per se.

In light of the obstacles outlined above, it seems imperative that we make a concerted effort to positively present the actual socioreligious position of women in Pauline Ephesus against the broader background of the whole of Ephesian society. This is not easy to do in such a brief space, so in the notes I will give many references to primary and secondary evidence that supports my more summary observations.

Because of this focus on Ephesus itself, I do not intend to spend much time critiquing today's reconstructions of the Ephesian situation in this essay. If I did, my line of argument would be entirely negative. For instance, one way to deny that this city was a bastion of women's rights or to deny that Artemis Ephesia was a fertility deity with eunuchs and sacred prostitutes among her cult personnel, and so on, is by evaluating the evidence (or lack of evidence) adduced by those who maintain the "feminist Ephesus" position.[15] We would find it wanting.[16] But this does not provide the reader with a feel for what Ephesus was truly like, and that is what I wish to do. When you know the real Ephesus, you will find the "feminist Ephesus" unacceptable.

My general purpose, then, is to present Pauline Ephesus to you. What was its culture like? Who was in charge? How did the Ephesians worship their state goddess, Artemis? What was she like? In the process of describing Ephesus in this general fashion, I hope to accomplish a secondary purpose as well: to show that the "feminist Ephesus" construct is not historically plausible. I will conclude by addressing some specific issues relating to the situation behind 1 Timothy.

Before we begin, let me emphasize from the start that there is indeed evidence that a few women held positions of high honors and patronage in the early centuries of the Christian era in Ephesus, Asia Minor, and elsewhere.[17] This essay is not intended to dispute such evidence. It is even possible that the church enjoyed patronage by some women, which might explain why Paul did not want that patronage to translate into the exercise of spiritual authority and entrance into the teaching office. But this plausible scenario is quite different from saying that Paul's injunction is restricted to ancient Ephesus and therefore not applicable today because of its peculiar socioreligious situation.

Historical Sketch

Ephesus, along with other colonies, was founded on the west coast of modern Turkey by Greek adventurers roughly around the time of the Israelite judges.[18] The physical setting for ancient Ephesus was highly favorable, especially for commerce. It had a natural harbor for overseas trade, and a royal road up the nearby Maeander River valley connected inland for important eastern passage and trade.[19]

Some myths have it that the Amazons were the original founders of Ephesus (Strabo, *Geogr.* 11.5.4; Pausanias, *Descr.* 7.4–5). This has been used as evidence of Ephesus's supposed "feminist" character. The Ephesians themselves, however, officially ascribed the foundation of their city to a Greek hero named Androclus. An oracle directed him to found the city at the site where he killed a boar while hunting (Strabo, *Geogr.* 14.1.3, 21; Pliny, *Naturalis historia* 5.115). The Ephesians called Androclus "the creator of our city" (*IvE* 501) and celebrated the city's foundation annually as "Androclus day" (*IvE* 644).[20]

Ephesus's cultural heritage was Greek. While it possessed the trappings of democracy, it had no grand tradition of equality like Athens, equality among male citizens, that is. What Theodor Mommsen said of Asia Minor in general was true of Ephesus specifically: "Asia Minor was just old subject-territory and, under its Persian as under its Hellenic rulers, accustomed to monarchic organization; here less than in Hellas did useless recollections and vague hopes carry men away beyond the limited municipal horizon of the present, and there was not much of this sort to disturb the peaceful enjoyment of such happiness in life as was possible under the existing circumstances."[21] From the time of its capture by King Croesus of Lydia in the sixth century BC, Ephesus never enjoyed independence from foreign domination. Croesus, Cyrus, Darius, Athens,

Sparta, Alexander, Lysimachus, the Seleucids, the Attalids, Mithridates, and finally the Romans had all captured or controlled Ephesus in their turns. The city's political life was dominated by kings, tyrants, satraps, bureaucrats, and proconsuls, but never by radical democrats. Ephesus never adopted an egalitarian democratic ideology that would necessitate feminism or, minimally, the inclusion of women in public offices.[22] Ephesus's mood was pragmatic and politically accommodating. "All is flux" was a famous dictum of the Ephesian philosopher Heraclitus, well expressing the city's adaptability to changing political climates. At the time of Paul, the political climate was Roman—not feminist.

Although Ephesus had suffered terrible economic and political turmoil in the first century BC, the Pax Augusta inaugurated a golden age of peace lasting roughly two centuries. Augustus himself, during a brief stop at Ephesus after Actium, confirmed the city's place as the provincial capital. Paul stepped into a city that was well on its way to eclipsing old rivals Miletus, Smyrna, and Pergamum as "the greatest and first metropolis of Asia" (*IvE* 22 et al.). With a population somewhere around one hundred thousand, Ephesus eventually was to become one of the largest and most important cities in the empire next to Rome.[23]

Political Institutions

The municipal organization of Ephesus had formal resemblance to the Athenian democratic model, with the male citizen body (δῆμος) divided into tribes (φυλαί) comprising the state assembly (ἐκκλησία).[24] The municipal ruling body was the 450-member state council (βουλή), presided over by the secretary of the people (ὁ γραμματεὺς τοῦ δήμου).[25]

There were a number of primary magistrates and civic groups at Ephesus. No women are known to have filled these magistracies at Ephesus in the first century. Furthermore, there were no women's civic groups to compare with the state council, *gerousia,* or *ephebia.*

Table 1.1
Male Magistrates of Ephesus

Roman Proconsul	ἀνθύπατος	Supreme de facto governor over all areas of life
Secretary of the People	ὁ γραμματεὺς τοῦ δήμου	Chief civil magistrate of Ephesus
Councilor	βουλευτής	Member of the state council (βουλή)
General	στρατηγός	Executive magistrate

Market Director	ἀγορανόμος	Control of grain supply, economy, and market
Gymnasiarch	γυμνασίαρχος	Oversight of culture and education in gymnasia; financial underwriting (a "liturgy," not a magistracy)

Table 1.2
Male Civic Groups in Ephesus

State Council	βουλή	Chief governmental body with oversight of all public affairs; 450 members
The People, Assembly	ὁ δῆμος ἐκκλησία	Male citizen body that ratified decisions of state council; 1,000–2,000 members
Gerousia	γερουσία	Broad extraconstitutional influence over religion, finances, culture, etc.; 300+ members
Ephebia	ἐφηβεία	Aristocratic cultural youth group (the group for younger boys is παιδές; older youths are νέοι); under an ephebarch and gymnasiarch

City councilors were normally chosen by lot from each tribe for an annual term. Under Roman influence, though, the Ephesian council began to resemble the aristocratic Roman senate, with perpetual, even hereditary terms of office.[26] This is just one example of extensive evidence for the growing influence of Roman cultural and political ideas (*Romanitas*) in Pauline Ephesus, which appears to have been more far-reaching than in Palestine.[27]

Roman *patria potestas* ("patriarchy"),[28] merged with the Greek institutions of male citizenship and male magistrates, *gerousia, ephebia,* and gymnasia, did not make for female cultural dominance. Even though women had some public roles at Ephesus, leadership in the political and social spheres was solidly in the hands of exclusively male institutions.[29]

Religious Climate

Although Artemis Ephesia dominated the public religion of her hometown, the Ephesians were ordinary Hellenic polytheists. A full house of Greek deities as well as some imports are in evidence from the temples, altars, and dedications in Ephesus. Familiar names include Aphrodite, Apollo, Asclepius, Athena, Dionysus, Pluto, Poseidon, and Zeus. The latter appears as Zeus Keraunios, Zeus Ktesios, Zeus Polieus,

Zeus Melichios, and Zeus Soter.[30] The more esoteric cults include the mysteries of Demeter Karpophoros, private house cults of Dionysus, the public cult of Dionysus "before the city,"[31] and a cult of God Most High ("Theos Hypsistos"), whose appellation may or may not have come about through Jewish influence.

Ephesus had earlier been under the control of the Ptolemies, so it is no surprise to find a fairly vigorous cult of Isis and Serapis, even Anubis (*IvE* 1231 and 1213), probably revived by Cleopatra's visit to the city in the days of Mark Antony.[32] Local Anatolian deities were represented at Ephesus by the Phrygian god Zeus Sabazios and by the Phrygian mother goddess, Meter. Some worshipers, covering all bases, dedicated their offerings "to all the gods and goddesses" (Neue Inschriften VIII, no. 131). At least one scholar believes that another dedication was made "to the Pantheion" in a truly pantheistic sense.[33]

The majority of these deities, even the goddesses, were served by male priests at Ephesus.[34] This is a bit unusual, since "a priestess very commonly officiated for goddesses and a priest for gods" in Greek cults.[35] Certainly "a bastion and bulwark of women's rights" would have had as many priestesses in evidence as in contemporary cities—not fewer as we find at Ephesus.[36]

The Artemisium

Ephesus was not a temple-city like the oracular centers of Claros or Delphi, yet the temple of Artemis dominated the city in many ways, partly by sheer size.[37] The Artemisium was the largest building in the Greek world, about four times larger than the Athenian Parthenon. It boasted 127 massive columns decorated with friezes. Its adornments by some of the most famous painters and sculptors of antiquity made it one of the Seven Wonders of the World (Pliny, *Naturalis historia* 16.213–14; 35.92–93; 36.95–97; Pausanias, *Descr.* 6.3.15–16).[38] Hence its fame: "What man is there after all who does not know that the city of the Ephesians is guardian of the temple of the great Artemis?" (Acts 19:35).[39] And its considerable tourist appeal brought "no small income" to many Ephesians outside the silversmith guild (Acts 19:24–27).

The Artemisium illustrates the intimate connection between the economic and the religious spheres of life at Ephesus, and it was the city's dominant economic power. The temple's influence was especially felt in two areas: banking and landholding. As a bank and moneylender, the Artemisium was "the common treasury of Asia" (Aelius Aristides, *Oratio* 23.24), holding in deposit "not alone money of the Ephesians but also of aliens and of people from all parts of the world, and in some cases

states and kings" (Dio Chrysostom, *Oratio* 31.54). The extant boundary stones show that Artemis, as a landholder, owned extensive, rich
farmlands in the Cayster River valley. A rough estimate shows her in
possession of about seventy-seven thousand acres of land, though she
may well have owned more lands whose boundary markers have not
yet been found.[40]

The Temple Hierarchy

Who held the actual reins of power over the considerable wealth
and sway of the Artemisium? We know of sacred guilds that administered Artemis's various resources, but they were probably bureaucratic
agencies that followed the policies of someone else.[41] What we find is
something entirely expected for a Hellenic city of the imperial era: su-
preme control over the Artemisium was exercised by civil magistrates,
with active meddling by Roman governors. There are various ways to
substantiate this, but the easiest is with one clear example deriving
from the lifetime of Paul. The following is a portion of an edict of the
provincial proconsul Paullus Fabius Persicus, possibly at the personal
direction of Claudius himself:

> The temple of Artemis herself—which is an adornment to the whole prov-
> ince because of the magnificence of the building, the antiquity of the
> worship of the goddess, and the abundance of the incomes granted to the
> goddess by the Emperor (or, Augustus)—is being deprived of its proper
> revenues. These had been sufficient for the maintenance and for the adorn-
> ment of the votive offerings, but they are being diverted for the illegal
> wants of the leaders of the *koinon*,[42] according to what they consider will
> bring them profit. . . . While using the appearance of the divine temple as
> a pretext, they sell the priesthoods as if at public auction.[43] Indeed, they
> invite men of every kind to their sale, then they do not select the most
> suitable men upon whose heads the crown would fittingly be placed.
> (Instead) they restrict incomes to those who are being consecrated to as
> (little) as they are willing to accept, in order that they themselves might
> appropriate as much as possible. (*IvE* 17–19 [AD 44])

This edict shows that the Roman government—and perhaps the emperor personally as *pontifex maximus*[44]—believed it held authority to
regulate and oversee religious affairs in Ephesus as in other provincial
cities.[45] Furthermore, the Persicus inscription shows that officials in
local government had direct control over access to the Artemisium's
priesthood. The wedding between civil government officials and religious

affairs was normal for Hellenic cities, where "a magistrate was usually a priest as a part of his official functions."[46]

If Ephesus truly "stood as a bastion of feminine supremacy in religion,"[47] we would expect to find either priestesses or other women controlling the resources of the Artemisium and appointments to its offices. Instead, Ephesian religious affairs were governed by the Roman and municipal authorities, who were decidedly male.

Table 1.3
Male Religious Groups in Ephesus

Priest of Artemis	ἱερεὺς Ἀρτέμιδος	Probably cultic duties and financial underwriting (not the same as the *megabyzos*)
Kouretes	κουρῆτες	Broad oversight over cult of Artemis and of Hestia Boulaia; important cultic duties; 6–9 members annually
Neopoios	νεοποιός (νεοποιής)	Oversight of Artemisium building and furnishings
Essene	ἐσσήν	Annual priesthood requiring cultic purity
Various bureaus and groups of the Artemisium		The rent office, sacred wine tasters, sacred victors, hierophants, etc.
Megabyzos	μεγάβυζος	Obsolete eunuch priest of the Artemisium
Prytanis	πρύτανις	Priesthood of Hestia Boulaia in Prytaneion (a few girls and women also served)
High Priest (of Asia), *Asiarch* (?)	ὁ ἀρχιερεὺς (τῆς Ἀσίας) ἀσιάρχης	Financial upkeep of imperial cult; ceremonial duties at festivals; sometimes called *neocoros* of the imperial cult (uncertain whether *asiarch* was synonymous with "high priest of Asia")

As implied in the Persicus edict, the "auctioning" of priesthoods of Artemis concerned "men" (ἄνθρωποι) who served as "priests" (ἱερεῖς) (*IvE* 18C.8 and 12). Although these terms could be used generically, other inscriptions name men who served as "priests of Artemis,"[48] so these were not necessarily priestesses. The financial costs and perquisites implied in the Persicus inscription are the only details we have for the character of the male priests of the goddess.

The next group of sacred officers, the κουρῆτες, was "doubtlessly the most important cult group connected to the temple of Artemis."[49] Strabo the geographer provides a helpful description of the *kouretes'* leadership in the annual ritual reenactment of the birth of Artemis Ephesia:

> Above the grove [Ortygia] lies Mt. Solmissus, where, it is said, the Curetes (*kouretes*) stationed themselves, and with the din of their arms frightened Hera out of her wits when she was jealously spying on Leto, and when they helped Leto to conceal from Hera the birth of her children. There are several temples in the place. . . . A general festival is held there annually; and by a certain custom the youths (*neoi*) vie for honour, particularly in the splendour of their banquets there. At that time, also, a special college (ἀρχεῖον, magistracy) of the Curetes (*kouretes*) holds symposiums and performs certain mystic sacrifices. (*Geogr.* 14.1.20 [LCL trans.])[50]

The epigraphical remains regarding the *kouretes* are extensive. We know that early in the reign of Augustus their headquarters was moved to the *prytaneion*, probably from the Artemisium.[51] The names of the six to nine annual *kouretes* were inscribed there each year during the imperial period, and over fifty of these lists are extant (*IvE* 1001–57 et al.). Two important facts emerge from these lists. First, the *kouretes* (and their assistants) were frequently also city councilors, illustrating the close integration of the civic and religious realms at Ephesus as was common in Greco-Roman cultures. Second, the *kouretes* were men.[52]

Hence, the following modern interpretation of the *kouretes* as priestesses epitomizes the kind of problematic historical imagination encountered in the interpretations of Ephesus as a feminist culture:

> In Ephesus women assumed the role of the man-slaying Amazons who had founded the cult of Artemis of Ephesus. . . . The female dancers at the temple of the Ephesian Artemis clashed their arms, so lethal weapons were part of the priestesses' religious accoutrements. There are reasons to suspect that the dances may have contained a simulated attack on males, especially as they were performed with spears. . . . They would surely have inspired terror; and this, Strabo tells us, was one of the purposes of the dance.[53]

These "female dancers" (*kouretes*) were men, and the goddess Hera was the one to be scared off in the ritual reenactment.

Another group associated with the Artemisium were the *neopoioi*, who functioned as something like a board of trustees for temple property (*IvE* 27, 1570–90b, 2212, et al.).[54] We know that the *neopoioi* held office for a term, since an aorist participle form of the word (νεοποιήσας) appears, and that the office involved significant financial commitment, since many *neopoioi* claimed that they were "voluntary" and served "generously."[55]

The sacred office of *essene* is of interest to New Testament scholars for its Qumran associations.[56] In the pre-Roman era, *essenes* appeared alongside the *neopoioi* as those charged with inscribing decrees of enfranchisement of new citizens in the Artemisium. In the imperial period, however, the Ephesian *essenes* held an annual priesthood with duties in cultic rites requiring chastity (even if married) and other kinds of ritual purity during their term of office (Pausanias, *Descr.* 8.13.1). The purity requirement is signified on the inscriptions by various forms of the phrase "completed my term as *essene* purely (ἀγνῶς)," and the financial obligations of office are indicated by their having served "generously."[57]

There were a number of other minor guilds and groups associated with the Artemisium that do not need elaboration here.[58] The men who filled these posts and the other major offices discussed were fully involved in the civic life of Ephesus. Many of them discharged a variety of sacred and civil offices during their lifetimes or served subsequent years in the same offices.[59]

In other treatments of the Artemis hierarchy, one figure frequently draws primary, indeed, sometimes sole attention: the *megabyzos*. This eunuch priest has fired the imagination of modern interpreters like no other.[60] The simple fact, however, is that this priesthood was obsolete by Paul's day; there were no more *megabyzoi*.[61] Hence, to speak of the *megabyzos* in connection with Pauline Ephesus is anachronistic.

The discussion of sacred offices thus far has shown that the cult hierarchy of Artemis Ephesia was securely under the control of the male political establishment of Ephesus. And many of the local civil magistrates themselves filled the priesthoods. There is nothing surprising about this; it was typical of Hellenic cults and cultures. Hence, to maintain that "the primary religious power [in Ephesus] lay with women by the first century CE"[62] runs counter to the clear and abundant evidence we have briefly reviewed.

Artemis Ephesia

A survey of some New Testament reference works on Artemis of Ephesus shows a consensus that she was "not the virgin huntress of Graeco-Roman tradition, but the many-breasted Asian mother-goddess, the symbol of fertility."[63] There are three interrelated components to this statement: (1) Artemis Ephesia was not the virgin huntress of Greco-Roman tradition; (2) (because) the adornments on her cult statues represent breasts; (3) (instead,) Artemis of Ephesus was a mother or fertility goddess. Although these seem to be well-entrenched opinions, they run counter to the judgment of specialists in Ephesian studies and should consequently be rethought. I will challenge each seriatim.

The character of the classical Hellenic Artemis (Diana to the Romans) is presented in this early hymn: "I sing of Artemis, whose shafts are of gold, who cheers on the hounds, the pure maiden, shooter of stags, who delights in archery, own sister to Apollo. . . . (After the hunt) she hangs up her curved bow and her arrows, and heads and leads the dances, gracefully arrayed (along with the Muses and Graces)" (*Homeric Hymns* 27 [LCL trans.]). Artemis was the ever-virgin consort of wild forest nymphs, who spurned marriage and relations with men. Her devotees, like priggish Hippolytus, were distinguished by perfect chastity (Euripides, *Hippolytus*). Should they lose their virtue—even innocently like Callisto—they were summarily banished from her presence as devotees defiled (Ovid, *Metamorphoses* 2.409–507). An even worse fate awaited unfortunate ones like Actaeon, who accidently came upon Artemis bathing: he was turned into a stag and torn limb from limb by his own hounds (Ovid, *Metamorphoses* 3.138–255). A wild huntress, remote and unpredictable, Artemis loved the chase and the bow; even though she was mistress of animals and helper in childbirth, one of her swift shafts might cause the sudden and inexplicable death of a maiden.

Some writers on the early history of Greek religion believe that Artemis originated in Asia Minor and that her role in childbirth points back to an origin as the Anatolian mother goddess.[64] This notion, of course, underlies modern opinions about Artemis Ephesia's identification as a mother or fertility goddess in Paul's day. But the origin of Artemis was long forgotten even by the classical period. Already in the earliest literature Artemis was "the virgin who delights in arrows" (*Homeric Hymns* 9), "the unbroken virgin" (*Odyssey* 6.109), and "the mistress of the beasts" (*Iliad* 21.470), but never a mother or confused with Aphrodite. "Whatever the roots of her fertility connections, the dominant conception of Artemis in the classical period is that of the virgin huntress."[65]

Richard Oster, who has worked extensively on Artemis and Ephesus, maintains that Artemis Ephesia herself conformed to this general Greco-Roman conception of Artemis-Diana and rejects the fertility associations for this goddess because of "the deafening silence from all the primary sources. None of the extant myths point in this direction, neither do the significant epithets of the goddess."[66]

The myths of Artemis Ephesia all refer to her as the classical "fair child of Leto (sired) from Zeus" (*IvE* 1383) and twin sister of Apollo,[67] or as the virginal guardian of maidenhood and of chastity.[68] As we saw earlier, the special priesthood of *essenes* maintained sexual purity during their terms of service for "the pure goddess,"[69] "the most-holy (ἁγιωτάτη) Artemis" (e.g., *IvE* 617 and 624).

The most significant evidence of Artemis Ephesia's virgin identity comes, again, from the epigraphical remains, the public records whereby the Ephesians displayed their conceptualization of their state goddess before the world. A lengthy record of a second-century AD oracle gives Artemis Ephesia's epithets in classic Homeric form and terms.[70] She is "the virgin" (παρθένον, line 14), the "renowned, vigilant maiden" (line 12), and "Artemis the pure" (line 16). As the goddess who watches over childbirth, she is the "midwife of birth and grower of mortals" and the "giver of fruit" (lines 3–4). And as huntress she is "Artemis with beautiful quiver" (line 2), the "arrow-pourer" (ἰοχέαιρα, line 11),[71] the "irresistible straight-shooter" (line 11).[72]

On the second point, the "breasts" on the cult statues, at the very least one must concede Robert Fleischer's conclusion from his exhaustive study of the representations of Artemis Ephesia: "Regarding the meaning of the 'breasts' it is still not possible today to advance beyond mere speculation."[73] More pointedly, William Ramsay noted long ago that "they were not intended . . . to represent breasts, for no nipple was indicated."[74] (They also begin well below the breast area on most representations.) And confirmation that they are not breasts comes from the fact that similar ornamentation appears on Anatolian reliefs of Zeus and on a statuette of Cybele below her breasts, which are discernable under her gown.[75]

We should also take into account that a statue of a classically Hellenic Artemis was found in an Ephesian home and that a similar cult statue of Artemis Ephesia with bow and torches is evidenced from the oracle inscription mentioned above, which "has an iconography radically different from what we know about the famous statue of Ephesian Artemis. . . . [It is] a statue of a more common type."[76] That the Ephesians had no trouble associating the deity symbolized by the exotic cult statue with the classical Artemis is illustrated by coins with the head of the maiden huntress with bow and quiver on one side and the polymastic cult statue on the other.[77]

Since "to write history on the basis of iconographic sources alone is a risky business that can lead only to the most dubious conclusions,"[78] we must rely more on the myths, epithets, and descriptions of Artemis Ephesia to discover how the ancients conceived of her. The ornaments on her representations cannot establish Artemis Ephesia as a fertility or mother goddess without corroborating evidence.

Finally, there should be no need to belabor point number three (Artemis as a fertility goddess) if we have presented sufficient evidence that her ornaments were not fertility symbols (breasts) and that she was otherwise identified with the typical Hellenic Artemis in contemporary Ephesian sources. There is simply no evidence from Artemis Ephesia's

cult practices to substantiate her as a fertility or mother goddess. Instead, what we do know of her worship shows it to have been a typical
Hellenic state cult, with "feasts," "festivals," and "public sacrifices"
(*IvE* 24), banquets (*IvE* 951; Strabo, *Geogr.* 14.1.20), processions (*IvE*
1577, 26–37, and 221), and contests of athletes, actors, and musicians
at the "Great Artemisia" and other sacred games in her honor (e.g., *IvE*
1081–1160).[79] Fertility and orgiastic rituals in the Greco-Roman world
were much different.[80]

None of this implies that the ancient Ephesians were uniform in their
theological conceptions, that they lacked a syncretistic spirit, or that
they rejected the worship of fertility deities out of some higher religious
principles. Nor was Ephesian paganism necessarily as innocent as the
inscriptions portray; certainly, the obsession with magic at Ephesus ex-
poses the demonic side of its religion (Acts 19:13–19).[81] But these things
are common elsewhere too; the Ephesians were little different in their
religious conceptions from inhabitants of other Pauline cities.

The Ephesians did worship fertility goddesses (Demeter, Gem, and
Meter), but so did most of their pagan contemporaries. Furthermore,
it cannot be shown that worship of such deities, or of any female deity,
translated into societal status, rights, or power for women in ancient
societies. To say that it did at Ephesus because of the centrality of the
worship of Artemis Ephesia is sheer speculation that runs counter to
the facts. One would have to say the same thing about Athens, which
is often used as a paradigm for a thoroughly patriarchal society, and
their cult of Athena Polias.

To this point, we have presented only males in politics and religion,
and we have seen them filling the principal positions. So far, the primary
sources have forced grave doubts on the "feminist Ephesus" thesis,
and this essay has particularly challenged the modern interpretation
of Artemis as a fertility or mother deity who sponsored the religious or
social superiority of women over men at Ephesus. However, we have
not yet discussed Ephesian women. What were their civic roles? Since
some did play a part in Ephesian public life, we must now give them
due attention. But first, the problems that this particular subject poses
to the scholar of ancient history need to be mentioned.

Women in Antiquity

The secondary works on women of antiquity understandably focus
on either classical Athens or imperial Rome, which makes our task
more difficult. For example, legal prerogatives of women in Rome are
frequently imputed to women in the free Greek city-states, which had

their own long-standing laws and traditions (developing *Romanitas* in the provinces notwithstanding).[82] Furthermore, changes in women's legal status are often used to posit a rise in their social status[83] even though there is no necessary correlation between the two.

A further condition that should limit blanket statements on women is the sharp distinction between cities like Ephesus and their rural possessions. Life was much different in the outlying hamlets and villages than in the cities, and the rural people easily comprised 75 to 80 percent of the total population in antiquity.[84] And of the metropolitan population, perhaps as many as one-third or more were slaves who lacked any sort of legal rights or social position.[85] Even if freed, slaves often remained in a subordinate role in the *oikos*, closely resembling their former service.[86]

In societies with at best a small middle class in the modern sense and with a minuscule urban elite, any assertion about "women's rights" is relevant for only a tiny fraction of all ancient women. Few had the leisure and social position to profit from legal rights or social openings, even if available. We will, therefore, proceed cautiously from evidence that is notoriously inadequate, often only partly understood, and at times self-contradictory.[87]

From our discussion thus far, one firm starting point has already been established: men filled Ephesian magistracies and its most prominent social positions. This alone rules out the kind of feminism sometimes conferred on Ephesus. In addition, we have blaring silence regarding feminism from curious explorers like Strabo and Pliny the Elder in their comments on Ephesus.[88] They give no hint whatsoever that women dominated this city.

And it is not as though the ancients would not have recognized a feminist society. They sometimes spoke about (fanciful) gynecocrats like the Amazons, who were supposed to rule foreign lands in distant times; yet with the notice: "What I have to say will appear, on account of its fabulous nature, to resemble tales from mythology (μῦθοι)" (Diod. Sic., *Bibl. hist.* 2.44.3; cf. 2.46.6). In such stories of "people among whom women possessed sovereignty" (ἔθνους . . . γυναικοκρατουμέ-νου—whence English "gynecocracy") (Diod. Sic., *Bibl. hist.* 2.45.1), only the women were involved in "manly military prowess," magistracies, and the affairs of state. Husbands were consigned to spinning and weaving—litmus tasks for dutiful Greek wives—and other domestic chores, including the care of children (e.g., Diod. Sic., *Bibl. hist.* 1.27.2; 2.44.1–5; 3.53.1–4). Family roles in Ephesus were not like this, however.

Are we correspondingly left with the position that "the opinion Thucydides imputes to Pericles reflects the ancient world's prevailing view of

women: the less said about them the better"?[89] Were Ephesian women
locked in their homes by jealous and severe patriarchs? And is it correct
to say that "old-fashioned women proved their modesty by going out
as little as possible and never showing themselves in public without a
partial veil"?[90]

It is true that women appear only rarely in the epigraphical remains
from Ephesus. Normally the city's patrons do not mention their wives at
all; if they do, it is something like: "P. Hordeonius Lollianus with wife"
(*IvE* 20). Wives do occasionally appear by name on Ephesian stones,
although frequently as models of classical female virtues, particularly
"modesty," or "prudence" (the term that appears in 1 Tim. 2:9, 15).[91]
For example, Laevia Paula was given this eulogy at her funeral procession: "The state council and people crown Laevia L. f. Paula, who lived
a modest and decorous life (σώφρονα καὶ κόσμιον ζήσασαν βίον)" (*IvE*
614B [AD 16–37]). It is clear from comparing her memorial with her
husband's—M. Antonius Albus, "the patron (προστάτης) of the temple of
Artemis and of the city" (*IvE* 614C)—that Laevia was honored because
of her husband's benefactions, not for her own public services. She did
not act as head of their *oikos*.[92]

Nevertheless, Ephesian women and girls do appear in some official
capacities, not just as the honorably mentioned wives of patriarchs and
patrons. Evidence to this effect picks up in the first century AD, so we
cannot trace it to a long-standing emphasis on a "feminine principle"
connected to Amazons, Ephesian culture, or Artemis Ephesia. Upon
examination, we find a few first-century women filling one or more of
four offices: priestess of Artemis, *kosmeteira*, *prytanis*, and high priestess of Asia.

Table 1.4
Female Priesthoods in Ephesus

Priestess of Artemis	ἱερεία Ἀρτέμιδος	Cultic duties in processions; financial underwriting of cult; some were young girls
Kosmeteira	κοσμήτειρα	Responsible for adornment of cult statue of Artemis for festival (?); often also the priestess of Artemis
Prytanis	πρύτανις	Priesthood of Hestia Boulaia in Prytaneion; financial underwriting of cult; some were young girls, but most *prytaneis* were male
High Priestess of Asia	ἀρχιερεία Ἀσίας	Financial upkeep of imperial cult; cultic duties probably focused on divinized empresses; only two known in Ephesus from the late first century

A first-century *kouretes* list serves as an example of relevant evidence (though it is rare that one woman filled all three offices): "In the prytany of Vedia Marcia, the daughter of Pu[blius], priestess (of Artemis) and high priestess of Asia" (*IvE* 1017 [AD 93–100]). Let us discuss each office in turn (combining the Artemis priestess and *kosmeteira*).[93]

Priestesses of Artemis

It should come as no surprise to find women serving as priestesses at Ephesus. In fact, women held a variety of priesthoods and unofficial functions in state cults throughout the Greco-Roman world.[94] As mentioned earlier, the ancients thought it especially fitting for a priestess to serve goddesses in the same way that sacrifices of female animals were normally offered to female deities. Furthermore, Greek women regularly participated in a variety of ways in state cults regardless of the sex of the honoree. Women might garland[95] or lustrate sacrificial victims, play musical instruments,[96] sing, shout a distinct cry (ὀλολυγή), chant, dance, pour libations, prepare sacred garments or sacrificial foods, bear water or sacred objects in processions, prophesy at the oracles, and so on.[97]

Who were the priestesses of Artemis of Ephesus? What do we know about them? As the example of Vedia Marcia illustrates, most of the priestesses had Roman names, suggesting that they were members of the municipal elite; perhaps some were even daughters of Roman immigrants.[98]

Vedia is identified as the "daughter of Pu[blius]," but not as the wife of anyone. In fact, many of the priestesses named on the inscriptions are identified only by the names of one or both parents or by their ancestors, leaving husbands unmentioned.[99] This is important, since most Ephesian women are identified as the "wife of so-and-so." "What's your husband's name?" (Aristophanes, *Thesmophoriazusae* 619) was the normal way to identify a married woman in the Greek world. Therefore, Vedia Marcia was not (yet?) married.

What should we make of this? Another priestess of Artemis, Ulpia Euodia Mudiane, daughter of Mudianus and Euodia, says that she "performed the mysteries and made all expenses *through my parents*" (*IvE* 989, emphasis added). This priestess of Artemis and others like her were unmarried girls.[100] Since Greek girls usually married soon after puberty, these priestesses of the "virgin" Artemis Ephesia must have been about fourteen years old or even younger (some Greek girls were married at age twelve).[101]

What were the duties of the priestesses of Artemis, especially given that some were young girls? Although our knowledge of their cultic responsibilities is sketchy and somewhat conjectural, they unquestionably did not engage in sacred prostitution.[102] These were the maiden daughters (and wives?) of the wealthy elite who served their goddess "circumspectly" (ἱεροπρεπῶς, *IvE* 987–88), "piously and with decorum" (εὐσεβῶς καὶ κοσμίως, *IvE* 3059), and "worthily of the goddess and of her family" (Neue Inschriften XIII, no. 160).[103] The idea is absurd for the priestesses of Artemis, "the unbroken virgin."[104]

We can say with some confidence, though, that (as with other priesthoods in this period) monetary obligations were paramount for priestesses of Artemis. We already saw that the parents of the priestess Ulpia Euodia Mudiane provided the requisite funds for her. Adding more details, two first-century (?) priestesses, Vipsania Olympias and her (adopted?) sister Vipsania Polla, "wreathed the temple and all its precincts in the days of the goddess' manifestations, making the public sacrifices and the distributions (of money) to the council and *gerousia*" (*IvE* 987–88). Another priestess "(made) all the distributions of her priesthood" (*IvE* 997) while the priestess Flavia Chrysanthe "fulfilled the myster[ies] generously" (Neue Inschriften IX, 123). The requisite donations and generosity for priestesses of Artemis were apparently set by the state council itself, since another stone reads: "(name lost) served as priestess of Artemis piously and generously . . . and gave five thousand denarii to the city in accordance with the state council's measure" (Neue Inschriften XI, no. 8, 176 [ca. AD 165]). We may suppose that at least part of the definition of "pious" service as priestess was serving "generously."

Another of the priestesses' duties beyond financial underwriting of the cult is suggested by the associated title *kosmeteira* ("adorner"), often held concurrently by the priestess (*IvE* 892, 983–84, 989, et passim). The etymology of this title suggests a duty connected with adorning the cult statue of Artemis with clothing and ornaments, which was common in the Greek world and clearly evidenced for Artemis Ephesia (*IvE* 2).[105] The role of the priestess and *kosmeteira* may have centered on providing sacred adornments for Artemis similar to the role of the girls and priestesses who made and presented an ornate new robe (*peplos*) to Athena during the Athenian Panathenaia.[106]

The priestesses of Artemis Ephesia fit the general picture of women's participation in Greco-Roman cults. These were sometimes the young daughters of municipal elites whose financial contributions to the cult festivals were important aspects of their sacred service. The fact that these were sometimes prepubescent girls makes the priestesses of Artemis Ephesia particularly unlikely material from which to posit a gynecocratic society. Their duties, beyond financial obligations, would have been necessarily ceremonial ones, perhaps connected with sacred clothing, rather than ones that evidence women "as prime movers and mediators in religion" at Ephesus.[107]

Prytanis

"I give thanks to Mistress Hestia and to all the gods," wrote the *prytanis* Aurelia Juliane, daughter of Paparion, "for they returned me safe and sound to my parents" (*IvE* 1066). In other Greek states, the prytany was a high-ranking executive magistracy of the state council, often the office whose annual incumbent's name dated state documents.[108] The pre-imperial Ephesian prytany possibly had this eponymous, magisterial character (cf. *IvE* 9), but not by the time Aurelia Juliane and other females served as *prytaneis;* the Ephesian office had changed.[109]

For some reason, after the reign of Augustus when the new *prytaneion* was built, the Ephesian prytany became a subordinate priesthood of Hestia of the Council (Hestia Boulaia), the flame goddess of the hearth. In a Greek *oikos,* keeping the hearth fire burning was an important task, and worship of Hestia as the eternal flame symbolized the family's continuity, health, and dependence on the gods for its basic needs, among which fire was the most important.[110] The cult of Hestia in the city's *prytaneion* was simply an extrapolation from the *oikos:* "The fire cult, then, proceeding from a necessary task in daily life, became a symbol for political unity embracing numerous families. . . . This cult of Hestia was thus a clear indication that the whole city was actually a single, big family."[111]

In the Greek *oikos,* a young girl tended the hearth fire, so it was natural for Hestia Boulaia to be served by a girl at the city's hearth as well. This is precisely the case with Aurelia Juliane, who was "returned to her parents" after her term of office. Like some of the priestesses of Artemis, some *prytaneis* were prepubescent girl-priestesses whose wealthy families acquired the honor for their daughters.[112]

The specific duties of the Ephesian prytany in the imperial era primarily involved significant monetary expenditures. The clearest evidence of this is a long inscription from the late second or early third century AD summarizing an "ancestral law" regulating the *prytanis's* duties (*IvE* 10).[113] The cultic duties were lighting the altar fires, making incense and herb offerings, and participating in animal sacrifices (daily), paeans, processions, and night festivals. The inscription explicitly says that the *prytanis* paid the bill "out of his private resources."[114]

Even if some female *prytaneis* were married, we must conclude that the prytany had no magisterial powers during the period when females served as *prytaneis,* though such service was a high honor for a *prytanis* and her family. Would a prepubescent girl—or boy, for that matter—be given magisterial responsibilities today?[115] For the same reasons, tenure in this office by girls cannot be viewed as a sign of a "women's rights" ideology. It shows rather that the city was willing to expand its base of individuals who would underwrite certain civic expenses in exchange for honors and priesthoods.[116]

High Priestess of Asia

The final official capacity in which we find women serving at Ephesus is as high priestesses of Asia, connected with the Roman imperial cult. This office in particular has been used as a sign of the advancement of women's social status in the province.[117] We will delve into this priesthood only briefly because, in the first place, its history and character have been fully explored in easily accessible works on the imperial cult in Asia Minor.[118] Second, the high priestesses of Asia represent nothing new; women held various priesthoods from the earliest times in the Greco-Roman state cults and particularly in earlier ruler cults honoring Hellenistic queens.[119]

The cult for the female personification of Roman power, the goddess Roma, is traceable in Asia to about 200 BC. The early forms of this cult were municipal establishments under the oversight of a magistrate who served as "priest of Roma" at an altar or sacred precinct.[120] After Augustus allowed the provincial league (*koinon*) of Asia to establish a temple for Roma at Pergamum in 29 BC (Cassius Dio, *Roman History* 51.20.6–8; Tacitus, *Annales* 4.37), the cult became a provincial affair, with priests participating in (and funding) regular sacrifices, festivals, and games.

Women (sometimes girls) held early priesthoods in honor of the wives and mothers of Roman rulers.[121] However, the earliest, single reference to a provincial high priestess of Asia dates to the reign of Nero, though the evidence for this early date is very tenuous.[122] At Ephesus, the earliest high priestess dates to Domitian (though male provincial priests are found there earlier), and only two high priestesses can be dated to the first century.[123] There were apparently no high priestesses in Ephesus until twenty-five to thirty years after 1 Timothy was written, making them slightly anachronistic as an institution for this period.[124]

The service of provincial high priestesses probably arose to accommodate the worship of the divinized empresses like Domitia, wife of Domitian, and "Sabina, the divine Augusta, wife of the Emperor (Hadrian)" (*IvE* 278).[125] Hence, the female high priesthood was analogous to the private priestesses of Hellenistic queens or of Livia Augusta, and it fits the general pattern of Greek religion for female divinities to be served ordinarily by a female priesthood.

The high priestesses of Asia probably did nothing out of the ordinary. Like the high priests, their most important function was financial; someone had to underwrite the sacrifices, banquets, games, buildings, and other elements of the imperial cult.[126] "The council and people honored Claudia Ammion, the wife of the high priest P. Gavius Capito, who was appointed high priestess of Asia, because of both her own and her husband's acts of generosity (φιλοδοξίας) to the city" (*IvE* 681 [first or second century AD]).[127] Unlike the male high priests who had political functions in the provincial league, the high priestesses of Asia had no governmental role in the *koinon*.[128]

To find women as high priestesses of Asia does not necessarily signal a shift of views on the familial roles of women in Asia or in Ephesus. This is witnessed by one Aelia Ammia from Phrygia, who served as "high priestess of the greatest temples in Ephesus." Among her chief virtues were her "humility and devotion to her husband" (σωφροσύνη τε καὶ φιλανδρία).[129] The few high priestesses of Asia simply demonstrate that some of the daughters and wives of the municipal elite moved in provincial circles and held priesthoods in that connection. This is not surprising in light of the "powerful international network of marriage ties and alliances" among some of these municipal elites in Asia Minor.[130]

In sum, priesthoods in various cults (especially where female divinities were concerned) were held by the daughters and wives of some of the wealthy families in Ephesus under the general oversight of male provincial and municipal authorities. This was the practice throughout the Greek world as well as in Ephesus. Specifically, that women—and young girls—served in priesthoods, though considered an honor,[131] had no demonstrable correlation with "emancipation" or domination in social, political, or religious affairs at Ephesus or elsewhere.[132]

Women and Education

Discussion of women from the Ephesian aristocracy brings up the question of women's cultural opportunities and the teaching of 1 Timothy 2:12. One egalitarian interpretation of this verse states that since Paul regularly supported the ordained teaching ministry of women, his prohibition must have been aimed simply at the *unlearned* women of Ephesus. After all, women in antiquity "were less likely to be educated than men."[133] This line of reasoning, however, requires us to accept a number of problematic assumptions and is hardly convincing.

Ephesus was "a center of philosophical and rhetorical studies" (Philostratus, *Vit. Soph.* 8.8),[134] and it possessed a well-known medical college in its center for the Muses. When modern analysts say that women were "uneducated" in antiquity, they usually mean that they were not in schools like this.[135] It is true that women do not appear as the sophists, rhetors, teachers, philosophers, doctors, and their disciples in ancient sources from Ephesus.[136] Although the extant evidence is not very extensive, it nevertheless forces the admission that women teachers were not integral to Ephesian society.[137]

However, to say that Ephesian women were *uneducated* because they did not appear in "graduate schools" of philosophy, rhetoric, and medicine is misleading. Few people in antiquity advanced in their formal education beyond today's elementary school levels, including men like Socrates, Sophocles, and Herodotus.[138] And there were other forms of education in which upper-class women participated at Ephesus, particularly private lectures in salons. For instance, false teachers mentioned in the Pastorals taught women in this venue: "They are the kind who worm their way into *homes* and gain control over weak-willed women" (2 Tim. 3:6 NIV, emphasis added).[139]

Because women's education in antiquity usually took place privately, we get only a glimpse of it here and there. As for women's literacy, daughters of the upper classes needed some level of education for their duties in managing large households.[140] And though they were not commonly found in fields like philosophy, women did read and write literature and poetry during this period.[141]

While women's literary works were usually designed for private consumption and are therefore lost for the most part, there are exceptions from Ephesus. For instance, we have several extant tributes to Hestia from female *prytaneis*.[142] Two poetic epigrams for Hestia ("sweetest of gods . . . ever-streaming light") in particular are said to have been written by the first-century *prytanis* Claudia herself (*IvE* 1062 [both epigrams]). These show that some upper-class Ephesian girls and women were among the known female devotees of literature in the Greek world.

From the foregoing, we can assume, then, that some female members of the Pauline church were at least literate and possibly had a modicum of formal or informal learning. The elaborate coiffures, jewelry, and clothing mentioned in 1 Timothy 2:9 and the warning to the rich in 1 Timothy 6:17–18 show clearly that there were wealthy women in the Ephesian congregation. At least some of these women were educated and possibly a few highly accomplished in letters or poetry.[143] Indeed, Paul probably knew Ephesian women who privately sat at the feet of teachers like Hymenaeus and Philetus, who were "ever learning, but never able to enter into knowledge of the truth" (2 Tim. 2:17; 3:7). Hence, I cannot agree that there were no literate or educated women in the church of 1 Timothy so that women would *eo ipso* be disqualified from teaching there.

Hairstyles and *Romanitas*

There was an increasing permeation of Roman culture in Ephesus during the first century. Interestingly enough, we may possibly see its effects in 1 Timothy 2 itself. Although Paul's exhortation for women to "adorn themselves with modesty and humility [σωφροσύνη]" (1 Tim. 2:9) fits the expectations of either Greek or Roman society, the adornment of the hair "with braids and gold or with pearls" (cf. 1 Pet. 3:3) fits a new trend originating in Rome.

During this period, Greek hairstyles for women were for the most part simple affairs: hair was parted in the middle, pinned simply in the back or held in place with a scarf or a headband. Roman coiffures were similar until the principate. The women of the imperial household originated new styles; by the Trajanic period they had developed into elaborate curls, braids, high wigs, pins, and hair ornaments that were quickly copied by the well-to-do throughout the empire: "See the tall edifice rise up on her head in serried tiers and storeys!" (Juvenal, *Satire* 6). One can even date representations of women by the increasing complexity of hair fashions.[144]

If Roman styles seem a bit too far away to affect Ephesian fashions, consider that portraits of reigning empresses often appeared on coins minted in Ephesus and other Asian cities and that they had prominent statues in both public and private places.[145] Portraits of provincial women from the era show that the imperial coiffures were copied in Ephesus and the other cities of Asia.[146]

Paul's injunction regarding elaborate hairstyles reflects the increasing influence of Rome at Ephesus during the third quarter of the first century AD. And his skeptical response to this trend was due to his judgment that simplicity and modesty in dress befit pious women rather than external extravagance.[147] Furthermore, his reaction to women's imitation of the latest hairstyles is understandable since it was quite a new trend, really begun only a decade or so earlier, and it carried connotations of imperial luxury and the infamous licentiousness of women like Messalina and Poppaea.[148] Today, it is the equivalent of warning Christians away from imitation of styles set by promiscuous pop singers or actresses.

Summary and Conclusions

Ephesus was in most ways a typical Hellenic society. It was a bur-geoning trade and commercial center somewhat like Corinth, though unlike Corinth (reconstituted as a Roman colony)[149] Ephesus's Greek roots were well preserved in its political and cultural institutions. The state council, *gerousia,* gymnasia, and religious hierarchies (including priestesses) were typically Hellenic.

Ephesus was also the center of Roman administration for the province, meaning that a Roman proconsul, like P. Fabius Persicus in Paul's day, might well give direction to its municipal government and religious af-fairs. Various pieces of evidence show that the city increasingly accepted Roman culture. For instance, the rising incidence of Roman names and Roman citizenship among Ephesians, the transformation of the demo-cratic state council into an aristocratic senate, the enthusiastic advance-ment of the imperial cult, and even the elaborate hairstyles referred to in 1 Timothy 2 attest to inroads of *Romanitas* at Ephesus.

Paul's injunctions throughout 1 Timothy 2:9–15, then, are not tem-porary measures in a unique social setting. Ephesus's society and reli-gion—even the cult of Artemis Ephesia—shared typical features with many other contemporary Greco-Roman cities. Ephesus was thoroughly Greek in background and character, yet influence of *Romanitas* is clearly discerned. Hence, we have every reason to expect Paul to apply the restriction of women from teaching and exercising official rule over a man to "every place" (v. 8).

Furthermore, there is no reason to suspect that the Christian women of Ephesus would regard Paul's exhortation to modesty and humility as unusual or necessarily unpalatable, even if they had earlier served as priestesses in pagan cults. As we saw, some of these elite girls and women were praised for their "modesty" and "devotion to husband." If they were to have read Plutarch's advice to a bride (*Coniugalia prae-cepta*)—and we believe that at least some Ephesian women were able and had the leisure to read such works—they would have encountered injunctions similar to Paul's on extravagance, modesty, and silence (*Mor.* 142C–D; 145A–B).

Indeed, Paul actually seems a bit more "liberal" than Plutarch, since the latter wants a virtuous wife to be hidden away when not accompanied by her husband and advises her not to make her own friends but to be content with her husband's (*Mor.* 139C; 140D). Paul positively opens the road to learning to all women by enjoining them to learn in the church. Furthermore, Paul does not tell women to remain cloistered at home but to exercise their gifts in the practice of public good works and especially in the discipleship of younger women (1 Tim. 5:9–10; Titus 2:4–5; etc.).

Even though Paul's first readers could not have read Plutarch—he was only a boy then—many of the inscriptions about first- and second-century women in Ephesus draw attention to their "modesty" and domestic fidelity in accordance with traditional Greco-Roman expectations for women. And there is explicit evidence that Ephesian women embraced this role in the person of Tullia. This young girl, after serving as *prytanis*, thanked Hestia with two metrical inscriptions (implying some degree of education). In the first she prays that "since she immaculately completed her obligations of patronage (προστασία), so grant children to her . . . because of (her) unimpeachable modesty (σωφροσύνη) and wisdom" (*IvE* 1063). This is hardly clamoring for women's rights by an Amazon-inspired female magistrate.

If this chapter has added anything concrete to this volume's discussion of 1 Timothy 2:9–15, it is that exegetical treatments can proceed with the assumption that Ephesus was not a unique society in its era. Specifically, it was not a feminist society as we read today in statements on 1 Timothy 2:12–13 like this:

> In a religious environment saturated with the "feminine principle" due to the Artemis cult, attitudes of female exaltation or superiority existed. Verse 13 attempts to correct such an emphasis. Also the myths of Cybele and Attis from which the Ephesian Artemis sprang emphasized the creation of the goddess first, then her male consort. Paul could be affirming the historical truthfulness of the biblical narratives to expose the fiction-based nature of the *Magna Mater* myths.[150]

The claims and assumptions here are a thorough misrepresentation of ancient Ephesus and of Artemis Ephesia. On the other hand, I do not intend to imply that the religious environment of Ephesus was "saturated with a 'masculine principle'" (whatever that might be). We have seen women given honors, public recognition, and religious functions at Ephesus within the general rubric of Roman and municipal magistrates' oversight. There is no evidence of Ephesian denigration of women per se.

Furthermore, the reader should be warned that some contemporary discussions of women in antiquity are so influenced by modern biases that they cannot appreciate and accurately describe the character and dynamics of the situation then. Ancient women's role in the home is frequently referred to today as "confinement"—a prejudicial term—and thus ignores a woman's sometimes extensive authority and management over domestic affairs.[151] Not very long ago, an American author could say, "Ma and her girls were Americans, *above doing men's work*."[152] Perhaps ancient women held a similar opinion. They may not have held public office or taught, not because it was forbidden by domineering men, but because they did not care to do so. They had their own spheres of influence.[153]

There is still work to be done to allow ancient women to speak for themselves as much as our limited sources allow. But the important points relevant to 1 Timothy may be considered as adequately attested in the sources reported here. These sources by their very nature refer to predominantly upper-class people. But there is good evidence that at least some women from such elite circles were part of the Ephesian congregation.[154]

In the course of our discussion, we have seen Ephesian girls and women in traditional Greco-Roman roles. Aristocratic women participated alongside their husbands as managers of sometimes extensive households:[155] "This memorial and the outlying area belongs to Pomponia Faustina, *kosmeteira* of Artemis (inherited) from her forebears,[156] and to Menander her husband. Myrrachis, Nico, and the rest of Menander's freedmen care for the tomb" (*IvE* 1655). Ephesian women's official functions were expressed almost entirely in the sacred priesthoods. Most, though, whose names would never be inscribed on stone, were much like women encountered anywhere else at the time: wives, mothers, and midwives; farmers, fullers, and fishmongers; scullery maids, bar-girls, and prostitutes; mediums, fortunetellers, and slaves. These women hardly had time for Amazonian phantasies.

In 1 Timothy 2, after reminding the wealthy women of Ephesus in particular about true piety in contrast to outward show, Paul anticipates that such women might misunderstand their inherited, worldly privileges to imply that they could step outside their divinely ordered role in the new covenant community. He points them instead to their distinct, profound, and significant roles in the church. And Paul's teaching on distinctly feminine virtues would have resonated with the ideals of their culture through the light of general revelation: "A woman's particular virtue is modesty (σωφροσύνη), for by it she is enabled to honor and love her husband" (Phintys, daughter of Callicrates, a Pythagorean philosopher).[157]

2

AN IMPORTANT WORD

Αὐθεντέω in 1 Timothy 2:12

HENRY SCOTT BALDWIN

The total vocabulary of the New Testament is a little over 5,400 words. With a knowledge of only 170 of the most frequently used words, the student of biblical Greek is able to recognize more than 70 percent of all the words in the Greek New Testament. With a vocabulary of 500 Greek words, one can read the New Testament without great difficulty. However, for careful study and exegesis of the text, a problem arises with the words that appear only once in the New Testament. These hapax legomena present a problem for both the reader and the scholar. The reader discovers that to learn every word in the New Testament, nearly 2,000 hapax legomena must be memorized. It is a formidable task to learn so many words so infrequently encountered in the text! But for the scholar, hapax legomena can present an even greater challenge. Since language usage is the key to understanding the meaning of a word, how does the New Testament scholar determine the meaning of words that appear only once in the New Testament or even in the whole Bible? Often context reveals the basic sense of a word. If the general flow of the text is understood, usually the meaning of the word will be evident. Occasionally, however, the context may make several different meanings for a hapax legomenon seem appropriate or at least possible. The scholar must then turn to sources outside the New Testament and evaluate other uses of the word to narrow the meaning. Such is the case with αὐθεντέω, which appears in 1 Timothy 2:12.

First Timothy 2:12 declares, "I do not permit a woman to teach or αὐθεντεῖν a man." What Paul intends to say by use of the word αὐθεντεῖν has been much debated in the past. The various definitions proposed resulted in surprisingly different interpretations of the verse. Thus, a careful analysis of the term is warranted. However, since the first edition of this volume was published, significant scholarly effort has been expended to understand the meaning of αὐθεντέω in 1 Timothy 2:12 and its larger usage and history among Greek speakers of the ancient world. Given the work offered here and the fine studies of Al Wolters[1] and David Huttar,[2] the time is now past for exegetes to claim lexical justification in support of idiosyncratic or tendentious interpretations of this critical text in 1 Timothy.[3]

Since αὐθεντεῖν is a New Testament hapax legomenon, the exegete must investigate extrabiblical materials to assist in analyzing Paul's meaning. Often turning to sources outside the New Testament can be as easy as consulting one of the standard New Testament or ancient Greek lexicons. However, in the case of the word αὐθεντέω, it is evident that many lexicons do not provide as thorough or comprehensive an explanation of the term as we might desire. A precise consensus as to the meaning of the word has not been achieved among well-known lexicographers. (Table 2.1 provides a summary of the conclusions of several modern lexicons.)

Partly because of the uncertainty in the lexicons, partly because of theological and practical concerns, scholars in the last decade undertook to study afresh this difficult word. There had been five significant word studies on the origin and meaning of αὐθεντέω in the fifteen years previous to the first edition. Some insight had been gained from each. However, methodological or technological shortcomings limited the extent to which each had been able to contribute to a satisfactory resolution of the meaning of the term.

In 1979 Catherine C. Kroeger asserted that αὐθεντέω was an erotic term whose essential meaning was "to thrust oneself."[4] Further, she asserted that the word was associated with fertility practices. Three years later, Carroll Osburn convincingly demonstrated that Kroeger's position was "more curious than substantive."[5] Osburn went on to make his own case for the meaning of αὐθεντέω: "to dominate or domineer." George W. Knight III produced a careful and detailed study of αὐθεντέω.[6] He concluded that the translation of the KJV ("to usurp authority") was

Table 2.1
Αὐθεντέω in Modern Lexicographers

Sophocles	1. to be in power, to have authority over
	2. to be the originator of anything
	3. to compel
	4. mid: to be in force
Preisigke	1. beherrschen (to rule, control, dominate)
	2. verfügungsberechtigt sein (to have legitimate authority to dispose of something)
	3. Herr sein, fest auftreten (to be master, to act confidently)[a]
Lampe	1. hold sovereign authority, act with authority
	2. possess authority over
	3. assume authority, act on one's own authority
	4. be primarily responsible for, instigate, authorize
Moulton and Milligan	1. from the word "master, autocrat"[b]
LSJ	1. to have full power or authority over
	2. to commit murder
Mayser	1. Herr sein, fest auftreten (to be master, to act confidently)
BDAG[c]	1. to assume a stance of independent authority[d]
Louw and Nida[e]	1. to control in a domineering manner—"to control, to domineer"
DGE	1. tener autoridad sobre andros [como algo prohibido a la mujer] (to have authority over a male [as something prohibited for a woman])

a. These English renderings are those of *The Oxford-Duden German Dictionary* (Oxford: Clarendon, 1990).

b. This is found under the heading αὐθεντέω. However, Moulton and Milligan begin their article with a discussion of the noun and cite only one instance of the verb.

c. For the use at 1 Tim. 2:12, Danker notes with the Jerusalem Bible that the word "practically = 'tell a man what to do,'" and suggests as a gloss for αὐθεντέω "give orders to, dictate to," the later gloss having the unfortunate connotation of meaning something socially undesirable. Danker acknowledges the articles of George Knight ("ΑΥΘΕΝΤΕΩ") and Leland Wilshire ("TLG Computer"), cited by me below, but

evidences no knowledge of the first edition of this present article, nor does he, understandably, have knowledge of Wolters ("Semantic Study") or Huttar ("ΑΥΘΕΝΤΕΙΝ").

d. The use of the term "domineer" appeared somewhere between the fifth edition of Walter Bauer's *Griechisch-Deutsches Wörterbuch* (Berlin: Töpelmann, 1958) and the English adaption and translation by BAGD. The negative term "domineer" became included perhaps mistakenly in the definition for αὐθεντέω. Bauer's German rendering, "herrschen über jemand," does not of necessity demand the negative "domineer" but merely "rule over" or "have absolute sway over."

e. Louw and Nida, 474.

"evidently erroneous" and that "the RSV, NAB, NIV and The Translator's Testament have caught the essence of the meaning of αὐθεντέω and present probably the most satisfactory rendering with their phrase 'to have authority.'" However, Knight's work, though exactingly executed, was not comprehensive enough to resolve the debate since it focused on a limited database.

In his study, Leland Wilshire remedied the deficiency of data.[7] Using the computer database of the *Thesaurus Linguae Graecae*, Wilshire was able to identify "314 or so references to αὐθεντέω and its cognates." Wilshire concluded that

> the 314 literary citations of the TLG computer (plus the pertinent references in BAGD analyzed by Knight along with others in the papyri) may be of help in understanding the meaning of 1 Tim. 2.12. Sometime during the spread of koine, the word αὐθεντέω went beyond the predominant Attic meaning connecting it with murder and suicide and into the broader concept of criminal behavior. It also began to take on the additional meanings of "to exercise authority/power/rights" which became firmly established in the Greek Patristic writers to mean "exercise authority."[8]

In this article, Wilshire came to no solid conclusion with respect to the definition of αὐθεντέω. However, he seemed to indicate that a notion of "exercising authority" should be associated with the term.[9] In a later clarifying article, Wilshire offered "instigating violence" as the best definition and averred that it was not until the time of the patristic fathers that the meaning "exercise authority" appeared.[10]

In 1992, Richard and Catherine Kroeger published an extensive study of αὐθεντέω as part of their treatise on 1 Timothy 2:12.[11] They concluded that αὐθεντέω has "a wide range of meanings." Among them are "(1) to begin something, to be responsible for a condition or action, (2) to rule, to dominate, (3) to usurp power or rights from another, (4) to claim ownership, sovereignty, or authorship." In particular, they find αὐθεντέω "has implications of killing, beginning, and copulating." Specifically, they preferred that at 1 Timothy 2:12 αὐθεντεῖν be taken to mean "proclaim oneself author of man."

Looking over the results of these studies, it seems their effect was to make the real meaning of αὐθεντέω more obscure than ever! Hence was born the need for this chapter. In it we seek to identify the most probable meaning of the verb in 1 Timothy 2:12 and to obtain data to critique the contributions of other scholars. This will also provide the basis for the syntactical and exegetical evaluation of 1 Timothy 2:12 in the chapters that follow. Specifically, (1) we will suggest a satisfactory method for analyzing αὐθεντέω. This may offer us a clue why scholars have reached widely differing conclusions about the meaning of the verb. (2) We will present an analysis of the meanings derived from every currently known instance of the use of the verb in ancient Greek literature with a summary in table 3.2.[12] (3) Finally, we will draw conclusions concerning the possible meanings of the word in 1 Timothy 2.

The Limitations of Word Studies

Before we begin, it is important to recognize the limitations of lexical studies. Following the older linguistic theories of the nineteenth century, there was a strong presumption that word studies would yield the meaning of a word with indisputable certainty. Newer linguistic investigations have brought this assumption under suspicion. Ferdinand de Saussure noted that in language, "tout se tient" (all things hold together). That is, language must be viewed as an interconnected system wherein the *context* provides the clues to the meaning of the words used.[13]

This principle has important implications. On the one hand, the competent user of a language can contextualize most anything. Every competent English speaker knows that "raise" may have several distinct meanings: "to raise the flag," "to raise corn in Nebraska," "to raise children." Our ability to contextualize alerts us to the fact that by "raise" we do not mean "nurture the flag," "hoist corn," or "plant and water children."

On the other hand, no word has a meaning value of zero, that is, no word is an entirely blank check, able to mean anything we choose depending on the context in which we choose to put it. Linguist Rudolf Carnap's sentence "Pirots karulize elatically!"[14] is perfect according to normal English syntax. Yet it means nothing at all because the three words have no known meanings from any other context. Linguist Roland Barthes points out that speech is not an act of pure creativity. (If it were, we would understand in what way the pirots are karulizing!) Rather, a speaker uses and combines what is already in the language to accomplish his or her ends.[15]

At the same time, speakers can use words in unusual or unique ways. This occurs regularly with metaphors or in poetry. Consider the following scene: "The caravan navigated the last stretch of sandy waste, piloting their sulking and knock-kneed ships safely into the harbor of the oasis." It is precisely because "ship" and "camel" have distinctive meanings that the unexpected substitution of one word for the other gives metaphor its memorable quality. But no reputable word study should conclude from such a use as this, for example, that one legitimate meaning of "ship" must be "camel."

All this places three practical limitations on word studies:

1. Lexical studies (properly conducted) are nothing more than sum-
   maries of contemporaneous uses of the word under consideration. Lexis is not a prescription of what a word must mean nor
   an absolute proscription of what a word cannot mean in a given
   context. Rather, it is a *description* of what people who use the word
   normally mean to indicate by its use.
2. No lexical study is a 100 percent guarantee that a word has a
   specific meaning in any given passage. The presence of poetics,
   metaphor, or the specialized use of a word by a subculture unknown
   to the lexicographer prohibits such certainty. However, when the
   semantic range of a word is established across a wide spectrum
   of language use, the burden of proof lies on the exegete to show
   why, in this particular case, the normal and well-attested usage
   should not be taken as the meaning in the passage at hand. With
   respect to the use of αὐθεντέω in 1 Timothy 2:12, this principle
   particularly has been repeatedly violated by exegetes.[16]
3. Understanding the meaning of a word in a specific context is a
   trial-and-error process. This process goes through the following
   steps: (a) We have a preunderstanding of the word based on its use
   in other contexts. This is the dictionary meaning (or denotation)
   we carry around in our heads or lexicons. (b) We attempt to apply
   the denotation to the present context. (c) We then check to see
   if the resulting sentence makes sense using this meaning. (d1) If
   it does, we search for the precise nuance of the context at hand.
   (d2) If it does not, we investigate why not. We may ask questions
   such as, Is the word misspelled? Is there a denotation to the word
   we did not know about? Is the writer using metaphor?

Limitation 3 will become particularly important to us in subsequent
chapters after we have the results of our study of αὐθεντέω in hand.

Methodology of Word Studies

Any formal attempt to discover the meaning of αὐθεντέω must be based
on sound methodology. In particular, in analyzing αὐθεντέω confusion
has arisen when some scholars have failed to distinguish the verbal
forms from the noun and adjectival forms of the word. Further, failure
to analyze the data by genre and date has resulted in unwarranted as-
sertions. These difficulties have led to faulty conclusions in some of the
word studies mentioned above.

The methodology employed in this study (separating verb and noun)
is justified for several reasons. First, there are numerous examples in

Greek where the verbal form does not correspond to all the meanings of the noun.[17] We cannot uncritically assume αὐθεντέω is exactly equivalent to "be an αὐθέντης" in every one of its senses. Our driving principle must be how people actually use language, not some theory about the origin of this or that word (etymology).[18] Second, this methodology (separating verb and noun) is the same methodology employed by all recent lexicographers. Third, we have precedent to separate verb and noun forms—particularly in the case of αὐθεντέω—from the ancient lexicographer Hesychius.[19] His is an important datum and a caution against careless etymologizing. Finally, though the verb αὐθεντέω is relatively rare,[20] the eighty-five references examined in this study are believed to be sufficient to give an adequate understanding of the meaning of the verb.[21] Furthermore, the oft-repeated argument—i.e., since the word is so infrequently found, Paul must have chosen it for some esoteric meaning it might carry—will be shown to be without merit.[22] This argument has more weight in light of the fact that the material presented here is drawn from an exhaustive list of the ancient uses of the verbal form known to scholars to date.[23] For these reasons we shall confine our study to the verbal form alone. This is a sound methodology.[24]

Results and Analysis of the Study

Upon analyzing these eighty-five[25] currently known occurrences[26] of the verb αὐθεντέω, it becomes evident that the one unifying concept is that of *authority*. Four outworkings of authority are reflected in the distinct meanings of the verb. Table 2.2 gives a summary of the meanings of αὐθεντέω for quick reference.

Table 2.2
The Meanings of Αὐθεντέω

1. To rule, to reign sovereignly
2. To control, to dominate
   a. to compel, to influence someone/something
   b. middle voice: to be in effect, to have legal standing
   c. hyperbolically: to domineer/play the tyrant
   d. to grant authorization
3. To act independently
   a. to assume authority over
   b. to exercise one's own jurisdiction
   c. to flout the authority of
4. To be primarily responsible for, to do or to instigate something[27]

Meaning 1, "to rule, to reign sovereignly," reflects unhindered authority to act based on inherent or divine right. Its thirteen uses are intransitive (simply, "I rule"). Philodemus uses it of officials, that is, of those who have authority by right of office. Chrysostom uses it of both humanity and deity. The church fathers use it frequently of members of the Godhead.

Meaning 2, "to control, to dominate," reflects authority from the standpoint of actually having control or ability to dominate an object. It may be used in this sense either transitively or intransitively. Ptolemy writes that Saturn dominates Mercury and the moon.[28] Didymus the Blind reports on the practice of his church, saying that women pray and prophesy just as Mary did. But though Mary did these things, she did not write Scripture so as not to exercise control over men. This meaning may imply a kind of control that can be employed in the legitimate exercise of an office.[29] This also, apparently, is the meaning Origen found for αὐθεντέω in 1 Timothy.[30]

Meaning 2a, "to compel, to influence someone/something," is to seek to exercise authority and/or possibly gain the ability to exercise authority/control. Athanasius employs this sense when speaking of the activity of the Holy Spirit. Chrysostom uses it of Jesus, who can compel dead bodies to rise. Ammonius uses it of the apostles, who write letters that compel obedience. These are clearly positive examples. However, the three remaining examples probably should not be understood to prove a negative meaning for αὐθεντέω in and of themselves. That is, they may not indicate "coercion" in its worst sense. In BGU 1208 the influence the writer exercises is based on his authority over his own funds and property. He is seeking to get what he considers an honest payment made to a boatman for services rendered in transferring his sheep across the Nile. In the other two cases, though the results of the act are negative (the fall, the crucifixion), we cannot say more than that the context indicates a negative connotation. There is not sufficient warrant to postulate a new meaning such as "tyrannize" or "coerce." To the contrary, Chrysostom says that Eve "exercised authority once *wrongly*" (ἠυθέντησεν ἅπαξ κακῶς). The implication, obviously, is that Chrysostom could not make the negative force felt without the addition of κακῶς, and he therefore did not regard the verb αὐθεντέω as negative in itself. Malalas's use is somewhat different: though the Jews pressured Pilate, influencing his decision, it cannot be said that they usurped his position or coerced his complicity in Jesus' death, as if Rome were subservient to Jerusalem. But at least we must say that "compel" is the intended meaning, if not something stronger.

Meaning 2b, "to be in effect, to have legal standing," occurs with the use of the middle voice. It is exceedingly rare, occurring only three times. Hippolytus uses it to describe the legal authority of a master over a slave. It is also found twice in the *Chronicon Paschale* with respect to a decree becoming authoritative at a certain point in time.

Meaning 2c, "to domineer/play the tyrant," is substantiated by only a single instance. From the context it is clear that Parker's translation ("do not act the despot") for αὐθέντει is correct. This is the sole unambiguous instance I have found where αὐθεντέω is plainly intended to convey the negative denotation "tyrannize." In this unique usage of the verb, Chrysostom has apparently transformed "exercise sole authority" into the intransitive, "play the tyrant."[31]

Meaning 2d, "to grant authorization," is found in the letters of Marcian and Pulcheria to Leo of Rome. The idea is that Leo has control and can say yes or no to a calling of a synod or a council. Athanasius tells us that Christ did not rain fire down on Sodom of himself, but that the Father authorized it.

Meaning 3, "to act independently," carries the idea of being one's own authority. This meaning appears eight times. The idea is not intrinsically negative. As Knight has pointed out, it does not mean in and of itself "usurp authority."[32] In PLond 1708, Psates has apparently acted on his own authority to cheat his siblings, and Chrysostom says we should not seek "to have our own way." Chrysostom also has Jesus say that he does not need to rebuild the temple of his own body by command of the Father but "exercises his own authority in the matter."

Meaning 3a, "to assume authority over," is a positive term that appears to imply that one moves forward to fill the leadership role. In BGU 103 the request is that the bishop "assume authority" over the matter and resolve a domestic squabble. The term appears to be used as an equivalent of the colloquial phrase "step up to the plate" or "take charge."

Meaning 3b, "to exercise one's own jurisdiction," is only found where αὐθεντέω is intransitive.[33] It occurs several times in negative contexts, where it refers to a condition that results when one has taken to himself or herself the judgments or authority belonging to another. Thus, the word is used three times to speak of an underlord who carries out an execution that ought to have been sanctioned by the king. It is used of other officials who release prisoners, lighten tribute, or convene assemblies without full authorization. In this it is like "usurp." However, "usurp" refers to the *action* of wrongfully appropriating or supplanting, while αὐθεντέω refers to the *state* in which one is when he or she has achieved independent jurisdiction. Further, for a speaker of English to say "to usurp wrongly" would be pleonastic, for "usurp" always has a negative denotation. In contrast αὐθεντέω with this meaning can be viewed positively. For example, when Victor Antiochenus discusses Jesus' rehearsal of David eating the holy bread, he says "For if a prophet assumes his own authority against the law . . . should you be vexed and judge the law?"[34] If the text has been properly reconstructed, the infinitive αὐθεντεῖν appears as a definition of αὐτοδικεῖν in Moeris's second-century AD lexicon. There he seems to indicate that the Attic αὐτοδικέω, "having independent jurisdiction," can be rendered by the Hellenistic αὐθεντέω. The sum of the above leads to the conclusion that the intransitive αὐθεντέω, with the meaning "to exercise one's jurisdiction," is not of itself positive or negative. What the author is trying to say must be determined from the context.

Meaning 3c, "to flout the authority of," is found three times. These all have a clearly negative denotation. John Malalas (ca. AD 690) uses αὐθεντέω transitively to indicate that the army has "sidestepped" the authority of the senate and, on its own, has selected an emperor. The same phrase as that used by Malalas is also found in the tenth-century work *About Strategy* with a similar sense. The transitive use with negative meaning may well be a later development arising from meaning 3b.

Meaning 4 is "to be primarily responsible for, to do or to instigate something." The meaning "to do" is claimed by Wolters in the sense of initiating an action.[35] The simple "to do" is a specific subset of "to be responsible for" and is defensible in the case of Eusebius[36] and the scholia on Homer's *Iliad*.[37] However, the instances in Leo's *Epistle 30*[38] and the *Second Council of Nicea*[39] require the meaning "instigate."[40] In the Suda Lexicon[41] "be responsible for" is taken as a meaning for the verb in contradistinction to "to do the thing with one's own hand." It then goes on to explain the word by the action of King Mithridates (the VI), who ordered murder to be done by letter but did not bear the sword himself.

Under this rubric αὐθεντεῖ has been erroneously taken by the Kroegers[42] to mean "to be the organic origin of something" with a sense analogous to the biological meanings of γεννάω or τίκτω.[43] This is clearly erroneous. A close examination of the eight occurrences of αὐθεντέω with this meaning shows they could all properly be subsumed under the meaning recognized by Lampe, "to be responsible for, to instigate." Indeed, in two of the eight uses under this meaning, αὐθεντέω is directly paralleled in the text by the verb προΐστημι, "to be the leader, to direct, to be the ringleader."[44]

We may note that the sometimes asserted meaning for αὐθεντεῖν, "to murder," is not substantiated for any period even remotely close to the period of the writing of the New Testament, and then by a single datum, a Byzantine scholarly note on a play by Aeschylus (d. 456 BC) from the fourteenth century AD.[45] As Huttar concludes, "The meaning 'murder' for αὐθεντεῖν is not attested in any living, natural Greek used in ordinary discourse, but only in the ingenuity of an etymologizing hypothesis on the past of some comparably late Byzantine scholar."[46]

Since the publication of the first edition, there has been significant discussion of what constitutes a "negative use," a "negative connotation," "positive meaning," and so on, for a particular use of αὐθεντέω. It is well to note that there are two definitions of αὐθεντέω offered here that are "morally negative," the intransitive meaning 2c "play the tyrant," which is attested by only a single datum, and the transitive meaning 3c, "flout the authority of," attested by three data. There are some six to ten instances, depending on how one interprets the larger discourse, where a positive meaning of αὐθεντέω is used in an overall negative context.[47] These, however, do not thereby create a transferable meaning that is "morally negative." Consider, for example, the English word "heal." In Luke 6:7 when the Pharisees wonder "if on the Sabbath Jesus heals,"[48] there is no question that, in the context, the enemies of Jesus would view it as a grievous moral error to heal on the Sabbath day. But that context would provide no justification to define "to heal" and use it in other contexts with a meaning such as "to commit grievous moral error." Much of the discussion of αὐθεντέω has been bedeviled by exegetes failing to recognize the difference between a transferable lexical meaning and the meaning that the total passage bears when a legitimate, transferable meaning is inserted in the context under investigation.[49]

A final observation may be made from the data of table 2.3. Among these data, there appears only limited historical development of the meaning of αὐθεντέω across fourteen centuries. The use of the word by Christian sources certainly brought it into a whole new sphere of application with respect to God and Christ. From the data presented here, it is possible that some of the meanings 2b through 3b *may* have developed after the New Testament period, and especially 3c, "to flout the authority of." What we can say with certainty is that we have no instances of a pejorative use of the verb before the fourth century AD.[50] The data available, however, provide clear indication that the widely understood meanings of αὐθεντέω were based on the idea of the possession or exercise of authority.

Table 2.3
Chronological Distribution of Various Meanings of αὐθεντέω

1. To rule, to reign sovereignly
   (1st cent. BC) Philodemus
   (AD 325) Eusebius
   (ca. AD 390) Chrysostom
   (6th cent. AD) Romanus Melodus
2. To control, to dominate
   (2nd cent. AD) Ptolemy
   (ca. AD 390) Chrysostom

(AD 790) Second Council of Nicea
(12th cent. AD) Michael Glycas
2a. To compel, to influence
(27 BC) BGU 1208
(AD 390) Chrysostom
(AD 690) John Malalas
2b. Middle voice: to be in effect, to have legal standing
(AD 235) Hippolytus
(7th cent. AD) Chronicon Paschale
2c. Uniquely: to domineer
(ca. AD 390) Chrysostom
2d. To grant authorization
(ca. AD 350) Athanasius
(AD 451) Marcian
(d. AD 638) Sophronius
  3. To act independently
(ca. AD 390) Chrysostom
(5th cent. AD) Ammonius Alexandrius
(6th cent. AD) PLond 1708
3a. To assume authority over
(ca. AD 390) Chrysostom
(6th–7th cent. AD) BGU 103
(9th cent. AD) Photius
3b. To exercise one's own jurisdiction
(2nd cent. AD) Moeris
(AD 450) Olympiodorus
(9th cent. AD) Photius
(13th–14th cent. AD) Thomas Magister
3c. To flout the authority of
(ca. AD 690) John Malalas
(10th cent. AD) Constantine VII
  4. To be primarily responsible for, to do, or to instigate
(ca. 1st cent. BC–1st cent. AD) Aristonicus
(ca. AD 325) Eusebius
(AD 449) Leo I
(10th cent. AD) Scholia on Homer

Conclusions

The four definitions (with seven subsets) for αὐθεντέω stand on firm ground. Further investigations will, no doubt, provide additional insights, but both the broad contours of meaning as well as the key details can be said to be understood with a high degree of clarity.[51]

With respect to αὐθεντέω in 1 Timothy 2:12 and the meanings identified in table 2.2, it may be concluded:

1. The root meaning involves the concept of authority.
2. The context of 1 Timothy 2 appears to make meaning 1, "to rule, to reign sovereignly," impermissible.
3. Meanings 2 or 2a, "to control, to dominate" or "to compel, to influence someone/something," are entirely possible.
4. Meaning 2c, "to play the tyrant," could only correspond to Chrysostom's unique usage if the context could be shown to intend the same clear use of hyperbole, and the context does not seem to do that. Of the possible choices, this would definitely be the *least* probable.[52]
5. Noting that αὐθεντεῖν in 1 Timothy 2:12 is transitive, a translation of "assume authority over" (i.e., meaning 3a) could be appropriate, while 3 or 3b, which are intransitive, are not possible. If a negative meaning were intended, meaning 3c, "to flout the authority of," could be possible, yet we have seen this meaning appears only well after the New Testament period.
6. It is difficult to imagine how meaning 2d, "to grant authorization," or meaning 4, "to instigate," could make sense in 1 Timothy.
7. Further syntactical/contextual studies of 1 Timothy (see chap. 3 below) are required to decide with certainty among meanings 2, 2a, 3a, and 3c.

We have come a long way in our understanding of the meaning of αὐθεντέω as it was used by speakers of Koine Greek. We have even been able to narrow the range of meanings that might be appropriate in 1 Timothy 2:12. But before we can enter into the trial-and-error process of identifying the meaning of αὐθεντέω in that verse (which we will do in chapter 4), we must examine the sentence structure of 1 Timothy 2:12 in the next chapter.

3

A COMPLEX SENTENCE

The Syntax of 1 Timothy 2:12

ANDREAS J. KÖSTENBERGER

What is so difficult to understand about Paul's statement "I do not permit a woman to teach or have authority over a man"? On the face of it, it seems clear that the apostle here sets boundaries for women's roles in the church, not just in ancient Ephesus, but in the church, which he later in the same epistle calls "the church of the living God, the pillar and foundation of the truth" (1 Tim. 3:15 NIV). In recent years, however, virtually every aspect of 1 Timothy 2:12 has been explained in a way that either limits the scope of the passage's application or makes the passage say something other than a plain, straightforward reading of it would suggest.

In the first chapter of the present volume, Steven Baugh shows that arguments for limiting the relevance of 1 Timothy 2:12 to the original context based on the ancient background of first-century Ephesus fail to convince. The role of women in first-century Ephesus was not sufficiently peculiar to suggest that Paul intended to curtail the role of women in the *Ephesian* church, but not elsewhere.

In the second chapter, Henry Baldwin carefully analyzes all the extant instances of the word αὐθεντεῖν, meticulously updating his original essay in interaction with subsequent scholarship. Over against efforts to construe the connotation of the term αὐθεντεῖν as negative, so that only women's *negative* exercise of authority would be proscribed by Paul, Baldwin has demonstrated that on the basis of lexical analysis there is no evidence that the word was used with a negative connotation in any of the instances prior to Paul or contemporaneous to him.

At the same time, as Baldwin himself acknowledges, there are limitations to word studies, since it could be argued that Paul used the word in a novel way (though this is not in fact what egalitarians *are* contending) or that an author could invest a basically positive or neutral term with a negative connotation in a particular statement. For this reason we must look at the word αὐθεντεῖν in its context in 1 Timothy 2:12 to confirm or disprove our understanding of Paul's words here.

Just as every nation has laws to govern the life of its citizens, so every language has a system of grammar and syntax that stipulates proper rules and conventions of usage for that language. Unless a writer wants to be accused of breaking the rules (and thus of writing improper Greek, in the present instance), he must conform to these rules of grammar and syntax. As will be seen, a careful study of the Greek grammar and syntax of the present passage goes a long way toward determining the meaning of the word αὐθεντεῖν. Thus the ensuing chapters on the exegesis, hermeneutics, and application of 1 Timothy 2:12 will be set on a firm foundation.

The Significance of Syntactical Background Studies for the Interpretation of 1 Timothy 2:12

The passage reads as follows: "I do not permit a woman to teach or have authority over a man" (or, in the original Greek, διδάσκειν δὲ γυναικὶ οὐκ ἐπιτρέπω οὐδὲ αὐθεντεῖν ἀνδρός, ἀλλ᾽ εἶναι ἐν ἡσυχίᾳ). The syntactical pattern found in 1 Timothy 2:12 can be laid out as follows:

- a negated finite verb ("I do not permit," οὐκ ἐπιτρέπω)
- governing a (preceding) infinitive ("to teach," διδάσκειν)
- which is connected by the coordinating conjunction οὐδέ ("or")
- with a second infinitive ("to have authority," αὐθεντεῖν);
- this phrase is then contrasted with the adversative ἀλλά ("but")
- and yet another infinitive ("to be in quietness," εἶναι ἐν ἡσυχίᾳ).

Or, in other words, the pattern is:

(1) a negated finite verb + (2) infinitive + (3) οὐδέ + infinitive + (4) ἀλλά + infinitive[1]

The need for syntactical background studies to understand 1 Timothy 2:12 has been recognized by P. B. Payne and D. J. Moo, who engaged in a detailed exchange on the syntactical significance of οὐδέ in the verse. Payne argued that οὐδέ connects the two infinitives διδάσκειν and αὐθεντεῖν "in order to convey a single coherent idea," that is, as a hendiadys, so that the passage should be rendered as follows: "I do not permit a woman to teach in a domineering manner."[2] Moo disputed this notion as firmly as Payne asserted it, arguing that, while οὐδέ "certainly usually joins 'two *closely related* items,'" it does not usually join together words that restate the same thing or that are mutually interpreting."[3] Moo concluded that, while teaching and having authority are closely related, "they are nonetheless distinct," referring also to 1 Timothy 3:2, 4–5 and 5:17, where these two concepts are distinguished.[4]

Indeed, Payne's study is subject to improvement at several points. First, Payne studies only Paul. A more comprehensive study of the uses of οὐδέ in the whole New Testament is needed, if for no other reason than that the Pauline authorship of the Pastorals, including 1 Timothy, remains in dispute. Second, Payne studies all the occurrences of οὐδέ in Paul, even where it joins nouns, not verbs. It would seem desirable to sharpen the focus by studying the passages where οὐδέ joins verbs.[5]

Third, Payne does not consider uses of μηδέ in Paul or elsewhere in the New Testament. Only seven instances remain where Paul uses οὐδέ to connect verbs (1 Cor. 15:50; 2 Cor. 7:12; Gal. 1:17; 4:14; Phil. 2:16; 2 Thess. 3:8; 1 Tim. 6:16). However, references including μηδέ in writings traditionally attributed to Paul provide eight further examples alone (Rom. 9:11, 16b; 14:21; 2 Cor. 4:2; Col. 2:21; 2 Thess. 2:2; 1 Tim. 1:3–4; 6:17). Notably, two of these, 1 Timothy 1:3–4 and 6:17, occur in the same letter. Fourth, Payne already starts with the assumption that αὐθεντεῖν means "domineer." However, that is the very thing that needs to be established, not asserted. What is called for is an inductive study of all the instances of οὐδέ joining verbs, both in the New Testament and in extrabiblical Greek literature. This investigation will distill the database for understanding the syntax of 1 Timothy 2:12 with implications for the meaning of αὐθεντεῖν.

Fifth, since Payne presupposes that αὐθεντεῖν means "domineer," he concludes that "teach" and "domineer" by themselves are conceptually too far apart to be joined by οὐδέ (which usually joins closely related terms) in a coordinating manner. Thus, Payne views the second term joined by οὐδέ in 1 Timothy 2:12, αὐθεντεῖν, as subordinate to the first, διδάσκειν. But if αὐθεντεῖν were to mean "to have authority" rather than "to domineer," it would be quite closely related to διδάσκειν, "to teach." In that case, consistent with Payne's own observations on how οὐδέ generally functions, οὐδέ could well link the two closely related terms, "to teach" and "to have authority," in a coordinating fashion. Payne's argument is circular, and his conclusion is unduly predetermined by his presupposition regarding the meaning of αὐθεντεῖν. Sixth, Payne's terminology is ambiguous when he calls two terms "closely related." He seems to use this terminology in the sense of "essentially one" so that he can conclude that in 1 Timothy 2:12 "οὐδέ joins together two elements in order to convey a single coherent idea." However, as will be shown below, two terms can be "closely related" and yet be distinct. For example, Matthew 6:20 refers to heaven, "where thieves neither break in nor steal." While "breaking in" and "stealing" are sequentially related and may be seen as components of essentially one event, burglary, the two activities are not so closely related as to lose their own distinctness. The burglar first breaks in and then steals.

Seventh, Payne is inconsistent in his use of terminology regarding his categories of the usage of οὐδέ. On page 1, he terms his second category "those which specify with greater clarity the meaning of one word or phrase by conjoining it with another word or phrase." Yet in his conclusion on page 10, he calls the same category those in which "οὐδέ joins together two elements in order to convey a single coherent idea." From the beginning of his paper until the end, Payne has subtly shifted from one definition of his crucial category to another. While his definition on page 1 allows for terms to be closely related and yet distinct, Payne's categorization on page 10 unduly narrows his earlier definition so that now closely related yet distinct terms seem excluded. Eighth, on page 10 Payne notes translations that render αὐθεντεῖν with "domineer" or similarly negative connotations. He fails to observe, however, that neither the NASB, the RSV, nor the NIV renders the term with a negative connotation. The NASB has "exercise authority"; the NIV and the RSV translate αὐθεντεῖν with "to have authority."

We may summarize the argument thus far. Two methodological paths have been taken to identify the proper rendering of 1 Timothy 2:12: word studies and syntactical studies. The rarity of the use of αὐθεντεῖν and other limitations impose certain restraints on word studies in the present instance. The major syntactical study on the passage is subject to some significant improvements. Therefore, a fresh study of New Testament syntactical parallels to 1 Timothy 2:12 needs to be undertaken.[6] Furthermore, extrabiblical Greek literature from the period preceding or contemporary with the New Testament should be consulted to supplement the study of syntactical parallels to 1 Timothy 2:12.

Syntactical Parallels to 1 Timothy 2:12
in the New Testament

Strictly speaking, there is only one close syntactical parallel to 1 Timothy 2:12 in the New Testament, Acts 16:21, where the same construction, a negated finite verb + infinitive + οὐδέ + infinitive, is found.[7] However, if one allows for verbal forms other than infinitives to be linked by οὐδέ, fifty-two further passages can be identified. These can be grouped into two patterns of the usage of οὐδέ:

- Pattern 1: two activities or concepts are viewed positively in and of themselves, but their exercise is prohibited or their existence is denied due to circumstances or conditions adduced in the context.
- Pattern 2: two activities or concepts are viewed negatively, and consequently their exercise is prohibited or their existence is denied or they are to be avoided.

In both patterns, the conjunction οὐδέ coordinates activities of the same order, that is, activities that are both viewed either positively or negatively by the writer or speaker.

Pattern 1, the prohibition or denial of two activities or concepts that are otherwise viewed positively, is found in the following New Testament passages: Matt. 6:26 = Luke 12:24; Matt. 6:28 = Luke 12:27; Matt. 7:6, 18; 10:14 = Mark 6:11; Matt. 13:13; 22:46; 23:13; Mark 8:17; 13:15; Luke 6:44; 17:23; 18:4; John 14:17; Acts 4:18; 9:9; 16:21; 17:24–25; 21:21; Rom. 9:11, 16; 14:21; 1 Cor. 15:50; Gal. 1:16–17; Col. 2:21; 1 Tim. 2:12; 6:16; Heb. 10:8; 1 John 3:6; and Rev. 12:8.

Pattern 2, the prohibition or denial of two activities that are both viewed negatively, can be seen in Matt. 6:20 = Luke 12:33; Matt. 12:19; Luke 3:14; John 4:15; 14:27; Acts 2:27; 2 Cor. 4:2; 7:12; Gal. 4:14; Phil. 2:16; 2 Thess. 2:2; 3:7–8; 1 Tim. 1:3–4; 6:17; Heb. 12:5; 13:5; 1 Pet. 2:22; 3:14; and Rev. 7:16. Overall, in the New Testament there are thirty-three examples of the first pattern and twenty of the second (see table 3.1).

Table 3.1
Patterns of the Usage of οὐδέ in the New Testament

Pattern 1: Two activities or concepts are viewed positively in and of themselves, but their exercise is prohibited or their existence is denied due to circumstances or conditions adduced in the context.

Matt. 6:26	οὐ σπείρουσιν (sow)	οὐδὲ θερίζουσιν (harvest)
		οὐδὲ συνάγουσιν εἰς ἀποθήκας (gather into barns)

Matt. 6:28	οὐ κοπιῶσιν (labor)	οὐδὲ νήθουσιν (spin)
Matt. 7:6	Μὴ δῶτε (give)	μηδὲ βάλητε (throw)
Matt. 7:18	οὐ δύναται ποιεῖν (can yield)	οὐδὲ ποιεῖν (yield)*
Matt. 10:14	μὴ δέξηται (receive)	μηδὲ ἀκούσῃ (listen)
Matt. 13:13	οὐκ ἀκούουσιν (hear)	οὐδὲ συνίουσιν (understand)
Matt. 22:46	οὐδεὶς ἐδύνατο ἀποκριθῆναι (could answer)	οὐδὲ ἐτόλμησεν ἐπερωτῆσαι (dared to ask)
Matt. 23:13	οὐκ εἰσέρχεσθε (enter)	οὐδὲ ἀφίετε εἰσελθεῖν (permit to enter)
Mark 6:11	μὴ δέξηται (receive)	μηδὲ ἀκούσωσιν (listen; cf. Matt. 10:14)**
Mark 8:17	οὔπω νοεῖτε (understand)	οὐδὲ συνίετε (understand)
Mark 13:15	μὴ καταβάτω (go down)	μηδὲ εἰσελθάτω (enter)
Luke 6:44	οὐ συλλέγουσιν (pick)	οὐδὲ τρυγῶσιν (gather)
Luke 12:24	οὐ σπείρουσιν (sow)	οὐδὲ θερίζουσιν (harvest; cf. Matt. 6:26)
Luke 12:27	οὐ κοπιᾷ (labor)	οὐδὲ νήθει (spin; cf. Matt. 6:28)
Luke 17:23	μὴ ἀπέλθητε (depart)	μηδὲ διώξητε (follow)
Luke 18:4	οὐ φοβοῦμαι (fear [God])	οὐδὲ ἐντρέπομαι (care [about man])
John 14:17	οὐ θεωρεῖ (behold)	οὐδὲ γινώσκει (know)
Acts 4:18	μὴ φθέγγεσθαι (speak)	μηδὲ διδάσκειν (teach)
Acts 9:9	οὐκ ἔφαγεν (eat)	οὐδὲ ἔπιεν (drink)
Acts 16:21	οὐκ ἔξεστιν παραδέχεσθαι (accept)	οὐδὲ ποιεῖν (practice)
Acts 17:24–25	οὐκ κατοικεῖ (dwell)	οὐδὲ θεραπεύεται (be served)
Acts 21:21	μὴ περιτέμνειν (circumcise)	μηδὲ περιπατεῖν (walk [in customs])
Rom. 9:11	μήπω γεννηθέντων (born)	μηδὲ πραξάντων (done)
Rom. 9:16	οὐ τοῦ θέλοντος (wishing)	οὐδὲ τοῦ τρέχοντος (running)
Rom. 14:21	μὴ φαγεῖν (eat)	μηδὲ πιεῖν (drink)
1 Cor. 15:50	κληρονομῆσαι οὐ δύναται (can inherit)	οὐδὲ κληρονομεῖ (inherit)*
Gal. 1:16–17	οὐ προσανεθέμην (consult)	οὐδὲ ἀνῆλθον (go up)
Col. 2:21	μὴ ἅψῃ (touch)	μηδὲ γεύσῃ μηδὲ θίγῃς (taste, handle)
1 Tim. 2:12	διδάσκειν οὐκ ἐπιτρέπω (teach)	οὐδὲ αὐθεντεῖν ἀνδρός (have authority over a man)
1 Tim. 6:16	εἶδεν οὐδείς (see)	οὐδὲ ἰδεῖν δύναται (can see)
Heb. 10:8	οὐκ ἠθέλησας (desire)	οὐδὲ εὐδόκησας (be well pleased)
1 John 3:6	οὐχ ἑώρακεν (see)	οὐδὲ ἔγνωκεν (know)
Rev. 12:8	οὐκ ἴσχυσεν (prevail)	οὐδὲ τόπος εὑρέθη (place be found)*

Pattern 2: Two activities or concepts are viewed negatively, and consequently their exercise is prohibited or their existence is denied or they are to be avoided.

Matt. 6:20	οὐ διορύσσουσιν (break in)	οὐδὲ κλέπτουσιν (steal)
Matt. 12:19	οὐκ ἐρίσει (quarrel)	οὐδὲ κραυγάσει (cry out)
Luke 3:14	μηδένα διασείσητε (extort money)	μηδὲ συκοφαντήσητε (accuse falsely)
Luke 12:33	κλέπτης οὐκ ἐγγίζει (thief come near)	οὐδὲ διαφθείρει (destroy; cf. Matt. 6:20)*
John 4:15	μὴ διψῶ (thirst)	μηδὲ διέρχωμαι ἀντλεῖν (come to draw)
John 14:27	μὴ ταρασσέσθω (let be troubled)	μηδὲ δειλιάτω (be afraid)
Acts 2:27	οὐκ ἐγκαταλείψεις (abandon)	οὐδὲ δώσεις ἰδεῖν διαφθοράν (give to see decay)
2 Cor. 4:2	μὴ περιπατοῦντες ἐν πανουργίᾳ (walk in deceit)	μηδὲ δολοῦντες (distort)
2 Cor. 7:12	οὐκ ἕνεκεν τοῦ ἀδικήσαντος (the wrongdoer)	οὐδὲ ἕνεκεν τοῦ ἀδικηθέντος (the injured party)
Gal. 4:14	οὐκ ἐξουθενήσατε (treat with contempt)	οὐδὲ ἐξεπτύσατε (scorn)
Phil. 2:16	οὐκ εἰς κενὸν ἔδραμον (run in vain)	οὐδὲ εἰς κενὸν ἐκοπίασα (labor in vain)
2 Thess. 2:2	μὴ σαλευθῆναι (become unsettled)	μηδὲ θροεῖσθαι (become alarmed)
2 Thess. 3:7–8	οὐκ ἠτακτήσαμεν (be idle)	οὐδὲ ἐφάγομεν (eat another's food)
1 Tim. 1:3–4	μὴ ἑτεροδιδασκαλεῖν (teach error)	μηδὲ προσέχειν μύθοις (pay attention to myths)
1 Tim. 6:17	μὴ ὑψηλοφρονεῖν (be arrogant)	μηδὲ ἠλπικέναι ἐπὶ πλούτου (put hope in wealth)
Heb. 12:5	μὴ ὀλιγώρει (despise)	μηδὲ ἐκλύου (consider lightly)
Heb. 13:5	οὐ μή ἀνῶ (leave)	οὐδ' οὐ μή ἐγκαταλίπω (forsake)
1 Pet. 2:22	ἁμαρτίαν οὐκ ἐποίησεν (commit sin)	οὐδὲ εὑρέθη δόλος (deceit be found)*
1 Pet. 3:14	μὴ φοβηθῆτε (be afraid)	μηδὲ ταραχθῆτε (be disturbed)
Rev. 7:16	οὐ πεινάσουσιν (hunger)	οὐδὲ διψήσουσιν (thirst)

*= change of subject; **= change from sing. to pl. verb form.

The first pattern can be illustrated by a few examples. In Acts 16:21, the closest syntactical parallel to 1 Timothy 2:12 in the New Testament, the two terms in the infinitive, παραδέχεσθαι and ποιεῖν, are conceptual parallels. "Accepting" and "practicing" do not carry negative connotations in and of themselves. However, due to circumstances indicated in the context, "being Romans," the exercise of these otherwise legitimate activities is considered "not lawful." In Acts 4:18, Luke reports that the authorities, because of their antagonism to Christ, forbid the early church

to speak and teach in the name of Jesus (two activities that carry no
negative connotations in and of themselves). In Acts 21:21, Paul is told
of reports that he forbids Jews living among Gentiles to carry out two
activities viewed positively by the speakers, circumcising their children
and living according to Jewish customs. In Galatians 1:16–17, to underscore that he had been divinely commissioned, Paul insists that, upon
his conversion, he did not immediately consult with others nor go up
to Jerusalem, two activities that are not intrinsically viewed negatively.
And in Colossians 2:21, the writer quotes the maxim "Do not touch, do
not taste, do not handle," as the (legalistic) prohibition of activities not
viewed negatively in and of themselves.

The following examples are instances of the second pattern, the prohibition or denial of two activities that are viewed negatively by the writer
or speaker. In John 4:15, the Samaritan woman expresses her desire to
avoid two things she views negatively, thirsting and having to come to the
well to draw water. In Philippians 2:16, Paul states that he wants to avoid
two activities he views negatively, running in vain and laboring in vain.
In 2 Thessalonians 3:7–8, Paul denies that, at his previous visit, he had
engaged in two activities that he views negatively, being idle and eating
another's food. A passage in the epistle under consideration, 1 Timothy
1:3–4, instructs Timothy to command certain ones to avoid two activities
the author views negatively, teaching error and holding to myths and endless genealogies. Later in the same epistle, in 6:17, one finds the instruction
to Timothy to command the rich in his congregation to avoid two things
viewed negatively by the writer, being arrogant and setting their hope on
the uncertainty of riches.

These examples set forth the New Testament evidence that οὐδέ joins
terms denoting activities that are both viewed either positively or negatively by the writer or speaker. The implication of this observation for
1 Timothy 2:12 is that there are only two acceptable ways of rendering
that passage: (1) "I do not permit a woman to teach [error] or to domineer over a man," or (2) "I do not permit a woman to teach or to exercise
authority over a man." In the first instance, both "teaching error" and
"domineering over a man" would be viewed negatively by the writer.
In the latter case, both "teaching" and "exercising authority" would be
viewed positively in and of themselves, yet for reasons to be gleaned
from the context, the writer does not permit these.

Before deciding on one of the two patterns for 1 Timothy 2:12, a preliminary clarification needs to be made. A distinction should be drawn,
especially in the first scenario, between the fact that two activities or
concepts are viewed positively in and of themselves and their prohibition due to circumstances. In the case of 1 Timothy 2:12, the writer's
"I do not permit" has apparently at times been taken to mean that he

views the two activities, διδάσκειν and αὐθεντεῖν, themselves negatively, in the sense of "teaching in a domineering way," or the like. However, one should keep in mind that it is possible for the writer, due to certain circumstances, to evaluate negatively the exercise of activities he generally views positively without tainting the two terms themselves.

For example, I may tell my pregnant wife that I do not want her to drive alone or be on the road at night. There is nothing wrong with driving alone or being on the road at night. It is just that, under the circumstances, my wife's pregnancy, I prefer for her not to engage in these activities. Or you may tell your child not to climb a ladder or to go near a cliff. There is nothing wrong with climbing a ladder or even going near a cliff. It is just that, since you fear for your children's safety, you do not permit them to engage in two activities that are otherwise viewed as permissible. In short, it remains a legitimate possibility for a writer to deny someone for certain reasons the exercise of activities he otherwise views positively.

In the light of this clarification, 1 Timothy 2:12 could legitimately be seen as an example of the first pattern, that is, the denial of two activities that are viewed positively in and of themselves, under contextually adduced circumstances. That this is indeed the case is strongly suggested by the use of the term διδάσκειν, which is consistently viewed positively in the New Testament, including the Pastorals, when used absolutely, that is, unaccompanied by contextual qualifiers such as those denoting the content of someone's teaching.[8]

The Kroegers' claim that "if the context of 1 Timothy 2:12 is neutral and refers only to the activity of teaching rather than to its positive or negative content, then it is the only time that διδάσκειν is so used in the Pastorals" is contradicted by passages such as the following:

- 1 Timothy 4:11: Παράγγελλε ταῦτα καὶ δίδασκε (Command and teach these things)
- 1 Timothy 6:2: Ταῦτα δίδασκε καὶ παρακάλει (Teach and encourage these things)
- 2 Timothy 2:2: Ταῦτα παράθου πιστοῖς ἀνθρώποις οἵτινες ἱκανοὶ ἔσονται καὶ ἑτέρους διδάξαι (Pass on these things to faithful individuals who will be able to teach others also)[9]

In each case, διδάσκειν is clearly viewed positively by the writer and is linked with activities such as encouraging, exhorting, and the passing on of apostolic tradition. And when the Kroegers contend that "the verb here [i.e., in 1 Tim. 2:12] forbids women to teach a wrong doctrine, just as 1 Timothy 1:3–4 and Titus 1:9–14 also forbid false teaching," it must be asserted that in 1 Timothy 1:3–4, it is ἑτεροδιδάσκαλειν, not διδάσκειν, that is used, while in Titus 1:9–14, there is ample contextual indication that false teaching is in view, a feature that is absent from the context of 1 Timothy 2:12.[10]

It should further be noted that the effort to make αὐθεντεῖν subordinate to διδάσκειν so that it in effect functions as an adverb and to give it a negative connotation, as in "to teach in a domineering way," is contradicted by the fact that οὐδέ functions not as a subordinating but as a coordinating conjunction. Neither the syntactical parallels in the New Testament nor the extrabiblical parallels lend support to the contention that the second term linked by οὐδέ modifies the first term adverbially. And while "teaching" and "exercising authority" may well be perceived jointly in 1 Timothy 2:12, these concepts do not blend to the extent that they become one concept in which the two constituent elements are no longer distinguishable.

Since, therefore, the term διδάσκειν is used absolutely in the New Testament for an activity that is viewed positively in and of itself, and since οὐδέ coordinates terms that are both viewed either positively or negatively, αὐθεντεῖν should be seen as denoting an activity that is viewed positively in and of itself as well. Thus, 1 Timothy 2:12 is an instance of the first pattern, in which the exercise of two activities is prohibited or the existence of two concepts is denied by the writer due to special considerations.[11]

The immediate context of the passage, 1 Timothy 2:11, supports this conclusion. Framed by the inclusio of ἡσυχία at the beginning of verse 11 and at the end of verse 12, there are two corresponding pairs of terms: "learning" in verse 11 corresponds to "teaching" in verse 12, and "full submission" in verse 11 relates to "having authority" in verse 12. The writer first expresses his desire for a woman to learn in full submission. Conversely, he then registers his prohibition of the opposite, a woman's teaching or being in authority over a man. He closes by reiterating his desire for a woman to learn in submission. "Learning" and "teaching," "full submission" and "having authority" are contrasted, the former terms being viewed positively in the case of women, the latter ones negatively. Thus, syntax and context join in suggesting that 1 Timothy 2:12 be rendered as "I do not permit a woman to teach or to have authority over a man."

Syntactical Parallels to 1 Timothy 2:12 in Extrabiblical Literature

The study of syntactical parallels to 1 Timothy 2:12 in the New Testament has yielded significant insights. Two patterns of the use of οὐδέ were identified, both consisting of coordinated expressions of the same order. However, since the New Testament contains only one exact syntactical parallel where οὐδέ links two *infinitives* governed by a negated finite verb, it seems desirable to extend the scope of this investigation to extrabiblical Greek literature preceding or contemporary with the New Testament era.

The IBYCUS system, a computer program with the capability of searching virtually all the extant ancient Greek literature, has enabled the researcher to study all Greek literature directly relevant to the study of the syntax used in 1 Timothy 2:12 (i.e., literature from the third century BC until the end of the first century AD)—the LXX, the papyri and inscriptions available on the IBYCUS, and all the extant works of Polybius, Dionysius of Halicarnassus, Diodorus Siculus, Josephus, Philo, and Plutarch.

Forty-eight syntactical parallels to 1 Timothy 2:12 in extrabiblical Greek literature were found: five in the LXX, two in inscriptions, six in Polybius, three in Dionysius of Halicarnassus, two in Diodorus Siculus, nine in Josephus, one in Philo, and twenty in Plutarch. Plutarch accounts for almost half of the references; Josephus and Polybius together provide another third. Following is a list of syntactical parallels to 1 Timothy 2:12.

LXX

1. 1 Maccabees 15:14: καὶ ἐκύκλωσεν τὴν πόλιν, καὶ τὰ πλοῖα ἀπὸ θαλάσσης συνῆψαν, καὶ ἔθλιβε τὴν πόλιν ἀπὸ τῆς γῆς καὶ τῆς θαλάσσης, καὶ (1) οὐκ εἴασεν οὐδένα (2) ἐκπορεύεσθαι (3) οὐδὲ εἰσπορεύεσθαι. "He surrounded the city, and the ships joined battle from the sea; he pressed the city hard from land and sea, and (1) permitted no one (2) to leave (3) or enter it."[12]

2. Sirach 18:6: (1) οὐκ ἔστιν (2) ἐλαττῶσαι (3) οὐδὲ προσθεῖναι, καὶ οὐκ ἔστιν ἐξιχνιάσαι τὰ θαυμάσια τοῦ κυρίου. "[Who can measure his majestic power? And who can fully recount his mercies?] (1) It is not possible (2) to diminish (3) or increase them, nor is it possible to trace the wonders of the Lord."

3. Isaiah 42:24b: οὐχὶ ὁ θεός, ᾧ ἡμάρτοσαν αὐτῷ καὶ (1) οὐκ ἐβούλοντο ἐν ταῖς ὁδοῖς αὐτοῦ (2) πορεύεσθαι (3) οὐδὲ ἀκούειν τοῦ νόμου αὐτοῦ; "[Who gave Jacob up for spoil, and Israel to plunderers?] Was it not God, against whom they have sinned, and in whose ways (1) they were not willing (2) to walk, and whose law (3) they did not obey?"

4. Ezekiel 44:13: καὶ (1) οὐκ ἐγγιοῦσι πρός με τοῦ (2) ἱερατεύειν μοι (3) οὐδὲ τοῦ προσάγειν πρὸς τὰ ἅγια υἱῶν τοῦ Ισραηλ οὐδὲ πρὸς τὰ

ἅγια τῶν ἁγίων μου καὶ λήμψονται ἀτιμίαν αὐτῶν ἐν τῇ πλανήσει, ᾗ ἐπλανήθησαν. "And (1) they shall not come near to Me (2) to serve as a priest to Me, (3) nor come near to any of the holy things of the sons of Israel, nor to the holiest of my holy things; but they shall bear their dishonor in their shame by which they have deceived."

5. Daniel 5:8 (Theod.): καὶ εἰσεπορεύοντο πάντες οἱ σοφοὶ τοῦ βασιλέως καὶ (1) οὐκ ἠδύναντο τὴν γραφὴν (2) ἀναγνῶναι (3) οὐδὲ τὴν σύγκρισιν γνωρίσαι τῷ βασιλεῖ. "Then all the king's wise men came in, but (1) they could not (2) read the inscription (3) [n]or make known its interpretation to the king."

Inscriptions

6. Attica.IG II(2).11589 (third century BC): (1) οὐκ ἄνσχετο (2) δῶρα δέχεσθαι (3) οὐδὲ κλύειν ἱκέτου Τισαμενοῖο πατρός. "(1) He did not stand up (2) to receive gifts (3) nor to give ear to the suppliant, Tisamenoios the father."

7. PZenPestm.21 (246 BC): Νίκων δὲ ὁ κρινόμενος πρὸς Ἀντίπατρον (1) οὐκ ἔφατο (2) εἰληφέναι τὸ παιδάριον παρ᾽ αὐτῶν (3) οὐδὲ ἔχειν αὐτὸ παρευρέσει οὐδεμιᾷ. "Nikon the judge (1) did not say to Antipater (2) to take the boy from them (3) nor to hold him under any pretense."

Polybius (202–120 BC)

8. *Hist.* 2.56.10: (1) δεῖ τοιγαροῦν οὐκ (2) ἐκπλήττειν τὸν συγγραφέα τερατευόμενον διὰ τῆς ἱστορίας τοὺς ἐντυγχάνοντας (3) οὐδὲ τοὺς ἐνδεχομένους λόγους ζητεῖν καὶ τὰ παρεπόμενα τοῖς ὑποκειμένοις ἐξαριθμεῖσθαι, καθάπερ οἱ τραγῳδιογράφοι, τῶν δὲ πραχθέντων καὶ ῥηθέντων κατ᾽ ἀλήθειαν αὐτῶν μνημονεύειν πάμπαν, κἂν πάνυ μέτρια τυγχάνωσιν ὄντα. "A historical author (1) should not (2) try to thrill his readers by such exaggerated pictures, (3) nor should he, like a tragic poet, try to imagine the probable utterances of his characters or reckon up all the consequences probably incidental to the occurrences with which he deals, but simply record what really happened and what really was said, however commonplace."

9. *Hist.* 5.10.5: (1) οὐ γὰρ ἐπ᾽ ἀπωλείᾳ δεῖ καὶ ἀφανισμῷ τοῖς ἀγνοήσασι (2) πολεμεῖν τοὺς ἀγαθοὺς ἄνδρας, ἀλλ᾽ ἐπὶ διορθώσει καὶ μεταθέσει τῶν ἡμαρτημέων, (3) αὐδὲ συναναιρεῖν τὰ μηδὲν ἀδικοῦντα τοῖς ἠδικηκόσιν, ἀλλὰ συσσῴζειν μᾶλλον καὶ οὐνεξαιρεῖσθαι τοῖς ἀνοιτίοις τοὺς δοκοῦντας ἀδικεῖν. "For good men (1) should not (2) make war on wrong-doers with the object of destroying and

exterminating them, but with that of correcting and reforming their errors, (3) nor should they involve the guiltless in the fate of the guilty, (4) but rather extend to those whom they think guilty the mercy and deliverance they offer to the innocent."

10. *Hist.* 6.15.8: τούτους (1) οὐ δύνανται (2) χειρίζειν, ὡς πρέπει, ποτὲ δὲ τὸ παράπαν (3) οὐδὲ συντελεῖν. "[For the processions they call triumphs, in which the generals bring the actual spectacle of their achievements before the eyes of their fellow-citizens,] (1) cannot (2) be properly organized and sometimes even cannot (3) be held at all, [unless the senate consents and provides the requisite funds.]"

11. *Hist.* 30.5.8.4–6: (1) οὐκ ἐβούλοντο (2) συνδυάζειν (3) οὐδὲ προκαταλαμβάνειν σφᾶς αὐτοὺς ὅρκοις καὶ συνθήκαις, (4) ἀλλ᾽ ἀκέραιοι διαμένοντες κερδαίνειν τὰς ἐξ ἑκάστων ἐλπίδας. "[As they wished none of the kings and princes to despair of gaining their help and alliance,] (1) they did not desire (2) to run in harness with Rome (3) and engage themselves by oaths and treaties, (4) but preferred to remain unembarrassed and able to reap profit from any quarter."

12. *Hist.* 30.24.2.3–4: (1) οὐ δοκοῦσι δὲ (2) γινώσκεσθαι παρὰ τοῖς ἀπαντῶσιν (3) οὐδὲ συνορᾶσθαι διότι λέλυνται σαφῶς, ἐὰν μή τι παράλογον ποιῶσι καὶ τῶν ἄλλων ἐξηλλαγμένον. "[The inhabitants of Peraea were like slaves unexpectedly released from their fetters, who, unable to believe the truth, take longer steps than their natural ones] and (1) fancy that those they meet will (2) not know (3) and see for certain that they are free unless they behave in some strange way and differently from other men."

13. *Hist.* 31.12.5–6: τὴν δὲ σύγκλητον (1) οὐ τολμήσειν ἔτι (2) βοηθεῖν (3) οὐδὲ συνεπισχύειν τοῖς περὶ τὸν Λυσίαν τοιαῦτα διεργασαμένοις. "[For the Syrians would at once transfer the crown to him, even if he appeared accompanied only by a single slave,] while the senate (1) would not go so far as (2) to help (3) and support Lysias after his conduct."

Dionysius of Halicarnassus (First Century BC)

14. *De Thucydide* 7.13–15: Θουκυδίδη δὲ τῷ προελομένῳ μίαν ὑπόθεσιν, ᾗ παρεγίνετο αὐτός, (1) οὐκ ἥρμοττεν (2) ἐγκαταμίσγειν τῇ διηγήσει τὰς θεατρικὰς γοητείας (3) οὐδὲ πρὸς τὴν ἀπάτην ἁρμόττεσθαι τῶν ἀναγνωσομένων, ἣν ἐκεῖναι πεφύκασι φέρειν αἱ συντάξεις, (4) ἀλλὰ πρὸς τὴν ὠφέλειαν. "Thucydides, however, chose a single episode in which he personally participated: (1) it was therefore inappropriate for him (2) to adulterate his narrative with entertaining fantasies (3) or to arrange it in a way which would confuse his readers, as

his predecessors' compositions would naturally do. His purpose was to benefit his readers."

15. *Antiquitates romanae* 10.12.3–5: ἢ ὡς (1) οὐ δεῖ (2) κοινωνεῖν (3) οὐδὲ παρεῖναι τῇ ζητήσει τοὺς ἀνειληφότας τὴν τοῦ δήμου ἀρχήν. "Or that the magistrates of the populace (1) ought not (2) to take part in or (3) be present at the inquiry."

16. *De compositione verborum* 23.2–5: (1) οὐ ζητεῖ καθ᾽ ἓν ἕκαστον ὄνομα ἐκ περιφανείας (2) ὁρᾶσθαι (3) οὐδὲ ἐν ἕδρᾳ πάντα βεβηκέναι πλατείᾳ τε καὶ ἀσφαλεῖ οὐδὲ μακροὺς τοὺς μεταξὺ αὐτῶν εἶναι χρόνους. "[The polished style of composition, which I placed second in order, has the following character.] (1) It does not intend each word (2) to be viewed from all sides, (3) nor that every word shall stand on a broad, firm base, nor that the intervals of time between them shall be long."

Diodorus Siculus (ca. 40 BC)

17. *Bibl. hist.* 3.30.2.8–9: (1) οὐ χρὴ δὲ (2) θαυμάζειν (3) οὐδὲ ἀπιστεῖν τοῖς λεγομένοις, πολλὰ τούτων παραδοξότερα κατὰ πᾶσαν τὴν οἰκουμένην γεγονότα διὰ τῆς ἀληθοῦς ἱστορίας παρειληφότας. "(1) Nor is there any occasion (2) to be surprised at this statement (3) or to distrust it, since we have learned through trustworthy history of many things more astonishing than this which have taken place throughout all the inhabited world."

18. *Bibl. hist.* 3.37.9.1–4: διόπερ τηλικούτου μεγέθους ὄφεως εἰς ὄψιν κοινὴν κατηντηκότος (1) οὐκ ἄξιον (2) ἀπιστεῖν τοῖς Αἰθίοψιν (3) οὐδὲ μῦθον ὑπολαμβάνειν τὸ θρυλούμενον ὑπ᾽ αὐτῶν. "Consequently, in view of the fact that a snake of so great a size has been exposed to the public gaze, (1) it is not fair (2) to doubt the word of the Ethiopians (3) or to assume that the report which they circulated far and wide was a mere fiction."

Josephus (AD 37–100)

19. *Contra Apionem* 2.6.1–3: (1) ἔστι μὲν οὖν οὐ ῥᾴδιον αὐτοῦ (2) διελθεῖν τὸν λόγον (3) οὐδὲ σαφῶς γνῶναι τί λέγειν βούλεται. "His argument (1) is difficult (2) to summarize and his meaning (3) to grasp."

20. *Contra Apionem* 2.212.1–2: (1) οὐ γὰρ ἐᾷ τὴν γῆν αὐτῶν (2) πυρπολεῖν (3) οὐδὲ τέμνειν ἥμερα δένδρα, ἀλλὰ καὶ σκυλεύειν ἀπείρηκε τοὺς ἐν τῇ μάχῃ πεσόντας καὶ τῶν αἰχμαλώτων προυνόησεν. "(1) He does not allow us (2) to burn up their country (3) or to cut down their fruit trees, and forbids even the spoiling of fallen combatants."

21. *Bellum judaicum* 5.199.3–5: κατὰ γὰρ τὰς ἄλλας (1) οὐκ ἐξῆν (2) παρελθεῖν γυναιξίν, ἀλλ᾿ (3) οὐδὲ κατὰ τὴν σφετέραν ὑπερβῆναι τὸ διατείχισμα. "For women (1) were not permitted (2) to enter by the others (3) nor yet to pass by way of their own gate beyond the partition wall."

22. *Ant.* 2.116.3–5: ὡς (1) οὐ προσῆκε μὲν αὐτὸν περὶ τἀδελφοῦ (2) δεδιέναι (3) οὐδὲ τὰ μὴ δεινὰ δι᾿ ὑποψίας λαμβάνειν. "[Judas, ever of a hardy nature, frankly told him] that (1) he ought not (2) to be alarmed for their brother (3) nor harbour suspicions of dangers that did not exist."

23. *Ant.* 6.20.3–5: (1) οὐκ (2) ἐπιθυμεῖν ἐλευθερίας (1) δεῖ μόνον, ἀλλὰ καὶ ποιεῖν δι᾿ ὧν ἂν ἔλθοι πρὸς ὑμᾶς, (3) οὐδὲ βούλεσθαι μὲν ἀπηλλάχθαι δεσποτῶν ἐπιμένειν δὲ πράττοντας ἐξ ὧν οὗτοι διαμενοῦσιν. "(1) Ye ought not to be content (2) to yearn for liberty, but should do also the deeds whereby ye may attain it, (3) nor merely long to be rid of your masters, while continuing so to act that they shall remain so."

24. *Ant.* 6.344.5–6: (1) οὐκ ἔγνω (2) φυγεῖν αὐτὸν (3) οὐδὲ φιλοψυχήσας προδοῦναι μὲν τοὺς οἰκείους τοῖς πολεμίοις καθυβρίσαι δὲ τὸ τῆς βασιλείας ἀξίωμα, ἀλλά. "[For he, although he knew of what was to come and his impending death, which the prophet had foretold,] yet (1) determined not (2) to flee from it (3) or, by clinging to life, to betray his people to the enemy and dishonour the dignity of kingship; instead."

25. *Ant.* 7.127.1–3: Τοῦτο τὸ πταῖσμα τοὺς Ἀμμανίτας (1) οὐκ ἔπεισεν (2) ἠρεμεῖν (3) οὐδὲ μαθόντας τοὺς κρείττονας ἡσυχίαν ἄγειν, (4) ἀλλὰ πέμψαντες πρὸς Χαλαμάν. "This defeat (1) did not persuade the Ammanites (2) to remain quiet (3) or to keep the peace in the knowledge that their enemy was superior. (4) Instead they sent to Chalamas."

26. *Ant.* 14.346.1–3: ὁ δὲ Ὑρκανὸν (2) ἀπολιπεῖν (1) οὐκ ἠξίου (3) οὐδὲ παρακινδυνεύειν τἀδελφῷ. "Phasael, however, (1) did not think it right (2) to desert Hyrcanus (3) or to endanger his brother."

27. *Ant.* 15.165.3–4: ὁ μὲν γὰρ Ὑρκανὸς ἐπιεικείᾳ τρόπου καὶ τότε καὶ τὸν ἄλλον χρόνον (1) οὐκ ἠξίου (2) πολυπραγμονεῖν (3) οὐδὲ νεωτέρων ἅπτεσθαι. "Now Hyrcanus because of his mild character (1) did not choose either then or at any other time (2) to take part in public affairs (3) or start a revolution."[13]

Philo (ca. 25 BC–AD 40)

28. *Posterity and Exile of Cain* 84.5–7: (1) οὐ γὰρ (2) ἀναπτῆναι, θησίν, εἰς οὐρανὸν (3) οὐδὲ πέραν θαλάσσης ἀφικέσθαι (1) δεῖ κατὰ ζήτη-

σιν τοῦ καλοῦ. "'For (1) it is not necessary,' he says, (2) 'to fly up into heaven, (3) nor to get beyond the sea in searching for what is good.' "

Plutarch (AD 40–120)

29. *Romulus* 9.2.4–5: ὅτι γὰρ (1) οὐκ ἠξίουν οἱ τὴν Ἄλβην οἰκοῦντες (2) ἀναμιγνύναι τοὺς ἀποστάτας ἑαυτοῖς (3) οὐδὲ προσδέχεσθαι πολίτας. "For that the residents of Alba (1) would not consent (2) to give the fugitives the privilege of intermarriage with them, (3) nor even receive them as fellow citizens [is clear]."

30. *Marcius Coriolanus* 27.4.1: τὰ γὰρ ἄλλα πάντα λυμαινόμενος καὶ διαφθείρων, τοὺς ἐκείνων ἀγροὺς ἰσχυρῶς ἐφύλαττε, καὶ (1) οὐκ εἴα (2) κακουργεῖν (3) οὐδὲ λαμβάνειν ἐξ ἐκείνων οὐδέν. "For while he maltreated and destroyed everything else, he kept a vigorous watch over the lands of the patricians, and (1) would not suffer anyone (2) to hurt them (3) or take anything from them."

31. *Timoleon* 37.2.1: ὧν Λαφυστίου μὲν αὐτὸν πρός τινα δίκην κατεγ-γυῶντος (1) οὐκ εἴα (2) θορυβεῖν (3) οὐδὲ κωλύειν τοὺς πολίτας. "Of these, Laphystius once tried to make him give surety that he would appear at a certain trial, and Timoleon (1) would not suffer the citizens (2) to stop the man (3) by their turbulent disapproval [lit., nor to prevent him]."

32. *Comparatio Aristidis et Catonis* 4.2.1: (1) οὐ γὰρ ἔστι (2) πράττειν μεγάλα φροντίζοντα μικρῶν, (3) οὐδὲ πολλοῖς δεομένοις βοηθεῖν πολλῶν αὐτὸν δεόμενον. "(1) It is impossible for a man (2) to do great things when his thoughts are busy with little things; (3) nor can he aid the many who are in need when he himself is in need of many things."

33. *Pyrrhus* 33.6.4: σπασάμενον γὰρ τὸ ξίφος ἢ κλίναντα λόγχην (1) οὐκ ἦν (2) ἀναλαβεῖν (3) οὐδὲ καταθέσθαι πάλιν, ἀλλ᾽ ἐχώρει δι᾽ ὧν ἔτυχε τὰ τοιαῦτα πάντα, καὶ περιπίπτοντες ἀλλήλοις ἔθνησκον. "For when a man had drawn his sword or poised his spear, (1) he could not (2) recover (3) or sheathe his weapon again, but it would pass through those who stood in its way, and so they died from one another's blows."

34. *Agesilaus* 32.3.3–4: ἐπεὶ δὲ φιλοτιμούμενος ὁ Ἐπαμεινώνδας ἐν τῇ πόλει μάχην συνάψαι καὶ στῆσαι τρόπαιον (1) οὐκ ἴσχυσεν (2) ἐξαγαγεῖν (3) οὐδὲ προκαλέσασθαι τὸν Ἀγησίλαον, ἐκεῖνος μὲν ἀναζεύξας πάλιν ἐπόρθει τὴν χώραν. "Epaminondas was ambitious to join battle in the city and set up a trophy of victory there, but since (1) he could (2) neither force (3) nor tempt Agesilaus out of his positions, he withdrew and began to ravage the country."

35. *Quomodo adulator ab amico internoscatur* 64.E.7–8: Ὁρᾷς τὸν πίθηκον; (1) οὐ δύναται τὴν οἰκίαν (2) φυλάττειν ὡς ὁ κύων, (3) οὐδὲ βαστάζειν ὡς ὁ ἵππος, οὐδ᾽ ἀροῦν τὴν γῆν ὡς οἱ βόες. "You must have noticed the ape. (1) He cannot (2) guard the house like the dog, (3) nor carry a load like the horse, nor plow the land like oxen."

36. *Consolatio ad Apollonium* 115.E.3.: ἀνθρώποις δὲ πάμπαν (1) οὐκ ἔστι (2) γενέσθαι τὸ πάντων ἄριστον (3) οὐδὲ μετασχεῖν τῆς τοῦ βελτίστου φύσεως (ἄριστον γὰρ πᾶσι καὶ πάσαις τὸ μὴ γενέσθαι). "But for men (1) it is utterly impossible (2) that they should obtain the best thing of all, (3) or even have any share in its nature (for the best thing for all men and women is not to be born)."

37. *Regum et imperatorum apophthegmata* 185.A.2: πρὸς δὲ τοὺς θαυμά-ζοντας τὴν μεταβολὴν ἔλεγεν ὡς (1) "οὐκ ἐᾷ με (2) καθεύδειν (3) οὐδὲ ῥαθυμεῖν τὸ Μιλτιάδου τρόπαιον." [Themistocles while yet in his youth abandoned himself to wine and women. But after Miltiades, commanding the Athenian army, had overcome the barbarians at Marathon, never again was it possible to encounter Themistocles misconducting himself.] To those who expressed their amazement at the change in him, he said that 'the trophy of Miltiades (1) does not allow me (2) to sleep (3) or to be indolent.' "

38. *Aetia romana et graeca* 269.D.8–9: (1) οὐ δεῖ δὲ τῶν ἡμερῶν τὸν ἀκριβέστατον ἀριθμὸν (2) διώκειν (3) οὐδὲ τὸ παρ᾽ ὀλίγον συκοφαν-τεῖν. "But (1) we must not (2) follow out the most exact calculation of the number of days (3) nor cast aspersions on approximate reckoning [since even now, when astronomy has made so much progress, the irregularity of the moon's movements is still be-yond the skill of mathematicians, and continues to elude their calculations]."

39. *Aetia romana et graeca* 273.E.9–10: Διὰ τί τοῖς μὴ στρατευομένοις μὲν ἐν στρατοπέδῳ δ᾽ ἄλλως ἀναστρεφομένοις (1) οὐκ ἐξῆν ἄνδρα (2) βαλεῖν πολέμιον (3) οὐδὲ τρῶσαι; "Why were men who were not regularly enlisted, but merely tarrying in the camp, (1) not allowed (2) to throw missiles at the enemy (3) or to wound them?"

40. *Aetia romana et graeca* 291.B.3–4: Διὰ τί τοῖς ἱερεῦσι τούτοις ἀρχὴν (1) οὐκ ἐφεῖτο (2) λαβεῖν (3) οὐδὲ μετελθεῖν; "Why were these priests (1) not allowed (2) to hold office (3) nor to solicit it?"

41. *De E apud Delphos* 385.A.9: (1) οὐκ ἦν εὐπρεπὲς (2) παράγειν (3) οὐδὲ παραιτεῖσθαι. "[On many other occasions when the subject had been brought up in the school, I had quietly turned aside from it and passed it over, but recently I was unexpectedly discovered by my sons in an animated discussion with some strangers, whom, since they purposed to leave Delphi immediately,] (1) it was not seemly (2) to try to divert from the subject, nor was it seemly for

me (3) to ask to be excused from the discussion [for they were altogether eager to hear something about it]."

42. *De defectu oraculorum* 426.B.1: (1) οὐ γὰρ ὡς σμήνους ἡγεμόνας δεῖ (2) ποιεῖν ἀνεξόδους (3) οὐδὲ φρουρεῖν συγκλείσαντας τῇ ὕλῃ μᾶλλον δὲ συμφράξαντας. "[Yet such an organization is altogether appropriate for the gods.] For (1) we must not (2) make them unable to go out, like the queens in a hive of bees, (3) nor keep them imprisoned by enclosing them with matter, or rather fencing them about with it."

43. *De tranquillitate animi* 474.A.12: (1) οὐ δεῖ τοῖς ἑτέροις (2) ἐξαθυμεῖν (3) οὐδ᾿ ἀπαγορεύειν. "(1) We should not (2) be disheartened (3) or despondent in adversity [but like musicians who achieve harmony by consistently deadening bad music with better and encompassing the bad with the good, we should make the blending of our life harmonious and conformable to our own nature]."

44. *De tranquillitate animi* 475.D.3: ὅθεν (1) οὐ δεῖ παντάπασιν (2) ἐκταπεινοῦν (3) οὐδὲ καταβάλλειν τὴν φύσιν. "Therefore (1) we should not altogether (2) debase (3) and depreciate Nature [in the belief that she has nothing strong, stable, and beyond the reach of Fortune, but, on the contrary, . . . we should face the future undaunted and confident.]"

45. *Quaestionum convivialum libri IX* 706.D.5: ἐρῶντι μὲν γὰρ πολυτελοῦς (1) οὐκ ἔστι τὴν Πηνελόπην (2) προσαγαγεῖν (3) οὐδὲ συνοικίσαι τὴν Πάνθειαν. "If a man has a passion for a costly harlot, (1) we cannot (2) bring Penelope on stage, (3) nor marry Pantheia to him [but it is possible to take a man who is enjoying mimes and tunes and lyrics that are bad art and bad taste, and lead him back to Euripides and Pindar and Menander, 'washing the brine from the ears with the clear fresh water of reason,' in Plato's words]."

46. *Quaestionum convivialum libri IX* 711.E.3: ὥσθ᾿ ὁ οἶνος ἡμᾶς (2) ἀδικεῖν (1) οὐκ ἔοικεν (3) οὐδὲ κρατεῖν. "The wine (1) seems not (2) to be harming us (3) or getting the best of us."

47. *Aetia physica* 918.B.4: ἡ δ᾿ ἄγαν περίψυξις πηγνύουσα τὰς ὀσμὰς (1) οὐκ ἐᾷ (2) ῥεῖν (3) οὐδὲ κινεῖν τὴν αἴσθησιν; "[Why is ground that has become dewy unfavorable for hunting so long as the cold lasts? . . . A spoor does this when there is warmth to free and release it gently] whereas excessive chill freezes the scents and (1) does not allow them (2) to flow (3) and affect [i.e., move] our perception."

48. *Bruta animalia ratione uti* 990.A.11: καὶ (1) οὐκ ἐᾷ (2) θιγεῖν (3) οὐδὲ λυπῆσαι τὴν γεῦσιν ἀλλὰ διαβάλλει καὶ κατηγορεῖ τὴν φαυλότητα πρὶν ἢ βλαβῆναι. "[It (our sense of smell) admits what is proper,

rejects what is alien] and (1) will not let it (2) touch (3) or give pain to the taste, but informs on and denounces what is bad before any harm is done."

Confirming the earlier study of the use of οὐδέ in the New Testament, these instances suggest that the construction "negated finite verb + infinitive + οὐδέ + infinitive" is used to link two infinitives denoting concepts or activities that are both viewed either positively or negatively by the writer. The same two patterns of the usage of οὐδέ are found: pattern 1, where two activities or concepts are viewed positively in and of themselves, but their exercise is prohibited or their existence is denied due to circumstances or conditions adduced in the context; and pattern 2, where two activities or concepts are viewed negatively, and consequently their exercise is prohibited or their existence is denied or they are to be avoided. Table 3.2 documents these two patterns.

Table 3.2
Patterns of the Usage of Οὐδέ in Ancient Greek Literature

Pattern 1: Two activities or concepts are viewed positively in and of themselves, but their exercise is prohibited or their existence is denied due to circumstances or conditions adduced in the context.

1. LXX: 1 Macc. 15:14	ἐκπορεύεσθαι (leave)	εἰσπορεύεσθαι (enter)
2. LXX: Sir. 18:6	ἐλαττῶσαι (diminish)	προσθεῖναι (increase)
3. LXX: Isa. 42:24b	πορεύεσθαι (walk)	ἀκούειν (obey)
4. LXX: Ezek. 44:13	ἱερατεύειν (serve as priest)	προσάγειν (come near)
5. LXX: Dan. 5:8 (Theod.)	ἀναγνῶναι (read)	γνωρίσαι (make known)
6. Inscr.: Attica	δέχεσθαι (receive gifts)	κλύειν (give ear to supplication)
10. Polyb., *Hist.* 6.15	χειρίζειν (be organized)	συντελεῖν (be held at all)
12. Polyb., *Hist.* 30.24	γινώσκεσθαι (know)	συνορᾶσθαι (see)
13. Polyb., *Hist.* 31.12	βοηθεῖν (help)	συνεπισχύειν (support)
15. Dion Hal., *Ant. rom* 10.12	κοινωνεῖν (take part in)	παρεῖναι (be present at)
19. Jos., *C. Ap.* 2.6.13	διελθεῖν (discern)	γνῶναι (know)
21. Jos., *B.J.* 5.199	παρελθεῖν (enter)	ὑπερβῆναι (pass by)
23. Jos., *Ant.* 6.20	ἐπιθυμεῖν (yearn for)	βούλεσθαι (want)*
25. Jos., *Ant.* 7.127	ἠρεμεῖν (remain quiet)	ἡσυχίαν ἄγειν (keep quiet)
28. Philo, *Post.* 84.5	ἀναπτῆναι (fly up)	ἀφικέσθαι (go beyond)*

*= preceding infinitive

29. Plut., *Rom.* 9.2	ἀναμιγνύναι (intermarry)	προσδέχεσθαι (receive as citizen)
32. Plut., *Comp. Arist. Cat.* 4.2	πράττειν (do great things)	βοηθεῖν (help)
33. Plut., *Pyrrh.* 33.6	ἀναλαβεῖν (take again)	καταθέσθαι (sheathe again)
35. Plut., *Adul. amic.* 64.E	φυλάττειν (guard)	βαστάζειν (carry)
36. Plut., *Cons. Apoll.* 115.E	γενέσθαι (obtain)	μετασχεῖν (have a share)
40. Plut., *Aet. rom.* 291.B	λαβεῖν (hold office)	μετελθεῖν (solicit office)
45. Plut., *Quaest. conv.* 706. D	προσαγαγεῖν (bring on stage)	συνοικίσαι (marry)
47. Plut., *Aet. phys.* 918.B	ῥεῖν (flow)	κινεῖν (move)

Pattern 2: Two activities or concepts are viewed negatively, and consequently their exercise is prohibited or their existence is denied or they are to be avoided.

7. Inscr.: PZenPestm.	εἰληφέναι (take away)	ἔχειν (hold in pretense)
8. Polyb., *Hist.* 2.56	ἐκπλήττειν (thrill)	ζητεῖν (seek to imagine)
9. Polyb., *Hist.* 5.10.5	πολεμεῖν (make war)	συναναιρεῖν (involve guiltless)
11. Polyb., *Hist.* 30.5	συνδυάζειν (run in harness)	προκαταλαμβάνειν (engage)
14. Dion. Hal., *Thuc.* 7.13	ἐγκαταμίσγειν (adulterate)	ἁρμόττεσθαι (confuse)
16. Dion. Hal., *Comp.* 23	ὁρᾶσθαι (be viewed)	βεβηκέναι (stand)
17. Diod. Sic., *Bibl. hist.* 3.30	θαυμάζειν (be surprised)	ἀπιστεῖν (distrust)
18. Diod. Sic., *Bibl. hist.* 3.37	ἀπιστεῖν (doubt)	ὑπολαμβάνειν (view as fictional)
20. Jos., *C. Ap.* 2.212.1	πυρπολεῖν (burn)	τέμνειν (cut down)
22. Jos., *Ant.* 2.116	δεδίεναι (be alarmed)	λαμβάνειν (harbor suspicions)
24. Jos., *Ant.* 6.344	φυγεῖν (flee)	προδοῦναι (betray)
26. Jos., *Ant.* 14.346	ἀπολιπεῖν (desert)	παρακινδυνεύειν (endanger)*
27. Jos., *Ant.* 15.165	πολυπραγμονεῖν (intrigue)	ἅπτεσθαι (start a revolution)
30. Plut., *Cor.* 27.4	κακουργεῖν (hurt)	λαμβάνειν (take from)
31. Plut., *Tim.* 37.2	θορυβεῖν (stop)	κωλύειν (hinder)
34. Plut., *Ages.* 32.3	ἐξαγαγεῖν (force)	προκαλέσασθαι (tempt)
37. Plut., *Reg. imp. apophth.* 185.A	καθεύδειν (sleep)	ῥᾳθυμεῖν (be idle)
38. Plut., *Aet. rom.* 269.D	διώκειν (follow out)	συκοφαντεῖν (cast aspersions)

39. Plut., *Aet. rom.* 273.E	βαλεῖν (throw missiles)	τρῶσαι (wound)
41. Plut., *E Delph.* 385.A	παράγειν (try to divert)	παραιτεῖσθαι (be excused)
42. Plut., *Def. orac.* 426.B	ποιεῖν ἀνεξόδους (make unable)	φρουρεῖν (keep imprisoned)
43. Plut., *Tranq. an.* 474.A	ἐξαθυμεῖν (be disheartened)	ἀπαγορεύειν (be despondent)
44. Plut., *Tranq. an.* 475.D	ἐκταπεινοῦν (debase)	καταβάλλειν (depreciate)
46. Plut., *Quaest. conv.* 711. E	ἀδικεῖν (harm)	κρατεῖν (get the best of)*
48. Plut., *Brut. an.* 990.A	θιγεῖν (touch)	λυπῆσαι (give pain to)

*= preceding infinitive

Again, we may consider a few examples of each pattern. Pattern 1 can be illustrated by the following instances. Polybius writes (10) that victory processions cannot be properly organized or sometimes be held at all unless the senate consents and provides the requisite funds. While Polybius views both "organize" and "hold" positively in and of themselves, he indicates that holding these processions is not possible unless certain conditions are met: the senate's consent and the requisition of appropriate funds. At another occasion (13) Polybius writes that "the senate would not go so far as to help or support Lysias after his conduct." Again, the writer views the two activities (here synonyms), "helping" and "supporting," positively in and of themselves, but the help is denied because of Lysias's (unacceptable) conduct. Josephus writes (23), "You ought not to be content to yearn for liberty . . . nor merely long to be rid of your masters." While the writer views his readers' yearning for liberty and their longing to be rid of their masters positively in and of themselves, he indicates in the context why these longings by themselves are insufficient unless accompanied by action and change in behavior.

A few examples of pattern 2 show instances where two activities or concepts are both viewed negatively by the writer and where consequently their exercise is prohibited or their existence is denied or they are to be avoided. An inscription (7) indicates that a judge ordered Antipater not "to take the boy from them or to hold him under any pretense." Clearly, both activities, taking the boy away from them as well as holding him under any pretense, are viewed negatively by the judge, who consequently denies the exercise of these activities. Josephus writes (27), "Hyrcanus because of his mild character did not choose . . . to meddle in state affairs or start a revolution." "Meddling in state affairs" and "starting a revolution" are both viewed negatively by the writer, who asserts that it was Hyrcanus's "mild character" that

kept him from engaging in these undesirable activities. In a writing by
Plutarch (46 above; note the preceding infinitive), the existence of two
negative effects of wine is denied: "The wine seems not to be harming
us or getting the best of us."

Conclusion

In analogy to the observations made in the study of New Testament
syntactical parallels to 1 Timothy 2:12 above, the following conclusions
may be drawn.[14] The implication of the identified patterns of the usage
of οὐδέ for 1 Timothy 2:12 is that the activities denoted by the two infinitives διδάσκειν and αὐθεντεῖν will both be viewed either positively
or negatively by the writer. That is, the passage should be rendered
either "I do not permit a woman to teach [error] or to usurp a man's
authority" or "I do not permit a woman to teach or to have (or exercise)
authority over a man."

The meaning of διδάσκειν in 1 Timothy 2:12 is therefore an important preliminary issue in determining the meaning of αὐθεντεῖν.
As was argued above, διδάσκειν, when used absolutely, in the New
Testament always denotes an activity that is viewed positively by the
writer, to be rendered "to teach" (cf. esp. 1 Tim. 4:11; 6:2; 2 Tim. 2:2).
If the writer had intended to give the term a negative connotation in
1 Timothy 2:12, he would in all likelihood have used the term ἑτεροδιδασκαλεῖν (as in 1 Tim. 1:3; 6:3) or some other contextual qualifier
specifying the (inappropriate or heretical) content of the teaching
(as in Titus 1:11).

Since the first part of 1 Timothy 2:12 reads, "But I do not permit a
woman to teach," and the coordinating conjunction οὐδέ requires the
second activity to be viewed correspondingly by the writer, αὐθεντεῖν
should be regarded as viewed positively as well and be rendered "to
have (or exercise) authority," and not "to flout the authority of" or "to
domineer."

Interaction with Responses to this Essay since Its Original Publication

1996–98

Responses to the present essay in the first few years subsequent to the
publication of *Women in the Church* were very positive, both overseas
and in North America. Peter O'Brien, in a review published in Australia,

concurred with the findings of this study,[15] as did Helge Stadelmann in an extensive review that appeared in the German *Jahrbuch für evangelikale Theologie*.[16] Both reviewers accepted the results of the present study as valid.

Even Alan Padgett, in a generally negative review in the egalitarian *Priscilla Papers*, calls the present chapter "a convincing syntactical analysis of v. 12," though he favors reading both infinitives as conveying a negative connotation.[17] Padgett disagrees that διδάσκω is always used positively in Paul, citing Titus 1:11; 1 Tim. 1:3; and 6:3, without, however, mentioning that in the second and third instances the word used is not διδάσκειν, but ἑτεροδιδασκαλεῖν.

Another egalitarian, Craig Keener, in a review that appeared in the *Journal of the Evangelical Theological Society*, says that while (in his view) the principle is not clear in all instances cited in the present study, "the pattern seems to hold in general, and this is what matters most." Keener concurs that the contention of the present essay is "probably correct that 'have authority' should be read as coordinate with 'teach' rather than as subordinate ('teach in a domineering way')."[18]

1999–2001

I. H. MARSHALL

The first substantive interaction did not appear until the publication of Howard Marshall's commentary on the Pastorals in 1999.[19] Marshall indicates his acceptance of the findings of the present study by noting that it has "argued convincingly on the basis of a wide range of Gk. usage that the construction employed in this verse is one in which the writer expresses the same attitude (whether positive or negative) to both of the items joined together by οὐδέ."

Marshall proceeds to suggest, however, that matters are "not quite so simple." In response to the point that Paul would have used the word ἑτεροδιδασκαλεῖν had he wanted to convey a negative connotation, Marshall avers that doing so would have implied that while women were not permitted to engage in false teaching, men were allowed to do so. However, as Blomberg points out in a later piece, this objection does not carry force, because the prohibition still could have been clearly framed to avoid this conclusion.[20]

Consequently, Marshall opts for a negative sense of both words because of the reference to Eve in verse 14, which he maintains would be pointless unless Paul here has "some particular false teaching by some women" in mind. Marshall concedes that the text does not say that Eve gave false teaching to Adam, but he claims such is nonetheless implied.

Again, however, Blomberg notes that, while women were clearly victimized by false teaching in Ephesus, "no passage ever suggests that they were numbered among the false teachers themselves."[21]

In a lengthy footnote, Marshall says the present study does not appreciate the point that, if the second unit is seen pejoratively, this will also be the case with the first unit. To the contrary, this is one of the two patterns shown throughout the entire essay. According to Marshall, Paul is using διδάσκειν with the same connotation as ἑτεροδιδασκαλεῖν, so the apostle is in fact telling women—but not men—not to teach falsely. How would that not still allow the same implication Marshall disavows, namely, that women and men are here treated inequitably?

As to the relationship between διδάσκειν and αὐθεντεῖν, Marshall presents two options: either these two terms are separate (citing Moo and the present study as favoring this option), or the former term represents a specific instance of the latter (i.e., teaching is an act by which authority is exercised). However, this does not quite capture matters accurately. The present analysis sees teaching as included in the exercise of authority, not as entirely separate. There is a partial overlap between the two terms, though exercising authority is the broader concept.

Finally, regarding the relation between verses 11 and 12, Marshall claims that the contrast is between learning in a submissive attitude and teaching in a manner "which is heavy-handed and abuses authority." However, there is no need to import the alleged negative sense of διδάσκειν into the way in which the contrast between verses 11 and 12 is construed.[22]

Overall, it appears that Marshall is not prepared to follow his acknowledgment that the present study "argued convincingly" for a particular understanding of the syntax of verse 12 to a conclusion that would require a nonegalitarian reading of the text. Hence, he opts for a negative sense of both "teaching" and "exercising authority" on the basis of his construal of the background and reading of the context, particularly verse 14.[23]

WILLIAM MOUNCE

Shortly after the publication of Marshall's commentary, William Mounce, in his contribution to the WBC series, comes to rather different conclusions than Marshall.[24] Mounce draws extensively on the present syntactical analysis of 1 Timothy 2:12 (quoting at length from its critique of Payne) and integrates it into a full-orbed and coherent exegesis of the passage. While there is no need to rehearse here all the details of his cogent discussion of the verse, it should be noted that Mounce frequently adduces data not adequately (or at all) considered or acknowledged by Marshall:

- διδάσκειν is almost always used in a positive sense in the Pastorals.
- If Paul is prohibiting women merely from teaching error, verse 13 seems irrelevant.
- The fact that διδάσκειν has no object strongly suggests that the verse is a positive command.
- διδάσκειν and αὐθεντεῖν are best seen as distinct yet related concepts.[25]

Mounce also points out that the two verbs are separated by five words in 1 Timothy 2:12, which further speaks against viewing them as forming a hendiadys, where words are usually placed side by side (citing BDF §442 [16]).[26] Following my identification of the pattern as from specific to general, Mounce concludes that "Paul does not want women to be in positions of authority in the church; teaching is one way in which authority is exercised in the church."[27]

KEVIN GILES

Remarkably, even Kevin Giles, who lodges a thirty-eight-page critique against the first edition of *Women in the Church*, finds himself in essential agreement with the present syntactical analysis of 1 Timothy 2:12.[28] However, by way of special pleading, Giles maintains that "people, even apostles, break grammatical rules at times," so that οὐδέ may function differently in the present passage than everywhere else in attested contemporaneous Greek literature.[29]

This, of course, is possible but highly unlikely. In my extensive research in both biblical and extrabiblical Greek literature, I found no evidence of anyone "breaking the rules" in his or her use of οὐδέ. It seems that even Giles himself does not trust this kind of reasoning, for he later floats the possibility that both διδάσκειν and αὐθεντεῖν are to be understood negatively—in keeping with the pattern of usage identified in the present study.[30]

LINDA BELLEVILLE

The most—in fact, the only—negative response to the present study comes from Linda Belleville.[31] She contends that the two verbs in 1 Timothy 2:12 connote "a single coherent idea in Greek."[32] In a discussion that blends instances of the noun αὐθέντης and the verb αὐθεντεῖν, Belleville maintains that the latter has a negative connotation.

Belleville also claims that the order of teaching first, and then authority, favors her interpretation: "If Paul had the exercise of authority in mind, he would have put it first, followed by *teaching* as a specific example." However, it is unclear why Belleville disallows the converse word order, especially in light of the occurrence of this pattern in Acts 21:21.[33] The upshot of her discussion is that she restates Payne's view that we here deal with a hendiadys, translating the phrase as "to teach a man in a domineering way."[34]

Belleville reiterates her opposition in her 2001 essay in *Two Views on Women in Ministry*. She charges that the present study "ignore[s] both the literary form and the nature of Greek correlatives."[35] According to Belleville, (1) infinitives are not verbs; (2) 1 Timothy 2:12 has to do with ideas, not grammar; and (3) "neither/nor" in 1 Timothy 2:12 constitutes a "poetic device." Belleville also contends that (4) the two infinitives modify "a woman" and that (5) the question answered by these infinitives is "What?" In response, however, it should be noted that Belleville herself misconstrues the grammar and syntax of 1 Timothy 2:12. What is more, her objection to the present study misses the mark in that the forty-eight syntactical parallels to 1 Timothy 2:12 identified in extrabiblical literature (as well as the one exact parallel in the New Testament, Acts 21:21; see above) all feature the construction negated finite verb + infinitive + οὐδέ + infinitive and in every instance yield the pattern positive/positive or negative/negative, confirming the conclusion that 1 Timothy 2:12 is to be rendered either "I do not permit a woman to teach [error] or to usurp a man's authority" or "I do not permit a woman to teach or to have (or exercise) authority over a man," the latter being preferred owing to the positive connotation of διδάσκειν elsewhere in the Pastorals. Hence, the question of whether infinitives are verbs or nouns is really irrelevant in the present case, since—however infinitives are classified—the present study focuses on exact syntactical parallels, comparing infinitives with infinitives. Beyond this, Henry Baldwin, in the preceding essay, has responded convincingly to Belleville's contention that nouns, rather than verbs, should be studied in relation to the syntax of 1 Timothy 2:12.

In addition, (1) Belleville's contention that infinitives are not verbs is hardly borne out by a look at the standard grammars. Her arguments (2) that 1 Timothy 2:12 has to do with ideas, not grammar and (3) that οὐδέ in 1 Timothy 2:12 constitutes a "poetic device" are unfounded, in that grammar is clearly involved, and the genre of the present passage is that of epistle, not poetry. As to Belleville's contention (4) that the two infinitives modify "a woman" and that (5) the question answered is "What?" it must be noted that, to the contrary, the infinitives modify the main verb in verse 12, ἐπιτρέπω (I permit), and the question answered is "To *do* what?"—the answer being "to teach or exercise authority." Hence, the two infinitives are found to convey the *verbal* notion of actions to be performed or not performed. This finds support in the standard Greek grammar by Daniel Wallace, who cites 1 Timothy 2:12 as an example of the "complementary" use of the adverbial infinitive, meaning that the infinitives work with the finite verb to convey the verbal notion.[36]

For these reasons Belleville's critique must be judged to be unpersuasive and unable to overturn the assured results of the present study.[37]

CRAIG BLOMBERG

Craig Blomberg, in an appendix included in the same volume, differs from Belleville and renders the following assessment:

> Decisively supporting the more positive sense of assuming appropriate authority is Andreas Köstenberger's study of pairs of infinitives in "neither . . . nor" constructions both throughout the New Testament and in a wide-ranging swath of extrabiblical Greek literature. Without exception, these constructions pair either two positive or two negative activities. So if the "teaching" in view in 1 Timothy 2:12 is not false teaching but proper Christian instruction, then *authentein* must be taken as appropriate authority as well.[38]

Blomberg proceeds to discuss the question of whether the two infinitives form a hendiadys. He contends that he has identified a "largely overlooked" "informal pattern throughout 1 Timothy of using pairs of partly synonymous words or expressions."[39] However, virtually all these examples are nouns. Blomberg concludes that the two terms are "closely related" (agreed) and "together help to define one single concept" (this may go a bit too far).

Blomberg finds it "overwhelmingly likely" that in 1 Timothy 2:12 Paul is referring to "one specific kind of authoritative teaching rather than two independent activities." However, this represents a false dichotomy, since no allowance is made for partially overlapping terms as in a pattern from specific to general.[40] Pointing to related passages such as 1 Timothy 3:2; 5:17; and Titus 1:5–7, Blomberg contends that the import of the two verbs in 1 Timothy 2:12 is one thing only: women "must not occupy the office of elder/overseer."[41]

To be sure, the parallels adduced by Blomberg suggest that 1 Timothy 2:12 clearly means at least that women ought not to serve in the office that epitomizes teaching and ruling authority.[42] Yet it appears that Blomberg's position, by reducing the issue solely to that of "no women elders/overseers," may be unduly minimalistic. The principles adduced by the quotations of Old Testament Scripture in 1 Timothy 2:13–14 would seem to suggest that 1 Timothy 2:12 is grounded in more foundational realities than a mere surface prohibition of women occupying a given office. For this reason a more nuanced application of the passage seems to be needed.[43]

WILLIAM WEBB

While critical of the chapter on hermeneutics in the first edition (see Robert Yarbrough's response in the present edition below), William Webb wrote that "I must commend the book for its exegesis in a number of the other chapters, written by other authors."[44] Later, he remarks, "In one of the finest *exegetical* treatments of 1 Timothy 2 available today, the authors of *Women in the Church: A Fresh Analysis of 1 Timothy 2:9–15* develop the text in its lexical and grammatical aspects in much the same way as I would be inclined."[45] Elsewhere, Webb comments that "the exegesis by Schreiner, Baldwin, Köstenberger, etc. is persuasive and will make a lasting contribution."[46] One surmises that this would include the syntactical analysis in the present chapter. This is all the more remarkable as William Webb is an egalitarian.

2002–4

ESTHER NG

In her critique of Elisabeth Schüssler Fiorenza's reconstruction of Christian origins, Esther Ng notes that Fiorenza apparently takes both infinitives in 1 Timothy 2:12 as having a neutral sense (meaning "teaching" and "having authority" respectively) and as linked to οὐδέ to mean two separable actions, though both related to men. This, she notes, puts the matriarch of feminist hermeneutics in agreement with "the more historical and conservative interpretation."[47] In the same note, Ng also refers to Wilshire's and Baldwin's studies and to the present study.

Later, Ng acknowledges that some "scholars with feminist inclinations" take αὐθεντεῖν in a negative sense (e.g., Payne, Fee) and then see the two infinitives as so closely related as to mean "teaching in a domineering way." She continues, "However, since a negative connotation of διδάσκειν is unlikely in this verse (see below), the neutral meaning for αὐθεντεῖν (to have authority over) seems to fit the οὐδέ construction better. . . . While the οὐδέ joins two separate activities, teaching and exercising authority are still closely associated, as the contrast with 'quiet learning in submission' makes clear."[48]

Hence it is clear that Ng follows the conclusions reached in the present study precisely and in their entirety.

JUDITH HARTENSTEIN

In a review published in the *Review of Biblical Literature,* May 2004, Judith Hartenstein of Marburg University, Germany, interacts with the reprint of my essay on 1 Timothy 2:12 in the essay collection *Studies on John and Gender: A Decade of Scholarship*.[49] She notes that "Köstenberger shows through a syntactical study that 1 Tim 2:12 forbids women to teach and to have authority over men, not only to abuse authority. . . . This teaching of 1 Timothy is consistent with the praxis in Pauline churches, as Köstenberger [in an essay on women in the Pauline mission] cannot find any evidence of contrary roles of women in the Pauline epistles. In Köstenberger's opinion, this role of women—where men bear ultimate responsibility—should be authoritative in the modern church."

While this reviewer has accurately summarized the contention of the present study, however, she proceeds to state: "I certainly do not agree with this result. My theological position is very different from that of Köstenberger. Nevertheless, I often find his analysis of texts and exegetical problems convincing and inspiring, especially if he uses linguistic approaches. . . . Likewise, I agree with Köstenberger's reading of 1 Tim 2. Köstenberger shows that the text demands a hierarchy between men and women and is meant as normative teaching. But with a different, far more critical view of the Bible, I need not accept it as God's word. (It helps that I do not regard 1 Timothy as written by Paul.)"

In a remarkably honest and candid fashion, therefore, Hartenstein affirms the present analysis of 1 Timothy 2:12 and acknowledges that she differs not for exegetical or linguistic reasons but because she holds a "far more critical view of the Bible." Especially since she does not regard 1 Timothy as having been written by Paul, she need not accept the teaching of 1 Timothy 2 as God's word, though it "is meant as normative teaching." While space does not permit a full-fledged critique of her stance toward Scripture in general or 1 Timothy 2 in particular, it seems clear that Hartenstein's presuppositions are problematic for, and unacceptable to, even inerrantist evangelical egalitarians.

This is not to say that *every* disagreement with the present essay by egalitarians must necessarily stem from an errantist stance toward Scripture, nor is it to imply that no exegetical or linguistic arguments could be advanced within an inerrantist framework. Nevertheless, Hartenstein's candor makes explicit what may often be an unacknowledged factor in feminist or egalitarian interpretations of 1 Timothy 2:12, namely, presuppositions that in fact override the actual exegesis of the passage. Whether or not this is acknowledged by egalitarian or feminist interpreters, their choice of which exegetical arguments to embrace may be (and often seems to be) motivated by their prior commitment to egalitarianism. How refreshing it is when this is openly acknowledged, as in the case of Hartenstein's review.[50]

LINDA BELLEVILLE—AGAIN

In the 2004 essay collection *Discovering Biblical Equality*, Linda Belleville ups the ante by claiming that I consider "a hierarchical interpretation of this passage [1 Tim. 2:12]" "a litmus test for the label *evangelical* and even a necessity for the salvation of unbelievers."[51] Belleville claims that I say (attributing a statement solely to me in a section that is signed by all three editors) "that a hierarchical view of men and women is necessary for 'a world estranged from God' to 'believe that God was in Christ reconciling the world to himself.'"

In context, however, the statement cited by Belleville refers not to the interpretation of 1 Timothy 2:12 but to "one's view of male and female gender identities and roles in the church" in general as of "the apprehension and application of his [God's] good gift of manhood and womanhood." A renewal of this understanding of what it means to have been created male and female in God's image in the beginning is presented as vital for our own deeper fulfillment and for our witness in the world.

Doubtless, Belleville and other egalitarians would see their vision of gender equality as vital for people's deeper fulfillment and witness in the world; it is unclear why the editors of the first edition of this volume are denied the same hope and conviction. In any case, contrary to Belleville's assertion, neither I nor the other contributors to this volume believe that what Belleville calls a "hierarchical" view of men and women is necessary for a person to claim the label "evangelical" or that such a view is "a necessity for the salvation of unbelievers."

In her discussion of the grammar of the present verse, Belleville states at the outset that "Andreas Köstenberger claims that it is the correlative that *forces translators in this direction*."[52] It is unclear, however, what in the original essay suggests to Belleville a claim that the correlative "forces translators" in a certain direction. I did not claim that a certain understanding of the Greek coordinating conjunction motivated translators in the past, but rather that a certain understanding of the Greek conjunction in 1 Timothy 2:12 most properly conforms to the way in which Greek grammar actually functions.

Belleville also misunderstands the argument of the original essay when she says that it "argues that the Greek correlative pairs synonyms or parallel words and not antonyms."[53] This is not in fact the argument I make. Rather, my point is that there are two patterns of usage found with regard to οὐδέ in the New Testament and extrabiblical Greek literature:

Pattern 1: Two activities or concepts are viewed positively in and of themselves, but their exercise is prohibited or their existence is denied due to circumstances or conditions adduced in the context.

Pattern 2: Two activities or concepts are viewed negatively, and consequently their exercise is prohibited or their existence is denied or they are to be avoided.

The issue here is not that of synonyms versus antonyms but that of a particular type of perception of a given activity by a writer or speaker. For example, in 1 Maccabees 15:14, we read that "he pressed the city hard from land and sea, and permitted no one to leave or enter it." Clearly, "leave" and "enter" are antonyms, but this is not the crucial point in the present analysis, but rather the fact that both "leaving" and "entering" are viewed positively (rather than one being viewed positively and the other being viewed negatively) by the perpetrator of a given action. This point may be subtle, but an understanding of it is crucial for one to appreciate the argument being made in the present essay.

Beyond this, Belleville merely repeats her earlier argument (noted above) that infinitives are nouns, not verbs, and disallows a progression from particular to general in 1 Timothy 2:12. Once again, however, it must be noted that the categorization of infinitives as verbs or nouns is not the critical issue, since the present study identifies a total of forty-nine exact syntactical parallels (negated finite verb + infinitive + οὐδέ + infinitive) in the New Testament and extrabiblical literature, so that infinitives are compared with infinitives, which clearly is the most accurate comparison possible. None of Belleville's arguments overturns the syntactical patterns identified and the implication of these patterns for the proper rendering of 1 Timothy 2:12.[54]

WAYNE GRUDEM

In his encyclopedic work *Evangelical Feminism & Biblical Truth: An Analysis of More Than 100 Disputed Questions*, Wayne Grudem accurately summarizes the contribution of the original essay and concurs with its findings.[55]

Grudem properly interacts with Sarah Sumner's objection that I have made a "mistake" in saying that the word διδάσκω in 1 Timothy 2:12 has a positive force, because the same word is used negatively in 1 Timothy 6:3 and Titus 1:11.[56] In fact, in 1 Timothy 6:3 it is not the same word but the word ἑτεροδιδάσκαλειν (to teach falsely) that is used, and in Titus 1:11 the context clearly indicates a negative connotation by the qualifier "teaching *for shameful gain what they ought not to teach.*" No such negative qualifier is found in 1 Timothy 2:12, however.

Grudem also deals with I. H. Marshall's objection to my taking the word διδάσκω in 1 Timothy 2:12 in a positive sense, claiming that this "overlooks the fact that to say 'But I do not permit women to give false teaching' in this context would imply 'But I do allow men to do so.'" Yet as Grudem rightly points out, Marshall himself argues that αὐθεντέω has a negative nuance of "exercising autocratic power."[57] Hence the same objection he lodges against my essay would apply equally to his interpretation.[58]

Conclusion

As the above survey of scholarly responses to the original essay on the syntax of 1 Timothy 2:12 has shown, the identification of two distinct syntactical patterns has met with virtually unanimous acceptance and has held up very well. Only Keener hinted at, and Belleville expressed, criticisms. Belleville alleged that (1) διδάσκειν and αὐθεντεῖν are not verbs, (2) the construction is a poetic device following grammatical rules of its own, and (3) there are no parallels for a pattern from specific to general.

However, all three objectons can be met. First, Greek grammars regularly and rightly treat infinitives under the rubric of verbs. Second, poetic device or not, Belleville has not overturned the clear and consistent syntactical patterns demonstrated in the present study, a pattern that has been accepted as valid even by virtually all other egalitarian scholars, including Marshall, Keener, Padgett, Giles, and Webb. Third, Belleville does not consider Acts 21:21, which constitutes a parallel. What is more, even if no parallel existed, this still would not mean that the pattern is illegitimate.

Marshall, finally, while accepting the overall validity of our syntactical analysis, contends that διδάσκειν is negative (see also Padgett, Giles). His arguments have been effectively refuted by Mounce and Blomberg.[59] For this reason, even after a decade of scrutiny, the results of the present study not only should be upheld as valid but also should now be considered as an assured result of biblical scholarship and hence ought to constitute the foundation upon which a sound exegesis of the present passage is conducted.

4

AN INTERPRETATION
OF 1 TIMOTHY 2:9–15

A Dialogue with Scholarship

THOMAS R. SCHREINER

The role of women in the church is probably the most emotionally charged issue in American evangelicalism today. I have been in public forums where the question has been debated, and the tension in the room is palpable. It is particularly difficult when I lecture on the issue at a seminary, for there are often women in the class who feel called to serve as pastors. To have a professor question the legitimacy of this call in a public setting is, to say the least, emotionally agonizing for women who feel called to pastor.[1] It also smacks of a public attack on a minority group since in my classes men usually outnumber women. Most of these women students have already been subjected somewhere in their journey to insensitive and cruel comments by men. Thus, the public examination of the issue by a professor who holds to the complementarian view can be almost unbearable.[2] Those of us who support the complementarian view on this question must bend over backward to love those with whom we disagree, and to assure them that we still hope and pray that God will bless their ministries, even though we believe that it is a mistake for women to take on a pastoral role.

In fact, I desired to believe that there are no limitations for women in ministry and that every ministry position is open to them.[3] As a student, I read many articles on the question, hoping that I could be exegetically convinced that all ministry offices should be opened to women. Upon reading the articles, though, I remained intellectually and exegetically unconvinced of the plausibility of the "new" interpretations of the controversial passages. Indeed, reading the egalitarian interpretations persuaded me that the complementarian view was true, since the former involved unlikely interpretations of the "problem" passages. I remember saying to a friend who is a New Testament scholar, "I would like to believe the position you hold. But it seems as if you have to leap over the evidence of the text to espouse such a position." He replied, "Tom, you are right. Take that leap. Take that leap." Leaping over the evidence is precisely what I am unwilling to do. Thus, I remain intellectually and exegetically unconvinced that the egalitarian position is tenable.

Many who are unfamiliar with the biblical text or have not engaged in much exegesis of the relevant passages (and this includes many pastors, unfortunately!) surrender the complementarian view rather easily.[4] To many the complementarian position seems unloving and discriminatory, and the general atmosphere of our society encourages people to liberate themselves from traditional views. American culture often lauds those who discard conventional positions and brands those who advocate "new" positions as courageous, creative, and thoughtful. On the other hand, those who hold the complementarian view are considered temperamentally contentious, narrow, and perhaps even psychologically hampered. These latter qualities are doubtless true of some (but obviously not all) who support the complementarian view, and yet it does not follow that the complementarian view is thereby falsified. The truth or falsity of both views must be established by an intensive exegesis of the biblical text.

Even though more and more people are temperamentally inclined to assume that the egalitarian position is correct, I will argue in this essay that the recent interpretations of 1 Timothy 2:9–15 in defense of the egalitarian position are exegetically unpersuasive.[5] The burden of my essay is to interact with this recent research and to set forth reasons for questioning its validity.[6] Scholars who embrace the feminist position, such as Paul Jewett, but argue that Paul was wrong or inconsistent in 1 Timothy 2, are exegetically more straightforward and intellectually more convincing than those who contend that Paul did not actually intend to restrict women teaching men in 1 Timothy 2.[7]

The Life Setting for the Text

One of the central planks for the egalitarian view is the occasional nature of 1 Timothy.[8] Too often, it is argued, scholars have seen 1 Timothy as a manual of church structure, so that the directives given are understood to be permanently binding on all churches.[9] What has not been sufficiently appreciated is that the Pastoral Epistles are addressed to specific situations; particularly they are aimed against false teaching that was imperiling the churches.[10] Thus, the letters should not necessarily be understood as timeless marching orders for the church but must be interpreted in light of the specific circumstances that occasioned them.

The emphasis on the specific situation and occasion of the letters is salutary. The Pastoral Epistles are not doctrinal treatises that float free from the circumstances that called them forth. In the case of 1 Timothy, it is clear that the letter is written to counteract false teaching (1:3–11, 18–20; 4:1–10; 5:11–15; 6:3–10, 20–21). Indeed, the transition between 1 Timothy 1:18–20 and 2:1 indicated by "therefore" (οὖν) shows that the following instructions relate to the charge to resist false teaching (cf. 1 Tim. 1:3, 18).[11] The letter is designed to correct the abuses introduced by the heretics into the community. Nevertheless, caution should also be the watchword in explaining the nature of 1 Timothy. Even though the presence of heresy is evident, it does not follow that every feature of the letter is explicable on the basis of the false teaching. Paul probably included some material for general purposes that did not address the deviant teaching directly. We could easily fall into the error of overemphasizing the ad hoc character of 1 Timothy. After Paul had functioned as a missionary and church planter for so many years, he likely had at least a general vision of how churches should be structured.[12] Hence, his instructions were not entirely situational but reflect the pattern of governance that he expected to exist in his churches.[13]

Even if 1 Timothy were written entirely to address specific circumstances (which is doubtful), it would not logically follow from the occasional nature of the letter that 1 Timothy has no application to the church today. It would be a grave mistake to argue as follows:[14]

1. First Timothy was written to counteract a specific situation in the life of the church.
2. Nothing written to a specific situation is normative for the church today.
3. Therefore, 1 Timothy contains no directives for the church today.

If we were to claim that documents written to specific situations are not applicable to the church today, then much of the New Testament would not be applicable to us either, since it is probable that many New Testament books were addressed to particular communities facing special circumstances. Universal principles are tucked into books written to respond to specific circumstances.

Of course, careful scholars who favor the egalitarian view do not argue that the directives in 1 Timothy are inapplicable merely because of the life situation that called them forth. They rightly insist that the specific life setting of the letter must inform our interpretation and application of specific passages. Thus, we must probe to see whether Paul's admonitions to women in 1 Timothy 2:9–15 are temporary directives in response to the impact of the false teachers. Can we show that Paul prohibited women from teaching men solely on the grounds of the false teaching afflicting the Ephesian church? The egalitarian view is not established merely by saying that the proscription on women teaching men emerged because of the impact that the false teachers had on women. There is little doubt that the heretics had an influence on the women in the community (cf. 1 Tim. 5:11–15; 2 Tim. 3:6–7), and it is possible that the issues of women's adornment and teaching arose as a consequence of the adversaries' leverage.[15] Nonetheless, Paul may have responded to these specific problems with a general principle that is universally applicable. Whether he does in fact appeal to a universal principle and what that principle is must be established by an interpretation of the verses in question.

Naturally, if one could show that the prohibition against women teaching men were explicable solely on the grounds of the false teaching and its specific features, then the egalitarian position would be greatly strengthened. For instance, Richard and Catherine Kroeger set forth the features of the heresy in amazing detail, seeing it as an amalgamation of Jewish-gnostic traditions and Ephesian devotion to Artemis.[16] They argue that the false teachers proclaimed the priority of Eve over Adam and that Eve enlightened Adam with her teaching.[17] Paul's words on Adam being created first and Eve's deception were intended to counterbalance the adversaries' exaltation of Eve. If this reconstruction is accurate, then the thesis that Paul's instruction contains temporary restraints on women is enhanced.[18] Unfortunately, the Kroegers' reconstruction is riddled with methodological errors. They nod in the direction of saying that the heresy is "proto-gnostic," but consistently appeal to later sources to establish the contours of the heresy.[19] The lack of historical rigor is nothing less than astonishing.[20] They have clearly not grasped how one should apply the historical method in discerning the nature of false teaching in the Pauline letters.[21]

The work of Sharon Gritz is much more restrained and sober than that of the Kroegers, though there are similarities in terms of her conclusions.[22] She posits that the restriction on women teaching men was due to the infiltration of the cult of the mother goddess, Artemis, in Ephesus.[23] Even if her case were established, this would hardly prove that the restriction on women was limited to the particular situation, for Paul could be giving a universal principle that was precipitated by special circumstances. The central weakness of Gritz's work, however, is that she nowhere provides any kind of in-depth argument for the influence of the Artemis cult in 1 Timothy. She records the presence of such a cult in Ephesus and then simply assumes that it functions as the background to the letter. To say that sexual impurity (1 Tim. 5:11–14) and greed (1 Tim. 6:3–5) are signs of the Artemis cult is scarcely persuasive.[24] Many religious and nonreligious movements are plagued with these problems. Gritz needs to show that the devotion to myths and genealogies (1 Tim. 1:3–4), the Jewish law (1 Tim. 1:6–11), asceticism (1 Tim. 4:3–4), and knowledge (1 Tim. 6:20–21) indicate that the problem was specifically with the Artemis cult.[25]

Many scholars who reconstruct the situation behind the Pastorals should pay greater heed to the fragmentary nature of the evidence.[26] Robert Karris observes that "it seems extremely difficult to infer from the polemic the nature of the opponents' teaching."[27] He concludes that "the author of the Pastorals is quite tight-lipped about the teachings of his opponents."[28] Karris is probably too pessimistic about our ability to delineate the heresy, but some scholars are far too confident about their ability to reconstruct the life setting in some detail.

A more promising and cautious approach has been proposed by Philip Towner.[29] He suggests that the problem in the Pastoral Epistles was a form of overrealized eschatology, analogous in many respects to a similar phenomenon in 1 Corinthians.[30] The belief that the resurrection had already occurred (2 Tim. 2:18; cf. 1 Tim. 1:20) was not a denial of resurrection altogether, but signals that the opponents believed in a spiritual resurrection with Christ.[31] Such overrealized eschatology could also explain their food prohibitions and dim view of marriage (1 Tim. 4:1–3).[32] Perhaps it could also account for the emancipation of women from previous norms (1 Tim. 2:9–15; cf. 1 Cor. 11:2–16; 14:33b–36). Towner's reconstruction is only a possibility. While it certainly does not answer all our questions, it has the virtue of being a reconstruction that does not depend on second-century evidence.[33] In addition, the nature of the false teaching is gleaned from the evidence of the Pastoral Epistles themselves. By contrast, those who see the Artemis cult as prominent appeal to a movement that is not mentioned or even clearly implied in the Pastoral Epistles.

Whatever the specific features of the heresy, firm evidence is lacking that the priority or superiority of Eve played any part in the false teaching. Nor is it clear that 1 Timothy 5:13 demonstrates that women were *teaching* the heresy.[34] Paul does not say that "they were *teaching* things that were not fitting," but that "they were *speaking* things that were not fitting."[35] It is scarcely clear in this context (although it cannot be dismissed as a possibility) that Paul is responding to false teaching as he does in other texts (e.g., 1 Tim. 1:3–11; 4:1–5; 6:3–10). The false teachers specifically named in the Pastorals are all men (1 Tim. 1:20; 2 Tim. 2:17–18; cf. 2 Tim. 4:14), and women are portrayed as being influenced by the heresy (1 Tim. 5:11–15; 2 Tim. 3:5–9) rather than as being its purveyors.[36] Towner is probably correct in concluding that an emancipation movement among women was a side effect rather than a specific goal of the teaching of the agitators.[37] Perhaps women began to engage in teaching because they had fallen prey to an overrealized eschatology.[38] They may have believed that the resurrection had already occurred (2 Tim. 2:18), and thus the distinctions between men and women were erased since the new age had dawned. In any case, the suggestion that women were prohibited from teaching because they were mainly responsible for the false teaching cannot be substantiated from the text. Even if some women were spreading the heresy (which is uncertain but possible), an explanation is still needed as to why Paul proscribes only women from teaching. Since men are specifically named as purveyors of the heresy, would it not make more sense if Paul forbade all false teaching by both men and women? A prohibition against women alone seems to be reasonable only if *all* the women in Ephesus were duped by the false teaching. This latter state of affairs is quite unlikely, and the probable presence of Priscilla in Ephesus (2 Tim. 4:19) also stands against it.

A Word on the Near Context

The first chapter of 1 Timothy demonstrates that the letter is in part a response to false teaching.[39] In 2:1–7 Paul emphasizes that God's desire is for all, including kings and other governing authorities, to be saved. Perhaps the adversaries used their myths and genealogies to argue that salvation was not possible for some people. Thus, Paul employs his apostolic authority (2:7) to pronounce upon God's universal purpose and intention in sending Christ as a ransom for all. Thereby believers are enjoined to pray for the salvation of all people.

A new section opens with verse 8, but the word "therefore" (οὖν) shows an intimate connection with verses 1–7. The link between the two sections is strengthened when we observe that Paul calls on the men to pray (v. 8), presumably for the salvation of all those referred to in verses 1–7.[40] Perhaps the anger and disputing that are forbidden in verse 8 were precipitated by the teaching of the agitators, which caused the church to veer away from its purpose of praying for the salvation of unbelievers.[41] The words "I want" (βούλομαι) do not merely express Paul's personal opinion and preference for prayer and the avoidance of anger. Indeed, they immediately follow verse 7, which is a powerful defense of Paul's apostolic authority. Thus, they express an authoritative command to pray.[42]

When Paul calls on men to pray "in every place" (ἐν παντὶ τόπῳ), this is probably a reference to house churches.[43] Thus, the directives here relate to a public church meeting when believers are gathered together.[44] The words "in every place" refer to all churches everywhere, not just those in Ephesus (cf. Mal. 1:11; 1 Cor. 1:2).[45] In any case, a public worship context is likely in view, whether the reference is to house churches in Ephesus or to all churches everywhere.[46] These observations on the public nature of the praying in verse 8 are significant, for verses 9–15 are also directed to public assemblies. This is clear in verses 11–12, where women are prohibited from teaching or exercising authority over men. George Knight questions whether verses 9–10 are limited to public meetings since wearing appropriate clothing and good works are necessary at all times, not just in worship services.[47] Knight correctly observes that proper clothing and good works extend beyond worship services, but Paul's exhortations on suitable attire probably stem from indecorous adornment being worn at public meetings.[48] The call to do good works is probably occasioned by an improper focus on adornment in the gatherings of the community, even though the works extend beyond church meetings. If the above observations are correct, there is no need to see a shift away from public worship in verses 9–10.[49]

Women's Adornment in 1 Timothy 2:9–10

The text is ambiguous regarding the connection between verses 8 and 9. Is Paul saying, "Likewise I want the women to pray with respectable adornment," or "Likewise I want the women to adorn themselves with respectable adornment"? Some scholars favor the idea that the infinitive "to pray" (προσεύχεσθαι) follows the implied verb "I want."[50] In support of this is the "likewise" (ὡσαύτως) linking verses 8 and 9. Just as Paul wants the men to pray in a certain manner ("lifting up holy hands without wrath and disputing"), so too he wants the women to pray with respectable deportment. It is more likely, however, that the infinitive "to adorn" (κοσμεῖν) completes the implied verb "I want."[51] The word "likewise" is a loose transition and does not indicate that the exact same activities are in mind (cf. 1 Tim. 3:8, 11; 5:25; Titus 2:3, 6). The connection between verse 8 and verses 9–15, then, is as follows: In verse 8, Paul considers the problem men have when gathered for public worship (anger and disputing in prayer), while in verses 9–15, two issues that have cropped up with the women in public gatherings (adornment and teaching men) are addressed. One should not conclude from the call to men to pray and women to adorn themselves properly that only men should pray in worship.[52] First Corinthians 11:5 clarifies that women are allowed to participate by praying in public meetings.[53]

What is meant by the word γυναῖκας in verse 9 and throughout the rest of this passage? Does it refer to women in general, or more specifically to wives? If it refers to wives both here and in subsequent verses, then women are not forbidden from teaching publicly in church. They are merely prohibited from teaching and exercising authority over their husbands. The idea that wives rather than women in general are the referent has been argued at some length by Gordon Hugenberger.[54] He contends that a reference to women and men in general is not demanded in writing to the church, for Peter in a text (1 Pet. 3:1–7) that is quite similar to 1 Timothy 2:9–15 only refers to husbands and wives. Moreover, appropriate dress for women (v. 9), good works (v. 10), and childrearing (v. 15) apply outside worship contexts. He thinks public worship is not necessarily in view, for the phrase "every place" does not refer to public meetings in 1 Corinthians 1:2 and 1 Thessalonians 1:8, and a public context is not needed for lifting one's hands in prayer. In addition, elsewhere in Paul the terms γυνή and ἀνήρ usually refer to wives and husbands, not to women and men in general. Further, he asserts that the parallels between Titus 2:4–5 and 1 Peter 3:1–7 are crucial for establishing the referent in 1 Timothy 2. In fact, Hugenberger thinks that the extensive verbal and conceptual parallels between 1 Timothy 2 and 1 Peter 3 "must be determinative for our exegesis" of 1 Timothy 2.[55] He believes it is unthinkable that no discussion of the family would occur in 1 Timothy.

The burden of Hugenberger's argument is that parallel texts show that Paul refers to husbands and wives in 1 Timothy 2:8–15. He especially leans on the parallels between 1 Timothy 2:8–15 and 1 Peter 3:1–7, seeing the latter as "determinative" for the meaning of the former. However, the texts hardly correspond in every respect, despite some impressive parallels. For instance, the 1 Peter text refers to *nonbelieving* husbands (3:1).[56] And in 3:7 husbands are addressed in terms of their specific responsibilities to their wives (cf. Eph. 5:25–30, 33; Col. 3:19). No admonition for husbands regarding their relationship with their wives is present in 1 Timothy 2. Finally, it is obvious that Peter has husbands and wives in view in 1 Peter 3 since he says wives should be subject to *their own* (ἰδίοις) husbands (v. 1; cf. v. 5). It is precisely this kind of clarifying evidence that 1 Timothy 2:8–15 lacks, with the result that most scholars detect a reference to men and women in general.

It is hardly impressive to say that elsewhere γυνή and ἀνήρ refer to husbands and wives since in those texts a reference to husbands and wives is indicated plainly in the context, and such passages are not even debated with respect to this issue.[57] Some examples will illustrate how clear the evidence is: "the married woman" (ἡ ὕπανδρος γυνή, Rom. 7:2); "each man should have his own wife" (τὴν ἑαυτοῦ γυναῖκα, 1 Cor. 7:2); "to the married" (τοῖς γεγαμηκόσιν, 1 Cor. 7:10); "if any brother has a wife" (ἀδελφὸς γυναῖκα ἔχει, 1 Cor. 7:12); "her husband" (ὁ ἀνήρ αὐτῆς, 1 Cor. 7:39); "Let them ask their own husbands at home" (τοὺς ἰδίους ἄνδρας, 1 Cor. 14:35);[58] "I betrothed you to one husband" (2 Cor. 11:2); "More are the children of the desolate one than of the one having a husband" (Gal. 4:27); "wives being subject to their own husbands" (αἱ γυναῖκες τοῖς ἰδίοις ἀνδράσιν, Eph. 5:22); "husband of one wife" (1 Tim. 3:2; cf. 1 Tim. 3:12; 5:9; Titus 1:6); "Instruct the young women to be lovers of their husbands (φιλάνδρους), . . . being subject to their own husbands" (τοῖς ἰδίοις ἀνδράσιν, Titus 2:5). By way of contrast, the lack of such qualifications in 1 Corinthians 11:2–16 shows that Paul is not referring to just husbands and wives, but to men and women in general. In Colossians 3:18–19, Paul could conceivably be referring to men and women in general, but the context (the next pericope deals with relations between parents and children, 3:20–21) and the call to "love your wives" (3:19) reveal that husbands and wives are in view. The very lack of such specificity in 1 Timothy 2:8–15 has rightly led most commentators to see a reference to men and women in general. Hugenberger demands that the Pauline usage elsewhere must obtain here, but he fails to notice the significant contextual differences between these other texts and 1 Timothy 2 and ends up imposing these other texts on the interpretation of 1 Timothy 2.[59]

Hugenberger's observations on the general applicability of appropriate dress, good works, and childrearing (better, childbearing) are apropos. And yet they call into question the thesis that only wives are being addressed, for it is quite improbable that Paul would be concerned about the adornment of wives but not the dress of single women.[60] Issues of adornment were probably occasioned by dress at public worship, even if they extend beyond that sphere.[61] The flow of thought of 1 Timothy as a whole commends a public setting. False teachers are threatening the church, and Timothy is charged to stem the tide of their influence. First Timothy 2:8–15 is succeeded by an exhortation to appoint over-

seers and deacons in the church (1 Tim. 3:1–13), and both are offices
that relate to public ministry in the church. The Pauline instructions
are designed to make the church a bulwark against the false teaching
(1 Tim. 3:14–15). Indeed, Paul immediately returns to the threat of false
teaching and the need to resist it (1 Tim. 4).[62] It seems improbable,
contrary to Hugenberger, that Paul would insert teaching on husbands
and wives at home in the midst of his polemic against false teachers.[63]
I conclude with most commentators that a reference to husbands and
wives in 1 Timothy 2:8–15 is quite improbable.[64] Instead, instructions
are given regarding proper behavior for men and women in public meetings of the church.

Advocates of the egalitarian view often raise the issue of women's
adornment in discussions about the legitimacy of women teaching men.
For example, Alvera Mickelsen says, "Those who believe that verse 12
forever bars all women of all time from teaching or having authority
over men usually ignore the commands in the other six verses in this
section. This is a classic case of 'selective literalism.' If this passage is
universal for all Christian women of all time, then no woman should
ever wear pearls or gold (including wedding rings) or have braided
hair or expensive clothing."[65] David Scholer argues that in the culture
of Paul's day proper adornment for women was linked to submission
to husbands.[66] He insists that women's adornment (vv. 9–10) must be
applied in the same way as the prohibitions against women teaching
(vv. 11–12).[67] One cannot legitimately claim that the latter is normative
whereas the former is culturally relative. Those who prohibit women from
teaching men should, to be consistent, also forbid the wearing of any
jewelry by women. Neither can they escape, he reasons, by saying that
submission is the principle that undergirds the wearing of appropriate
attire, so that the wearing of jewelry is permitted as long as one has a
submissive spirit. Suitable adornment and submission are inextricably
linked, and one cannot surrender the former and maintain the latter.
Scholer concludes that a careful interpretation of the text in its histori-
cal-cultural setting neither proscribes a woman from wearing jewelry
nor from teaching men, but that those who uphold the complementarian view have inconsistently enforced the proscription on teaching men
while ignoring the verses on proper adornment.[68]

The questions raised by these scholars are crucial and will be addressed in my explanation of these verses. We begin, though, by noting what the verses actually say. Paul calls upon the women to "adorn
themselves with respectable deportment" (v. 9). The word καταστολῇ
(deportment) probably refers to both suitable clothing and suitable
behavior.[69] The rest of verses 9–10 elaborates on proper deportment.
It consists of modesty and discretion with respect to dress instead of

enticing and ostentatious clothing. Attire that is immodest and reflects a lack in mature judgment includes braiding the hair, gold, pearls, and expensive clothing. Women who profess godliness should focus on good works rather than outward adornment.

Precisely what is Paul's intention here? Scholer and others rightly conclude that a proscription of all jewelry on the basis of these verses alone can fall into the error of excessive literalism. We should not rule out too quickly, though, the possibility that we have ignored these verses because they indict our culture.[70] Nonetheless, we have an important clue to Paul's intention in the words "expensive clothing" (ἱματισμῷ πολυτελεῖ).[71] The proscription is against not all wearing of clothing, but luxurious adornment, an excessive devotion to beautiful and splendid attire.[72] The similar text in 1 Peter 3:3 supports this interpretation, for read literally it prohibits all wearing of clothing, which is scarcely Peter's intention. The words on clothing provide help in understanding the instructions on braids, gold, and pearls. Paul's purpose is probably not to ban these altogether, but to warn against expensive and extravagant preoccupation with one's appearance. James Hurley suggests that the command is directed against the elaborate hairstyles that were worn by fashionable women and wealthy courtesans.[73] Probably the plaiting of hair with gold is indicted since braiding hair was common, enhancing the thesis that what is being forbidden is an excessive devotion to outward adornment.[74] In the Greco-Roman world, a polemic against ostentation of wealth was common (Juvenal, *Satires*, 6.352–65, 457–73; Plutarch, *Mor.* 142ab).[75] And the wearing of jewelry was not absolutely forbidden in Judaism (Gen. 24:22; Exod. 35:22; Babylonian Talmud *Šabbat* 64b; *Joseph and Aseneth* 18.6).[76] In conclusion, the text does not rule out all wearing of jewelry by women but forbids ostentation and luxury in adornment.[77]

It is also likely that these words on adornment contain a polemic against seductive and enticing clothing.[78] This is suggested by the words "modesty and discretion" (αἰδοῦς καὶ σωφροσύνης, v. 9).[79] In both Jewish and Greco-Roman literature, sexual seductiveness is linked with extravagant adornment (*Testament of Reuben* 5.1–5; *Testament of Judah* 12.3; *Testament of Joseph* 9.5; *1 Enoch* 8.1–2; Judith 10:3–4; Rev. 17:4; 18:16).[80] Thus, we can draw two principles from these verses. Not only is extravagant and ostentatious adornment prohibited but also clothing that is seductive and enticing.[81] These words are desperately needed in our culture, for materialism and sexual seductiveness with respect to adornment still plague us.

We have already noted that some scholars argue that suitable clothing was linked with submission to one's husband in Paul's day. Scholer, in particular, cites a number of texts to support this view.[82] Nonetheless, that these two themes are wedded to the extent that Scholer argues is unpersuasive. In 1 Peter 3:1–6, for instance, the two themes are found side by side, but it goes beyond the evidence of the text to say that submission is expressed by one's attire. In the other texts that Scholer cites, the vice that is specified with regard to the women is unchastity, not insubordination or lack of submission.[83] The demanded devotion to and the honor of the husband probably relate to faithfulness to the marriage bed rather than submission.[84] In any case, not a word is said about lack of submission in 1 Timothy 2:9–10, and thus reading this theme into the text is questionable.

For the sake of argument, though, we will assume for a moment that Scholer and others are correct about suitable adornment being tied to submission. Even if this is the case, it does not logically follow that the principle of submission must be jettisoned if one does not literally apply the words regarding proper attire. Of course, the principle regarding suitable adornment needs to be taken seriously today, for the instructions on adornment prohibit ostentation and seductiveness in clothing. However, *if* such adornment were banned by Paul for the sole reason that it expressed lack of submission, then it seems that the principle informing the commands could be retained in our culture without requiring the first-century cultural expression of that principle. No one in our culture would believe that a woman wearing jewelry or a wedding band was declaring her independence from a man. In fact, wearing a wedding band is often taken to mean just the opposite. In our culture such adornment would not communicate lack of submission. Submission to one's husband would be expressed in other ways.

Scholer's conclusion that a principial application of the biblical text would be illegitimate is unconvincing. We rightly apply the principle from other biblical texts without requiring the literal practice that communicated the principle in Paul's day. For instance, we are not *required* to drink wine for stomachaches today (1 Tim. 5:23), but the principle behind Paul's admonition still applies to us. We should use an antacid or some other medicine when suffering from stomach problems. So too, in American culture we do not typically express our affection with a holy kiss (1 Cor. 16:20). We should not conclude from this that we *must* greet one another with a holy kiss. Nor should we argue that if we do not literally practice the holy kiss, then this verse is inapplicable to us. The principle is that we should greet one another with warm affection, and in our culture that may be expressed by a warm handshake or a hug. In our culture, therefore, the admonitions in verses 9–10 contain the principle that women should not dress ostentatiously or seductively. The intention of the text is not to ban the wearing of all jewelry. This raises, of course, the question as to how the principle in verses 11–12 should be applied today. Perhaps the principle undergirding those verses is not violated if women teach men today. Such an application of these verses is certainly possible, and thus we must interpret those verses carefully to see what the principle is.

Should a Woman Teach or Exercise Authority over a Man?

Virtually every word in verses 11–12 is disputed. Thus, I will attempt to construct my argument piece by piece, although it is impossible to interpret the parts without appealing to the whole, and so other issues must be broached in the midst of the analysis of individual elements as well. Verse 11 is translated as follows: "A woman should learn quietly with all submission." The singular "woman" (γυνή) is generic, and thus should not be limited to an individual woman. The alternation from the plural "women" in verses 9–10 to the singular "woman" in verses 11–12 reveals that the latter is generic and all women are included.[85]

Paul enjoins all women to learn (μανθανέτω). It has often been pointed out that this represents an advance over some traditions in Judaism that forbade women from learning.[86] The exhortation implies a belief in the intellectual capability of women and their ability to profit from instruction and education. Certainly those of the complementarian position should also encourage women to grow in their knowledge of the Scriptures. Philip Payne says that the injunction for women to learn is the only command in this text.[87] When we analyze the verb "I permit" (ἐπιτρέπω), however, it will be argued that this observation is linguistically naïve, even if it is rhetorically impressive. The injunction to learn, many aver, implies that the women could teach after they learn. Therefore, it is claimed that the only reason for the prohibition on women teachers was lack of education or the influence of the false teachers.[88]

Several things need to be said in response to the above observations. Even though egalitarians are right in detecting a commendation of women learning in verse 11, the thrust of the command is obscured in their exegesis by abstracting the imperative verb from the rest of the sentence. Paul does not merely say, "Women must learn!" He says, "Women must learn quietly and with all submission." The focus of the command is not on women learning, but *the manner* and *mode* of their learning.[89] Egalitarians are correct in seeing a commendation of women learning, for the propriety of women learning is implied in the use of the imperative verb. But Paul's main concern is the way they learn, that is, quietly and with all submissiveness. An illustration might help. If I were to say to my son, "You must drive the car carefully and wisely," the sentence assumes that driving the car is permissible and suitable for my son. Nonetheless, the focus of my instruction is not on permission to drive the car; that is assumed. What I am mainly concerned about is the *manner* in which he drives it. Similarly, that women should learn is undoubtedly commended, and yet the central concern is the manner in which they learn.

Neither is it convincing to say that permission to learn implies that women can teach once they have sufficient learning.[90] Such exegesis overlooks what we have just pointed out, that the command concentrates not on the fact that women should learn but on the manner in which they should do so. Moreover, Paul could have easily said in verse 12, "But I do not permit a woman to teach a man until she is sufficiently educated." Instead, verse 12 says that women cannot teach or exercise authority over men. Egalitarians read out of the injunction to learn, permission to teach, but verse 12 prohibits this very activity.[91]

The two adverbial phrases in verse 12 regarding the mode in which women should learn should be noted. First, Paul says they should learn "quietly" (ἐν ἡσυχίᾳ). Most scholars today argue that this word does not actually mean "silence" here, but refers to a quiet demeanor and spirit that is peaceable instead of argumentative.[92] The use of the same word in 1 Timothy 2:2 supports this thesis, for there not absolute silence but rather a gentle and quiet demeanor is intended. The parallel text in 1 Peter 3:4 also inclines us in the same direction, since the "gentle and quiet spirit" of the wife in the home can scarcely involve absolute silence! In addition, if Paul wanted to communicate absolute silence, he could have used the noun σιγή (silence) rather than ἡσυχία (quietness). The resolution of this question is not of prime importance for the debate before us, for the meaning of the text is not drastically changed either way. Some prefer "silently" on the basis of the context of verse 12.[93] There women are proscribed from teaching and exercising authority over men; instead, they are εἶναι ἐν ἡσυχίᾳ. It is argued that the most natural antonym to teaching in this context is "silence," and the word group does bear the meaning "silence" in some texts (e.g., Luke 14:4; Acts 22:2). Thus, the question comes down to what the word means in this specific context. It seems more likely that Paul refers to a quiet and nonrebellious spirit instead of absolute silence.[94]

Second, women should learn ἐν πάσῃ ὑποταγῇ (in all submission). Probably the word "all" has an elative sense, meaning "with entire submissiveness."[95] To what are the women to be submissive? It has been suggested that women are to be submissive to God,[96] the congregation in general,[97] sound teaching,[98] the contemporary social structure,[99] or the women's teachers.[100] We are aided in answering this question by the parallels between verses 11 and 12. Verses 11 and 12 constitute an inclusio; verse 11 begins with "quietly" and verse 12 concludes with "quietly." The permission for women to "learn" is contrasted with the proscription for them "to teach," while "all submissiveness" is paired with "not exercising authority over a man." The submission in view, then, is likely to men, since verse 12 bans women from exercising authority over men. Yet the context of verse 12 (more on this below) suggests that the submission of all women to all men is not in view, for not all men taught and had authority when the church gathered. Thus, we should not separate submission to what is taught from submission to those who taught it. Women were to learn with entire submissiveness from the men who had authority in the church and manifested that authority through their teaching.[101]

The δέ introducing verse 12 is a mild adversative that clarifies more precisely the command in verse 11.[102] The two verses are closely tied together, and perhaps even chiastic.[103] The phrase ἐν ἡσυχίᾳ (quietly) introduces verse 11 and concludes verse 12, and thus functions as an inclusio for these verses. "Women should learn quietly" (ἐν ἡσυχίᾳ μανθανέτω, v. 11) but are not permitted "to teach" (διδάσκειν, v. 12).[104] They are to learn "in all submission" (ἐν πάσῃ ὑποταγῇ, v. 11) but are not "to exercise authority over men" (αὐθεντεῖν ἀνδρός, v. 12). These correspondences and antitheses between verses 11 and 12 indicate that Andrew Perriman's view that verse 12 is parenthetical is unconvincing.[105] Verse 12 follows on the heels of verse 11 and clarifies its meaning. Missing the relationship between verses 11 and 12 has the consequence of vitiating Perriman's exegesis of this text, since his interpretation depends on this analysis.

The verb "I do not permit" (ἐπιτρέπω, v. 12) has been the subject of controversy. It is often said that the verb reflects only a temporary prohibition. Scholars appeal to the verbal form being a present active indicative first singular, concluding from this that Paul is not permitting women to teach or exercise authority over men *for a restricted period of time*.[106] It is also claimed that the intrinsic meaning of ἐπιτρέπω demonstrates that a temporary prohibition is intended, for the verb elsewhere never indicates a universally applicable command. Indeed, as noted above, some even capitalize on the form being indicative and state that the only imperative in the text is in verse 11.

This latter point should be taken up first, for it is extraordinarily misleading and betrays a wooden view of Greek by implying that one can only have commands if the imperative mood is used. On the contrary, Paul often uses present indicatives in cases where the context reveals a command is intended. For instance, in 1 Timothy 2:1 the call to pray for all people is introduced by a present indicative (παρακαλῶ, "I exhort"; cf. Rom. 12:1; 1 Cor. 1:10; Eph. 4:1; Phil. 4:2; 2 Tim. 1:6). So, too, the directive for men to pray without wrath and disputing is introduced by a present indicative (βούλομαι, "I want," 1 Tim. 2:8; cf. 1 Tim. 5:14; Titus 3:8). The assertion that verse 11 contains the only command in the text, therefore, can hardly be taken seriously.[107]

But does the present active indicative first singular form reflect a temporary prohibition, or is it merely Paul's personal opinion? Once again, the answer is negative on both counts.[108] Numerous injunctions are given by Paul in the present active indicative first singular that are universal commands. For instance, the command to present one's body to God as a living and holy sacrifice is introduced with a present active indicative first singular (παρακαλῶ, "I exhort," Rom. 12:1), and it is obviously a universally applicable command. In many other instances such universal commands exist with present active indicatives in the first person (e.g., Rom. 15:30; 16:17; 1 Cor. 1:10; 4:16; 7:10; 2 Cor. 10:1; Eph. 4:1; Phil. 4:2; 1 Thess. 4:1, 10; 5:14; 2 Thess. 3:6, 12; 1 Tim. 2:1, 8; 5:14; 2 Tim. 1:6; Titus 3:8). The point is not that the present active in- dicative first person form in 1 Timothy 2:12 *proves* that the command is universal and for all time. My point is more modest. Those who appeal to the form of the word as if it established the temporary nature of the prohibition transcend the evidence. The form does no such thing, and such a thesis must be established on other grounds.

More promising, on first glance, is the contention that ἐπιτρέπω con- tains the idea of a temporary limitation by virtue of its intrinsic meaning. That the verb may relate to a specific situation is obvious in a number of contexts (Matt. 8:21 par.; Mark 5:13 par.; John 19:38; Acts 21:39, 40; 26:1; 27:3; 28:16). Nonetheless, the argument is again dubious. The specificity of the situation is plain not from the verb itself but from the context in which it occurs. For instance, in Matthew 8:21 we know that the request for permission to bury one's father before following Jesus relates to a specific situation that will not last forever. But this is scarcely explicable from the verb ἐπιτρέπω itself; we know this because one can bury one's father only once.[109] In other contexts ἐπιτρέπω is not necessarily limited to a specific situation (cf. 1 Cor. 14:34; 16:7; Heb. 6:3; Ignatius, *To the Ephesians* 10.3; *1 Clement* 1.3; *Ant.* 20.267). Whether what is permitted or forbidden is universal cannot be determined by the tense of the verb nor by its intrinsic meaning. It is the context in which the verb occurs that is decisive. If I say to my daughter, "You are not permitted to drive the car one hundred miles per hour," it is obvious (or should be!) that this is a universal prohibition. But if I say, "You are not permitted to go into the street," it is also plain that this is a temporary restriction given to a young girl of two years of age who is not yet able to handle herself safely in the street. In conclusion, the mere presence of the word ἐπιτρέπω cannot be used to establish the temporary nature of the restriction, nor can it establish that we have a universal principle for all time.[110] Only the context can resolve that question, and verse 12 alone does not contain sufficient evidence to answer it, although it will be argued below that verse 13 establishes that the prohibition is a universal one.

Two things are forbidden for a woman: teaching and exercising authority over a man.[111] The emphatic position of "to teach" at the beginning of verse 12 does not show that the verse is a parenthesis.[112] Instead, Paul emphasizes that although women are permitted to learn, they cannot teach. Teaching here involves the authoritative and public transmission of tradition about Christ and the Scriptures (1 Cor. 12:28–29; Eph. 4:11; 1 Tim. 2:7; 2 Tim. 3:16; James 3:1).[113] It is clear from the rest of the Pastoral Epistles that the teaching in view is the public transmission of authoritative material (cf. 1 Tim. 4:13, 16; 6:2; 2 Tim. 4:2; Titus 2:7). The elders in particular are to labor in teaching (1 Tim. 5:17) so that they can refute the false teachers who advance heresy (1 Tim. 1:3, 10; 4:1; 6:3; 2 Tim. 4:3; Titus 1:9, 11). It is crucial that the correct teaching and the apostolic deposit be passed on to the next generation (2 Tim. 1:12, 14; 2:2).

The prohibition against women teaching is not absolute and is probably given because some women were teaching both men and women when the church assembled.[114] The object of the infinitive "to teach" (διδάσκειν) is "man" (ἀνδρός), indicating that women teaching men is what is forbidden.[115] The distance between the two infinitives is exaggerated by those who think that ἀνδρός is not also the object of διδάσκειν.[116] Those who advocate the egalitarian position point out that Timothy was taught by his mother and grandmother (2 Tim. 1:5; 3:15); that Priscilla and Aquila taught Apollos (Acts 18:26); that women are permitted to teach elsewhere (Titus 2:3); and that all believers are to teach one another (Col. 3:16).[117] But those who hold to the complementarian view do not doubt that women can teach children or other women. It should be noted that Titus 2:3–4 speaks specifically of women teaching other women, and thus the appeal to women teaching here hardly violates what Paul says in 1 Timothy 2:12. Neither does the private teaching of Apollos by Priscilla and Aquila contradict what is said here, for this is profoundly different from the public and authoritative teaching in view in the Pastoral Epistles. Colossians 3:16 (cf. 1 Cor. 14:26) could be taken to say that women can teach men publicly and officially.[118] But the teaching described there is the mutual instruction that occurs among all the members of the body. Unfortunately, some churches ban women from doing even this, although it is plainly in accord with Scripture. Yet this is quite different from the authoritative transmission of tradition that Paul has in mind in the Pastoral Epistles. Such authoritative teaching is usually a function of the elders/overseers (1 Tim. 3:2; 5:17), and it is likely that Paul is thinking of them here.[119] Thus, women are proscribed from functioning as elders/overseers, but Knight also correctly observes that they are prohibited from the function of public and authoritative teaching of men by this verse as well.[120]

A more powerful objection against the complementarian position is the assertion that prophecy is just as authoritative as teaching (1 Cor. 12:28; Eph. 2:20; 4:11).[121] Since it is clear that women could prophesy in the public assembly (Acts 2:17–18; 21:9; 1 Cor. 11:5), it is therefore concluded they should also be permitted to teach. In response, Wayne Grudem has distinguished prophecy and teaching, saying that the latter is based on the apostolic deposit for the church and is more authoritative. Prophecy involves spontaneous revelations in which truth is mixed with error so that the content of the prophecies needs to be sifted.[122] According to Grudem, the nonauthoritative nature of New Testament prophecy explains why women can prophesy but not teach. Grudem's understanding of New Testament prophecy would explain why women could prophesy but not teach, for the nature and authority of prophecy are quite different from teaching.[123] Even if Grudem is incorrect regarding the nonauthoritative character of New Testament prophecy, the gifts of prophecy and teaching are still distinct.[124] Prophecy is more vertical in nature, while teaching is more horizontal; the former involves spontaneous revelation and in that sense is more charismatic. Prophecy applies to specific situations and is less tied to the consciousness of the individual than teaching. Moreover, 1 Corinthians 11:2–16 shows that women with the prophetic gift should exercise it in such a way that they do not subvert male leadership.[125] This does not mean that the prophecies given by women are any less authoritative than those of men. It does signal that the gift of prophecy can be exercised by women without overturning male headship, whereas 1 Timothy 2:11–15 demonstrates that women cannot regularly teach men without doing so.[126]

Not only does Paul forbid women to teach men, but he also says that they should "not exercise authority over" (αὐθεντεῖν) them. The debate over the meaning of αὐθεντεῖν has been vigorous. The meaning "exercise authority" is most likely.[127] In particular, Henry Scott Baldwin has pointed out that the verb must be separated from the noun in constructing the definition of the term.[128] Moreover, the near context also suggests that αὐθεντεῖν means "exercise authority," for it functions as the antonym to "all submissiveness" in verse 11.[129] Catherine Kroeger proposed the interpretation "engage in fertility practices" for the verb in 1979,[130] but the evidence for this meaning was virtually nonexistent, and her interpretation has not gained acceptance.[131] The Kroegers have recently suggested that the sentence should read, "I do not allow a woman to teach nor to proclaim herself the author or originator of a man."[132] This suggestion is faring little better than the first one and shows no signs of gaining any adherents.[133] Leland Wilshire's 1988 study led most scholars to believe that he was adopting the meaning "exercise authority" as the most probable in 1 Timothy 2:12.[134] In a recent article, he complains that Paul Barnett wrongly read this conclusion out of his work.[135] If there is any deficiency here, it lies with Wilshire rather than Barnett, for a number of scholars have understood Wilshire's 1988 article this way.[136] Now Wilshire suggests that the meaning in 1 Timothy 2:12 is "instigate violence."[137] This latter suggestion is flawed.[138] Even in the first article he failed to distinguish between the meaning of the noun and that of the verb. In the latter study Wilshire speculates that the problem with women was violence or conflict, but the text gives no indication that women were actually involved in such. Indeed, verse 8 says it was the men who were involved in arguing and disputation, whereas Wilshire concludes that the problem of disputing and arguing, which Paul limits to the men in verse 8, was actually the main problem with the women! Nor does Wilshire's view explain how the alleged prohibition against violence is related to teaching, and thus his proposal makes little sense in context. Perhaps I can be forgiven for thinking that the evidence actually leads to the conclusion Wilshire seemed to suggest in 1988, but his preference is for another translation, and this led him to write an article that lacked the high quality of his 1988 piece.[139]

Some scholars have said that αὐθεντεῖν cannot mean "exercise authority" because Paul would have used the more common ἐξουσιάζειν (to exercise authority), κυριεύειν (to exercise authority), or ἔχειν ἐξουσίαν (to have authority) if he had wanted to communicate this idea.[140] They claim that the hapax legomenon αὐθεντεῖν reveals that a distinct meaning is in view. This argument is not as convincing as it might appear. Αὐθεντεῖν and ἐξουσιάζειν have overlapping semantic fields. A review of Baldwin's data shows that the two words are used synonymously in at least eight different contexts. The expression "have authority" (ἔχειν ἐξουσίαν) does not convey the same meaning as "exercise authority," since it focuses on possession of authority instead of use (cf. Rom. 9:21; 1 Cor. 7:37; 9:4, 5, 6; 11:10; 2 Thess. 3:9). And one might get the impression that Paul frequently uses the verbs ἐξουσιάζω and κυριεύω for "exercise authority," but he uses the former only three times (1 Cor. 6:12; 7:4 [twice]),[141] and the latter on six occasions (Rom. 6:9, 14; 7:1; 14:9; 2 Cor. 1:24; 1 Tim. 6:15). The statistical significance of selecting αὐθεντεῖν instead of ἐξουσιάζειν or κυριεύειν, therefore, is overrated.[142] Moreover, ἐξουσιάζω has a clearly negative sense in Luke 22:25 but a positive one in 1 Corinthians 7:4. Thus, one cannot say that Paul had to use this verb to indicate a positive use of authority. What indicates a positive or negative use of authority is the context.[143] The verb κυριεύω is hardly a better choice. When used of God or Christ, it has a positive meaning (Rom. 14:9; 1 Tim. 6:15), but elsewhere in Paul it bears a negative meaning (Rom. 6:9, 14; 7:1; 2 Cor. 1:24; cf. Luke 22:25). If Paul had wanted to communicate a positive meaning of exercising authority, the verb κυριεύω would not qualify as a better candidate than αὐθεντέω. Neither ἐξουσιάζω nor κυριεύω necessarily includes a positive concept of exercising authority. Whether the authority is positive or negative is contextually determined. Too much has been made, therefore, of a distinct verb being used in 1 Timothy 2:12. Surely, we need to investigate carefully the meaning of the term in extrabiblical literature, so that the semantic range of the term is known. In most cases αὐθεντέω has a positive meaning along the lines of "exercise authority." Nonetheless, in context αὐθεντεῖν can have a negative meaning. We should not rule out the possibility that the context will incline us toward the meaning "domineer" or "play the tyrant" rather than "exercise authority."[144] But we shall see shortly that the definition "exercise authority" is constrained by the context.

The relationship between the two infinitives "to teach" and "to exercise authority" should also be explored. Philip Payne has argued that these two infinitives joined by the word "neither" (οὐδέ) communicate a single coherent idea.[145] Andreas Köstenberger, in a wide-ranging and impressive study of both biblical and extrabiblical literature, demonstrates that Payne's database was too small and that he misinterpreted the evidence.[146] The two ideas are closely related, but two different injunctions are intended.[147] Women are forbidden both to teach and to exercise authority over men.[148] Köstenberger's study also reveals that in constructions with οὐδέ both items proscribed are viewed either negatively or positively. Thus, the verse means either "I do not permit a woman to teach falsely or domineer over a man" or "I do not permit a woman to teach or exercise authority over a man." The latter option is demanded, for there is no evidence here that the infinitive διδάσκειν should be rendered "to teach falsely."[149] If Paul had wanted to communicate that the teaching prohibited was false teaching, then he would have used ἑτεροδιδασκαλεῖν (to teach false doctrine), which he uses to convey this very idea in 1 Timothy 1:3 and 6:3; or he would have given some other clear contextual clue (such as an object clause or an adverb) to indicate that the teaching in view is false teaching.[150] The verb διδάσκω (I teach) has a positive sense elsewhere in the Pastoral Epistles (1 Tim. 4:11; 6:2; 2 Tim. 2:2). The only exception is Titus 1:11, where the context clarifies that false teaching is the object.[151] But no indication is given in this text that false teaching is what is proscribed for women,[152] and thus the verse should be translated as follows, "But I do not permit a woman to teach a man or to exercise authority over a man, but [I want her] to be quiet."

The Reason for the Prohibition

Why does Paul command women to learn quietly and submissively and forbid them from teaching or exercising authority over men? The reason is provided in verse 13: "For Adam was formed first, then Eve." The second creation account (Gen. 2:4–25) is clearly the text Paul has in mind, for there we find the narrative of Adam being created before Eve.[153] The use of the word "form" (πλάσσω; cf. Gen. 2:7, 8, 15, 19) instead of ποιέω (make; cf. Gen. 1:26–27) also indicates that the reference is to the second creation account in Genesis. The proscription on women teaching men, then, does not stem from the fall and cannot be ascribed to the curse. Paul appeals to the created order, the good and perfect world God has made, to justify the ban on women teaching men.[154] Gordon Fee has recently seemed to suggest that Paul is not appealing to the created order here,[155] but his objections fly in the face of the clear meaning of the text. The created order is invoked; the question is whether this constitutes verses 11–12 as a universal principle.

Those who adhere to the egalitarian position argue that the γάρ (for) introducing verses 13–14 does not give *reasons* why women should not teach; instead, *illustrations* or *examples* are provided of what happens when women falsely teach men.[156] This understanding of the γάρ is singularly unconvincing. When Paul gives a command elsewhere in the Pastoral Epistles, the γάρ that follows almost invariably states the reason for the command (1 Tim. 4:7–8, 16; 5:4, 11, 15, 18; 2 Tim. 1:6–7; 2:7, 16; 3:5–6; 4:3, 5–6, 9–10, 11, 15; Titus 3:1–3, 9, 12).[157] So, too, a command is given in verses 11–12, and the reasons for the command are enunciated in verses 13–14.[158] Frankly, this is just what we would expect since even in ordinary speech reasons often follow commands. The implausibility of the egalitarian view is sealed when we begin to probe how verse 13 functions as an example. Alan Padgett interprets the verse in a highly allegorical manner to yield an illustrative sense, even though such an allegory is scarcely apparent in the text.[159] Padgett says that the text is typological; Eve functions as a type of the rich Ephesian women and Adam as a type of the teachers. Thus, the teachers, like Adam, are formed first in the spiritual sense of being older in the faith and possessing a more accurate understanding of the Old Testament. This is certainly a creative reading of the text, but it does not qualify as serious exegesis. Rather, such an approach is reminiscent of Philo's allegories on the Old Testament.[160]

The complementarian view has the virtue of adopting the simplest reading of the text.[161] Paul maintains that the Genesis narrative gives a reason why women should not teach men: Adam was created first and then Eve. In other words, when Paul read Genesis 2, he concluded that the order in which Adam and Eve were created signalled an important difference in the role of men and women. Thus, he inferred from the order of creation in Genesis 2 that women should not teach or exercise authority over men. It is customary nowadays for evangelical scholars to claim that a distinction between the roles of men and women cannot be justified from Genesis.[162] But many remain unpersuaded by their exegesis because it seems quite apparent both from 1 Timothy 2:13 and 1 Corinthians 11:8–9 that Paul interpreted Genesis 2 to posit legitimate role differences between men and women.[163] A difference in role or function does not imply that women are inferior to men.[164] The Son will submit to the Father (1 Cor. 15:28), and yet he is equal to the Father in essence, dignity, and personhood.[165] It is a modern, democratic, Western notion that diverse functions suggest distinctions in worth between men and women. Paul believed that men and women were equal in personhood, dignity, and value but also taught that women had a distinct role from men.

Egalitarians back away from verse 13 because it calls into question the exegetical edifice they have built to justify women teaching men. For example, Mary Evans says that the relevance of verse 13 for verse 12 is unclear, and that verse 13 merely introduces the next verse about Eve.[166] Gordon Fee asserts that the verse is not central to Paul's argument.[167] Timothy Harris says that the verse "is difficult to understand on any reading."[168] Craig Keener thinks that the argument here is hard to fathom.[169] David Scholer protests that the text is unclear and that Paul cites selectively from Genesis.[170] Steve Motyer says that logic and justice are nullified if the complementarian position of verses 13–14 is accepted.[171] It seems that unclarity is in the eye of the beholder, for the thrust of the verse has been deemed quite clear in the history of the church. The creation of Adam first gives a reason why men should be the authoritative teachers in the church.[172] Egalitarians often say that the argument from the order of creation does not work because it would also imply that animals have authority over humans since they were created first.[173] This objection is not compelling. For it is obvious in Genesis that only human beings are created in God's image (Gen. 1:26-27) and that they are distinct from animals. Paul, as a careful reader of the Hebrew narrative, under the inspiration of the Spirit, detected significance in the order of creation for the roles of men and women. James Hurley notes that the reasoning would not be obscure to people of Paul's time, for they were quite familiar with primogeniture.[174]

William Webb protests, however, that arguments from primogeniture are flawed.[175] In Scripture, God often overrides the principle of primogeniture (choosing Jacob instead of Esau), and hence primogeniture cannot be a transcultural principle. Indeed, according to Webb, primogeniture is tied to ancient agricultural societies, and we must not impose the agrarian culture of the past onto contemporary cultures. Webb suggests that the intimations of patriarchy in the garden represent literary foreshadowing of the curse, so that the writer accommodates to the readers by describing the social conditions that existed in Moses's day as if such conditions were actually present in paradise. Webb's criticisms of appealing to primogeniture are not compelling, for he misunderstands the position. In referring to primogeniture, complementarian scholars are scarcely suggesting that the cultural practice of primogeniture should be enforced today, nor do they think that Paul is endorsing primogeniture per se. Nor would they deny the many examples from the Old Testament, adduced by Webb, in which primogeniture was overturned. Instead, they appeal to primogeniture to explain that the notion of the firstborn having authority would be easily understood by Paul's readers. The readers of 1 Timothy would not have scratched their heads with perplexity and amazement when Paul says that women should not teach because Adam was created first. The priority of Adam in creation would have naturally suggested his authority over Eve to the original readers. Paul does not endorse primogeniture per se in 1 Timothy 2:13; he appeals to the creation of Adam first in explaining why women should not teach men. For Webb to convince, he needs to explain why Paul refers to the creation of Adam first in writing a letter to the city of Ephesus (not simply to an agricultural community). Paul's prohibition of women teaching has nothing to do with the cultural limitations of primogeniture mentioned by Webb: land-based cultures, elderly parents, large families, age, sibling rivalry, parental death, and survival/success of lineage. But Paul does maintain that Adam being created first (not all other dimensions of primogeniture mentioned in the Old Testament!) supports the notion that men are to be those who teach and exercise authority rather than women. At the end of the day, Webb does not take seriously what Paul says as an argument.

Even more troubling is Webb's claim that the Genesis account contains "whispers of patriarchy" because the writer of Genesis accommodates what he says to the patriarchal society in which he lives.[176] Webb thereby concedes that patriarchy is present in the creation account, but he attempts to explain it away as accommodation. This is hardly comparable to biblical writers who use the language and culture of their own day in prophesying about the future, as Webb suggests. Webb's position implies that the biblical writers distorted the true nature of paradise since they suggested that it was patriarchal, when it fact, according to Webb, it was not. Webb's "whispers of patriarchy" in paradise and his attempt to explain such as accommodation illustrate his commitment to sustain an egalitarian reading of the text, even at the cost of finding fault in paradise.[177]

Even egalitarians acknowledge that role differences were common in ancient societies. The original readers would have understood Paul, then, to defend such role differences, and he does so on the basis of the created order. In other words, Paul thinks such differences are good and proper and not the result of sin or the fall. Scholer's observation that Genesis is cited in a selective manner is irrelevant. Douglas Moo rightly observes that the Old Testament is *always* cited selectively.[178] The question is how the citation fits into the flow of the argument in which it is used.

Some scholars contend that Paul's interpretation here is forced and illogical.[179] This position at least has the virtue of understanding the Pauline intention and meaning, even though his argument is rejected as inferior. My purpose is not to engage in an apologetic for the Pauline position here; it should simply be noted that most evangelicals have a higher view of biblical authority than these scholars. We should note, however, that these scholars agree exegetically with the complementarian position, although they see a contradiction with Pauline teaching elsewhere because of their own philosophical commitments.

Many scholars suggest that the reason women could not teach men is because they were promulgating the heresy or were uneducated.[180] This theory cannot be exegetically validated because it reads something into the text that is not present. Paul could have easily said that the women were prohibited from teaching because they were spreading the heresy or were uneducated.[181] Yet he does not breathe a word about these matters.[182] Instead, he appeals to the created order. Those scholars who posit that false teaching or lack of education was the reason for the prohibition upon women ignore the reason the text actually gives (the created order) and insert what is not said in the text (false teaching and lack of education) to explain the proscription. I do not deny that women were influenced by the false teaching (1 Tim. 5:11–15; 2 Tim. 3:6–9), and it is even possible (though not certain) that some of the women were teaching the heresy.[183] But this alone does not explain the Pauline wording here. If both men and women were involved in the heresy, why does Paul forbid only the women from teaching men?[184] If the reason for the limitation were participation in the heresy or lack of education, then we would expect Paul, as a good egalitarian, to prohibit all men and women, who were spreading the heresy or who were uneducated, from teaching. This point is particularly important because we know without a doubt from the Pastoral Epistles that men were spreading the heresy (1 Tim. 1:20; 2 Tim. 2:17–18; 3:5–9). Yet he forbids only women from teaching. As Don Carson says about another text, the Pauline limitation on women would be sensible only if *"all* the women and *only* women . . . were duped—which perhaps I may be excused for finding hard to believe."[185]

Philip Towner says the real point of the passage is that one must adapt to societal norms and institutions, but this can take place as time progresses.[186] Once again, though, he leaps over the argument given to provide one not stated in the text. Towner's view is attractive, yet Paul's appeal to creation shows that the proscription here is not just part of societal norms but is rooted in the created order. Richard Longenecker avers that redemption transcends creation, and thus creational norms are not necessarily binding.[187] Again, this would neatly solve the problem, but it stumbles on the stubborn fact that Paul himself apparently did not believe redemption in Christ overturned the created order. We must bypass Paul, then, to say that redemption transcends creation in the relationship between men and women. Those who erase the distinction in roles between men and women in the present age are probably guilty of falling prey to a form of overrealized eschatology, for the creational order established with reference to men and women will be terminated in the coming age (cf. Matt. 22:30).

Others protest that we are selective in what we accept as universally valid.[188] We do not, for instance, command all younger widows to marry (1 Tim. 5:14), and little is said today about the applicability of 1 Timothy 5:3–16. We all have blind spots and thus we need to beware of bracketing out texts that are distasteful to us. Perhaps we have not been serious enough about applying 1 Timothy 5:3–16 to our culture. But if we have been avoiding the message of this passage, it does not logically follow from this that we can also jettison the prescriptions in 1 Timothy 2:9–15. Our responsibility in such a situation is to obey both texts. A full exegesis of 1 Timothy 5:3–16 cannot be engaged in here, but it seems that one principle in the text is that godly widows in financial need, who can no longer support themselves, need to be supported by the church. If widows in our churches need financial help, then the church should provide it. Bruce Waltke rightly observes that Paul's authorial intent must be gleaned in his advice to the younger widows (1 Tim. 5:11–15).[189] He recommends marriage for the younger widows to restrict sexual sin (cf. 1 Cor. 7:9). One principle here is that believers should not pledge themselves to a life of celibacy without taking into account the strength of their sexual desires. Paul commends the single state (1 Cor. 7), but even then (vv. 2, 9) he recognizes that sexual desires may be one indication that one should marry. In any case, the prohibition in 1 Timothy 2:12 is grounded by an appeal to creation, indicating that the command has universal validity.

Ronald Pierce, in dependence on Sherwood Lingenfelter, asserts that women are often banned from ministry on the basis of verse 13 because we assume that Paul is using Western logic when he is actually using "practical logic."[190] Lingenfelter says that Paul taps into the "generative core of beliefs" to justify his prohibition. But how does labeling this "practical logic" show that the prohibition is no longer applicable? If this represents Paul's "generative core of beliefs," on what basis do we discard it today? Interestingly, Pierce slides from this observation to the thesis that Paul wanted women to practice humility and patience as they slowly moved from their lowly status to their new liberty in Christ.[191] But Pierce reads this latter idea into the text, for it is hardly apparent from verses 13–14 that Paul envisions a time when the restriction in verse 12 will be lifted.[192]

One might object, however, that not all commands rooted in creation are normative. Paul commends food and marriage as good since they are grounded in creation (1 Tim. 4:1–5), yet we know from 1 Corinthians 7 and from Romans 14–15 and 1 Corinthians 8–10 that in some situations he counsels believers to abstain from marriage and from certain foods. Is this not an indication that an appeal to creation is not necessarily normative? Actually, a subtle equivocation has occurred in such an objection. What Paul argues in 1 Timothy 4:1–5 is that all foods and marriage are good, *not that one must eat all foods and must get married*. Thus, the fact that some believers are called to celibacy or should abstain from certain foods in particular situations hardly constitutes an exception to the argument from creation in 1 Timothy 4:1–5. In 1 Corinthians 7, Paul continues to maintain that marriage is good and counters the idea that marriage and sexual relations must be eschewed. Moreover, in Romans 14–15 and 1 Corinthians 8–10, those who abstain from certain foods are even considered weak in faith, and the strong must abstain occasionally so as not to offend the weak. What would violate the principle of 1 Timothy 4:1–5 is if one were to argue that marriage and certain foods were always to be avoided because they were inherently defiling, and this is precisely what the false teachers in the Pastoral Epistles were saying.

Even if we were to accept the analogous argument from 1 Timothy 4:1–5, so that the argument from creation in 1 Timothy 2:11–13 admits exceptions, the conclusion egalitarians want to draw from the parallel does not follow logically. For at least in the case of 1 Timothy 4:1–5, the principle of the goodness of the created world stands, whereas in the case of 1 Timothy 2:13, egalitarians would have to argue that the exception exists when women are prohibited from teaching men, but the norm permits them to do so. In the case of 1 Timothy 2, then, the appeal to the created order would justify *the exception*, not the rule. The parallel from 1 Timothy 4:1–5 falters on this analysis because in that text the created order is invoked to support the *rule*, not the exception.

In other words, Paul supports the idea that women cannot teach men by invoking the created order, and yet egalitarians who would use this argument do not say that women may in some exceptional circumstances teach men (in analogy with the argument from 1 Tim. 4:1–5). Instead, they insist that prohibiting women from teaching men is the exception. The analogy from 1 Timothy 4:1–5, therefore, is turned around. And if women can usually teach men, we are left wondering why an argument from creation is given at all. In principle, one could similarly argue that the prohibitions against polygamy and homosexuality are exceptional, even though an argument from creation is used to support the commands (Matt. 19:4–6 par.; Rom. 1:26–27). The fundamental problem with this suggestion, then, is that it provides no explanation as to why an argument from creation is given.[193] It appeals to alleged exceptions and renders no account as to why Paul appeals to a creational norm. This seems to be a clear case of evading the positive reason given for the prohibition.

Perhaps we can preserve the principle of the command in verse 12 without denying women the right to teach men. After all, it was argued that the principle underlying verses 9–10 permits women to wear jewelry and clothing that is not seductive or ostentatious. However, the principle in verse 12 cannot be separated from the practice of teaching or exercising authority over men.[194] There are some instances in which the principle and practice (e.g., polygamy and homosexuality) coalesce. This is one of those cases. Public teaching of men by women and the concomitant authority it gives them violate the principle of male leadership.

The Argument from the Woman Being Deceived

If verse 13 is a strong argument for the complementarian view, egalitarians claim that verse 14 is quite problematic for the complementarian position.[195] For instance, Towner notes that the former position would seem to lead to the conclusion that women are more easily deceived than men.[196] Bruce Barron says that the complementarian position cannot explain how Adam was not deceived, for he was as guilty as Eve.[197] And if Adam sinned rebelliously with his eyes wide open, and Eve sinned because she was deceived, then why would this qualify men to teach women? It would seem the more serious sin would be the blatant rebellion practiced by Adam, and thus men would be disqualified from teaching. Egalitarians believe they have a much more credible solution to the meaning of this verse. They argue that the reference to Eve's deception points either to women being responsible for the heresy or to the influence of false teachers on women and/or their lack of education.[198]

It is suggested, for instance, that Adam knew of God's prohibition in the garden firsthand, while Eve only knew the command secondhand. Thus, Eve sinned because she was ignorant of God's command, and so too the women in Ephesus were being deceived by the false teachers and, in turn, were propagating the heresy. They could not teach until they were adequately educated.

Doubtless the verse is difficult, but I would like to suggest that defenders of the egalitarian view have a weaker interpretation of the text than defenders of the complementarian interpretation.[199] It cannot be stressed enough that verse 14 scarcely justifies the thesis that women were *teaching* the heresy, although it is certainly possible that the prohibition is given because some women were teaching men.[200] Neither Genesis nor Paul suggests that Eve taught Adam. Instead, both texts affirm that she was deceived (cf. Gen. 3:13).[201] The emphasis is on what transpired in Eve's heart—deception—not on the fact that she wrongly taught Adam.[202] Verse 14, therefore, does not provide any clue that women were forbidden from teaching because they were spreading the heresy. Verse 14 can only be used by egalitarians to say that the women of Ephesus—like Eve—were *influenced* by false teaching and thus fell into sin. Egalitarians can only reasonably argue, therefore, that the women in Ephesus were prohibited from teaching because they were temporarily deceived by the false teachers, and they could later function as teachers by acquiring sound doctrine. But again it must be emphasized that verse 14 does not provide any evidence that women were promulgating false teaching.

Neither does the appeal to the Genesis narrative in verse 14 support the idea that women were disallowed from teaching merely because they were duped by false teaching or uneducated.[203] If Eve was at a disadvantage in the temptation, as some egalitarians declare, because she received the commandment from God secondhand through Adam, then the implication is that Adam somehow muddled God's command in giving it to Eve. If he gave it to her accurately and clearly, then we are back to the view that Eve (before the fall!) could not grasp what Adam clearly said, which would imply that she was intellectually inferior.[204] But if Adam bungled what God said, so that Eve was deceived by the serpent, the argument of 1 Timothy 2:11–15 makes little sense in its historical context. For then Eve was deceived because Adam muddled God's instructions. And if Eve sinned because a man communicated God's command inaccurately, then why would Paul recommend here that men should teach women until the latter get their doctrine right? If a man teaching a woman is what got the human race into this predicament in the first place, Paul's appeal to Eve's being deceived would be incoherent and would not fit the argument he is attempting to make in 1 Timothy 2.

What I am suggesting is that egalitarians, who often complain that the proponents of the complementarian view cannot handle verse 14, are actually in an even more indefensible position. The verse cannot be used to say that women were teaching the heresy. Nor does it make sense to say that women were deceived because they lacked knowledge. Such a view would pin the blame on Adam as a teacher, not Eve. If such were Paul's understanding of the events associated with the fall, his admonition that men should teach women (even temporarily) on the basis of the Genesis narrative would be incoherent.

Moreover, the author of Genesis is not suggesting that Eve was at a disadvantage because she was ignorant of or poorly instructed in God's command (Gen. 3:2–3). What Genesis 3 indicates (and Paul is a careful interpreter of the account here in 1 Tim. 2:14) is that the serpent deceived Eve, not Adam. We should not read into the narrative that Eve was at any disadvantage in terms of knowledge during the temptation. Deceit may occur because of lack of knowledge or education, but Genesis does not attribute Eve's deception to her being uneducated. Indeed, the idea that sin originated because of ignorance is a Platonic view, not a biblical one. The serpent deceived Eve by promising her that she could function as a god, independent of the one true God (Gen. 3:4–6). Eve was deceived not because she had an intellectual deficiency, but because of a moral failing.

In conclusion, egalitarians cannot provide an interpretation of verse 14 that makes sense of the contexts of both Genesis 2–3 and 1 Timothy 2:9–15. What we need to probe is the significance of this verse in the context of 1 Timothy 2. Some scholars, depending on parallels in Jewish tradition, suggest that Eve was sexually seduced by the serpent.[205] But this is unwarranted. The appeals to Jewish parallels are unpersuasive since the latter postdate the New Testament.[206] And the word ἐξαπατάω (I deceive) elsewhere in Paul does not refer to sexual seduction (cf. Rom. 7:11; 16:18; 1 Cor. 3:18; 2 Cor. 11:3; 2 Thess. 2:3). The parallel from 2 Corinthians 11:3 is particularly illuminating, for Paul fears that the entire church will fall prey to the same deception Eve did. His concern is scarcely that the whole church will fall into sexual sin.

Others argue that the point is that Adam sinned with full knowledge and rebelliously, for the text says that "Adam was not deceived," whereas Eve was deceived and committed transgression.[207] The verse thereby signals that Adam was responsible as the leader and the religious teacher. This interpretation is surely a possibility, and it has the virtue of taking the words "Adam was not deceived" straightforwardly. Nevertheless, it is hard to see how this argument would function as a reason for men teaching women. An appeal to Adam sinning willfully and Eve sinning mistakenly (because deceived) would seem to argue against men teaching women, for at least the woman wanted to obey God, while Adam sinned deliberately.[208] This view would be strengthened if the corollary were also drawn: Paul implies that women are more prone to deceit than men. Yet most of the modern adherents of this view are reluctant to draw this latter conclusion.[209]

Historically, a common interpretation is that Paul is forbidding women from teaching because they are more liable to deception and more easily led astray than men.[210] This interpretation is usually dismissed out of hand today because it is so shocking to modern sensibilities. Our task, though, is to interpret texts according to the intention of the author, and thus we must be careful that an interpretation is not rejected merely because it offends our sense of justice. For those who hold a high view of biblical authority, the text must reign over and correct what we think is "just." This interpretation, then, is possible and less speculative than those advanced by egalitarians. Still, this interpretation should be rejected since it implies that women are ontologically and intellectually inferior. Other serious objections have also been raised against this view.[211] Women teaching other women and children is saluted elsewhere in the Pastorals (2 Tim. 1:5; 3:15; Titus 2:3–4). It is unlikely that Paul would commend this if women are prone to deceit by nature, for then their error would be passed on to children and other women. Moreover, if women are inherently prone to deceit, it calls into question the goodness of God's creation.

Paul Barnett intriguingly suggests that the point of the text is that Adam was not deceived first, but Eve was deceived first.[212] The word "first" (πρῶτος) would be implicitly understood from verse 13. Timothy Harris objects that the text does not say that Eve was deceived first, and this weakens Barnett's suggestion.[213] But Barnett's suggestion is a possibility when we recall that Paul was writing to Timothy, who was quite familiar with his theology. Paul would be reminding Timothy that Eve transgressed first, and yet Adam was held responsible for the sin that was imputed to the whole human race (Rom. 5:12–19). The reference to Eve sinning first along with the recognition that Adam bore primary responsibility for sin entering the world (note in Gen. 3 that God approached Adam first after the sin) reveals the reality of male headship. In this scenario, then, verse 14 would function as a second argument for male leadership in teaching.[214]

We can supplement what Barnett says with the following.[215] What Paul emphasizes is that it was Eve (not Adam) who was deceived *by the serpent*. Thus, we need not conclude that Adam was undeceived in every respect. The latter would contradict Romans 5:12–19, and the former is hard to understand in any case, for it seems that all sin involves deceit. Do people sin with their eyes wide open, understanding the nature and consequences of their sin? Paul's purpose is more restricted here. He wants to focus on the fact that the serpent approached and deceived Eve, not Adam. The significance of the serpent targeting Eve is magnified, for apparently Adam was with Eve (Gen. 3:6) during the temptation.[216] In approaching Eve, then, the serpent subverted the pattern of male leadership and interacted only with Eve during the temptation.[217] Adam was present throughout and did not intervene. The Genesis temptation, therefore, is indicative of what happens when male leadership is abrogated.[218] Eve took the initiative in responding to the serpent, and Adam let her do so.[219] Thus, the appeal to Genesis 3 serves as a reminder of what happens when God's ordained pattern is undermined.[220]

Women Being Saved through Childbirth

Verse 15 reads, "But she shall be saved through childbirth, if they remain in faith and love and sanctification along with discretion" (my translation). Susan Foh's opinion that the verse is "a puzzle and a sort of non sequitur" is unsatisfying, for the verse functions as the conclusion to the paragraph and must be integrated with the rest of the argument.[221] On the other hand, some scholars think that this verse is climactic, the key to the whole text.[222] This latter opinion goes to the other extreme.[223] It is better to take the verse as providing a qualification to what is said in verse 14 and as rounding out the argument.[224]

Many questions emerge from this verse.[225] What is the subject of the verbs σωθήσεται (she shall be saved) and μείνωσιν (they remain)? Does the verb σωθήσεται refer to spiritual salvation, spiritual preservation, or physical preservation through childbirth? What does the noun τεκνογονία (childbirth) refer to: the birth of Christ, bearing children, or rearing children? What is the precise meaning in this context of the preposition διά? Does this text teach salvation by works? How does it fit with the rest of the paragraph?

We will begin by examining the meaning of the verb σωθήσεται. Some understand it to mean "preserve," so that the verse says that women shall be preserved safely through childbirth.[226] Craig Keener defends this interpretation by appealing to parallels in Greco-Roman literature, where women often prayed for safety in childbirth; the verb σώζω (save) most commonly bears the idea of physical preservation.[227] This interpretation should be rejected for at least two reasons. The fact that Christian women have often died in childbirth raises serious questions about this interpretation.[228] More important, σώζω always has the meaning of spiritual salvation in the Pastoral Epistles (cf. 1 Tim. 1:15; 2:4; 4:16; 2 Tim. 1:9; 4:18; Titus 3:5) and the other Pauline writings.[229] Keener commits the error of making the meaning of the term in other writings more important than in the Pauline writings. In addition, since σώζω always refers to eschatological salvation in Paul, it is also not compelling to say that women "are saved" from the error of usurping authority over men by keeping to their proper function.[230] Once again a definition is supplied for σώζω that does not accord with the Pauline usage. In addition, verse 12 is too far from verse 15 for this latter interpretation to be plausible.[231] The difficulty of this verse, therefore, cannot be swept aside by finding a different meaning for σώζω; the verse does say that a woman will be spiritually saved through bearing children.[232]

Perhaps the biting edge of this verse can be explained by investigating the meaning of the word τεκνογονίας. A common view in the history of the church is to detect a reference to the birth of Christ.[233] The near context is invoked by supporters of this reading, for the reference to the deceit and transgression of Eve (v. 14) is qualified by the promise that she will be saved by the childbirth, that is, the birth of Christ. Since Paul had just cited Genesis 3 in verse 14, it is argued that he would have naturally turned to the promise of salvation through the seed promised in Genesis 3:15. The singular "she" could be ascribed to Eve as the representative of all women or to Mary, who gave birth to the Messiah. The definite article τῆς (the) preceding τεκνογονίας is also cited to defend the idea that Paul was thinking of the birth of Christ.[234]

The unpalatable flavor of this verse would certainly be removed if it says that salvation comes through the birth of Christ. This view, unfortunately, is quite improbable. Anthony Hanson says that it "is more romantic than convincing."[235] Donald Guthrie trenchantly observes that Paul "could hardly have chosen a more obscure or ambiguous way of saying it."[236] One must also slide from seeing Eve as the subject of σωθή-σεται to Mary, but to read the latter into the verse is highly arbitrary.[237] Moreover, even if we accept Mary as the subject, the meaning is still problematic. Mary was not saved by virtue of giving birth to Jesus, nor does Paul elsewhere say that salvation is through the incarnation. The noun τεκνογονία emphasizes the actual giving birth to a child, not the result or effect of childbirth.[238] Those who posit a reference to Jesus' birth have subtly introduced the notion that salvation is secured as a *result* of giving birth to him, whereas the text speaks not of the result of birth but of the actual birthing process. A defense of the christological interpretation cannot be sustained by the presence of the article. The article is notoriously perplexing in Greek since it has a wide range of uses and is thereby difficult to categorize definitively. Thus, we should be wary of concluding that the presence of the article indicates particular reference to Christ's birth.[239] The article is probably generic in any case.[240] A reference to the birth of Christ, although immensely attractive, must be rejected. Neither is it persuasive to see in the word τεκνογονία the idea of rearing children.[241] The word τεκνοτροφέω (I bring up children) was available and used in 1 Timothy 5:10 to communicate this idea, while the verbal form τεκνογονέω (I bear children) by contrast is used in 1 Timothy 5:14 for the bearing of children.[242]

The significance of διά is also a matter of debate. E. F. Scott tried to soften the scandal of the verse by saying that a woman shall be saved "in spite of" or "even though" having children.[243] Any notion of women being saved "through" having children is excluded. Unfortunately, the semantic range of διά is violated by this interpretation, and thus Scott's proposal has been consistently rejected.[244] Neither is it persuasive to see διά referring to attendant circumstances, so that women will be saved "in the experience" of childbirth.[245] This interpretation is dictated by theology rather than syntax.[246] Probably the common instrumental sense of διά is intended here (cf. Titus 3:5).[247] Shortly, I shall take up how this fits with Paul's theology of salvation.

Who is the subject of the verbs σωθήσεται and μείνωσιν, and why does the tense switch from the singular to the plural? It has already been argued above that we can eliminate the options that Eve or Mary is the subject of σωθήσεται. The context clarifies that nonbelievers are not included, for they will not be spiritually saved. Thus, the reference is to the Christian women of Ephesus and by extension to all Christian women everywhere.[248] The switch from the third singular to the third plural is awkward.[249] It has been suggested that the third plural refers to the children of the women or to husbands and wives.[250] It is too jarring, though, to detect a sudden reference to children or husbands here. The third singular at the beginning of the sentence refers to women generically, and thus Paul shifts to "women" plural in the latter half of the verse.[251] This fits with the structure of the passage as a whole, where Paul begins by speaking of women in the plural (vv. 9–10), shifts to the singular (vv. 11–15a), and then reverts to the plural.[252] The singular in verse 15a may also be accounted for from the reference to Eve in verses 13–14, for the latter is understood as representative of all Christian women.

The discussion so far has simply established that the verse says what it appears to say on first glance, and thus the theological and contextual questions posed earlier remain.[253] If women are saved by bearing children, then is this not salvation by works and a contradiction of Pauline theology?[254] Understanding the historical situation will aid us in answering this question. The false teachers, in trumpeting an over-realized eschatology, prohibited marriage and certain foods (1 Tim. 4:1–5). If marriage was banned, then bearing children was probably also criticized.[255] Childbearing was selected by Paul, then, as a specific response to the shafts from the false teachers. Referring to childbearing is also appropriate because it represents the fulfillment of the woman's domestic role as a mother in distinction from the man.[256] Childbearing, then, is probably selected by synecdoche as representing the appropriate role for women. This rounds out the passage because a woman should not violate her role by teaching or exercising authority over a man; instead, she should take her proper role as a mother of children. It could be argued that the reference to women bearing children is culturally limited to the domestic and maternal roles of Paul's day.[257] More likely, Paul saw in the woman's function of giving birth a divinely intended and ongoing difference of function between men and women.

This does not mean that all women must have children in order to be saved.[258] Paul is hardly attempting to be comprehensive here. He has elsewhere commended the single state (1 Cor. 7). He selects childbearing because it is the most notable example of the divinely intended difference in role between men and women, and many women throughout history have had children. Thus, Paul generalizes from the experience of women in using a representative example of women maintaining their proper role. To select childbearing is another indication that the argument is transcultural, for childbearing is not limited to a particular culture but is a permanent and ongoing difference between men and women. The fact that God has ordained that women and only women bear children indicates that the differences in roles between men and women are rooted in the created order.

When Paul says that a woman will be saved by childbearing, he means, therefore, that they will be saved by adhering to their ordained role.[259] Such a statement is apt to be misunderstood (and often has been), and thus a further comment is added for explanation. Women will be saved "if they remain in faith and love and sanctification along with discretion." Thereby Paul shows that it is not sufficient for salvation for Christian women merely to bear children; they must also persevere in faith, love, holiness, and presumably other virtues.[260] The reference to "discretion" (σωφροσύνης) harkens back to the same word in verse 9 and also functions to tie the entire text together.[261] Paul does not imply that all women must bear children to be saved. His purpose is to say that women will not be saved if they do not practice good works. One indication that women are in their proper role is if they do not reject bearing children as evil but bear children in accord with their proper role.

Many will object that this is salvation by works and contradicts Pauline theology. A contradiction with Pauline theology would only exist if the text were claiming that one must do these good works in order to *earn or merit* salvation, or that works are the grounds of one's salvation. Elsewhere Paul insists that good works are a necessary consequence of salvation (e.g., Rom. 2:6–10, 26–29; 1 Cor. 6:9–11; Gal. 5:21).[262] Paul is not asserting in 1 Timothy 2:15 that women *merit* salvation by bearing children and doing other good works. He has already clarified that salvation is by God's mercy and grace (cf. 1 Tim. 1:12–17). The term σωθήσεται is used rather loosely here, so that Paul does not specify in what sense women are saved by childbearing and doing other good works. Since Paul often argues elsewhere that salvation is not gained on the basis of our works (e.g., Rom. 3:19–4:25; Gal. 2:16–3:14; 2 Tim. 1:9–11; Titus 2:11–14; 3:4–7), I think it is fair to understand the virtues described here as evidence that the salvation already received is genuine.[263] Any good works of the Christian, of course, are not the ultimate basis of salvation, for the ultimate basis of salvation is the righteousness of Christ granted to us.

The same problem arises in 1 Timothy 4:11–16.[264] There Paul exhorts Timothy to live a godly life ("be an example for believers in speech, in conduct, in love, in faith, in purity," v. 12) and to keep instructing believers in the truth of the gospel. Paul sums up these instructions in verse 16. He says to Timothy, "Pay heed to yourself and to your teaching; remain in them." In other words, Timothy is to keep practicing the virtues specified in verse 12 and to continue instructing the church. In verse 16b a reason is supplied as to why Timothy should be virtuous and keep teaching: "For by doing this, you will save both yourself and your hearers." Once again the verb σώζω is used with reference to spiritual salvation. Paul certainly does not mean that Timothy and his hearers will be "physically preserved" if they live godly lives and continue in godly instruction. One could protest that Paul is teaching salvation by meritorious works here, since he says that Timothy and his hearers will be saved *if* they live godly lives and continue in right instruction. But this would be a mistake. What Paul means is that abiding in godly virtues and obeying apostolic instruction are the necessary evidences that one has been saved.[265] Those who fall away have no assurance that they belong to the redeemed community (cf. 1 Cor. 9:24–10:22). Indeed, the necessity of doing good works or persevering to the end in order to realize salvation is often taught in the New Testament (cf., e.g., Heb. 2:1–4; 3:7–19; 5:11–6:12; 10:26–31; 12:25–29; James 2:14–26; 2 Pet. 1:5–11; 1 John 2:3–6).[266]

The parallel text in 1 Timothy 4:11–16 indicates that it is too simplistic to wave aside the reference to salvation by bearing children as salvation by meritorious works. Upon examining the context and historical situation carefully, we see that Paul selected childbearing because of the emphasis of the false teachers who denigrated marriage and the maternal role of women. Other virtues are added in the conditional clause to prevent misunderstanding. Salvation is not evidenced by childbirth alone. But the genuineness of salvation is indicated by a woman living a godly life and conforming to her God-ordained role. These good works are necessary to obtain eschatological salvation.

Conclusion

I can scarcely claim that I have given the definitive and final interpretation of this passage. I would argue, however, that verses 9–15 yield a coherent and comprehensible meaning. Paul has argued that women should adorn themselves appropriately with good works, not with ostentatious or seductive clothing. Moreover, women should not arrogate a teaching role for themselves when men and women are gathered in public meetings. They should learn submissively and quietly and not engage in teaching or the exercise of authority. Women are prohibited from teaching or exercising authority because of the creation order. The creation of Adam before Eve signaled that men are to teach and exercise authority in the church. Moreover, the events in Genesis 3 confirm the necessity of male leadership. Eve, beguiled by the serpent, took leadership in responding to the serpent. Adam, although he was with Eve, did not intervene and properly exercise leadership. Instead, he allowed Eve to respond improperly to the serpent. Even though Eve was the first to sin, the responsibility for sin is assigned primarily to Adam (Rom. 5:12–19). Women, Paul reminds his readers, will experience eschatological salvation by adhering to their proper role, which is exemplified in giving birth to children. Of course, adhering to one's proper role is not sufficient for salvation; women must also practice other Christian virtues in order to be saved.

Our problem with the text is in the main not exegetical but practical. What Paul says here is contrary to the thinking of the modern world. We are confronted here with a countercultural word from the Scriptures. This countercultural word should modify and correct both our thinking and our behavior. In the next chapter, we will explore the basis for applying of Paul's teaching to our modern world. These are not idle topics, for the happiness and strength of the church today will be in direct proportion to our obedience to the biblical text.

5

PROGRESSIVE AND HISTORIC

The Hermeneutics of 1 Timothy 2:9–15

ROBERT W. YARBROUGH

Exegesis and 1 Timothy 2:9–15

How should we interpret the Bible? Some say the answer is easy: just read what it says. While ultimately too naive, those words can be valuable initial counsel. In a sense "reading what it says" has been the focus of this book thus far. The technical name for such "reading," for determining textual meaning in the light of a text's historical setting broadly conceived, is *exegesis*. Preceding chapters have reexamined the *exegetical* ABCs of 1 Timothy 2:9–15. Various writers have sought to shed fresh and, to the extent possible, definitive light on basic questions of word meaning, syntax, background, "signification"[1] (meaning of the passage in its original setting), and other matters.

"What the Bible says" (to keep the matter simple for a moment), the signification of 1 Timothy 2:9–15, is tolerably clear, as the preceding chapter shows. In Paul's understanding men and women, while equal in value and importance before the Lord, were not regarded as unisex components with swappable functions in home and church.[2] In the overall scope of biblical teaching this was not, apparently, felt to be a penalty or restriction.[3] Women's gifts, callings, and ministries are delineated and even exalted in numerous passages both in Paul's letters and across the whole of Scripture. Women are hallowed in the innumerable situations arising in home, church, and public life that call for those expressions of Christian graces that lie uniquely within the purview of regenerate[4] female nature and competencies. But a corollary to this is that at certain points women's gifts, callings, and ministries were differentiated from the gifts, callings, and ministries of men.[5] The historic position of the church on the sanctity of motherhood (for married females only), fatherhood (for married males only), and certain church offices (only males were chosen as apostles and elders) recognizes this.

William J. Webb has argued that this position is not "historic" and that a hermeneutic that arrives at this conclusion is "static," a term to which he attaches strongly negative associations.[6] He therefore subjects the earlier version of this chapter in *Women in the Church* to harsh criticism. By way of reply, I offer three comments.

First, it seems that Webb mistakes the intent and outcome of my chapter (then and now). He speaks of "the static hermeneutic developed by Yarbrough,"[7] as if my essay were a miniversion of his book, which *does* develop a hermeneutic and takes nearly three hundred pages to do so. On the contrary, I am aware I cannot "develop" anything in one short chapter; I simply describe features of an approach that has been around a very long time and point out liabilities to newer and (to me) suspect readings and their underlying rationales. I made this intent and limitation explicit in the chapter Webb critiques.[8] Webb apparently bases his criticism in part on how well I achieved an aim that I never set out to fulfill.

Second, I agree with Webb that something like his "redemptive-movement hermeneutic" has been a feature of exegesis in the church on various topics and at various times throughout the centuries. But I continue to maintain that my hermeneutic, which affirms some form and degree of male headship in home and church, is the "historic" one compared to his. Historically, the "redemptive-movement hermeneutic" in the particular form Webb constructs it, with its implications for 1 Timothy 2 and associated texts, did not exist until a generation or two ago. My hermeneutic, which interprets the Bible to teach that women should not be church leaders on strict equivalency with men and that fathers and husbands have a leadership prerogative in marriages and homes, seems to resemble more closely than Webb's the approach taken by biblical writers and their interpreters (as diverse as they are) through the centuries. How can we call Webb's approach "historic" when it demands that we change the general understanding of biblical teaching on men and women that prevailed for nearly twenty centuries? So I am not trying to claim any high moral ground by the label, just appealing to fairly self-evident fact.

Third, a "static" hermeneutic may not be all bad in a belief system that prizes being steadfast and immovable (1 Cor. 15:58), warns about doctrinal innovation (2 John 9), appeals to the teaching of the apostles (2 Thess. 3:14; Jude 17), urges believers to be "constantly nourished on the words of the faith and of the sound doctrine which you have been following" (1 Tim. 4:6), and calls Christians children of Abraham (Gal. 3). Christians are rightly wary of new teaching that calls for fundamental revision of what Scripture affirms. To the charge that this is "static," it should be pointed out that an opposite approach ("manic"?) would be no better. This is my concern about Webb's proposal, which for all its sophistication is, as he admits, "hardly completely new" in conception.[9] Church history offers examples of "static" recalcitrance (those holdouts today who attack all Bible translations but the King James might be an example), but it is also replete in recent centuries with "redemptive-movement" practitioners who have led the church away from historic Christian belief in most if not all cardinal Christian doctrines and demanded change in Christian teaching and practice. Examples here abound in the form of scholars who on the basis of contemporary conviction have taken offense at biblical miracles, or blood atonement, or divine sovereignty, or biblical authority, or Jesus' divinity, or some combination of the preceding.

Therefore, if I may define "static" as "holding the line on what Western society is intent on destroying," foremost among which I see to be God's authority and the Bible's view of personhood, I will accept the term and bear the consequences of Webb's disagreement. Because on the whole, especially in view of world Christendom (see last pages of this chapter), I think the inferences drawn from passages like 1 Timothy 2 for Christian doctrine and practice were a greater force for good than ill in past centuries[10] and will prove to be vastly redemptive, civilizing, and transformative as the gospel goes forth in coming generations—if they are not compromised (as I would see it) by the interpretive strategy emerging from Webb's proposals.

To return to our main argument: 1 Timothy 2, it has been maintained above, lends support to what is justly termed the historic position, in spite of proposals to the contrary that have proliferated in the last half-century.

Earle Ellis has pointed out that this understanding of 1 Timothy 2 is no anomaly in early Christian teaching. In fact, it is quite in keeping with parallel passages in earlier Pauline and Petrine texts:[11]

> *The women* should keep *silent* in the churches. For they are not *permitted* to speak, but they are to *subject themselves*, as the law says. If they wish to *learn*, let them ask *their own husbands* at home. For it is disgraceful for *a woman* to speak in church. (1 Cor. 14:34–35)

> Likewise also [I want] *women* [everywhere] to *adorn* themselves in *respectable* deportment with modesty and decency, not in *braids* and *gold* or pearls or *high-cost clothing, but rather* [in] that which befits women professing godliness, with good works. Let *a woman learn* in *silence* in *full submission*. Teaching is something I do not *permit a woman* [to do], nor to exercise authority over *a man*; she is to be *quiet* [not teach]. For Adam was formed first. (1 Tim. 2:9–13)

> Likewise you *wives* . . . let not your *adornment* be the outward *braiding of hair*, wearing *gold jewelry*, or *putting on dresses, but rather* . . . *quietness* of spirit, which is *costly* in the sight of God. For thus also the holy *women* who trusted in God formerly *adorned* themselves, *subjecting themselves to their own husbands*, as Sarah obeyed Abraham. (1 Pet. 3:3–6)

Because this kind of biblical teaching is *not* restricted to 1 Timothy 2,[12] interpreters with a high view of Scripture—a view that seeks to let "signification" determine "significance" as much as possible—will be slow to reject it as merely the product of culpably patriarchal writers[13] or relativize it as culturally outmoded.[14]

The findings of the previous chapters, however, will not bring an end to the debate over the responsibilities and offices most appropriate to women in the body of Christ generally or even over the significance of 1 Timothy 2:9–15 in particular. This is because the discussion is not guided by *exegesis* alone (nor can it be); it is influenced by *hermeneutics* as well.

The Need for Hermeneutical Wisdom

Exegesis (determining the "signification") of a text must be informed by sound *hermeneutics* to determine "significance," or the present implications, with any degree of validity.[15] *Hermeneutics* refers to the principles (and other factors, whether acknowledged by the interpreter or not) that tend to govern interpretation. "Hermeneutics" is a broader term than "exegesis," and the relationship of the two calls for clarification. It is easy to see why.

The matter of moving from the original message of the text in its historic setting to today, from "signification" to "significance," is complicated. Exegesis, determining "what the Bible says," is always informed by the hermeneutics of the exegete. This is a constellation of theological convictions, assumptions, principles, and frequently social forces that affect how exegetes go about their work. And this hermeneutical orientation is, in turn, likely informed by previous exegesis, which has been influenced by an earlier level of hermeneutical understanding, and so on. The spiral extends back endlessly into the imponderables of each individual interpreter, the interpretive community he or she inhabits, and the full range of experiences and native tendencies that lie behind the exegesis he or she performs.

But while the spiral is endless with respect to the circumstances of each interpreter, it is not endless with respect to the object to be interpreted, in this case the text of 1 Timothy 2. These words stand before all interpreters in their literary, historical, cultural, and theological givenness. The canon of Scripture "has been assembled and handed down to us; it contains words that stand over against us and judge us; and we have to come to grips with it."[16] Both better and worse interpretations of Scripture's words are conceivable. They can be appropriated faithfully or wrested wrongfully. Some interpretations do more justice to the whole range of relevant factors that bear on what a biblical author wrote and its best present application, and others do less.[17]

With respect to any given question aimed at any given text—for example, does a passage like 1 Timothy 2:9–15 accord to women in Christ precisely the same position in the family and offices in the church as men?—there is in theory one truly best answer. That answer will be the one that best accords with the author's meaning in the text under scrutiny, given certain hermeneutical considerations that permit exegesis, "reading what the Bible says," to liberate the biblical message for contemporary application rather than confine it due to the interpreter's restrictive assumptions, principles, or procedures. By "liberate" I mean permit the message to convey to the reader the signification that inheres in the original document and that the author intended to pass on to readers whether in the near or the distant future.

This is not the place for a hermeneutical guidebook; this need is amply provided for in other studies.[18] Even if we could canvass such works, we might be disappointed with the results, for as Howard Marshall comments, "discussions on biblical hermeneutics have given us a fair amount of guidance on how to elucidate what the text said" but "have not done a lot to help us take the passage from what the text said to what the text says."[19] Nor will an attempt be made to arrive at a full-orbed application of 1 Timothy 2:9–15.

We will rather survey a selection of hermeneutical issues bearing on the move from our text's signification in Paul's day to its significance for the present day. Perusal of current literature indicates that for many readers the major impediment to applying what 1 Timothy 2 says, as interpreted in earlier chapters of this volume, lies in arguments based on (1) Western culture's liberalized views of women; (2) the putative meaning of Galatians 3:28; and (3) an alleged tie between women's subordination and slavery. In the following discussion, I point to the liabilities of the views in each of these three areas that hinder the scriptural testimony from being accepted as the authors of this volume think it should be.

More broadly, the survey below will serve to make understandable major features of the hermeneutical rationale informing previous and following chapters. It will provide a hermeneutical framework[20] for cautious but firm affirmation[21] of the reading of 1 Timothy 2:9–15 that has the weight of historic Christian interpretation, as well as the most plausible understanding of related biblical passages, to commend it. And it will constitute a challenge to those who take exception with those chapters to examine their own hermeneutical outlook lest it prevent them from coming to grips with the divine word addressed to us all.

Copernican Revolution and Aftermath

No single hermeneutical question is of greater consequence than this one: Was it, is it, and will it continue to be well advised for Christians to follow the recent lead of Western society in liberalizing attitudes toward women's and men's identities and roles?[22]

By "liberalizing" I have in mind not theological liberalism (though that is an important concern too) but rather the individualistic "liberal faith," the "particular social doctrine," that stresses individual rights rather than social or institutionally mandated responsibilities in both civil and moral matters.[23] I have in mind the view of persons that dominated the West at the twentieth century's end and that persists today, a view that stresses self-realization and personal fulfillment rather than fellowship and self-sacrifice for others by involvement in an inherited or adopted family and perhaps also religious tradition. Liberalism in this sense is the grand "cause of the liberty of the human spirit, the cause of opportunity of human beings for full development of their powers."[24] While it is tempered today by impulses calling for selective subordination of personal good or freedom to collective ideals (national health care, gun control, submission to mandatory drug testing in workplace and school, mandatory seat-belt laws), a dominant trend in the United

States, at least, is still toward an "expressive individualism"[25] that tends to "obliterate all prior culture"[26] in its own narrow liberal self-interest.

The harrowing fascist and communist experiments of the twentieth century did not provide promising models or motivation for an alternate socialist[27] vision that would check America's seemingly endless self-obsession. Instead, successive philosophical movements stretching back as far as John Stuart Mill (1806–73) have fueled feverish demands for "the rights and liberty of individuals" along lines "supportive of today's feminist principles."[28] These movements (and representative seminal thinkers) were utilitarian (Mill), existential (Simone de Beauvoir [1908–86]), Marxist (Friedrich Engels [1820–95], Lenin [Vladimir Ilyich Ulyanov, 1870–1924], Herbert Marcuse [1898–1979]), and analytic (Bertrand Russell [1872–1970]).

In its views of women's roles, the church in the West has followed the world's lead. On this point there can hardly be debate. "Feminism originated as the handmaid of individualism and, from the start, has been tied to and informed by the ideals of individual liberty and the equality of individual rights."[29] In the 1830s, Mary Stewart advanced issues of gender equality and social justice in the United States, and the Grimké sisters, Angelina and Sarah, wrote "Appeal to the Christian Women in the South" (1836) and "Letters on the Equality of the Sexes and the Condition of Women" (1837) respectively. In 1849, Antoinette Brown published an article in the *Oberlin Quarterly* in which she argued that 1 Corinthians 14:34–35 and 1 Timothy 2:12 merely proscribe inappropriate teaching by women. In 1895 and 1898, Elizabeth Cady Stanton edited the *Women's Bible*, in which she contended that women's emancipation was impossible if Scripture's position was accepted.[30]

After a weakening of the women's movement in the decades subsequent to women in America gaining the right to vote in 1919, "the women's movement of the 1960s and 1970s and the increasing number of women attending seminaries renewed interest in what it might mean to read the Bible self-consciously as a woman."[31] Today it is a commonplace that biblical authority for much feminist biblical interpretation is secondary to feminist experience,[32] although some feminists are owning up to and addressing the downside of this tendency.[33] "In sharp contrast to the uniquely normative character of scripture, white feminist theologians view scripture as only secondarily normative, subjecting scripture, with other sources, to another norm: the liberation of women from oppressive, patriarchal structures, of which scripture and its interpretation is one."[34]

While evangelical feminist interpreters seek to maintain full biblical authority, it has been the larger sanction of liberalizing feminist social forces that has given both impetus and credence to new interpretations (or dismissals) of key texts like 1 Timothy 2 in evangelical circles.[35] Krister Stendahl speaks for a great many in arguing that the two questions of societal liberation for women and full ecclesiastical powers for women (their ordination on exact parity with men) ultimately cannot be separated; a positive answer to the former inexorably requires a "progressive" view regarding the latter.[36] "The only alternative . . . is to recognize the legal, economic, political, and professional emancipation of women . . . as a great achievement. . . . If emancipation is right, then there is no valid 'biblical' reason not to ordain women."[37]

So significant are the changes taking place that one scholar observes: "Women's entrance into ordained ministry represents the single most significant transformation of the clergy profession since the Reformation."[38]

Relatively ignored in the wrangling over Christian women's demands to be as free from traditional constraints in church and marriage as their non-Christian sisters has been the plight of women and children in the years since the Copernican social revolution of the 1960s. This deserves more scrutiny than it tends to receive.

The very institution of marriage is coming under increasing attack.[39] Gay marriage is in the process of normalization in many quarters, with implications for children, homes, localities, and perhaps whole nations. These implications are unlikely to be favorable in the sight of the God of Scripture. The destruction of Sodom and Gomorrah may seem remote to us today, but it was much on the minds of biblical writers. Not only did Moses narrate the account (Gen. 18–19); he also cited it twice in his Deuteronomic preaching. Sodom receives significant reference in the major prophets (Isaiah, Jeremiah/Lamentations, Ezekiel) as well as the minor ones (Amos, Zephaniah). It figures in the teaching of Jesus, according to Matthew and Luke. Other New Testament writers mentioning Sodom or its sin are Paul, Peter, Jude, and John. If certain sexual practices and gender outlooks at variance with God's revealed will are known to have brought divine judgment on society as a whole, how much more cautious should the church be about embracing similar or even identical views? For today's assault on marriage is of a piece with demands for revolution in how the church views gender.

True, we have not seen the fall of literal fire and brimstone. Yet it can be said that disaster has overtaken women and children[40] (to cite social subgroups whom the God of Scripture is particularly concerned to protect) as divorce rates more than doubled from 1970 to 1980, eventually leveling off at a distressingly high rate.[41] "The War against Women: Violence, Poverty and Abuse" trumpeted a *U.S. News & World Report* cover story. Its theme: "Women are falling further behind in country after country—and their men like it that way."[42] *U.S. News* focused on the international scene, but the domestic picture is disconcerting enough. As M. N. Ozawa notes:

> Something extraordinary is happening to American women. Although their individual economic capability has never been as great as it is today, their economic well-being in relation to that of men has been slipping. . . . Women's economic lot is deteriorating in comparison to that of men.[43]

Women have gained great freedom—but not without tragic cost.

And there are other significant dimensions to the problem. For example, sexual promiscuity (attested, for example, by illegitimacy rates that have skyrocketed by historic standards) has increased due to the nature of "the changes of sexual behavior of the last thirty to thirty-five years."[44] Women are arguably more the victims of male tyranny or indifference (as well as of their own misguided complicity) than ever before.

> The determining factor [of women's increasing social plight] is social, not economic: *the weakening tie between men and women* as a result of the increasing incidence of childbearing out of wedlock (whether by teenagers or by adults), divorce, and the growing likelihood that women will become widows.[45]

The plight of children, however, is perhaps even more depressing to contemplate.[46] The ills besetting women "have profound ramifications" for "the future of American children—the future of American human capital."[47] The issue is both social and economic. "For the first time in American history, the educational skills of the current generation of children will not surpass, will not equal, and will not even approach those of their parents."[48] "Never before has one generation of American children been less healthy, less cared for, or less prepared for life than their parents were at the same age," according to the National Commission on the Role of School and the Community in Improving Adolescent Health Care.[49] There is annual fluctuation in the situation, but the status quo and discernible trends give little cause to think that we are turning back the distressing preponderance of bad news when it comes to the overall welfare of our children.[50]

On a closely related front, adolescents who are not yet legally adults wield lethal weapons and murder not only adults but one another by the hundreds on America's streets. Youth deaths by homicide have doubled since 1985, with a child dying from gunshot wounds at the rate of one every two hours.[51] The whole world was shocked in the 1990s by details of a trial in Britain of two boys who lured a mere toddler away from his mother, then tortured him much as boys in other times might have tormented a toad. It is unlikely that we should take much solace in an apparent slight reduction in U.S. male youth homicides in the 1990s overall, said to be due to the legalization of abortion[52]—in other words, thanks to the deaths of some four thousand babies a day in the United States following *Roe versus Wade*, we have come to a time when there are fewer young people left for belligerent peers to target. This, too, is part of the legacy of recent social change, much of it not for the better.

The short- and long-term emotional and psychological effects of divorce on the high percentage of American children affected by it are far more damaging than once thought.[53] "Research evidence has clearly demonstrated that, on average, children from divorced families are not as well adjusted as those in intact families."[54] Judith S. Wallerstein's research has documented "the sleeper effect."[55] This means that children may not show the trauma of divorce for a decade or more after it occurs. Even if Wallerstein's groundbreaking work proves flawed at points,[56] the fact remains that "each divorce is the death of a small civilization."[57] And the problem is worsening, it seems, with the passage of time.[58] "The growing percentage of children who experience parental divorce will increase the likelihood that the 'epidemic' of single-parent households will last well into the next century."[59] Yet there "remains extraordinary reluctance to acknowledge its seriousness and its enormous impact on all our lives."[60]

Society has changed markedly in recent decades. A revolution has occurred. The symptoms are numerous and defy easy quantification and definition. "Compassion fatigue" (cf. "battle fatigue") among teachers and school psychologists has resulted from "child abuse . . . occurring at alarming rates," with 40 percent of school psychologists exhibiting burnout symptoms and 35 percent, in one study, considering leaving their profession.[61] Communities across the United States are continually scandalized today by accounts of local men—often public figures such as teachers, coaches,[62] and journalists—being caught in Internet stings where they have solicited sex with minors[63] or victimized the subjects of their research.[64] And it is not only men whose morals have crumbled: outwardly respectable wives and mothers have been arrested for analogous criminal activity. Anyone with an Internet connection can see that teachers, many women among them, are being arrested for sexual contacts with students to an extent unthinkable not many years ago.[65]

While there is no easy turning back in all this, adjustments must be made. And for Christians the question remains: Is it responsible for the church to assume the intrinsic desirability for the church of ideals—such as the liberalization of views of women's (and corresponding shifts in men's) roles as defined above, with all the accompanying consequences—that appear to be linked with bringing such woe to the world?

It is not being argued here that all these woes are the direct result of the liberalization of women's and men's roles. Nor is it being argued that all social change affecting women since the 1960s has been bad. I am neither overlooking nor demonizing what Giles calls "the radically changed status and the greatly changed opportunities for women in modern society."[66] But it would be unconscionable special pleading to deny that the "emancipation" of women and men from the moral and familial expectations common until the 1960s (reflected, for example, in strict divorce laws) has nothing to do with the breakdown of marriages, debasing of morals, and increasing plight of women and children since the 1960s. The connection between these woes and liberalization has been sufficiently demonstrated, and the church is well advised to be wary of the latter if it wishes to avoid being implicated in the former. Too often the church has been uncritical on this score.

From a Christian perspective both sexes have sinned grievously against each other in rampant divorce, the sexual infidelity that often attends it, the killing (abortion) and other victimization of children, and the ripple effects of drastic lifestyle changes. Corporate adult offense, and increasingly offense by children or minors against one another, is incalculable.

Adult women themselves have been adversely affected in areas other than economics: Between 1980 and the end of 1992, the number of women in state and federal prisons increased 275 percent.[67] A recent study concludes:

> The number of adult females under correctional supervision rose 120% from 37,200 in 1990 [to] 81,700 in 2003, with an average annual increase of 6.2% over the 13-year period. The largest percentage increase during the 10-year period occurred in 1994, amounting to 10.0%, followed by an increase of 8.6% in 1996. The lowest percentage increase in adult female jail inmates between 1990 and 2003 occurred in 1992, amounting to 3.0%, an increase of 2,300.[68]

Yet remarkably the implicit assumption has been and continues to be that changes in society require parallel changes in the church. Nowhere has this been truer than in the area of biblical teaching on sex and gender roles.[69] As Spencer Perkins remarks with an eye to the African-American inner-city scene:

> After three decades of civil rights laws, wars on poverty and drugs, and billions of dollars in urban programs we have not fewer but more dead young Black men, more babies born out of wedlock, and an overall decrease in the quality of life in our inner cities. And still we have been unwilling to look at the obvious connection between family breakdown and the growing instability of our cities.[70]

All this points to a hermeneutical watershed. Those who feel justified in endorsing our zeitgeist's convictions that women ought to hold church office and be on radically equal footing with husbands in marriage will continue to hold 1 Timothy 2:9–15 as interpreted elsewhere in this volume at arm's length. But for others, omnipresent heartbreaking social carnage, the scope of which we have only sketched briefly, could encourage a new sympathy with much-vilified "traditional" Christian teaching.

Some will claim that the challenge is to appropriate society's positive new direction without succumbing to its evils.[71] Yet this is to overlook that numerous passages in the Bible may be understood as forbidding the people of God facilely to adopt the liberal (in the political sense sketched earlier) attitudes toward personhood, sexuality, morality, marriage, children, and (if this book's thesis proves correct) church leadership that have arisen in recent decades. As we will see below, these attitudes have spawned much debate and many creative new renderings of passages like 1 Timothy 2 that are taken to legitimate the essential implications of society's new direction. But viewing society's drift in its application for Christian gender roles as essentially "positive" could only have taken place when key biblical texts were set to the side long enough for the drift to be endorsed in the first place. This, in turn, enabled creative renderings of the problem texts so as to reinterpret them, declare them culturally relative, or both. The soundness of this interpretive strategy deserves careful questioning.

It might also be argued that endorsement of the liberalizing agenda that has taken shape since the 1960s was required because of the evils of bourgeois society and attendant victimization of women stemming from the 1950s or before. Here the reply must be that Christians should not have been letting some earlier sordid status quo determine treatment of women either. When they were doing so—and they often did—they should have repented. But repenting of the 1950s should have taken some other form than acquiescence to the social debacle chronicled above. It should have involved a renewed draught of grace and compassion from Christ and submission to Scripture by all parties, not attenuation of the Bible's counsel. Chapters elsewhere in this volume suggest ways in which 1 Timothy 2:9–15 might conduce to the proliferation of biblical ministry by both sexes rather than to the curtailment or abbreviation of it.

To summarize, a fundamental hermeneutical question is whether the prevailing secular mind-set and practices should continue to exercise the strong influence on the exegesis of biblical texts that they have in the recent past. An affirmative answer here is conceivable from those who choose to ignore the mounting social devastation, for others who think that the gains for some women are worth the pain for other women and

millions of children, and for all who believe that continued liberalization will at some point begin to reverse the current vast and burgeoning
misery.[72] Rebecca Groothuis offers rallying words: "We must weather the
storm of change—keeping our wits about us and our spirits submitted
to the truth that sets us free."[73]

Others, however, may find veteran social critic John Perkins's counsel
worth pondering: "We are fools if we depend on the same people that
got us into the mess to get us out of it."[74] Or as William Ramsay more
temperately states, bringing us back to Paul and 1 Timothy 2:

> How far Paul's opinions about women should be regarded as springing
> from his insight into the divine force that moves the world, we do not
> venture to judge; they are out of harmony with ours; but the fault may well
> lie with us, and we may be judging under the prepossession of modern
> custom, which will perhaps prove evanescent and discordant with the
> plan of the universe and the purpose of God.[75]

Even secular authors weigh in with similar words. James Tooley sees
women today as brainwashed due to "education policy . . . stuck in a
time warp, circa 1975"; women should be encouraged to pursue family
and mothering priorities that societal thought-police work[76] assiduously
to discourage but that many of them are longing to embrace.[77] "To raise
the very idea of psychological sex differences was risky" until recently,[78]
and still is, but there is increasing willingness to question what the late
twentieth century deemed sacrosanct.[79] Maggie Gallagher notes that
current "equal-regard advocates" (feminists in outlook if not in name)
"seem to argue that Christian ideals of mutuality and neighbor love at
a minimum imply, if they do not command, that Christians ought to
reject all but the most minimal sexual scripts. Roles must remain conceptually androgynous, fluid, the subject of intersubjective dialogue, if
women and men are to be 'free.'"[80] In contrast to this, non-Christian
mainline publishers are recognizing the appeal of ideas that sound in
certain respects much like traditional biblical teaching on how women
and men will find the most mutual happiness, fulfillment, and success
in life.[81]

Are "Progressive" Readings of 1 Timothy 2:9–15 Capitulations to the Spirit of the Age?

Some will be loath to concede what the previous section argues: that
the "progressive" interpretation of Paul is indebted significantly to the
prevailing social climate rather than to the biblical text. Such reticence

is conceivable from two groups. One would be those who fail to realize how novel some of the arguments currently being advanced for "progressive" readings of 1 Timothy 2 are.[82] A second group would be those who are probably aware that the arguments are novel but who feel they are justified by an equally novel assessment of another Pauline text: Galatians 3:28. This will be seen below when we deal with the views of K. Stendahl and F. F. Bruce.

By way of reply to the first group, the first edition of this chapter scrutinized *New Testament Abstracts* since 1956 as a rough barometer of contemporary discussion on the topic of 1 Timothy 2:9–15 and its relation to the question of women's role in the church. Some ten articles over nearly a forty-year period supported a "historic" view, while more than twice that many (twenty-three) argued for a "progressive" interpretation. The year 1969 marks the beginning of the "progressive" voice. Prior to that time, apparently, while there is no lack of rejection of Paul's teaching in 1 Timothy 2:9–15 on other grounds,[83] the distinctive features of "progressive" understanding as these have taken shape in contemporary discussion had not emerged.

One can, therefore, hardly argue that social pressure did not exert considerable influence on how 1 Timothy 2 gradually came to be understood in "progressive" circles today. It simply strains credulity to maintain that it is mere coincidence that "progressive" readings of 1 Timothy 2, which are at most marginally attested in church history prior to the women's movement of the 1960s[84] and since, are not indebted to that movement in fundamental respects for their plausibility. "Contemporary interest in vindicating the pastoral ministry of women"[85] is at work from about 1970 onward, so that today progressive interpreters speak confidently of "the egalitarian hermeneutic that has earned its rightful place in the theological forum of the evangelical community."[86]

A brief look at the Religion Index One database, which casts a slightly broader bibliographic net than *New Testament Abstracts*, indicates much the same trend (see first edition of this essay for detailed tally). Prior to 1970–74, Religion Index One cites no "progressive" articles, that is, articles arguing that 1 Timothy 2 gives no impediment to women holding pastoral office at full parity with men. After that time articles on the subject, whether "progressive" or "historic" in orientation, swelled by the mid-1990s to account for about 40 percent of all cataloged published discussion on Timothy or 1 Timothy generally. While lulls did occur, in some years the percentage was much higher. Not all of the 40 percent argued the "progressive" view, it is true, but many did.[87] And virtually all of the 40 percent are best accounted for as symptomatic of the rise and onward march of the "progressive" outlook. We conclude that the "progressive" claim simply to be interpreting the text with no fundamental indebtedness to the larger social milieu should be taken with a sizable grain of salt.

This conclusion is confirmed by a look at the pioneering arguments for "progressive" understanding of 1 Timothy 2 marshaled years ago by Krister Stendahl and F. F. Bruce, whose point of departure was a novel reading of Galatians 3:28: "There is neither Jew nor Greek, there is neither slave nor free, there is neither male nor female; for you are all one in Christ Jesus" (RSV).

Stendahl's voice[88] was seminal in raising the issue of hermeneutics and the interpretation of New Testament passages dealing with women's roles. Bruce will go down as perhaps the most influential evangelical New Testament scholar in English-speaking Christendom in the latter half of the twentieth century. In handling New Testament passages on gender roles, both employ methods fundamentally indebted to contemporary conviction rather than to the ancient sources. In other words, they impute a signification to the biblical writings that does not inhere in them but is imported from twentieth-century beliefs.

Stendahl's essay was written to further the cause of women's ordination in the Church of Sweden in the late 1950s. He criticizes liberal theology for its "conscious or unconscious tendency to judge and evaluate texts and ideas from the first century by the anachronistic standards of modern Western values and sentiments."[89] He praises what he calls "realistic interpretation," by which he appears to refer to what others called the "biblical theology movement" with roots in the 1920s and whose flower lasted from about the end of World War II to sometime in the late 1950s. "Realistic interpretation" is invaluable because, unlike both liberal and fundamentalist interpretation, it recognizes the enormous gap "between the first and the twentieth centuries."[90] The realistic interpreter "is a good enough historian to recognize that everything is conditioned by the actual situation of the time," so that "Jesus and Paul shared the exegetical and cultural presuppositions of their time" even when speaking of matters that "they considered . . . 'timeless truths' of fundamental significance."[91] The realistic interpreter "may even question whether the idea of 'timeless truth' is congenial to the biblical material in which the revelation in the Scriptures is always open to interpretation."[92] Such statements indicate already that Stendahl is prepared to sweep aside the Bible's certainties—even those stated by Christ himself—when these conflict with modern cultural presuppositions.

Stendahl's key insight is that rightly interpreting the New Testament requires a sense for what is absolute and enduring in its pages, on the one hand, and what is ephemeral and nonbinding for later times, on the other. This is the heart of his call for attention to "hermeneutics." For Stendahl, "the center of revelation" in the Bible is "God and his mighty acts." In contrast, biblical statements about persons are peripheral and nonrevelatory: "The understanding of man in the biblical view is valuable for our reading of the content and consequences of revelation, but it can hardly be the revelation itself."[93] He concludes:

> Against this background it seems natural to see the understanding of man in the New Testament—an integral part of the "biblical view"—as distinct from the revelation itself, as anchored in the event, in the Christ event. Then this must also refer to the question concerning the relationship between male and female both in home and congregation.[94]

For Stendahl, then, when the Bible speaks of humans, its outlook is not authoritative for later times. (This foreshadows the view of Kevin Giles, treated in more detail in the next section.) This approach enables him to preserve the theory of biblical authority in purely theological matters, while at the same time admitting that there is hardly any "element in the gospels which transcends the essentially Palestinian Jewish frame of ideas. Jesus' sayings touching on the relationship between men and women all fall within this fundamental view,"[95] a patriarchal[96] outlook quite out of line with modern convictions about persons and roles. The claim to hallow the Bible by frankly critiquing and finally correcting it is a clear indicator that Stendahl's method is bound to construe biblical statements in ways inimical to the original writers' intent when he finds those statements to be incompatible with what he takes to be correct modern conviction.

Yet even in the New Testament, if not in Jesus' example or teaching then at least in the course of early-church developments, there is hope. This hope rests in Galatians 3:28 ("There is neither Jew nor Greek, slave nor free, male nor female, for you are all one in Christ Jesus"), which represents a "breakthrough."[97] It is the wave of the future for those "in Christ" and in fact for the world as a whole.

Stendahl's "progressive" hermeneutic thus involves pitting Galatians 3:28 (and a few other Pauline phrases that he thinks hint in the same egalitarian direction) against other passages that speak of women's subordination. This includes 1 Timothy 2:9–15. What the Bible repeatedly states (classic passages include Eph. 5:22–6:9; Col. 3:18–4:1; Titus 2:2–10; 1 Pet. 2:13–21) and everywhere assumes[98] is set aside by the hermeneutical move of declaring the Bible culturally bound when it speaks about people. Prophetic, dominical, and apostolic insight take a back seat to the presumed superior vantage point of the modern or postmodern West.

Stendahl's "breakthrough" verse, Galatians 3:28, carries virtually the whole weight of Stendahl's argument because of its reference to "slave and free." If this verse is properly understood to mandate the abolition of slavery in society, or even declare it to be sinful, then why cling to distinctions that fail to realize that "male and female" are likewise distinctions requiring abolition in ecclesiastical and home settings?[99] This is an important issue and one to which we will return when we discuss the slavery issue and its relation to the hermeneutics of 1 Timothy 2.

For now, we note that Stendahl calls for doing away with the "serious hermeneutical naïveté" that failed to realize that "the New Testament contain[s] elements, glimpses which point beyond and even 'against' the prevailing view and practice of the New Testament church."[100] Christians dare not play "First-Century Semites," accepting some "static 'biblical view'" of the past that is no longer appropriate today, nor pursue a "nostalgic attempt to play 'First Century'" or "First-Century Bible Land."[101]

Stendahl's confident, even flippant ad absurdum argumentation in these passages is a clue to his confidence in the plank on which he builds: contemporary affirmation of women's liberation or "emancipation." "If emancipation is right, then there can be no valid 'biblical' reason not to ordain women."[102] He candidly admits that "the ideology or dogma which underlies both the movements of emancipation and the demand for the ordination of women is a secularized philosophy of equality with roots in the Enlightenment or in Hellas or in the cult of Baal—in any case alien to the Bible."[103] But he thinks the "fruits" of recent social developments confirm their rightness. The basis, then, for his hermeneutical move is pragmatic. On that basis secular Western society's "belief in unlimited human freedom"[104] must be true, at least for the present world, while the Bible's counsel about persons and social order even in the church are wrong. Stendahl would perhaps say "wrong for today," though adequate for its own time.[105] This outlook seems reasonable in the current hermeneutical climate in which there are no universal transcendent verities. But is it compatible with a Christian view of revelation that takes the Bible as its authority?

Ironically, Stendahl is as guilty of letting modern certainties determine his exegesis as the liberal and fundamentalist elements he opposes. For as Madeleine Boucher states in a study rejecting Stendahl's exegesis (though agreeing with his hermeneutics), "the ideas of equality before God and inferiority in the social order are in harmony in the New Testament. To be precise, the tension did not exist in first-century thought, and it is not present in the texts themselves. The tension arises from *modern man's* inability to hold these two ideas together."[106]

F. F. Bruce takes up the matter where Stendahl leaves off. If the latter argues for the need to appreciate the phenomenon of cultural relativity and incorporate it into one's hermeneutic, Bruce baptizes it at the outset; the first words of his treatment are "The phenomenon of cultural relativity, with the adaptations it imposes, is repeatedly illustrated within the Bible itself."[107]

The problem that Stendahl, writing in Swedish in the mid-1950s, could not have anticipated, and of which Bruce, writing in the late 1970s, seems unaware, is the meaning of "cultural relativity" in postmodern parlance. It is fundamental to what Diogenes Allen calls the "postmodern creed."[108] This is not simply a matter of cultures differing (the fact to which Bruce probably means to point). It is the claim that all science, literature, philosophy, and religion generally are "wholly imbedded in culture" (which Stendahl seems prepared to accept).[109] This is the entrée into what Diogenes Allen has called

> a particular kind of relativism. We not only construct the world, so that all knowledge, value, and meaning are relative to human beings, as Idealists since Kant have argued, but now the radical conclusion is drawn that there is no reality that is universally constructed because people in different periods of history and in different societies construct it differently. There is no definitive procedure or universal basis to settle disputes in the natural sciences, in ethics, and in the interpretation of literature. Every domain of inquiry and every value is relative to a culture and even to subcultures.[110]

Bruce would doubtless not have agreed with such an approach to knowledge, but his hermeneutical method in the question at hand does little to discourage it. He calls for separating the temporal husk from the enduring kernel[111]—a hermeneutical tool so reminiscent of rationalists like Lessing that the student of the Enlightenment may be shocked to witness an evangelical scholar wielding it with such aplomb.[112] How do we know what is permanent? Whereas we might expect an appeal to Scripture, Bruce's sole stated criterion is that "whatever in Paul's teaching promotes true freedom is of universal and permanent validity; whatever seems to impose restrictions on true freedom has regard to local and temporary conditions."[113] Such language can only be understood as positing an extrabiblical standard—true freedom—which we may use to recognize the Bible's true utterances and to cancel out teachings of less lofty quality.

Given Bruce's restrained but consistent suspicion of the written word (the Bible)[114] as inferior to the insight given by the living Spirit, there seems little to distinguish his approach to the question at hand from Stendahl's, in which the "fruit" and social acceptability of liberalized understanding of women's roles is decisive for determining what Christians today should make of the Bible's counsel. Bruce, like Stendahl, ultimately calls for pragmatics to determine hermeneutics: "Experience shows that [the Holy Spirit] bestows ... gifts, with 'undistinguishing regard,' on men and women alike. ... That being so, it is unsatisfactory to rest with a halfway house in this issue of women's ministry, where they are allowed to pray and prophesy, but not to teach or lead."[115]

And for Bruce as for Stendahl, Paul's "revolutionary sentiment" of Galatians 3:28[116] serves to qualify 1 Timothy 2:9–15 in such a way as to set it to the side.[117] Bruce does affirm the pastoral epistles' canonicity and acknowledges that in 1 Timothy 2:11–12, "women are quite explicitly not given permission to teach or rule."[118] But he claims to be puzzled by verses 13–14 and unable to see how they support verses 11–12.[119] Galatians 3:28 plays a key role in his puzzlement, since for Bruce it mandates what Paul in 1 Timothy 2 seems to forbid. Bruce cuts the Gordian knot by declaring, "Nothing that Paul says elsewhere on women's contribution to church services [he refers to 1 Cor. 14 and 1 Tim. 2] can be understood in a sense which conflicts with these statements of principle"[120] related to Galatians 3:28. De facto abrogation of 1 Timothy based on Galatians 3, grounded in the foundation of a pragmatic hermeneutics of cultural relativity, is Bruce's way of settling the impasse.

The problem with Bruce's and Stendahl's method is not that it recognizes tensions in the Bible. The Reformation principle that Scripture interprets Scripture (*sacra scriptura sui interpres*) implies the presence of obscure or ostensibly conflicting passages. The problem lies in the recourse to a distinctly modern consciousness to adjudicate Scripture's meaning. This is to step outside the horizon of Scripture to determine Scripture's significance. It is to imperil the *sola scriptura* doctrine of the Reformation and similar affirmations of earlier periods.[121]

The Hermeneutical Problem of Slavery

The case for an updated handling of New Testament passages like 1 Timothy 2:9–15 received notable support from Kevin Giles a decade ago.[122] His article is ultimately not so much about slavery as about what he calls "the subordination of women," by which he appears to mean applications of exegesis following a "historic" rather than a "progressive" line. His thesis nicely summarizes what both Stendahl and Bruce argued with less comprehensiveness and verve:

> If it can be shown that the Bible does in fact unambiguously endorse both the institution and the practice of slavery, although we cannot now accept slavery in any form, then we will have discovered something about the nature of biblical revelation which will help resolve the present debate about the status and role of women. We will have learnt that Scripture

can endorse social structures no longer acceptable, just as we have learnt that the Bible can endorse scientific ideas no longer tenable. *The Bible is authoritative in matters of faith and conduct but not necessarily in science, or on how to order social relations.*[123]

Before interacting with Giles here, I should comment on his critique of the version of this chapter that appeared a decade ago.[124] In most respects, I find the response by A. Köstenberger to be a satisfactory reply.[125] In addition, I should say that I disagree with Giles's point that his essay was primarily about slavery. I argued that he was wrong about slavery (for reasons made more explicit below), but my main point was that he declares the Bible to be nonauthoritative in the area of social relations (see italics in the preceding paragraph). This move may clear the ground for his view of gender roles in the church, but it is a Pyrrhic victory, I argued then and still think now, because while it may help the church seem more acceptable to the world, it robs the church of the revelatory guidance for men and women that I believe Scripture intends for us to accept and cherish.

Giles claims that my earlier chapter was "an apologetic for slavery," attacked him personally, and made claims that are "reprehensible in a supposedly scholarly work."[126] I have shaped my comments below so as to avoid these charges (which, not surprisingly, I found inaccurate in the first place) this time. In addition, I have dropped reference to the "Cartesian" approach favored by Stendahl, Bruce, and Giles, because I have concluded that it is an argument too extended and subtle for this discussion. Also, the main implication of my "Cartesian" charge is that Stendahl and others are letting contemporary concerns dictate their application of Scripture's message. I continue to think so; I try to argue it in this version of my essay and do not need to discuss the "Cartesian" factor in post-Enlightenment exegesis to make my point.

To return to Giles's original essay, at a number of points one can only agree with Giles's analysis, which centers on American slavery in the Old South and its purportedly biblical defense by Reformed theologians like Robert Dabney, James Henry Thornwell, and Charles Hodge. Southern slavery was a great evil. Much of the defense mounted in its favor deserves criticism. Racism is roundly condemned by the Scriptures of both Testaments. Devout Christians with sophisticated hermeneutical understanding and formidable learning can be wrong in interpreting and applying the Bible. Giles rightly drives these important points home.

Nevertheless, Giles's point is not well taken that the slavery analogy as he presents it proves that those who hold the "historic" view of women's roles in church and home stand in the tradition of Old South slaveholders and those who defended them, while "progressive" interpreters are the modern equivalent of righteous abolitionists. A number of considerations serve to vitiate Giles's claims.

First, by Giles's logic his own "progressive" hermeneutic is responsible for the social evils of post-Enlightenment, postslavery liberal governments and nations. For if Southern Reformed "historic" hermeneutics should be blamed for endorsing the social order of its day with its attendant ills such as slavery, then Giles's theology, which defends and enshrines the modern liberal social order of emancipation, must share the guilt of the wars, injustices, and inequities that the liberal social order since, say, the American or French Revolution, has produced. Extending this logic, we could argue that Christians who argue a just-war theory in the modern world should be blamed for Hiroshima and Nagasaki. Or American Christians whose (not unfounded) fear of government intrusiveness moves them to oppose the abolition of the constitutional right for citizens to bear arms are guilty for the thousands of homicides committed with handguns. Such charges are illogical. But if they are, then so is the basic logic on which Giles depends.

Second, Giles too facilely equates biblical teaching on slavery and its teaching on male-female relations.[127] There are in fact important differences to note.

1. Neither God nor Scripture ordained slavery, though biblical law and doctrine did regulate and limit it. Slavery is never said by Scripture to have been created by God. Marriage and men's spiritual leadership in home and church, however, were ordained if Scripture is the measure.
2. Slavery in Israel had a six-year limit (with one exception; see Lev. 25:39–43; Deut. 15:12–18). M. A. Dandamayev notes, "We have in the Bible the first appeals in world literature to treat slaves as human beings for their own sake and not just in the interest of their masters."[128] But no time limit is stated for men to continue as husbands to particular wives or as elders of churches.
3. In New Testament times Paul advises slaves to gain their freedom if they can lawfully do so (1 Cor. 7:21). No such counsel is given to wives or to people in churches with male leaders.
4. Far from mandating slavery in biblical times and even now "by permitting the ownership of slaves today,"[129] New Testament teaching was the foundation for abolishing the institution of slavery in the Roman world. Bruce notes that the little Epistle to Philemon alone "brings us into an atmosphere in which the institution could only wilt and die."[130] "The early Christian ideology undermined the institution of slavery, declaring an equality of all people in Christ."[131] But we have argued above that it is unwarranted to view Scripture

as mandating the termination of male leadership.[132] Those who would do so must follow a trajectory beyond and outside the New Testament to arrive at that conviction.

A third and final hermeneutically significant objection to Giles's case is the gravity of his claim: "The Bible is authoritative in matters of faith and conduct but not necessarily in science, or on how to order social relations."[133] It is not clear how this can be taken seriously as a credibly Christian understanding of scriptural authority. How much of life can be safely regarded as bereft of implications related to "social relations"? The great commandment to love others is surely inseparable from "social relations." Yet in Giles's view we are now suddenly without necessarily trustworthy biblical counsel for our lives in this crucial area of spiritual response. The leap from the correct observation that God contextualizes his message for the peoples and times he addresses through Scripture to the programmatic assertion that we do not regard Scripture as necessarily authoritative when it touches on "social relations" is a fateful hermeneutical move that many will rightly hesitate to endorse.[134]

Giles's contentions epitomize a stock justification for "progressive" reinterpretations of biblical pronouncements about men, women, and their respective places in God's economy.[135] If Giles be followed and the implications of his views traced out fully in years ahead, then we may have seen only the beginning of revised understandings of social, and inevitably sexual, relations in ostensibly Bible-believing circles. We may be at the threshold of any number of behavioral and philosophical adjustments rendered plausible even in evangelical churches by unfolding social mores now that the Bible is silent for us, if not flatly wrong, on these topics. (In many nonevangelical circles, of course, society's mores long ago replaced the Bible in the area of social relations.) To take one example, D. W. Jones has shown that egalitarian hermeneutics as deployed in various churches frequently "so minimize gender that once biblical feminism is embraced, it is but a small logical step to accept homosexuality."[136] He shows how this has happened in recent years in various denominations.[137]

But if Giles's arguments lack the sweeping powers to validate "progressive" hermeneutics that he claims, then that hermeneutic loses the powerful rhetorical and comparative validation of the slavery analogy in interpreting 1 Timothy 2:9–15. It must be content to bear responsibility for its procedure in which some parts of Scripture (in this case Gal. 3:28) serve to cancel out others. And it must face squarely the exegetical liabilities set forth elsewhere in this volume. We are amply justified in declining to follow Giles's startling counsel that the Bible may not be authoritative for Christians in the area of social relations.

Toward a Progressive "Historic" Hermeneutic

To the extent that the preceding arguments are sound, the hermeneutics informing the "progressive" interpretation of 1 Timothy 2:9–15 deserve to be called into question. The "historic" exegesis of the passage should be allowed to stand, as earlier chapters of this book maintain. Some offices and responsibilities in church and home are biblically mandated as the peculiar province of men and husbands. We have tried to show that certain hermeneutical moves to circumvent "historic" exegesis fall short of being persuasive.

In conclusion, we wish briefly to summarize the liabilities of the "progressive" hermeneutic. We will also call for refinement of the hermeneutic underlying the "historic" exegesis of 1 Timothy 2:9–12 for which this book argues.

Summary Reflections on a "Progressive" Hermeneutic

The Stendahl-Bruce approach, now widespread in evangelical circles,[138] has serious drawbacks. It is novel and depends largely on contemporary culture for its persuasive power.

We have seen above that American society, since the retooling of conceptions of men and women and morality and marriage in recent decades, has witnessed sinister outcomes when it comes to the lot of women and children. The developments we observed argue for critical, not unthinking, church endorsement of social trajectories that have brought such woes into being and promise to extend them to the next generation, if not longer. For the cycle will not be easy to break. But it is unlikely that the so-called feminization of poverty, to take just one of the issues, will be effectively addressed by further feminization of what male leadership in Christian homes there may still be and of the ministry of Christian churches.[139] Something far more profound and less cosmetic is called for.

Or, to make an anecdotal observation: men I know who are unchurched are generally united in their acceptance of stereotypes of wives (typically including their own) that are not very attractive. (Wives, of course, share corresponding stereotypes that apply to their husbands.) The best insurance I can imagine that these men will never darken a church's door is to increase the extent to which women will be the leadership figures in churches they might someday have occasion to attend.

To phrase the matter positively, there is freedom, emancipation, liberty, whatever it be called, only in Christ. This is true for all, Jew and Greek, slave and free, male and female.[140] Embracing the modern social order as somehow pre-evangelistic for a newly discovered gospel of equal rights in church and home is a dubious strategy for at least two weighty reasons.

First, it would appear to be disobedient to those Scriptures that call for reflection of the creation order in marriage (e.g., Eph. 5:31–33) and ministry (e.g., 1 Tim. 2:13–14). We may perhaps scoff at what harm could come from disobeying Scripture's commands when current social conditions make it seem not only expedient but necessary to do so. But unless weighty hermeneutical considerations constrain us to transpose the form (never the substance) of what Scripture commands (an example might be the biblical kiss of greeting, for which some modern cultures possess different equivalents),[141] we do well to keep transgressions as defined by Scripture to a minimum. To love God and one another involves more than obeying his commands, but it does not involve less.

Second, "progressive" hermeneutics removes the social scandal of the cross of subordination—for husbands the call to place their wives' welfare above their own, for wives the call to respond to their leadership as they do so; for men the solemn charge that some of their number will give account of the souls under their ordained oversight (Heb. 13:17), for women the mandate to minister aggressively in the expansive spheres delegated to them. True, there is here a reciprocity that forbids a simplistic "chain of command" schema (1 Cor. 11:11). Spouses are partners, not master and slave. Pastors are shepherds, not commandants. But the Bible does envisage a divine ordering within redeemed human relationships, domestic and ecclesial, redolent of God's own diversity in unity, which humans together bear and mirror in their divinely bestowed social potential and destiny. The Bible does this, among other reasons, because of its high view of persons and the intrinsic connections it affirms between sexuality and identity. Groothuis writes, "Sexual identity is not conflated with personal identity" in the evangelical feminism she urges as middle ground in the current debate.[142] This is hardly middle ground at all, since it is a direct challenge to the scriptural claims that each of us is, essentially, human *qua* male or female. Our corporate wholeness as divine image-bearers emerges through our respective acquiescence to God's will in creating us as he did, with all that implies for our respective stations in his household.

To obliterate our God-given gender distinctions (or to follow Marxist or other social theories in declaring all such distinctions to be no more than social conditioning) on the flimsy grounds offered by postmodern humanism is an affront and basic alteration to the message of the cross. On the contrary, our call is to renounce treasured societal values, where necessary, in order to follow Christ.[143] In the current climate it is becoming increasingly necessary. *"The cross transforms present criteria of relevance; present criteria of relevance do not transform the cross. Salvation is pro-active, not re-active, in relation to the present.*"[144]

It is not enough, however, to point to deficiencies in "progressive" thought or practice. There must also be renewal among those who affirm "historic" exegesis.

Refining a "Historic" Hermeneutic

In kingdom hermeneutics the interpreter's own life and soul are integral to the blessedness of the message he or she propounds.[145] This means that rightly applying 1 Timothy 2:9–15 is not only, and in a sense not primarily, about exegetical rigor and conceptual sophistication. It has everything to do with how the Lord regards the state of our hearts, the intent behind the arguments we marshal, and the way we treat other persons.

There is need for détente in the "historic"-"progressive" debate. This will be no easier in days ahead than it has been in times past. Both sides sling stinging salvoes. Strong differences of opinion are unavoidable. There is need for the inevitable conflicts over different points of view to be waged "with honorable and clean weapons."[146] It is helpful to note that there is a wide range of mediating positions between hard-core male dominance views and full-blown biblical feminist positions—even among those who claim the highest possible understanding of scriptural authority.[147] In the end we may be convinced that the other side's understanding of what the Bible says is wrong and feel that this vitiates its claim to be honoring Scripture's authority. But we should strive to keep lines of peaceable exchange open.

We should, however, not be oblivious to voices that see evangelicalism as in trouble. A full decade ago, *Christianity Today*'s 1994 book awards were dominated by jeremiads: "Many of the titles communicate anxiety—we are concerned that we may be ignoring the institutional church, that we no longer value truth or theology, that we have been unduly influenced (and harmed) by psychology and marketing techniques, that heresy is creeping into our churches."[148] This trend has only accelerated in the years since, in my view. "Progressive" hermeneutics may be contributing to the drift. A Neville Chamberlain response to gathering doctrinal storm clouds, whether we detect them in the opposing camp or in our own, will not do. At a time when the basic parameters of evangelical theology, and even the nature of God (as in the open theism debate), are being questioned and repositioned, we must be as wary of untoward innovation as we are hopeful of positive alteration. For the time may come, if it is not already here, when the issue at hand will not merely comprise a secondary matter (like mode of baptism or form of church government) but an essential one. It will become a confessional issue, a question on which hinges one's understanding of the essence of the gospel itself.

Communities who affirm "historic" exegesis should be aware that their own hierarchical excesses are probably the most effective apologetic for the "progressive" view at the popular level. When wives are less loved than utilized, when their myriad legitimate ministries are repressed or trivialized rather than respected and furthered, when women continue to be the objects of thin humor and innuendo, when husbands fob off on long-suffering spouses all the drudgery of housework and childcare and make no attempt to share the burden, no amount of biblical evidence can legitimate a "historic" community hermeneutic.[149] There arises a relative justification for "progressive" understanding of biblical texts that are being used to subjugate women rather than to accord them the dignity that even the "subordination" passages presuppose.[150]

By the same token, male pastoral incompetence or chauvinism or laziness gives point to the argument that some women could do the job a whole lot better. In the end, this pragmatic argument should not overrule Scripture's insistence that men bear a few strategic burdens that women normally[151] do not. The Lord reigns; we gain nothing by mistrusting his counsel and taking matters into our own hands. But men must be careful not to hide their own sinfulness behind the presumed privilege that pet verses seem to afford. Too many confuse the *necessary* condition of maleness for certain biblically mandated responsibilities with a *sufficient* condition. Being male alone is not a sufficient qualification for proper execution of leadership responsibilities in the household of God, in either church or home.

Finally, the call for renewed affirmation of a "historic" hermeneutic is a call for repentance. Where that hermeneutic has not been abandoned today, it tends to be in such ill repair as to be, so far, largely undiscovered in its fullness. Just as the church through its neglect of social need was in some ways responsible for the rise of anti-Christian socialist forces in Europe during the nineteenth century,[152] the church in the late twentieth century brought sex-role confusion on itself by a variety of quintessentially male sins often tolerated in its own midst. In some churches these are even legitimated by male-exalting mores or teachings: failure to love wives and children even in intact families as Scripture calls for; bogus division of labor in the home so that childcare and housework were unjustly heaped exclusively on the wife (and daughters when available); throwaway attitudes toward marriage and family leading to divorce and followed by negligence in child support; use of the family as chattel rather than cultivating it as a dynamic center for spiritual renewal and ministry through the church;[153] idolization of crass materialism leading to occupational or leisure fixations (sports, hunting, fishing) at the expense of loving God and others wholeheartedly; indulgence of moral double standards that exploited wives by cheating on them and other women by misusing them. Even this representative sampling of historic male malfeasance ought to make "historic" proponents wince, since churches in the past that championed their hermeneutic often failed to address, much less rectify, such evils.

Behind every confirmed "progressive" exegete there is probably some personal experience of self-serving "historic" use of the Bible.[154] My source of information for many of the male sins just listed was the (nominally Protestant) home I grew up in; the (Irish Catholic) childhood home life of my wife of over thirty years was no better. As a result we began married life as self-centered egalitarians. We came of age in the Woodstock era and had a view of marriage to match. But we repented, in part due to the stubborn testimony of passages like 1 Timothy 2, and are still discovering how glad we are that we did. The good news is that many modern women and men alike are discovering the grace to abide in the "subordinate" roles Scripture sets for us all under Christ as a "historic" gospel and companion hermeneutic work their transforming grace.

A missiological note in closing. A continual concern of progressives is that the Christian message will be ignored or scorned by people in our society because of its perceived retrogressive teaching on gender: "Many people believe that Christianity is the major cultural carrier of the subordination of women."[155] We need to be reminded, however, that the bulk of the world church, and its leading edges of growth, are and long have been in South America, Africa, and Asia. Even if we can enhance evangelism and church ministry in some Western locales by revamping biblical teaching to bring it in line with local social standards—and to my knowledge this has not been shown to be a successful strategy in the long run and on a broad scale[156]—most of the world church does not relate to our social standards. The high regard for women that helped Christianity win social domination in cultural settings of ancient times[157] is the best hope for women and children (to say nothing of men) in those lands at present. A message that calls for "equal regard" in marriage and church—when the historic reading of the Bible and the one most likely to strike the reader unschooled in certain Western sensitivities is one of some form and degree of male headship—is not apt to sit well in these non-Western settings.

For over a decade I have served twice annually in an Eastern European setting (Romania) and a site in Muslim Africa (Sudan). Host church and academic bodies in both settings are courageously Christian and eager for solid biblical and theological instruction. They are also magnanimous in bearing with me as a teacher from the outside doing my fitful best to give them tools for understanding that they can ply in their own language and cultural settings. But one thing, I think, they would not tolerate for long is any fundamental divergence on my part from the Bible's clear (to them) teaching on marriage and the family and church order.[158] In Sudan, for example, Paul's advocacy of dignity and freedom for women to speak and pray in the worship assembly (1 Cor. 11) and be loved sacrificially by their husbands (Eph. 5), yet to be silent at points in church (1 Cor. 14; 1 Tim. 2) and pursue loving submission in marriage, seem to be a quantum advancement beyond the social regard for women in the dominant Muslim culture. Christians there would perceive a progressive hermeneutic as cutting the biblical ground out from under the church in a setting where it lives on the edge of survival anyway, in part by giving Muslims occasion to charge the church with not believing its own Scriptures.

People in Western circles hope to gain approval for the gospel by moderating biblical teaching on gender. In regions characteristic of "the next Christendom,"[159] however, this hermeneutic would frequently bring reproach and not approval.[160] "The West as a modern progressive society is committed to live as if God does not exist, *etsi deus non daretur*, or at any rate to live with no sense of the devil."[161] The progressive hermeneutic seeks to make a strategic partnership with this society. In choosing between a historic or a progressive hermeneutic, a pressing question is, Which segment of the world church is missing the point of God's intent in the teaching on men and women set forth in Scripture? How that question is answered is fateful for determining the hermeneutic we endorse for reading 1 Timothy 2.

6

WHAT SHOULD A WOMAN DO IN THE CHURCH?

One Woman's Personal Reflections

DOROTHY KELLEY PATTERSON

How well I remember my first introduction to theological studies! My husband had suggested that I take New Testament Greek with him during our university studies. The distinguished scholar who taught the language was an all-business, no-nonsense professor and a well-prepared instructor who also expected his students to be prepared. On the first day of class, he announced that to miss even one class would hamper the learning process; to miss several days would mean a letter's difference in one's grade; to miss more than a week of classes would be to forfeit the entire course! I took him very seriously and applied myself rigorously to the study of Koine Greek.

Midway through the first semester of my first year, I became pregnant unexpectedly and inconveniently (or so I thought at the time). I still remember my initial irritation and grave concern that the baby would arrive just as I needed to complete Greek translation work and the final examination. However, these concerns quickly evaporated;

early in the second semester of my studies, I began to miscarry my baby. My maternal instincts kicked in quickly and without prompting, so that soon I didn't care whether or not I completed my Greek studies; I just wanted my baby. In the weeks that followed, I was forced to complete bed rest and even so lost my baby while at home and alone. The physical pain was greatly surpassed by the mental anguish and spiritual turmoil. I did manage to keep up with my Greek through the patient help of the professor, who indeed did have a pastor's heart, and the careful tutoring of my husband, who passed on each day's classwork with amazing exactitude. In fact, I excelled enough to keep my A and to be named the grader for that esteemed professor during my second year of Greek.

What is the point of such a personal illustration in an academic book? This incident in my personal life began the constant tension I was to have between my womanhood, on the one hand, and my passion for learning the truths of Scripture and doing the work of the kingdom, on the other. Within my womanhood, because of my choice to marry, I am a helper; because of the maternity that was mine by divine design, I am a natural nurturer. These predetermined roles are augmented by a hunger to follow Christ and a desire to serve him. The callings to marriage and to serve Christ—are they antithetical to each other? Or can they be linked in tandem? If so, are my responsibilities in the home simple "life support"—mundane tasks that become the rudiments for living in the world? Do these everyday routines come even close to being on a par with tasks to be done in kingdom service to Christ?

First Timothy 2:9–15 is a passage that brings this tension to the forefront for me and for every woman. By context, the passage is set within a framework of apostolic instruction concerning church order. By content, its message is to every woman who affirms her desire to learn. Nevertheless, that desire for knowledge is set within boundaries that will make a woman's learning, and the outworking of that learning, most meaningful to her, most edifying to the kingdom, and above all most God-glorifying in the overall schema of the Father's plan.

The approach of this chapter is to build on firm theological foundations with *presuppositions* that are rooted in the creation order and that are forever bound to honor Holy Scripture as divine truth and thus the ultimate authority for faith and practice. The hermeneutical tools used by the interpreter to discern this divinely imparted truth have stood the test of time from generation to generation, unlocking the Scriptures with faithful consistency worthy of the timeless principles embodied therein. The verses in 1 Timothy 2:9–15 address women with a noteworthy warning concerning the boundaries for their roles within the church. There are unique lessons for women to be gleaned from the apostle's injunctions. Yet the application of biblical truth in one's life must never overshadow the accuracy of the words of the text itself.

Some believe that instructions given to women—most of whom did not have access to formal education, much less to the public platform—in the first century by the apostle Paul are either wrong or at least could not be applicable to women living in the enlightened and progressive culture of the modern era.[1] In other words, personal situation or existential circumstances have begun to take priority over Scripture. Others may suggest that Scripture is not clear on what a woman can and cannot do in the church, especially in light of different settings and circumstances.

Many interpreters are attempting to frame these boundaries for women found within the section in 1 Timothy that deals with church order in terms of *positions*. Can a woman be a missionary, a children's minister, a youth pastor, a worship leader, a church planter, the teacher of a coed Sunday School class, an author of commentaries, a professor in theological studies, a crusade evangelist, an associate pastor, a senior pastor? The Scripture does not furnish a gender-based list of appropriate ministries using the terminology of this generation. In fact, because its principles are timeless, the biblical discussion is fashioned around functions—what you *do* and not what position you *hold*. Therefore, one passage complements another; all passages are in harmony and without contradiction; and finding a word from God on such an important matter is within reach of every seeker who is eager to learn and committed to obey.

With unparalleled educational options and increasingly recognized giftedness as well as diverse opportunities for service, women can be distracted and enticed to accept responsibilities outside biblical boundaries. For example, the point is not that women cannot or should not serve as missionaries, sharing Christ and edifying their converts here and around the world, nor are they forbidden the important kingdom task of teaching in the church. However, Scripture does provide clear and consistent boundaries (1 Tim. 2:9–15) for what women may or may not do in the church. This passage addresses the church of all generations. Its timeless principles are not directed so much to defining positions or offices to be assigned to women in the church but rather are aimed at providing guidelines for how a woman is to pursue her functions or tasks in the kingdom of Christ. The divine mandate is then easily understood and expectantly applicable to women in every generation.

Based on this understanding, one is wise to approach each decision on how to use personal giftedness and when to pursue specific opportunities according to a positive biblical admonition, that is, "older" or spiritually mature women (πρεσβύτιδας) are to teach "younger" or new-to-the-faith women (νέας; Titus 2:3–5), while noting clear biblical boundaries, namely, that women not teach men or rule over men in the church (1 Tim. 2:12). Adding to these clear specifics, one can move to make decisions with a determination not to violate explicit directives given or to cause division or confusion in the church (1 Cor. 14:26, 33, 40). How much better it is for one to miss an opportunity for service than to cause confusion through her service. A wise woman would rather give up an opportunity to show and use her giftedness if by using that giftedness she would risk bringing dishonor to God's Word and thus to him (Titus 2:5). A woman committed to the Lord Jesus dare not do even what she is trained or gifted to do if by so doing she is disobedient by calling into question her accountability to a clear teaching of Scripture.

The movement of this chapter is designed to complement the biblical exegesis and the historical discussion found in other chapters. The hopeful result is to guide the reader through a difficult passage with biblical interpretation that is further illuminated through personal testimony and practical insights gleaned from living life as a woman committed to husband and children while simultaneously nurturing a passion to serve Christ along the way. The following discussion is not fashioned as a point-by-point discussion of the text but rather as a means of fleshing out the truths taught in these verses as worthy of direct application to the life and ministry of a woman who wants to maximize her giftedness in service without compromising her commitment to obedience.

Rooted in Creation: First Principles

By explicitly referring to the creation of Adam, and then Eve, in 1 Timothy 2:13, the apostle Paul directs the readers' attention to the foundational narrative of the creation of humankind, where the first man and the first woman were placed in the Garden of Eden, which became their home. At the dawn of creation God established his first and primary institution (Gen. 2:8, 15). One man and one woman were created and then challenged to commit themselves to binding their lives together as one flesh (Gen. 2:24). Because of the priority of the home—in times past as it was established at the beginning of creation, and in the present and in the future as God uses the home and its familial relationships to reveal himself (John 14:2–3; Eph. 5:1, 25–27)[2]—one must consider the theology of the home as well as the divine design for manhood and womanhood in general as part of the theological underpinnings for God's plan for men and women in the church.

The home is God's tangible illustration to humankind of his perfect love, which is portrayed in the Father; it is the dramatic stage for complete sacrifice as shown in the Son; and it is the object lesson for his illuminating teaching as manifested through the Holy Spirit. Because the apostle Paul supports his principles of church order with references to creation, it stands to reason that the role of the woman in the church is assuredly based on and irrevocably tied to God's divine order for the first institution he established. The home as we know it—that is, the divinely appointed union in which the husband's servant leadership of his wife and the wife's submission to and honor of her husband is the bedrock—is obviously born in the Garden of Eden with the union of Adam and Eve. Yet their union continues to provide a worthy metaphor through which God reveals himself in this and every generation.

There is a close tie between the home and the church. The home is used as a metaphor for heaven, the dwelling place of God (John 14:2); John uses wedding imagery as he describes the church as the bride and Christ himself as the bridegroom (Rev. 19:7; 21:9; 22:17). Therefore, a woman must look carefully at what Scripture has to say about both the home and the church in order to determine her place in each.

A Hard Word but a Sure Word: The Blessings Resulting from Obedience

Most of what Scripture has to say to women is presented in positive challenges, but there are also warnings. For many women, 1 Timothy 2 is indeed a "hard word" that is difficult to understand. The feminine intellectual prowess coming out of this new and enlightened age and the giftedness that has become more apparent as women are breaking through the so-called glass ceilings of the world, not to mention the obvious cultural trends moving modernity toward a unisex society—all these factors add to the confusion and self-centeredness that character- ize a postmodern world.

One might, for example, consider women in the Bible—the promi- nent civil servant Deborah, whose wisdom was sought by women and men; the brilliant and resourceful widow Abigail, who moved from the household of a foolish and abusive husband to the throne room of the king of Israel; the beautiful and courageous Queen Esther, who became the mediator and deliverer of her people; the humble and determined Gentile Ruth, who made her way into the lineage of the Messiah; the perceptive and articulate tentmaker Priscilla, who was able to hold her own in discussions even with the most learned theologian Apollos. These women found their greatness and usefulness, and thus their respective places in history, not only by moving against the grain of their culture but also by being obedient to God.

Women in church history, too, have made their mark. Consider the faithful and dedicated mothers like Anthusa, whose son Chrysostom preached such powerful sermons that centuries after his death he remains a model for biblical exposition in modern classrooms. Monica, despite the absence of a godly husband in her household, nurtured and prayed until her son Augustine was drawn into the kingdom, and Augustine's theological discourses are still honored today as classic and foundational for study in seminaries throughout the world.

Susannah Wesley bore and reared many children, but she is most remembered for the impact of her life on her sons, John and Charles, who shook two continents for Christ. Katie Luther and Susannah Spurgeon were greatly admired household managers and ministry partners during their respective lifetimes. Both biblical and secular histories are replete with vignettes of brilliant and gifted women who recognized and functioned within biblical guidelines—imperfectly, of course, as one would expect in dealing with frail and vulnerable humanity.

Nevertheless, my own experience—inspired by godly women who have gone before—has evolved to trust the providence of God to open opportunities for me and to give me usefulness beyond what appear to be my human limitations, while utilizing my academic preparation and perceived giftedness. I find in Scripture a "sure word" that frees me to offer to the Father whatever giftedness or creativity I may have as well as my personal energies and passions—whether in teaching biblical truth, extending Christian hospitality, or engaging in individual ministries.

As a believing woman, I do not feel a freedom to allow my theological training or giftedness for ministry to elevate personal experience, modern cultural perception, or ministry opportunities above biblical boundaries. Rather, I feel a compulsion to work under the clear mandates of Scripture, recorded in centuries past, yet protected and preserved to guide me now. With God's help, I will neither seek recognition nor demand higher office, but I will make every effort to serve *him* who is Lord according to *his* terms.

If I may be allowed yet another personal vignette, I remember a stimulating encounter with a young female theologue. She had read an interesting paper but one that opened countless questions, which, by the way, were not asked because of the courteous behavior of the predominantly male audience. In our conversation afterward, she queried, "Would you like to know what other women are saying about you?" I thought to myself, "Not really," but I also sensed that I was about to know. As I recall the gist of that conversation, she indicated that "other women" (who, of course, went unnamed) were saying that if *they* had husbands with positions like that of my husband (a seminary president) and if *they* were in the heart of a theological campus like the one where my husband and I live, with teaching opportunities like those accorded *me*, they would gladly hold my theological positions on the role of women in ministry. Recovering from the initial insult to my personal integrity, which suggested that I might be a woman whose experience and whose desire for expediency would dictate my faith and practice, I was able to respond with references to a public record that was clear—if any of "these women" cared to research it.

While at the small college where my husband and I began our ministry in theological education (twelve full-time students upon our arrival) about thirty years ago, I practiced and put into print the same principles to which I am now committed.[3] Of course, as I have studied and researched the treasures of Scripture through the years, I have learned more about those passages; but my path, as well as my determination to stand under Scripture, was set from the earliest study I made of these key passages pertaining to the role of women in the church.

The first priority for me, beyond consistently nurturing my personal relationship with Christ, is the responsibility to help my husband, followed closely by the task of nurturing my children (and now enriching the lives of my grandchildren), then my personal ministries to our extended family, and finally, beyond my home, the challenging ministries to other women that come to me in the course of ministry with my husband on the seminary campus. Along the way, I have had some "Priscilla" ministries even to godly men, who on a personal level have sought my counsel. I am humbly grateful if in those cases the Lord can speak through me. However, whether I have five women or fifty women or a thousand women who want to sit under my teaching, the point is that the biblical mandate is for woman-to-woman teaching. Yes, men have inquired about the courses I have offered in Women's Studies; yes, I have had men come into gatherings of women where I am the speaker. I do not exercise authority and throw them out. However, I remain very clear about my ministry assignment from God: it is woman-to-woman teaching. There is no question in the minds of my colleagues—whether complementarian or egalitarian—about my position on this matter. Of course, I can be misrepresented, as everyone is at some point; but, although I do not reply to personal attack, I do respond to misrepresentation that could be hurtful to the kingdom of Christ. For example, a reporter once listened to a taped message I delivered and wrote that I did not believe that the Bible had answers to questions concerning what a woman can do in the church.[4]

What I actually said from the platform in the message being reported was that between what is absolutely forbidden and what is clearly mandated is a gray area of questions and choices. However, I simultaneously clearly affirmed that the timeless principles given in Scripture were sufficient for timely applications in the past, present, and future. I contacted the reporter, furnished a copy of the tape, and corrected the misunderstanding; he acknowledged what I had actually said.

What everyone else is doing, whatever ideas the world may have on how a woman should use her gifts, even what the need for her gifts may seem to be—none of these factors is equal to or more important than biblical guidelines. Every woman is responsible for her testimony, which is often formulated by the choices she makes. She is also responsible for using her giftedness within biblical boundaries.

Although women are certainly not bound by the past and what their foremothers have done, neither do they have the option of revising, updating, or adding to Scripture just because they are part of a new generation. Many of the decisions a woman faces over a lifetime are not covered by a specific verse of Scripture, and yet they must make choices and come to decisions concerning their personal faith, beliefs, and the practical outworking of these factors in life. Between what is clearly recorded in Scripture as right, on the one hand, or wrong, on the other, one makes decisions every day. The Bible gives basic principles, but it does not speak in specific detail to thousands of real-life situations and choices that come before a woman. Yet she must preserve whatever God says without questioning his wisdom and without attempting to shift his clear boundaries to suit her personal whims or the modern cultural consensus and without adding her own ideas to what God has already clearly mandated. At the same time, one must be just as careful not to prohibit what the Bible does not prohibit or insist on restrictions based on one's tradition or personal preference rather than accepting the boundaries of Scripture itself (Mark 7:1–13, esp. vv. 6–8). Both the harmony between faith and practice and the mutuality manifesting itself in a uniquely effective reciprocity between men and women are interwoven into God's plan.

In the Garden of Eden, Eve faced a dilemma, a choice to be made. Satan used the serpent to tempt Eve by questioning the word she had received from God concerning the tree of the knowledge of good and evil. God warned Adam that he and Eve should not eat of the fruit of this tree. Satan questioned this word from God: "Did God really say that?" (Gen. 3:1). Eve responded with her own rendition of what God said, "Neither shall you touch it, lest ye die" (Gen. 3:3 KJV). Eve took it on herself to add to what God had actually said. He had forbidden *eating* the fruit; she added her own caveat—don't even touch the fruit. Distorting God's Word (even with good intentions) is a serious matter. One must be cautious in pushing the divine directive beyond what God says. Often, making the directive more restrictive than is indicated in Scripture is a ploy to prepare for disobedience by making the divine commandment appear foolish to consider, severe in its parameters, beyond reason in its expectations, and thus impossible to obey.

A Firm Foundation: The Role of Presuppositions

Every interpreter of Scripture starts with certain presuppositions or assumed principles. A believing woman, too, has and should acknowledge her own presuppositions. Owing to the nature of divine revelation, truth is absolute, not relative, and therefore unchanging. In other words, God's overall plan for women is the same today as it was for women in the first century. I believe that God exists and that he has revealed himself in his written Word and through the illumination of the Holy Spirit. I believe that God's revelation of himself is absolutely reliable and trustworthy. However, I also know that his revelation is *sufficient* for me. It is possible for me not only to know God but also to know what he wants me to do and how he wants me to live.

The world was created by God and is sustained by him. Concerning man and woman as God's highest creation, Scripture says that both are created "in his image" (Gen. 1:26–27). Therefore, I am capable of understanding God's revelation and of choosing how I will respond to him. I am dependent on God, but I have a choice as to how I will relate to him—whether in obedience or disobedience. If I choose obedience, I am forgiven and become his by adoption (Rom. 8:15). But obedience is never optional. If anything, obedience must become an even more serious commitment as one grows from infancy in Christ (the salvation experience through which Jesus becomes one's Savior) to a mature relationship of living one's life according to his will.

The theological foundation for manhood and womanhood is found in the Genesis account of creation. As principles for how the man and the woman are to relate to each other unfold in Scripture, this unique creative design is a frequent point of reference, including what we find in 1 Timothy 2:13. God's design is based neither on women's intellect and giftedness nor on her cultural setting or circumstances. Rather, God designed marriage in the beginning according to his own plan. This design has been woven into the fabric of manhood and womanhood from creation until now and will ever be so—an intricate and colorful tapestry to bring unity and happiness to the man and the woman and to facilitate their usefulness in the kingdom. At the heart of this design is an unchanging principle that *the man and the woman are equal in their essential being but different in their role assignments* (Gen. 1:26–27; 2:15–18). In other words, the divine design calls for the man and the woman to be *equal* to each other, but not for one to be the *same* as the other. To express it yet differently, each is both *equal to* the other and yet *different from* the other.

Some try to pit Scripture against Scripture and claim that equality must mean no distinction. For example, they point to Galatians 3:28 to affirm the equality of the believer "in Christ" as meaning that both the man and the woman are to have the same functions in the church and the same assignments in the kingdom.[5] Even aside from the contextual problem with such a position and the fact that the context in Galatians 3 involves a discussion of salvation, not gender roles in the church, there is a problem of logic. Would any woman really stand before a mirror and claim that she is made exactly as a man? I do not think so. God himself is without form, and thus to be "in his image" must mean something other than human appearance. Nevertheless, both man and woman can affirm an equal status *in Christ*, that is, the road to a personal relationship with Christ is the same regardless of one's family position, ethnic heritage, or gender. That message is clearly not only the truth enunciated in Galatians 3:28 but also the message of the whole of Scripture (see also 1 Pet. 3:7).

Coupled with this unique creative design is a distinctive role assignment. Within the framework of our family, I gladly have a different job description or function than my husband. We do not both do the *same things*, but we *each contribute* to our relationship and ministry in keeping with our respective functions as we live our lives together according to God's plan and offer to the Lord our respective and joint ministries. Amazingly, what seem to be weaknesses in each of us are coupled with the strengths of the other so that in our complementarity there is ultimate usefulness not only in the home but also in the kingdom.

The Tools: Some Guidelines for Interpreting Gender Passages

Followed closely by presuppositions are the *tools* one chooses to use for interpreting Scripture. Hermeneutics is an ever-burgeoning field with new guidelines multiplying faster than rabbits. However, in the process of unlocking the Word of God, a few basic hermeneutical principles have stood the test of time and have been useful to this interpreter in unlocking the treasures of Holy Scripture.

- All verses have to be understood in the light of context—that of the immediate passage, of the broad paragraph discussion, of the book itself, of the Old or the New Testament as a whole, and finally of the Bible in its entirety. The passage is to be interpreted *contextually*.

- Looking at the historical situation out of which the passage comes, weighing the various grammatical structures found within the passage, and using lexicons and dictionaries to determine the range of definitions for the words themselves are *grammatical-historical* aspects that are important to the interpretation of the text.
- Difficult verses must be interpreted in light of verses that are clear in order to maintain *consistency* in interpretation.
- The verses that describe or make application ought to be set in relationship to the *overall teaching of Scripture* and be used to further eludicate the message of the teaching text. Verses that are part of a particular historical *narrative* ought not to be interpreted apart from *didactic* passages.
- Pertinent verses must not be discarded simply because they seem irrelevant or out of step with modern culture. One must yield to the principles found in the whole counsel of God as recorded in Scripture under the illumination that comes from the *Holy Spirit*, who ultimately opens the Word to the diligent and faithful interpreter (John 14; 16; 2 Pet. 1:21). The Holy Spirit, as he interprets a passage in the heart of an individual, will not contradict what he has written in the biblical record.

Some Foundational Observations for Interpreting Gender Passages

As I have personally struggled with the challenge of these issues regarding a woman's place in church order, I have noted some additional guidelines for biblical interpretation that have been helpful to me, especially in considering passages such as 1 Timothy 2.

1. The spiritual privileges in the body of Christ come equally to men and women. In Genesis 1:27, the man and the woman are given joint dominion over the world, which in no way precludes each having unique functions and both fulfilling their respective complementary assignments. In 1 Peter 3:7, both the man and the woman are declared to be "joint heirs" in Christ; and Galatians 3:28 clearly teaches that no distinction exists between men and women with regard to their salvific position "in Christ." At the same time, this does not mean that *equality* with regard to *salvation* equals *sameness* with regard to *role*.
2. Sharing in the same position and privilege on the part of the woman and the man does not amount to uniformity of practice,

nor does it entail the obliteration of all differences between the sexes. The conclusion is evident in Genesis 2:15–25, where God's creative purposes for the man and the woman are clearly laid out within the context of the man's priority in creation and the woman's clearly designated position as the man's "helper." The man's assignment, coming directly from the Creator, is to tend the garden, to guard it, and especially to exercise leadership in obedience to the important spiritual directive concerning the tree of the knowledge of good and evil in the midst of the garden.

Also in these verses, the woman is described as a "helper" to the man, a term carefully chosen by the Creator to unveil his purposes for the woman in her complementarity to the man. In Ephesians 5:21–33, the wife is admonished to submit herself to her husband's leadership even as he submits himself to assuming the responsibility of exercising loving servant leadership in the home, following the example of Christ. First Corinthians 11:1–16 and Colossians 3:18–19, together with 1 Peter 3:1–7, consistently affirm the same teaching as Ephesians 5 concerning how husbands and wives are to relate to each other within the home.

3. The New Testament contains numerous regulations concerning activities of women "in the church." An understanding of this important matter does not rest on narrative passages that are relevant only in an indirect sense, such as the pericope in John 4, where Jesus shares the gospel with the woman at the well. The Samaritan, having been introduced to the Messiah, returned to her village and shared her testimony in the marketplace and neighborhood with anyone who would listen. Nothing in the text indicates that she held evangelistic crusades or addressed the synagogue or even delivered her message in the local amphitheater (John 4:5–30).

Mary Magdalene was instructed by Jesus himself to go to his disciples and share her personal testimony that she had found the tomb empty and had seen Jesus risen from the dead. This witness Mary was faithful to discharge: "I have seen the Lord" (John 20:18). Mary of Bethany took advantage of a unique opportunity to sit at Jesus' feet to learn the deep truths of Scripture (Luke 10:38–42). Both clear examples and straightforward directives related to church order are readily available in Scripture for women who earnestly seek a word from God concerning their roles in the kingdom.

4. Underlying Paul's answers to these difficult questions concerning the role of women in the church is the apostle's own deep concern for the preservation of the Christian home according to the plan God had from the very beginning as to how men and women are

to relate to each other. Although the apostle ascribes to women a different position than that assigned to men, he does not regard a woman's role in the church to be any less important (1 Cor. 14:33–35; 1 Tim. 2:8–15; Titus 2:3–5).

An Important Practical Warning

In 1 Timothy 2:11–12, women are encouraged to learn. The passage is both a challenge to women and a commendation of their efforts. Women are given the opportunity to model one of the highest callings found in the church: They are to listen quietly to the voice of the Lord and then to use what they learn in arenas of influence appropriate for them. The boundaries for exercising their spiritual gifts are clearly given. There are only two biblical restrictions: Women are prohibited from teaching men or ruling over men in the home (Eph. 5:21–31) and in the church (1 Tim. 2:9–12).

In 1 Timothy 2:9–12, Paul begins with a general statement admonishing women to practice quiet receptivity in their hearts as the Word of God is given. God's teaching for a woman is expressed in a consistent and appropriate manner. For example, the call for "quietness" (sometimes translated "silence") is a concrete example and a consistent expression of the overarching principle of submission. In all the household codes (Eph. 5:21–31; Col. 3:18–19; Titus 2:3–5; 1 Pet. 3:1–7), passages penned by Paul and Peter, submission is a unique assignment to the wife in relating to her husband. This admonition underscores Paul's emphasis on a woman's heart attitude as the basis for her relationship to God and to others. *Clearly human learning is not an excuse to overturn the divine order.* The heart desire of a woman ought not to be construed as permission to pass on the fruit of her learning in any forum she chooses. Nevertheless, this caution negates neither the opportunity nor the mandate for women to study and learn and even to teach—within the boundaries given in Scripture.

In addition to the general statement found in 1 Timothy 2:9–11, the apostle continues with very specific boundaries. Paul even used his own personal authority to affirm what the Holy Spirit had inspired him to record as the boundaries to guide women in exercising their gifts and accepting their opportunities for service (1 Tim. 2:12). He also tied these boundaries to theological moorings—the creation order and its concomitant design for the family.

The first prohibition is that women should not teach men (1 Tim. 2:12). No one should be confused by the meaning of this clear directive. These words under the protection of the infallibility of Scripture say precisely what God means, and the Lord does not bring confusion: He means what he says. In the New Testament, the Greek word διδάσκειν, with its derivatives, occurs almost one hundred times, of which only three seem to refer to *individual* instruction, making it clear that the reference here is probably to the teaching of a *group* of men.

The individual instruction of Apollos shared by Priscilla and Aquila does not fall into the category of group instruction. Nor does one find another specific New Testament reference in which a woman instructs a man! It is interesting to note that διδάσκω is used to describe the "teaching" done by Apollos, whereas a different word, ἐκτίθεμαι (lit., "to set forth, explain"), is used in the interchange of Priscilla and her husband, Aquila, with Apollos. The former word—usually both linguistically and theologically—refers to a uniquely faithful proclamation of God's Word that involves authority beyond the mere sharing of general information.

Perhaps this distinction should not be summarily dismissed. The difference in words could affect the meaning of the passage even if only subtly or indirectly. Even if both words are treated as virtually synonymous, nonetheless the text in question awards no official ecclesiastical status to whatever expounding was done by Priscilla and Aquila to Apollos. Although one cannot build a system of theological understanding or base a thorough exegesis on the use of different words or on the nuances of meanings found in those words, one must still consider that the selection of a specific word and the nuances of the meaning of that word are factors to be considered. Nevertheless, no one passage, and certainly no single word, builds a case for ferreting out a theology of what women can or cannot do in the church. The challenge is to fit all the passages together and identify the diverse factors in each so that when jointly understood this word from God is consistent, free from confusion, and adequate to supply principles needed for faith and practice.

The second prohibition, "not to exercise authority over men" (αὐθεντεῖν), makes use of a hapax legomenon (i.e., the word's only appearance in the Greek New Testament). Egalitarians regularly contend that only a woman's *abuse* of authority is here proscribed by Paul. This argument is of doubtful merit, however. Scott Baldwin has documented the lack of evidence for a negative use of this expression prior to Paul.[6] Furthermore, Andreas Köstenberger has conclusively demonstrated that if "teaching" is to be understood as a positive term in 1 Timothy 2:12—a highly plausible assumption—then the syntax of the verse necessitates that "exercising authority" is to be understood positively as well.[7] Therefore, the prohibition is understood as being general in nature—a woman is not to teach men or to exercise authority over men—and not merely a reference to forbidding the oppressive or improper exercise of these functions by a woman.

Also interesting is the limitation for these prohibitions, which actually serves as further protection for women. The setting is obviously within the realm of religious instruction in the life of the church. However, what is prohibited is not couched in a particular office or position but rather in the exercising of specific activities or functions. The apostle does not mention official positions like pastor or elder or bishop/overseer in these verses directed to women, but he chooses to use functional terms, "teaching" and "exercising authority."[8] In the process, Paul never states that women should be banned from the work of the church, nor does he suggest that they be denied any leadership roles in the church. In fact, the apostle commends women who are active in church work (e.g., Phoebe, Rom. 16:1; Priscilla, Rom. 16:3). He notes the importance of women teaching other women and describes the *spiritually mature women* (πρεσβύτιδας), who are to be leaders among women, especially those *new to the faith* (νέας; Titus 2:3–4). He also notes the vital assignment women have to instruct children (as Lois and Eunice were commended for doing in 2 Tim. 1:5; 3:15; see also Prov. 1:8). Paul also records an instance of a woman teaching a man in private conversation (Priscilla and Aquila with Apollos, Acts 18:25–26).[9]

Clearly, then, these prohibitions specifically pertain to the teaching of men by a woman and to a woman's exercising authority over men. The passage is set in a section discussing *church* order and does not specifically address *every* gathered assembly of believers.[10] Nevertheless, one is wise to remember that to live as the scribes and Pharisees, with one's heart and mind sold out only to the *letter* of the law, is insufficient. Rather, one's desire should be to live life within the *spirit* of the law, looking for ways to bend the will to that of the Father, not for how close one can come to acquiescing to personal desires without outright disobedience. The choice ought to be: How far away can one move from avoiding disappointing the Father and marring his clear principles? One's personal testimony must be clear and free from compromise. The most logical application for these prohibitions is to the pastoral office,[11] which in the collective passages describing the pastor combines the activities of both prohibitions. Also under consideration must be either function as it may appear within the work of the church and the kingdom. Timeless principles are not limited to the terminology of official positions.

Paul does not leave future generations to conjecture that these directives recorded in the first century are for that time alone. Rather, he ties his guidelines to theological foundations, arguing for the man's natural and spiritual headship and the woman's role as his helper by appealing to creation itself (1 Tim. 2:13; see Gen. 2:4–24). To do so is to preclude the view of those who hold that male/female roles are simply a direct result of the fall.

Paul argues from creation and then illustrates this argument, albeit negatively, from the fall. Paul appeals to the fall as an event that demonstrates in the starkest terms the dire consequences of a reversal of leadership roles. The apostle moves to the pericope detailing the fall, showing the disastrous effect of the role reversal that occurred in the garden (1 Tim. 2:14; see Gen. 3:1–24). He notes Eve's violation of the divine command and alludes to the ensuing reversal of the divine order prompted by Eve's fateful decision. By her act, Eve took leadership that was not hers, while simultaneously Adam abdicated his divinely assigned spiritual leadership by following the woman in contradiction to the clear directive he personally received from God (Gen. 2:16–17). There is a lesson to be learned: Nothing should be done in the church that undermines God's order in the home.

Some maintain that this passage is not to be taken at face value because of cultural influences on Paul's interpretation of the fall narrative. Paul is accused of clinging to objectionable rabbinical interpretations. These detractors appeal to "the attitude of Jesus" and "the spirit of Christ" in an effort to suggest that some alleged position of Jesus outweighs the apostle's clear teaching. To be sure, much that the New Testament explicitly condemns is approved today as acceptable with the excuse that a particular action expresses "Christian love" or the "spirit of Christ." The problem is resolved by answering the question of how one knows the "spirit of Christ" or anything else about Jesus. Scripture is God's revelation of himself and his Son. One dare not suggest that Christ would be in opposition to what is inspired by the Holy Spirit, whose purpose is to glorify the Son. If Paul's epistle is to be regarded as inspired by the Spirit of God, then its words cannot be in contradistinction to the words or the life of Christ.

Some Unique Lessons for Women

What woman who enjoys study and the opportunity to learn is not especially grateful for the Pauline exhortation encouraging women to "learn"? Paul obviously assumed that women could and would learn. The command implies the apostle's confidence in the intellectual capabilities of women. The focus of the command is without doubt on the manner and method of learning. Silence or listening is prerequisite to the learning process since a submissive spirit is essential for one who genuinely wants to learn. Can anyone learn except in "quietness"? Charlotte von Kirschbaum remarks that women in silence are the "listening church—which the teaching church must constantly revert to being."[12]

Silence or quietness is an attitude of the heart that prepares one for learning. It is also a concrete expression of the principle of submission, through which the pupil opens herself to hear first and then to do. It is a prerequisite to becoming a learner or disciple. In no sense is a woman given carte blanche to go about the task of learning in any way she chooses. Nor should the permission, or even encouragement, to learn be tantamount to a mandate to teach in any setting one might choose. An attitude of quietness and submission prepares the heart for receptiveness to and respectfulness for what is taught.

A careful reading of the text indicates that this prohibition is not limited to wives but that it is addressed to women in general.[13] Paul is addressing women and men as a worshipping community rather than as a family unit. The family is often included within more general terms and without question is the basic component in communities, churches, and civilization itself. However, Paul's words are certainly not a blanket command to eliminate all feminine teaching and leadership. To the contrary, women may instruct men in certain instances, if this function is specified in Scripture. Priscilla, together with her husband, Aquila, instructed Apollos in a personal and private setting (Acts 18:26); Timothy's grandmother Lois and his mother, Eunice, nurtured him and equipped him for ministry (2 Tim. 1:5). Throughout the generations women have exerted influence and shared wisdom for the glory of God through the channels he created for their participation in kingdom ministries—channels that do not contradict the clear boundaries of Scripture.

The prohibitions are qualified and clarified with the clear indication that the assignments within the church should be in harmony with the divinely mandated relationships between husbands and wives in the home. Perhaps Paul was encouraging women to exercise their spiritual gifts in the church, while being careful not to violate the headship of their respective husbands in the home. A wife and mother should be encouraged to know that her home is important to the Father. Without doubt God laid upon men and husbands the primary responsibility for Christlike, servant leadership in the church and in the home. His reasons are not necessarily deemed clear enough or palatable enough to satisfy modern minds, but one can certainly see the divine use of the metaphor of the family and familial relationships woven throughout the Scripture as a tool for God's revelation of himself.

One must not assume that any restriction, even if it does exclude women from certain aspects of ecclesiastical leadership on the basis of gender, is a new or unusual way for God to work. No one appointed himself to the priesthood; in fact, the priests came from a particular lineage (Exod. 28:43–29:9; Lev. 8:1–36). The priests were limited to Aaron and his descendants. Yet even those who qualified as descendants of Aaron could not serve if they did not meet other criteria. For example, among men in the Old Testament, there were specific requirements for those entering the priesthood (Lev. 10:8–11; 21:1–15). Not every man in the priestly tribe could serve as a priest. Those with certain physical defects were forbidden to serve (Lev. 21:5, 16–21). God has sovereignly reserved the right to set the general boundaries for leadership in the church. The criteria he uses, for whatever reasons, are not limited to or based on a person's ability or on her giftedness to perform a given service.

God chose to reveal himself primarily through masculine imagery. Therefore, within the framework of religious instruction and the structure of church order, doctrinal teaching, that is, the shaping of the will and the doctrinal oversight and care of believers (Luke 22:26; 2 Cor. 10:8; 1 Pet. 5:3) were assignments for men. The divinely imputed holiness of the priests enabled them to handle the holy or set-apart articles contained in the Lord's sanctuary. Most important, neither the priests themselves nor the people they served determined the criteria and boundaries by which their selection and fulfillment of duties were governed. They did not set themselves apart; rather, they were set apart for their task by God's representative.

Again, the general concept is that nothing should be done in the *church* that would undermine God's order for the behavior of a wife toward her husband in the *home*. J. I. Packer described the man-woman relationship as "intrinsically nonreversible."[14] One could easily see how a wife who teaches in the church could become so proud and autocratic that she would lose sight of her proper place in submission to her husband in the home. In this case, she would be destroying the object lesson ordained of God to reveal himself and his relationship to his creation through the metaphor of marriage. Seldom would a woman who slips into this trap be aware of her own failing. God does not leave matters of such importance to human judgment. He lays out the guidelines in such a way as to keep these important choices within his domain.

In moving away from the church and home, questions arise concerning how these directives might affect women in civic and community life. To answer these questions, one must move from what is explicitly clear, that is, the apostolic discussion of church order, a topic addressed throughout the New Testament (especially the Epistles) and grounded in creation, to what one must infer without an explicit word from Scripture. These directives may become more subjective and even ambiguous. For a woman genuinely committed to stand under Scripture, the spirit of the explicit commands can and does serve as a backdrop to all decisions that must be made in such cases where Scripture does not provide express guidelines. Believers can be grateful that God does not leave his children bewildered in a sea of confusion but has put within the grasp of everyone the ability to understand a sure and clear word from him.

The Virtue of Modesty

Modesty is not a virtue reserved for the environs of the church or for the character of those who are "church" people. However, it is a quality uniquely associated with women, even a God-given part of a woman's feminine nature. For that reason one is not surprised to find the subject at the heart of two passages directed to women—1 Timothy 2:9–15 and 1 Peter 3:1–7. Again, one can be encouraged by the apostle's reminder of an important lesson for women.

Modesty is creeping back into the arena of life even in the twenty-first-century world through books like *A Return to Modesty* by Wendy Shalit or *Secret Keeper: The Delicate Power of Modesty* by Dannah Gresch. One can hope that modesty never really left the conscience of the church, and there is a trail of popular volumes to show its presence—*Passion and Purity* by Elisabeth Elliot or *Christian Modesty* by Jeff Pollard.[15] Nevertheless, the age has been permeated with immodesty in the public sector through movies graced by scantily clad women, through television with explicit sexual encounters portrayed in the living rooms of American homes, and in the local bookstores through romantic novels that would make even the most cavalier reader blush. The decadence of modern society is on view for the entire world to see. How grateful believing women ought to be that God affirms the beauty of this virtue so ingrained in femininity by addressing the matter clearly in Scripture.

Women are enjoined to clothe themselves with modesty as a way of life—in all their interactions with others. First, women who are believers represent the Lord as his daughters. Second, godly women should not want to tempt men to impure thoughts. Finally, women who bear the name of Christ also should remember their personal influence on other women, who can observe the chaste behavior of spiritually mature women and thus be called to personal purity.

Modesty creates a mystique that gives a woman added charm and wholesome appeal. And it also endears her to the Father in a wonderful way. Modesty moves the emphasis to what is within—what Peter describes as the "gentle and quiet spirit"—and enhances a woman's testimony, while framing that testimony in a God-honoring way.

At the same time, Paul says nothing to discourage women from enhancing their own attractiveness. Of interest to women may be the fact that the words κόσμιος (translated "modest") and κοσμέω (translated "adorn") have both found their way into the English word "cosmetics."[16] The primary issue clearly seems to be *attitude* rather than *appearance*. What an exciting affirmation! Any woman will have limitations associated with her outer appearance. Age, physical deterioration, suffering and pain, even economics, can affect the outer frame and hamper all a woman wants to do on the outside. But God's focus on the inside turns a woman's attention to a task she can pursue with his help. It would be incorrect to assume that this text prohibits a woman from fixing her hair a certain way or wearing jewelry, since to do so would also suggest that she ought to do away with clothing as well. Rather, the underlying principle seems to be that beauty of the inner self and the development of an attitude of godliness, accompanied by its outward manifestation of good works, should be the focus for every woman, rather than ostentatious hair, flashy jewelry, or inappropriate garments.[17] Apparently, a woman's demeanor in church is expected to be different from a man's. She is marked by "a quiet spirit," which is consistent with the "helper" motif (Gen. 2:18, 20) and with the mandate for her to be submissive to the headship of her husband (1 Cor. 11:1–16).

The Ministries of Women

Another special lesson for women in this text is the necessity of recognizing what is entailed in a faith relationship, that is, trusting the promises of God rather than embracing the agendas of the age. On the one hand, Paul clearly states his own commitment to role distinctions (1 Cor. 11:3–10; 1 Tim. 2:12). At the same time, the apostle indicates that he does not consider women to be inferior or less vital to the kingdom (1 Cor. 11:11–12; 1 Pet. 3:1–7). To suggest that a woman may not teach anyone under any circumstances exceeds what is taught in Scripture. First Corinthians 11 clearly affirms that a woman is allowed to pray and prophesy in church. To be sure, Paul placed restrictions on the didactic ministry of women in the church. Nevertheless, the restriction pertains to women teaching *men* or exercising authority over *men*. The directive should not be extended beyond this boundary except as the "spirit" of the passage might dictate on an individual basis.

Women may indeed pray and prophesy in the church, although they are not *commanded* to do so. But if they do pray or prophesy, they are admonished to do so with an attitude of submission to the male leadership of the church, which for women in the Corinthian culture may have been illustrated by the wearing of a head covering (1 Cor. 11:3–15). This passage is especially helpful in distinguishing between those *timeless principles*, such as headship and submission, which are linked to *theological foundations*, and the *timely manifestations* of these principles in particular cultural contexts. These timely manifestations may be considered as one would view any outer adornment and thus appropriated according to the contemporary setting. In other words, reasoned principles manifest themselves in relevant ways. The principles not only transcend the modern context; they also supersede cultural practices.

Only in the *contextualization* of these principles is it appropriate to be influenced by a particular cultural response and the corresponding contemporary application.

Another lesson from 1 Timothy for women is that differences between men and women are to be both accepted and appreciated. The differences embedded in the creation order are not to be summarily abolished or rudely ignored; rather, they are inextricably linked to God's plan for redemption. The apostle Paul never considered equality of roles and distinctions within roles as antithetical or contradictory ideas. To the contrary, he presents both concepts with amazing balance and as complementing each other. This understanding preserves male leadership not only in the home but also in the house of worship.

G. K. Chesterton has much wisdom on the "woman question." He suggested that women display extraordinary skill in keeping their families running smoothly and then posed the question: What job could be more important or rewarding? He argues that a woman who is employed outside the home becomes independent of her own husband and dependent on her employer, a shift that inevitably takes a toll on home life. While not doubting that women could achieve many things out in the world, Chesterton proposed that women ought to be at their happiest and best in the home, a conclusion he made based on his own observations of his mother and of his wife.[18]

Preaching to and ruling over men are not the only frontline ministries in the kingdom. Women are called just as men are and sometimes to the same tasks, but these tasks are often set within different venues. The boundaries are not determined by giftedness or even opportunity but by divine assignment. Women, as men, are equally called, but as women they are not necessarily assigned the same tasks as men. In 1 Timothy, the boundaries happen to be based on gender. Women must also be warned that success in ministry is not the divine criterion for what they can or should do in the kingdom. One may even be recognized by others as effective in ministry when she is violating biblical boundaries, but the end does not justify the means when a person stands before the Creator God.

First and foremost, the Holy Spirit who calls the believer to a particular task is also the Holy Spirit who inspired Scripture. Because he is God with the same attributes and character as God the Father and God the Son, he will not be inconsistent or contradictory. There is no greater challenge than putting yourself at the disposal of the God of the universe and allowing him to place you in his design. Women, then, must embrace the authority structures placed in their lives by God. These lines of authority are good, wise, and worthy reflections of God himself. Women are uniquely blessed to be able to honor God with emulating both sides of the authority-submission relationship, which is modeled within the Godhead. Jesus humbled himself and became obedient or submissive to the Father; the Father then expressed his loving approval by exalting the Son in heaven. Jesus is also the Lord and head of the church, which becomes occasion for the church to submit to her Lord's authority and leadership.

Contextualizing the Passage

One cannot apply 1 Timothy 2:9–15 without a careful review of one's personal presuppositions, especially with regard to the role of Scripture. Many want to move the interpretation into an existential arena with the influence of culture as the primary yardstick for interpretation. Yet culture must not be allowed to supplant the immutable Word of God. If allowed to stand, this premise illegitimately dethrones Scripture from its rightful place as the Word of God. In such a scenario, the cultural setting becomes more important and more binding than the principles from the text that are tied to its interpretation. Any accommodation of Scripture to human preference or cultural custom lifts the person who engages in such a practice above his or her Creator. The recipients of the mandate become more important than the One who bestows the guidelines. The relevance of application overwhelms the reliability of the text. No—what God says must be preserved and honored without question.

Is the Issue Salvation of Soul or Reality of Role?

The role of motherhood has been distorted and misconstrued, especially since the onslaught of feminism. The Bible is clear that bearing a child and nurturing the life of that living gift from God is a unique and cherished honor bestowed by the Creator. By divine design, the responsibilities of motherhood call for a woman to link hands with the heavenly Father to mold and fashion a life. In no way can one extricate the impact of a woman's God-designed nature from the assignments and directives she is given in Scripture.

First Timothy 2:15 is a difficult verse to understand, but it is also an affirming verse for biblical womanhood. The reference to childbearing is appropriately presented because maternity represents one of the most vital aspects of femininity. Women are uniquely designed to be mothers and nurturers. Catherine Kroeger, although a prominent proponent of egalitarianism, expresses the importance of motherhood:

> Especially we hail those engaged in the tremendously important task of childbearing and childrearing. Above all, it is they who teach the next

generation and win the little ones to Christ. Verse 15, for all its difficulties, affirms the significance of mothers in God's scheme. They are the primary evangelists in the Christian church, and from their homes will come the replacements for the leaders of this generation.[19]

Motherhood was a role clearly understood as right and proper for women in Paul's day, and one would hope that such would be true even today. Children are undoubtedly a blessing and a reward and not a burden or an obstacle.

"Childbearing" becomes a synecdoche (a figure of speech citing a part as standing for the whole) encompassing a woman's role related to her familial and domestic responsibilities, and maternity most certainly is a crucial part of the feminine nature that helps a woman accomplish her God-given role. Maternity is neither limited to conceiving and bearing a child nor to childrearing, but rather is a nurturing sensitivity that God can use in a variety of ways in the whole scope of every woman's life and ministry. Bearing children is the most notable example of the maternity that is an integral part of the feminine nature. It becomes a generalizing example that is taken from, and is representative of, the experience of most women. Any woman can understand that, assuming she has accepted God's gift of salvation by faith alone, she works out that faith by fulfilling the divine purpose for her life—a purpose well represented by her role as wife and mother and one that is representative of her divine assignment. With her salvation secure, out of gratitude of heart she wants to offer back her own committed obedience and service.

No woman who has chosen to marry should violate her God-given role as wife and mother in order to move on and pursue other callings, even when those pursuits might seem to be more worthy of her time and energies. The apostle simply affirms the function of giving birth and a woman's associated responsibilities as the divinely bestowed role that sets women apart from men. Childbearing is not limited to a particular culture but rather is permanent and transcultural, making this awesome privilege for the woman yet another indication that manhood and womanhood—with the God-ordained differences in each nature—are rooted in creation. Childbearing is typical of the feminine role and, in fact, is the most exclusive aspect of that role.[20]

Conclusion

First Timothy 2:9–15 expresses a prohibition for women that must not be ignored as being merely cultural because divine order in the home was not established to conform to the cultural tradition of a particular people or to a specific era of history. Rather, the passage is predicated on God's timeless design for male-female relationships. God established the home in the beginning as part of the creation order—before a well-established culture existed or history had been recorded. However, these principles are also imbedded in church order as laid out by the apostle Paul in the Pastoral Epistles.

The prohibition in these verses cannot be restricted only to a wife relating to her husband since the greater context does not confirm such a narrow limitation. Rather, God's design for the man and the woman corresponds to their respective natures assigned to each by divine fiat in the order of creation.

The reasons for the prohibition are clear in the text: (1) the order of creation—the man was formed first (1 Tim. 2:13); (2) the purpose in creation—the man was assigned the task of providing, protecting, and leading, and the woman was created to be a helper suitable to assist the man in his vast responsibilities in dominion (1 Tim. 2:13; see also Gen. 2:15–24); (3) the marring of creation when the woman usurped the man's responsibility in leadership, ignoring the divine directive that must have come to her through her husband, and then making a decision on her own to eat the fruit, while at the same time the man listened to her and evidently followed her leadership, eating of the fruit as well (1 Tim. 2:14; see also Gen. 3:6).

Both the man and the woman decided to go their own way rather than God's. However, it was Adam who was ultimately held accountable for their disobedience, because he was the one who had received the prohibition concerning eating the fruit directly from God himself (Gen. 2:15–17; see also 1 Tim. 2:14). The text makes no mention of the woman's presence at the time God gave Adam the prohibition concerning the tree in the midst of the garden (Gen. 2:17). In 1 Timothy, when Paul refers to the testing of the woman in that same garden, he notes that she was deceived by the serpent, while mentioning also that Adam was not deceived (1 Tim. 2:14; see also 1 Cor. 15:22). There obviously are connecting links between the passage in 1 Timothy and the Genesis account of creation.

Scripture affirms that women with varied positions of service and influence, including functions of leadership and teaching, fulfilled their assignments in the early church with modesty and orderliness, and did not teach or exercise authority over men.[21] In fact, to argue that women in our day should serve in the same roles as men is one thing; to read that modern "ideal" back into the biblical text and records of early church history, both of which speak for themselves, is quite another.

From the outset of God's creative activity, he moved toward establishing his first and primary institution—one man and one woman, who choose to link their lives together as one to engage in spiritual ministry. The home and the familial relationships have been designed for the purpose of revealing God's nature. His perfect love, which is beautifully portrayed in the Father; his amazing sacrifice, which is lived out in the Son and his atonement on the cross; and his masterful teaching of his children about himself through the Holy Spirit—all are at the heart of that revelation.

Because the biblical directives recorded by the apostle Paul are founded on unchanging historical facts with specific theological significance (1 Tim. 2:13–14), they are authoritative for all times and cultures. The divinely instituted order recorded by the apostle is to be respected in the church. The role of the woman in the church is clearly in harmony with God's divine order for the home—the wife's submission to, and honor of, the husband. Whether in teaching biblical truth (as the spiritually mature women are admonished to do in Titus 2:3–5, especially giving instructions on the character traits of a godly woman, on relationships within the home, and on the importance of working at tasks within the home), extending Christian hospitality (as New Testament women were faithful to do, 1 Tim. 5:10), or engaging in personal ministries to individuals (as Priscilla with her husband, Aquila, did for Apollos, Acts 18:26), New Testament women have given to women in succeeding generations a pattern for working under the clear authority of God's revealed will. That pattern will remain the same until the Lord comes.

Paul does not provide a comprehensive discussion of the teaching role of women in one single passage. While his epistles address a variety of issues, the full extent of every situation may not be clearly spelled out in a particular passage. This lack of thorough discussion of a certain theological issue may impose certain limitations on the interpreter and even keep one from completely understanding a particular passage or doctrine. A believer must be content with such limited knowledge. Nevertheless, the personal conviction of a God-fearing woman must surely be that timeless principles are available to equip her to make timely applications in the decisions of her life and in what she does for the kingdom of Christ. To claim from the Holy Spirit a word of knowledge or a calling, however high and holy, while setting aside the teaching of Scripture and engaging in a task prohibited by Scripture but acceptable in modern culture is to involve the divine triunity in contradiction and to transfer divine authority into human hands.

My prayer is that I, as a woman, will always work within the clear authority of God's written Word and accordingly follow as perfectly as my own human frailty allows me the example of the living Word. The revision of this excellent resource volume has no need for a woman's touch in its superb exegesis and extensive historical discussions, but perhaps

I have added what no man can pen—the testimony of a woman who is equipped professionally in theological training to deal with the text, who is established personally in relationships to husband and children and grandchildren, and yet who spiritually has tried and found worthy of obedience the directives given to me in the home and the church. I will never have perfect obedience to God any more than I will have perfect submission to my husband. I will make wrong choices, and the kingdom of Christ may suffer from my mistakes. But I can say that these will be mistakes of the head—a lack of understanding of what Scripture says—and not of the heart—a lack of desire to be obedient to God's Word. My heart is full; my joy is overflowing; I have gained and not lost the freedom my spirit craves as I willingly stand under Scripture, accepting and assuming the divine mandates in my own home and in the Lord's church. God grant that I will never focus on my own opportunities while losing sight of the responsibilities before me to become through my life and testimony a Christ-honoring and formative influence on the generations to come, especially on my own children and grandchildren.

Jesus, as the Son of God and one with the Father—my Lord as well as my Savior—humbled himself and became obedient even to death on the cross. He seemed to lose all; yet because of his obedience, he was exalted above all. As a woman, I, too, have the opportunity to humble myself in obedience to God through my voluntary submission to my husband and to any authority God has placed over me. In doing so, I will not nor should I be personally exalted; but I will be lifting up him whose Word I honor.

Most of all, I am bound by the teachings in his Holy Word, the Bible. I then want to submit, to humble myself, to relinquish my rights voluntarily, to yield to the principles found in his Word. I want no confusion or divisiveness in his church. I may seem to be oppressed, but in reality I am freed—I am under his protection. My attitude must be to maintain a servant's heart. My goal is to be obedient to the biblical mandate. My reward will come from him: "A woman who fears the Lord, she shall be praised" (Prov. 31:31).[22]

EPILOGUE

The controversy over the role of women in the church has gripped virtually every denomination in Christendom. The Roman Catholic Church resists the ordination of women, at least in part if not primarily because of church tradition. Notwithstanding the recent watershed decision to ordain women in the Anglican Church, there, too, a significant number oppose such a practice, be it on scriptural grounds (evangelicals) or for traditional reasons (High Church Anglicans). This book could easily be assessed by some as a defense of the church's traditional position on the issue and an effort to resist the new winds of freedom that are blowing in the churches. The contributors to this volume, as evangelicals, do not grant ultimate authority to tradition, for practices and beliefs contrary to the Scriptures can infiltrate the church. We are not committed to defending the historic view on women in the church merely because it is the venerable tradition of the church.

Of course, long-held traditions in the church should not be jettisoned casually or without careful reflection, for we are all liable to the chronological snobbery of the modern age and apt to dismiss the contribution of thoughtful Christians who have preceded us. Indeed, the virtually universal agreement on the role of women in the church by Christian believers from a variety of communions in the nineteen centuries of the Christian era constitutes presumptive evidence against the progressive view. Nonetheless, Scripture functions as our sole authority only if we are willing to reexamine every cherished doctrine and practice. New circumstances may provoke us to see that we have defended a certain view of women in the church because of our prejudices and cultural encumbrances. Thus, we have attempted to probe in this book whether the central biblical text that forbids women from teaching or ruling men,

1 Timothy 2:11–15, actually justifies role distinctions between men and women in the church.

The aim of this book is to interpret carefully and rigorously, using all the available scholarly resources, the meaning of 1 Timothy 2:9–15. Further, the book does not conclude merely by setting forth the exegesis of the text in question. We proceed to probe the text in terms of its hermeneutical implications and its application in today's world. In some ways our book represents, it is hoped, a model of how to proceed in interpreting a text in its historical and linguistic context and then discerning its implications for the contemporary church.

At this juncture it might prove helpful to summarize the book. S. M. Baugh explores the social world that must inform any rigorous exegesis of 1 Timothy—the world of first-century Ephesus. He demonstrates that the "feminist Ephesus" is a figment of the modern imagination. The role of women in Ephesian society was not vastly different from that in other Greek cities of that period. That role has both significant points of continuity and some discontinuities with the role of women in modern societies. Too often scholars have interpreted the text on the basis of a reconstructed situation that cannot be vindicated by sober historical evidence. Indeed, some of the alleged reconstructions have been wildly speculative.

Scott Baldwin then conducts an exhaustive analysis of the term αὐθεν-τέω, demonstrating that the word means "to have or exercise authority" in 1 Timothy 2:12. Often scholars have failed to distinguish between the nominal and verbal form in deciphering the meaning of αὐθεντεῖν. Baldwin remedies that deficiency, thereby establishing his own conclusions on a firmer foundation than some previous studies. Incidentally, the definition suggested by Baldwin fits with the interpretation proposed throughout the centuries, showing that his conclusion cannot be dismissed as novelty for novelty's sake.

Andreas Köstenberger examines the syntactical structure of 1 Timothy 2:12 in both biblical and extrabiblical writings. This fresh and sophisticated analysis of the structure reveals that teaching and exercising authority are a conceptual pair, so that both terms are to be interpreted positively or negatively. Köstenberger rightly argues there is no evidence that teaching and exercising authority are negative concepts in 1 Timothy 2:12 (cf. 1 Tim. 4:11; 6:2; 2 Tim. 2:2). When teaching bears a negative meaning, this is clear from context (Titus 1:11) or Paul uses the term ἑτεροδιδασκαλέω (1 Tim. 1:3; 6:3). The same phenomenon is evident with the use of the noun διδασκαλία, which is used fifteen times in the Pastoral Epistles, and in only one of these instances is the term used negatively.[1] What is also remarkable is that since its publication ten years ago, the Köstenberger study has not been seriously challenged. Indeed, some egalitarians have even endorsed his analysis of the structure, without, of course, retreating from their egalitarian views overall. Given the constant controversy that attends 1 Timothy 2 and the incessant study of the text, the staying power of Köstenberger's analysis indicates that he rightly interprets the data.

Thomas Schreiner, drawing on the research of the first three chapters, conducts an intensive exegesis of 1 Timothy 2:9–15. Schreiner interacts extensively with recent scholarship on the passage, and he demonstrates that the prohibition in 1 Timothy 2:12 is not based on an ephemeral or culturally conditioned situation. Rather, the prohibition is grounded in the created order, and hence represents God's pattern for the church in all times and all places. Egalitarian attempts to explicate the text are shown to be exegetically unsatisfying and are to be rejected because they conform to modern cultural aspirations instead of faithfully conveying the Pauline meaning.

The meaning of 1 Timothy 2:9–15 having been established, Robert Yarbrough considers further the hermeneutical significance of the text for today. He reminds us that texts are not interpreted in a sociocultural vacuum. The "new view" of 1 Timothy 2 emerged in a Western context where Enlightenment views of freedom and feminism were trumpeted. Modern-day egalitarians often disparage the mistreatment of women in previous eras, and they are partially right, for the sins of men against women have contributed to the rise of feminism. On the other hand, Yarbrough demonstrates that egalitarians have failed to see the massive social consequences engendered by an Enlightenment view of freedom. Egalitarians have overreacted to the sins of the past and have inadvertently contributed to the cultural disarray so evident today. Scholars like Stendahl and Bruce set Galatians 3:28 over against 1 Timothy 2:12, but in doing so they reveal their own philosophical and cultural commitments instead of recognizing what interpreters all throughout history had recognized previously, namely, that the two texts do not contradict each other. A contradiction exists only if one has accepted the egalitarian agenda. Finally, many attempt to diminish the Pauline admonition regarding women by appealing to slavery as a parallel. Yarbrough demonstrates persuasively that the comparison is not apt. Slavery is not rooted in the created order, and it is never mandated by God as a necessary or good element of the social order. Indeed, Paul urged slaves to acquire their freedom if possible (1 Cor. 7:21). There is no corresponding word from Paul that women should express their freedom in serving as pastors if possible.

Dorothy Patterson concludes the book by reflecting on the role of a woman today. How does a woman live out the biblical truth as it has been set forth in this book? Patterson appropriately considers the question from an autobiographical standpoint, though her own experience does not function as the Archimedean point for what is permissible for women, for it is evident throughout her essay that Patterson's desire is to conform to biblical admonitions regarding men and women. Patterson does not attempt to write up a "Mishnah" in which she passes judgment on every possible situation that arises in working out the biblical teaching today. She makes it clear, however, that the biblical word is her norm. First Timothy 2:12 prohibits women from serving as pastors, but Patterson maintains it also addresses the question of whether women should function as teachers of men more generally. Her conclusion is that it is wrong, for example, for a woman to regularly teach the Scriptures to both men and women and to claim that she does not violate biblical authority since she does so with the blessing of her pastors.

Many other practical questions could be considered. What is required is that we are faithful to the biblical mandate found in 1 Timothy 2:12. At the very least this prohibits women from serving as pastors or elders and as those who preach the word of God. Some will object to this book by claiming that it deals only with a "problem passage" or that it does not consider all the texts on women in ministry. It is important, of course, to include all the biblical texts in constructing our view of women in ministry. We would argue that a consideration of all the texts does not call into question the conclusions set forth here but demonstrates even further the credibility of the case advanced here.[2] Moreover, the notion that 1 Timothy 2:9–15 is a problem text is a curious way of speaking of this passage. Doubtless the text has its difficulties, but those who speak this way about the text have often already determined that Galatians 3:28 is the clear text and that nothing can contradict their alleged understanding of Galatians 3:28. Hence, 1 Timothy 2:9–15 may be eliminated from consideration from the outset. We are arguing in this work that the main teaching of 1 Timothy 2:9–15 is clear and that the church of Jesus Christ will be holier and healthier if we obey what the Scripture says.

Those who maintain that the Scriptures affirm functional gender distinctions in church and home are often considered to be male chauvinists, or, if they are women (such as Mary Kassian and Susan Foh and many women in churches throughout the world), betrayers of the feminist cause. They appear to some as "doctrinaire reductionists" who resist the swift progress of a gender-blind, discrimination-free society. But is the church to take its cue from the world and succumb to its pressure? In a climate of religious freedom, all Christians should resist the effort on the part of the larger society to squeeze the church into its mold. To contend that the Scriptures prohibit women from functioning in roles of ultimate responsibility and authority over Christ's church does not amount to devaluing women's contributions in the church or to relegating them to roles of insignificance, as is often alleged. While there is room for disagreement and constructive dialogue—hence this book—each person ultimately stands before God himself, with the responsibility to search the Scriptures with an open mind and a heart ready for obedience. If such obedience involves a certain amount of suffering and being misunderstood, this, after all, has always been part of the calling of followers of Christ, and we live in a time where being conservative may be the most radical thing of all.

NOTES

Chapter 1: A Foreign World

1. Still the best general survey of ancient Asia Minor is David Magie, *RRAM*. General overviews of Ephesus include D. Knibbe, "Ephesos: Historisch-epigraphischer Teil," PWSup 12:248–97; and D. Knibbe and W. Alzinger, "Ephesos vom Beginn der römischen Herrschaft in Kleinasien bis zum Ende der Principatszeit," in *ANRW*, 2.7.2:748–830. More popular are D. Knibbe and B. Iplikçioglu, *Ephesos im Spiegel seiner Inschriften* (Vienna: Schindler, 1984); and W. Elliger, *Ephesos: Geschichte einer antiken Weltstadt* (Stuttgart: Kohlhammer, 1985). For bibliography, see Richard E. Oster, *A Bibliography of Ancient Ephesus*, ATLA Bibliography Series 19 (Metuchen, NJ: Scarecrow, 1987). More recent resources are Traute Wohlers-Scharf, *Die Forschungsgeschichte von Ephesos*, 2nd ed., Europäische Hochschulschriften 38, vol. 54 (Frankfurt am Main: Lang, 1996); Helmut Koester, ed., *Ephesos: Metropolis of Asia* (Valley Forge, PA: Trinity, 1995); Werner Thiessen, *Christen in Ephesus*, Texte und Arbeiten zum neutestamentlichen Zeitalter 12 (Tübingen: Francke, 1995); and Paul Trebilco, "Asia," in *The Book of Acts in Its Graeco-Roman Setting*, ed. David W. J. Gill and Conrad Gempf, The Book of Acts in Its First Century Setting 2 (Grand Rapids: Eerdmans; Carlisle, Eng.: Paternoster, 1994), 291–362.

Unless otherwise noted, all translations appearing in this chapter, including those of Scripture, are my own, except for ancient authors included in the Loeb Classical Library.

2. Paul R. Trebilco, *Jewish Communities in Asia Minor* (Cambridge: Cambridge University Press, 1991), 104–26, with quote from 126.

3. The notion of "leadership" in ancient religions and societies needs more careful definition. For instance, a woman who was granted public honors for certain benefactions or who served as a priestess may suggest to a modern reader that women were making authoritative decisions that shaped institutions in the political, social, or religious realm analogous with a modern politician, judge, pastor, elder, or bishop. But this is not necessarily the case. Such ancient institutions were usually shaped through a long historical process; for instance, Plutarch's *Roman and Greek Questions* shows how traditions whose origins and meaning were long lost had shaped their fundamental institutions and customs (*Mor.* 263D–304F).

4. Yet it is obvious that twenty-eight women in eight cities over a three-century span averages to only about one woman per city every one hundred years.

181

5. First- to early-second-century Ephesian *prytaneis* include men like Apollonius Passalas (*IvE* 902), along with his son Alexander Passalas (*IvE* 257), Tib. Claudius Aristio (*IvE* 425), T. Flavius Perigenes (*IvE* 1270), P. Vedius Antoninus (*IvE* 728), and T. Flavius Aristobulus (*IvE* 1384), to name just a few. The handful of female Ephesian *prytaneis* are discussed below.

6. One should also keep in mind the transforming socioreligious influence of Christianity in Ephesus during these later centuries.

7. Marcus Barth, *Ephesians 4–6*, Anchor Bible (Garden City, NY: Doubleday, 1974), 661.

8. "For a man to be ruled by a woman is the very height of hubris" (Democritus).

9. Catherine Clark Kroeger, "1 Timothy 2:12—A Classicist's View," in *Women, Authority and the Bible*, ed. A. Mickelsen (Downers Grove, IL: InterVarsity, 1986), 227–28; cf. Edith Specht, "Kulttradition einer weiblichen Gottheit: Beispiel Ephesos," in *Maria, Abbild oder Vorbild?* ed. H. Röckelein et al. (Tübingen: Edition Diskord, 1990), 41.

10. Marcus Barth, "Traditions in Ephesians," *NTS* 30 (1984): 16.

11. "Matriarchy" is used with various meanings in Richard Clark Kroeger and Catherine Clark Kroeger, *I Suffer Not a Woman: Rethinking 1 Timothy 2:11–15 in Light of Ancient Evidence* (Grand Rapids: Baker, 1992).

12. Hubert Martin, "Artemis," *ABD*, 1:464; cf. W. K. C. Guthrie, *The Greeks and Their Gods* (Boston: Beacon, 1950), 101.

13. Camden M. Cobern, *New Archeological Discoveries*, 2nd ed. (New York: Funk & Wagnalls, 1917), 465; Sharon Hodgin Gritz, *Paul, Women Teachers, and the Mother Goddess at Ephesus: A Study of 1 Timothy 2:9–15 in Light of the Religious and Cultural Milieu of the First Century* (Lanham, MD: University Press of America, 1991), 39–40, 116; and Kroeger and Kroeger, *I Suffer Not a Woman*, 93, 196.

14. Kroeger and Kroeger, *I Suffer Not a Woman*, 93. Cf. John W. Cooper, *A Cause for Division? Women in Office and the Unity of the Church* (Grand Rapids: Calvin Theological Seminary, 1991), 50.

15. On the issue of sacred prostitution, see my "Cult Prostitution in New Testament Ephesus: A Reappraisal," *JETS* 42, no. 3 (1999): 443–60.

16. For a critique of *I Suffer Not a Woman* along these lines, see Baugh, "The Apostle among the Amazons," *WTJ* 56 (1994): 153–71.

17. For instance, see R. A. Kearsley, "Women in Public Life in the Roman East: Iunia Theodora, Claudia Metrodora and Phoebe, Benefactress of Paul," *TynBul* 50, no. 2 (1999): 189–211. Note especially Kearsley's qualification that Corinth (and other Hellenic cities in my opinion) were dominated by a "high-ranking, predominantly male world of government and commerce" (197). Nevertheless, Kearsley's thesis in this essay that women like Phoebe could well have served the ancient church as important benefactresses (and deaconesses) is well established.

18. Technical overviews are D. Knibbe, "Ephesos: Historisch-epigraphischer Teil," and D. Knibbe and W. Alzinger, "Ephesos vom Beginn der römischen Herrschaft in Kleinasien bis zum Ende der Principatszeit," in *ANRW*, 2.7.2:748–830. More popular are D. Knibbe and B. İplikçioglu, *Ephesos im Spiegel seiner Inschriften;* and W. Elliger, *Ephesos: Geschichte einer antiken Weltstadt.* For a full bibliography, see Richard E. Oster, *Bibliography of Ancient Ephesus;* cf. G. H. R. Horsley, "The Inscriptions of Ephesus and the New Testament," *Novum Testamentum* 34 (1992): 105–68.

19. This was possibly Paul's route when "he passed through the upper regions and arrived at Ephesus" (Acts 19:1); see Stephen Mitchell, *Anatolia* (Oxford: Clarendon, 1993), maps 3 and 7. But compare David French, "Acts and the Roman Roads of Asia Minor," in *The Book of Acts in Its Graeco-Roman Setting*, ed. David W. J. Gill and Conrad Gempf,

The Book of Acts in Its First Century Setting 2 (Grand Rapids: Eerdmans; Carlisle, Eng.: Paternoster, 1994), 55–57.

20. Androclus and his boar were also minted on Ephesian coins; see Barclay V. Head, *Historia Numorum: A Manual of Greek Numismatics*, 2nd ed. (Oxford: Clarendon, 1911; repr., Chicago: Argonaut, 1967), 577.

21. Theodor Mommsen, *The Provinces of the Roman Empire*, 2 vols. (1909; repr., Chicago: Ares, 1974), 1:354.

22. William Ramsay's work has sometimes been used to impute an indigenous Anatolian matriarchal influence on Ephesus. The idea of matriarchy in Asia Minor finds little support among historians today, and Ramsay himself explicitly says that matriarchy made little headway in the Hellenic cities; see his *Cities and Bishoprics of Phrygia* (Oxford: Clarendon, 1895), 94–96; cf. Edwin Yamauchi, "Ramsay's Views on Archaeology in Asia Minor Reviewed," in *The New Testament Student and His Field*, ed. J. Skilton, New Testament Student 5 (Phillipsburg, NJ: Presbyterian & Reformed, 1982), 27–40. On the related issue of matrilinearity, see Baugh, "Apostle among the Amazons," 163–64.

23. Some higher estimates of Ephesus's population—such as 200,000+ by T. R. S. Broughton ("Roman Asia Minor," in *An Economic Survey of Ancient Rome*, ed. T. Frank [Baltimore: Johns Hopkins University Press, 1938], 4:812–13) and David Magie (*RRAM*, 1:585; 2:1446n50)—are based on a misreading of an inscription (*IvE* 951); cf. Preston Duane Warden and Roger S. Bagnall, "The Forty Thousand Citizens of Ephesus," *ClPhil* 83 (1988): 220–23.

24. The mob is addressed in Acts 19 as though an ordinary meeting of the ἐκκλησία—"Men, Ephesians" (Ἄνδρες Ἐφέσιοι, vv. 35, 39)—recalling that women were technically not citizens of Hellenic poleis. See an inscription from Magnesia-on-Maeander, where prayers are offered at a festival of Artemis Leucophryene "for the safety of the city and countryside, *citizens* and *women* and children and all resident aliens" (*IvM* 98, emphasis added). Cf. E. L. Hicks, ed., *IBM*, 68–71; Dieter Knibbe, *Der Staatsmarkt: Die Inschriften des Prytaneions*, vol. 1, *Die Kureteninschriften und sonstige religiöse Texte*, Forschungen in Ephesos 9.1 (Vienna: Österreichische Akademie der Wissenschaften, 1981), 107–9; and Guy M. Rogers, "The Assembly of Imperial Ephesos," *ZPE* 94 (1992): 224–28.

25. We know the names of scores of these men. From the first century are Heraclides III (*IvE* 14); Tatianus (*IvE* 492); Tib. Claudius Aristio (*IvE* 234–35 et al.); C. Julius Didymus (Neue Inschriften IX, 120–21); Alexander Memnon, son of Artemidorus (*IvE* 261); and L. Cusinius (either *episkopos* or *grammateus;* Barclay V. Head, *BMC*, no. 205; and *IvE* 659B, 716, et al.). Either Alexander Memnon or L. Cusinius could be the *grammateus* of Acts 19:35.

26. For an Ephesian councilor who served nineteen consecutive years, see *IvE* 1017–35 (under Trajan and Hadrian). Roman officials like Pliny might deliberately limit councilors to "free men from the better class families (*honestorum hominum liberi*)" than from the commoners (*plebs*)" (*Epistulae* 10.79). Cf. G. W. Bowersock, *Augustus and the Greek World* (Oxford: Clarendon, 1965), 87–88.

27. Another important indication of acceptance of *Romanitas* is the high incidence of Roman citizenship among Ephesians. For Roman citizens among the Ephesian "fishermen and fishmongers" (*IvE* 20), see S. M. Baugh, "Paul and Ephesus: The Apostle among His Contemporaries" (Ph.D. diss., University of California, Irvine, 1990), 165–93, 222–25; cf. G. H. R. Horsley, in *New Docs*, 5:95–114.

28. See esp. W. K. Lacey, "Patria Potestas," in *The Family in Ancient Rome*, ed. B. Rawson (Ithaca, NY: Cornell University Press, 1986), 121–44. His thesis: "*Patria potestas* was the fundamental institution of the Romans which shaped and directed their world-view" (140).

29. The *asiarchs*—mentioned in Acts 19:31—were another, especially prominent group of men. Whether this was a priesthood or an honorary title is subject for debate, but the *asiarchs'* high social status is not. See Kearsley, in *New Docs*, 4:46–55; Steven J. Friesen, *Twice Neokoros: Ephesus, Asia, and the Cult of the Flavian Imperial Family* (Leiden: Brill, 1993), 92–112; and Baugh, "Paul and Ephesus," 132–63, 214–21.

30. Many epigraphical references to the deities at Ephesus are collected in *IvE* 1201–71; cf. Dieter Knibbe, "Ephesos—nicht nur die Stadt der Artemis: Die 'anderen' ephesischen Götter," in *Studien zur Religion und Kultur Kleinasiens*, ed. S. Sahin et al. (Leiden: Brill, 1978), 2:489–503; and Richard Oster, "Ephesus as a Religious Center under the Principate, I: Paganism before Constantine," *ANRW*, 2.18.3:1661–728.

31. See R. Merkelbach, "Die ephesischen Dionysosmysten vor der Stadt," *ZPE* 36 (1979): 151–56.

32. See Günther Hölbl, *Zeugnisse ägyptischer Religionsvorstellungen für Ephesos* (Leiden: Brill, 1978).

33. Chr. Börker, "Eine pantheistische Weihung in Ephesos," *ZPE* 41 (1981): 181–88.

34. For example: P. Rutelius Bassus Junianus, priest of Demeter Karpophoros (*IvE* 1210); Isidorus, son of Apollonis, son of Apollonis, priest of "Karpophoros Earth" (*IvE* 902) (apparently different from Demeter Karpophoros; so Walter Burkert, *Greek Religion* [Cambridge, MA: Harvard University Press, 1985], 175); C. Sossianus, priest of Isis and Serapis (*IvE* 1213); Nic[ius?], priest of Theos Hypsistos (*IvE* 1235); Demetrius, son of Myndius, son of Nester, priest of Zeus Keraunios (*IvE* 1239); and a few named priests and unnamed priestesses of Dionysus (*IvE* 902, 1600–1601, et al.). See also priests of civic groups: priests of the council (*IvE* 941; and Neue Inschriften XII, no. 22); a priest of the *ephebes* (*IvE* 836); and a priest of the *molpoi* (a guild of musicians) (*IvE* 901 and 3317).

35. Burkert, *Greek Religion*, 98.

36. Women served as priestesses in more than forty Athenian cults during the classical era when women's public functions outside the home were scarce; cf. Michael Grant, *A Social History of Greece and Rome* (New York: Scribner's, 1992), 8.

37. The temple did not dominate the city's skyline, though, since it was situated about a mile (2 km) from downtown Ephesus.

38. Cf. Anton Bammer, *Das Heiligtum der Artemis von Ephesos* (Graz, Austria: Akademische, 1984).

39. The cult of Artemis Ephesia was spread throughout Asia Minor and Syria, and was found even in Italy: "Whereas the leader of our city, the goddess Artemis, is honored not only in her hometown—which she has caused to be honored more than all cities through her own divinity—among both Greeks as well as barbarians, so that her rites and precincts have been set up everywhere" (*IvE* 24B [AD 160]). Cf. Robert Fleischer, *Artemis von Ephesos und verwandte Kultstatuen aus Anatolien und Syrien* (Leiden: Brill, 1973).

40. The boundary-stone inscriptions are collected in *IvE* 3501–12, including a map of the area and the location of the stones; cf. Dieter Knibbe et al., "Der Grundbesitz der ephesischen Artemis im Kaystrostal," *ZPE* 33 (1979): 139–46.

41. "The Sacred Rent (or Wage) Office" (*IvE* 1577A, 3050, et al.) probably administered leases on temple lands to peasant farmers and larger agricultural concerns. One such concern was represented by another bureau known variously as "Those Engaged in the Taste" (*IvE* 728), "The College of the Sacred Tasters" (*IvE* 2076), or more fully, "The College of the Sacred Wine Tasters," an association engaged in the production and distribution of wine grown on the sacred soil of Artemis (so SEG 35, no. 1109). One sacred association of the Artemisium (*hieropoioi*) apparently owned its own land (Neue Inschriften IX, 118–19).

42. The term κοινόν in the singular normally refers to the provincial League of Asia, while the plural form (κοινά), used elsewhere in this inscription, corresponds to res pu-

blica, the city-state. Although it is not certain whether these are precisely city or provincial officers, the same city magistrates were the ones who filled the provincial posts, so the distinction is not critical here. Cf. Baugh, "Paul and Ephesus," 159–61.

43. A "donation" for the honor of serving in various priesthoods was common in the Greek world. For instance, in Egypt, a certain priest offered 2,200 drachmas for his temple's prophetic office (A. S. Hunt and C. C. Edgar, *Select Papyri*, 2 vols., LCL [Cambridge, MA: Harvard University Press; London: Heinemann, 1932–34], 2, no. 353). But this practice upset Roman sensibilities. They preferred to grant and acquire priesthoods through patronage. Pliny the Younger, for example, was appointed to the college of augurs through imperial patronage, not through payment (*Epistulae* 10.13 and 4.8). This confined membership of priesthoods to "people of the right sort," which, of course, is what Persicus had in mind. Perhaps among the "wrong sort" acquiring priesthoods of Artemis were freedmen like Domitian's procurator Tib. Claudius Clemens, who became a "trustee" (*neopoios*) of the Artemisium (*IvE* 853 and 1812). Cf. Magie, *RRAM*, 1:545–46; and esp. 2:1403–4n17.

44. In Greek, ἀρχιερεὺς μέγιστος (*IvE* 259B [Claudius]).

45. Earlier Augustus had personally limited the boundaries of the asylum area of the Artemisium (Strabo, *Geogr.* 14.1.23; Cassius Dio, *Roman History* 51.20.6). See also Pliny and Trajan's correspondence for rulings on religious matters in Bithynia (*Epistulae ad Trajanum* 10.49–50, 68–71); cf. A. N. Sherwin-White, *The Letters of Pliny: A Historical and Social Commentary* (Oxford: Clarendon, 1966), 632, 655–59. Further evidence of Roman oversight of Ephesian religion is as follows: (1) The city petitioned Roman proconsuls for permission (a) to perform mysteries "to Demeter Karpophoros and Thesmophoros and the divine emperors . . . with all sanctity and lawful customs" (*IvE* 213 [AD 88–89]); and (b) to carry on festivals throughout the month of Artemision in honor of Artemis (*IvE* 24 [AD 162–64]). (2) The municipality and temple establishment placed themselves under the patronage of individual Romans: "Lucius Antonius son of Marcus (a brother of Mark Antony) . . . patron (πάτρων) and benefactor of Artemis and of the city" (*IvE* 614A [ca. 49 BC]); and the same for Marcus Messalla Corvinus, a prominent figure under Augustus (Neue Inschriften XII, no. 18). Cf. R. P. Saller, *Personal Patronage under the Early Empire* (Cambridge: Cambridge University Press, 1982).

46. "Priests," *OCD*; cf. Burkert, *Greek Religion*, 95–98. In Acts 19:35 the *grammateus* mentions that the city (i.e., its magistrates) was "*neocoros* of the great goddess" (cf. *IvE* 647). *Neocoros* refers to the individual or group charged with the oversight of a cult; cf. R. A. Kearsley, in *New Docs*, 6:203–6.

47. Kroeger and Kroeger, *I Suffer Not a Woman*, 54.

48. C. Julius Atticus was "priest of Artemis Soteira (and) of the family of Caesar" (*IvE* 1265), Apollonius Politicus was "the priest of Artemis" who dedicated a local altar (Neue Inschriften IX, 120–21), and Servilius Bassus was "(priest) of Artemis" under Augustus (*IvE* 4337). An imperial freedman under Nero, C. Stertinius Orpex (whose daughter was a priestess of Artemis), says that he donated five thousand denarii "to the council of the Ephesians and to the priests" (*IvE* 4123). Also, a "priest of Artemis" figures prominently in Achilles Tatius's second-century novel when the story's venue shifts to Ephesus (*Leucippe and Clitophon*, books 7–8).

49. Ellinger, *Ephesos*, 127; cf. Knibbe, *Kureteninschriften*, and the brief treatment by R. A. Kearsley, in *New Docs*, 6:196–202.

50. In the myth of Artemis's birth, Hera, wife of Zeus, tried to destroy Leto's children, the twins Artemis and Apollo. Their birthplace was believed by most of the Greek world to be on Delos, called Ortygia in earlier days, but the Ephesians claimed that it was in their mountain grove of that name (Tacitus, *Annales* 3.61); cf. "Ortygia," *Kl. Pauly*.

51. The *prytaneion* is the building housing the state cult of Hestia and the prytany (see below). The move of the *kouretes* may indicate the consolidation of control over the

affairs of the Artemisium by municipal powers through Roman influence (cf. Kearsley, in *New Docs*, 6:197). Their close alliance with the municipality explains why Strabo calls their office a "magistracy," even though they retained priestly functions in the birthday festival.

52. For example, here is one of the lists: "In the prytany of Tib. Claudius Tib. f[ilius] Quirina Romulus the emperor-loyal priest for life, the pious, emperor-loyal *kouretes*, all city councilors (βουλευταί) were M. Pompeius Damonicus; Tib. Claudius Capito; C. Numicius Peregrinus; Tib. Claudius Claudianus; Alexander, son of Alexander, the *ephebarch*; Ephesius, son of Aristonicus. The sacred assistants were P. Cor(nelius) Aristo, [victim inspector and city councilor]; Myndicius, hierophant and city councilor; Epikrates, sacred herald; Atticus, incense bearer; Trophimus, flute player at the drink-offering" (*IvE* 1020 [AD 100–103]).

53. Kroeger and Kroeger, *I Suffer Not a Woman*, 186–87.

54. Since the discovery of an inscription mentioning a first-century *neopoios* named Demetrius (*IvE* 1578A), it has been debated whether this might be the silversmith of Acts 19. A first-century silversmith, M. Antonius Hermias, served as *neopoios* (*IvE* 2212), so it remains possible, though not proven. See Horsley, in *New Docs*, 4:7–10, 127–29.

55. For instance: "The loyal C. Mindius Hegymenus, who served as *decemprimus*, *ephebarch* with distinction, harbor master, superintendent of education, and as voluntary *neopoios* piously and generously, the father of Mindia Stratonike Hegymene, high priestess of Asia of the temples in Ephesus and *theoros* of the Great Olympiad, and of Mindia Soteris Agrippine, priestess of lady Artemis, the grandfather of a sacred herald [broken off]" (Neue Inschriften IX, 125). The *decemprimus* (δεκάπρωτος) was probably a financial officer of the Artemisium; cf. SEG 38, no. 1181.

56. See Hicks, *IBM*, 3:85; A. H. Jones, *Essenes: The Elect of Israel and the Priests of Artemis* (New York: University Press of America, 1985); and J. Kampen, "A Reconsideration of the Name 'Essene,'" *HUCA* 57 (1986): 61–81, esp. 68–74.

57. For example: "To Good Fortune. I give thanks to you, Lady Artemis. C. Scaptius Frontinus, *neopoios*, city councilor, along with my wife, Herennia Autronia. I completed a term as *essene* (ἐσσηνεύσας) purely and piously. The drink offering was performed by Theopompos III (great-grandson) of Menecrates, the votary" (*IvE* 1578B; first or second century AD); and, "In the year of the chief staff bearer, M. Aurelius Poseidonius. I give thanks to you Lady Artemis. Aur. Niconianus Eucarpus son of Agathemerus, voluntary *neopoios*, *chrysophorus*, member of the *gerousia*, and *gymnasiarch* of the *gerousia*, in that I piously and generously fulfilled two terms as *essene*" (Neue Inschriften IX, 120).

58. For example, sacred victors (ἱερονεῖκαι) of the games in honor of Artemis were supported after their victories as "votaries" (ἱεροί) of the goddess (*IvE* 18, line 22; 17, lines 46–50) and may also have been called "crown bearers" (χρυσοφόροι). Cf. Hicks, *IBM*, 3:85–87; and Oster, "Ephesus as a Religious Center," 1722.

59. For example: "The most sacred association of *neopoioi* of our lady, the goddess Artemis, have honored the loyal Cornelius Gamus, high councilor, general, sheriff, *neopoios*, *decemprimus*, twice secretary (of the people), *chrysophorus*, superintendent of education (*paidonomon*) [broken off]" (Neue Inschriften IX, 121–22); and, "I give you thanks, Lady Artemis. Metrodorus Damas Jr., grandson of Alexas, Teïos tribe, Eurypompios division; I completed a term as *neopoios* piously and [two as *es*]*sene*, (I dedicate this) with my three children, and [my w]ife, and brother" (*IvE* 1588).

60. The Kroegers connect the *megabyzos* with possible ritual castration in the Christian community of 1 Tim. 2 (*I Suffer Not a Woman*, 94).

61. Richard Oster attributes the disappearance of the *megabyzos* to the rise of Roman hegemony at Ephesus ("Ephesus as a Religious Center," 1721–22). Strabo, in the late first century BC, speaks of the *megabyzos* as something from the past: "[The Ephesians] used

to have (εἶχον) eunuch priests, whom they would call (ἐκάλουν) *Megabyzoi*. They were ever looking elsewhere for people worthy of such a high position (προστασία), and they used to be held (ἧγον) in high honor. It was necessary (ἐχρῆν) for virgins to serve with them. Nowadays, some of their customary practices are preserved, and others less so" (*Geogr.* 14.1.23). Note that *megabyzos* does not appear on any of the roughly four thousand inscriptions from Ephesus. The only epigraphical reference to this figure occurs in two connected honorary inscriptions from Priene from 334–333 BC (*IvPr* 3, 231).

62. Kroeger and Kroeger, *I Suffer Not a Woman*, 71, 196.

63. J. B. Prichard, ed., *The Harper Atlas of the Bible* (New York: Harper & Row, 1987), 175. See also L. R. Taylor, "Artemis of Ephesus," in *The Beginnings of Christianity*, ed. F. Foakes Jackson and K. Lake (London: Macmillan, 1933), 5:253; H. Martin, "Artemis," *ABD*, 1:464–65. Cf. Lynn LiDonnici, "The Images of Artemis Ephesia and Greco-Roman Worship: A Reconsideration," *Harvard Theological Review* 85 (1992): 389–415.

64. But compare Louise Bruit Zaidman and Pauline Schmitt Pantel (*Religion in the Ancient Greek City*, trans. P. Cartledge [Cambridge: Cambridge University Press, 1992], 5), who challenge this interpretation of Artemis and the "origins-theory" methodology behind it.

65. Mark P. O. Morford and Robert J. Lenardon, *Classical Mythology*, 4th ed. (New York: Longman, 1991), 182; see esp. 173–84. Cf. "Artemis" in *Kl. Pauly* and *OCD*; and Burkert, *Greek Religion*, 149–52.

66. Oster, "Ephesus as a Religious Center," 1725–26; cf. his "Ephesian Artemis as an Opponent of Early Christianity," *Jahrbuch für Antike und Christentum* 19 (1976): 28; and Paul Trebilco, "Asia."

67. See Leto and the nativity of Artemis depicted on Ephesian coins (e.g., *BMC*, no. 374) and in Strabo (*Geogr.* 14.1.20); cf. Oster, "Ephesus as a Religious Center," 1711–12.

68. Achilles Tatius, *Clitophon and Leucippe* 8.11–14.

69. ἡ καθαρὰ θεός from Tatius, *Clitophon* 8.8. In the same passage, Tatius's priest of the "virgin" (παρθένος) goddess is accused of defiling his priesthood by allowing illicit sex in the Artemisium's precincts. See also Pseudo-Heraclitus, who interpreted the (pre-Pauline) Ephesian custom of having a eunuch as priest of Artemis (the *megabyzos*) as based on fear "lest a man as a priest service her virginity!" (David R. Worley, trans., "Epistle 9," in *The Cynic Epistles*, ed. A. Malherbe, SBLSBS 12 [Atlanta: Scholars Press, 1977], 213).

70. Neue Inschriften XII, no. 25; cf. Fritz Graf, "An Oracle against Pestilence from a Western Anatolian Town," *ZPE* 92 (1992): 267–79.

71. A poetic epithet found in Homer and the Homeric Hymns (above); cf. LSJ.

72. In the novel by Xenophon of Ephesus, the Ephesian heroine dresses in a fawn-skin hunting costume complete with quiver and arrows. In consequence, "Ephesians would reverence her as Artemis when they saw her in the sacred precincts" (*Ephesiaca* 1.3; probably second century AD).

73. Fleischer, *Artemis von Ephesos*, 87. Cf. Fleischer, "Artemis von Ephesos und verwandte Kultstatuen aus Anatolien und Syrien Supplement," in *Studien zur Religion und Kultur Kleinasiens*, ed. S. Sahin et al. (Leiden: Brill, 1978), 324–31; and A. Hill, "Ancient Art and Artemis: Toward Explaining the Polymastic Nature of the Figurine," *Journal of the Ancient Near Eastern Society* 21 (1992): 91–94. Fleischer covers all interpretations of the "breasts" to date, observing that the breast interpretation did not originate from pagan worshipers of Artemis but from secondary Christian writers Minucius Felix and Jerome. Other interpretations include pendants from a necklace, sacred grapes, bee eggs, and scrota of sacrificed bulls (!); cf. Fleischer, *Artemis von Ephesos*, 74–88. In favor of the "grape thesis," there is an interesting painting of Bacchus covered with large grapes at Pompeii; cf. T. Feder, *Great Treasures of Pompeii and Herculaneum* (New York: Abbeville, 1978), 14–15.

74. *Asianic Elements in Greek Civilisation* (1927; repr., Chicago: Ares, 1976), 82. Ramsay took the objects to be bee eggs.

75. Fleischer, *Artemis von Ephesos*, plates 58, 138–41; cf. LiDonnici, "Images of Artemis," figs. 2–3.

76. Graf, "Oracle against Pestilence," 269–70. For the classical statue, see Anton Bammer et al., *Führer durch das archäologische Museum in Selçuk-Ephesos* (Vienna: Österreichisches Archäologisches Institut, 1974), photo 9. For torches of classical Artemis, see Pausanias, *Descr.* 8.37.1 (from Arkadia).

77. Stefan Karwiese, "Ephesos: Numismatischer Teil," PWSup 12:311. Karwiese references several other types: "griech(ische) Artemis m(it) Bogen u(nd) Köcher," "jagende Artemis," kneeling stags, torches, etc. (ibid., 307–14); cf. Head, *Historia Numorum*, 571–77. One coin from the third century AD has "Artemis of the Ephesians" riding a chariot drawn by stags; see Peter Robert Franke, *Kleinasien zur Römerzeit: Griechisches Leben im Spiegel der Münzen* (Munich: Beck, 1968), no. 355; cf. nos. 350–51; 353.

78. Stella Georgoudi, "Creating a Myth of Matriarchy," in *A History of Women in the West*, ed. P. Pantel (Cambridge, MA: Harvard University Press, Belknap Press, 1992), 1:460.

79. See, for example, the procession in honor of Artemis Ephesia described by Xenophon of Ephesus, "The Ephesian Tale," trans. G. Anderson, in *Collected Ancient Greek Novels*, ed. B. P. Reardon (Berkeley: University of California Press, 1989), 128–69. Cf. I. Ringwood, "Festivals of Ephesus," *AJA* 76, no. 1 (1972): 17–22. It has been said that the cult of Artemis Ephesia was a mystery religion in the technical sense fulfilled only by women (hence, a fertility cult); so Kroeger and Kroeger, *I Suffer Not a Woman*, 97–98, 186–88, et al. The term μυστήρια occurs on Ephesian inscriptions, but it refers to rituals depicting the nativity of Artemis (involving the male *kouretes*; see above), according to Oster, "Ephesus as a Religious Center," 1711–13; Kearsley, in *New Docs*, 6:196–202; and Rogers, *Sacred Identity*, 81. And men did "fulfill the mysteries" at Ephesus as well as young girls and women (*IvE* 26, 1069; Neue Inschriften XII, no. 6).

80. For example, see the worship of Cybele in Juvenal, *Satire* 6.512–20; 2.82–99. There is, by the way, scant evidence for the worship of Cybele at Ephesus; cf. Oster, "Ephesus as a Religious Center," 1688.

81. Cf. Clinton E. Arnold, *Ephesians: Power and Magic; The Concept of Power in Ephesians in Light of Its Historical Setting*, SNTSMS 63 (Cambridge: Cambridge University Press, 1989).

82. Cf. Jane F. Gardner, *Women in Roman Law and Society* (Bloomington: Indiana University Press, 1991).

83. For example, Everett Ferguson, *Backgrounds of Early Christianity*, 2nd ed. (Grand Rapids: Eerdmans, 1993), 72; and Gritz, *Paul, Women Teachers*, 16–18. Cf. Eva Contarella, *Pandora's Daughters* (Baltimore: Johns Hopkins University Press, 1987), 140–41; and Ramsay MacMullen, "Woman in Public in the Roman Empire," *Hist.* 29 (1980): 208–18.

84. See, for example, Apuleius, *Metamorphoses*, and Longus, "Daphnis and Chloe," for somewhat idealized portraits of Greek rural life in the imperial period. Cf. Fergus Millar, "The World of the Golden Ass," *JRS* 71 (1981): 63–75; and Ramsay MacMullen, *Roman Social Relations 50 BC to AD 284* (New Haven: Yale University Press, 1974), 1–56.

85. Galen estimates that one-third of second-century Pergamum's population were slaves; see Géza Alföldy, *The Social History of Rome* (London: Croom Helm, 1985), 137. In first-century Ephesus, even some slaves owned slaves to perform their service (*IvE* 18, lines 18–22).

86. That freed slaves remained in the *oikos* is illustrated by their inclusion in family grave plots: "I desire that my slaves, freedmen, and slave girls be placed in this tomb" (*IvE* 2414). Cf. "Freigelassene," *Kl. Pauly*; "Freedmen," *OCD*; and Thomas Wiedemann, *Greek and Roman Slavery* (Baltimore: Johns Hopkins University Press, 1981), 3–4, 52–56.

87. For example, Plutarch gives contradictory views of Spartan women within one essay: They were famous for ruling over their men, yet one Spartan woman said, "When I was a child, I learned obedience to my father . . . and since I became a wife, now I obey my husband" (*Lacaenarum apophthegmata* [*Mor.* 240E and 242B]). Which was the real Spartan woman? The ruler, the ruled, or a *tertia quis*?

For similar cautions, see Hugo Montgomery, "Women and Status in the Greco-Roman World," *ST* 43 (1989): 115–24; and Averil Cameron, "Neither Male nor Female," *G&R* 27 (1980): 60–68.

88. Not to mention Achilles Tatius, Aelius Aristides, Dio Chrysostom, Diodorus Siculus, Herodotus, Pausanias, Plutarch, and Xenophon of Ephesus.

89. Pauline Schmitt Pantel, "Representations of Women," in *A History of Women*, 1:2; cf. Thucydides, *Peloponnesian War* 2.44; Plutarch, *De mulierum virtutes* (*Mor.* 242E–F).

90. Paul Veyne, "The Roman Empire," in *A History of Private Life: From Pagan Rome to Byzantium*, ed. P. Veyne (Cambridge, MA: Harvard University Press, Belknap Press, 1987), 1:73. On veils, see Richard Oster, "When Men Wore Veils to Worship: The Historical Context of 1 Corinthians 11.4," *NTS* 34 (1988): 481–505.

91. The noun σωφροσύνη can also mean "good judgment," "moderation," "self-control," "esp. as a woman's virtue *decency, chastity*" (BDAG; LSJ). Sometimes seen as part of a New Testament "code of conduct"; see David C. Verner, *The Household of God: The Social World of the Pastoral Epistles*, SBLDS 71 (Chico, CA: Scholars Press, 1983), 134–39; cf. Hermann von Lips, "Die Haustafel als 'Topos' im Rahmen der urchristlichen Paränese," *NTS* 40 (1994): 261–80.

92. An even more pointed illustration of the value placed on female modesty at Ephesus is demonstrated in this honorary inscription of unknown date: "(Heraclides Didymus) . . . [unknown office] of Artemis and was benefactor of the people because of his personal, universal excellence, his piety toward Artemis, his acumen and trustworthiness in learning, and his goodwill toward the people. [Ammion, daughter of Perigenus,] wife of Heraclides Didymus son of Menis (was honored) because of her personal modesty (σωφροσύνη) and because of the goodwill of her husband, Heraclides, toward the demos" (*IvE* 683A; lacunae supplied from *IvE* 683B). It is explicitly stated that Ammion received honorable mention because of her husband's public benefactions; her own praise consists of the stock expression of "modesty."

See also a grave inscription from Prusias-on-Hypius (Bithynia), where "Aur(elia) Chrestiniane Rufina, known as Himeris, was the modest and husband-honoring wife (ἡ σώφρων καὶ φίλανδρος γυνή) of the silversmith Aur(elius) Socratianos Pasikrates, she lived a decorous life (κοσμίως) for 31 years" (*IvPrusias* 89). The editor calls the phrase in question "eine typische Formulierung für eine Frau" and cites other examples.

93. A few Ephesians served as priestesses of Leto, Athena, and other gods (e.g., *IvE* 4107; Neue Inschriften IX, 142–43); cf. honors for a Magnesian woman who was "priestess also of Demeter in Ephesus" (*IvM* 158). Women also appear as "envoys" (θεωροί) to the Ephesian "Olympic games" (e.g., *IvE* 891–96). The *theōros*, often a priestess, represented the state's matrons at the sacred games as at Olympia (Pausanias, *Descr.* 2.20.8–9); cf. H. Engelmann, "Zu Inschriften aus Ephesos," *ZPE* 26 (1977): 154–55.

There is also some evidence for women as benefactresses of public works, although after the first century AD; cf. G. M. Rogers, "Constructions of Women at Ephesus," *ZPE* 90 (1992): 215–23.

94. See Mary Lefkowitz and Maureen Fant, eds., *Women's Life in Greece and Rome: A Source Book in Translation* (Baltimore: Johns Hopkins University Press, 1982), 113–27, 249–62; Ross Kraemer, *Maenads, Martyrs, Matrons, Monastics: A Sourcebook on Women's Religions in the Greco-Roman World* (Philadelphia: Fortress, 1988), 11–38, 211–17; cf. Louise

Bruit Zaidman, "Pandora's Daughters and Rituals in Grecian Cities," in *A History of Women*, 338–76; John Scheid, "The Religious Roles of Roman Women," in ibid., 377–408.

95. The στέμματα in Acts 14:13.

96. See Johannes Quasten, *Music and Worship in Pagan and Christian Antiquity*, trans. B. Ramsey (Washington, DC: National Association of Pastoral Musicians, 1983), 1–31, esp. 17, where two female flutists and two veiled girls appear on the pedestal of a statuette of Artemis Ephesia in Rome. Quasten interprets the scene as an incense offering.

97. "Whereas inequality between the sexes was the rule in the political sphere, it appears that honors and responsibilities in the religious sphere were divided according to some other principle. Priestesses seem to have had the same rights and duties as priests" (Zaidman, "Pandora's Daughters," 373).

Also, women alone performed certain mystic rituals in the Thesmophoria festival celebrated in many Hellenic cities, including Ephesus. See the parody by Aristophanes (*Thesmophoriazusae*); cf. "Thesmophoria," *Kl. Pauly*; Marcel Detienne, "The Violence of Wellborn Ladies: Women in the Thesmophoria," in *The Cuisine of Sacrifice among the Greeks*, ed. M. Detienne and J.-P. Vernant (Chicago: University of Chicago Press, 1989), 129–47; and Burkert, *Greek Religion*, 242–46.

98. An inscription of Trajanic date was dedicated *favisori civitatis Ephesiorum qui in statario negotiantur*, "To the patron of the Ephesian citizenry who conduct business in the slave market" (*IvE* 646). These were Roman businessmen who also possessed local citizenship.

99. For priestesses of Artemis named by their parents and ancestors, see, for example, *IvE* 492, 508, 980–989A, 3059, 3072.

100. *IvE* 3072 (ca. AD 270) is a lengthy memorial for "the most missed daughter" of Vedius Servilius Gaius, who similarly "fulfilled the mysteries through her father Gaius." It is not certain whether she was a *prytanis* (below) or priestess of Artemis (especially since the Artemisium was sacked by raiding Goths only a few years earlier if the date is accurate). The *prytanis* and *gymnasiarch* Ploutarchos inscribed a prayer to Hestia and Artemis on behalf of his children, "priestesses of Artemis" (*IvE* 1068).

101. That such young girls could serve as priestesses of Artemis Ephesia fits Plutarch's comparison of her priestesses with the Roman vestal virgins (*Mor.* 795D–E). Along with this, one broken inscription of a priestess of Artemis mentions that she came from a line of ancestors who served in the "virgin-office" (ἐκ παρθενῶν|ος]; *IvE* 990).

For possible married priestesses, see Auphidia Quintilia, "priestess (of Artemis) and high priestess (of Asia) of the temples in Ephesus," who paid for an honorary statue of her husband, "Tib. Claudius Aelius Crispus the *asiarch, agonothete* of the great Ephesian (games), secretary of the people, secretary of the state council, and all other liturgies" (*IvE* 637). We know that the priestesses Kallinoe and Hordeonia Paulina had sons (*IvE* 615A, 981; cf. 690), but we cannot tell whether they had served their terms in the temple before their marriage or afterward.

Achilles Tatius says: "From ancient days this temple [the Artemisium] had been forbidden to free women who were not virgins. Only men and virgins were permitted here. If a non-virgin woman passed inside, the penalty was death" (*Leucippe et Clitophon* 7.13) (trans. J. Winkler, in *Collected Ancient Greek Novels*, 267). There is some doubt about whether Tatius had firsthand knowledge of Ephesus, though.

102. Compare note 12.

103. At the very least, most priestesses had Roman names and were presumably the daughters of Roman citizens. Under Roman law, strict penalties for prostitution applied to them; see Gardner, *Women in Roman Law*, 127–34, 250–53.

104. While sacred prostitution is sometimes proposed, say, in Aphrodite's cult at Corinth ("Prostitution," *Kl. Pauly* [4.1192]), it is a disputed question; see Burkert, *Greek Religion*,

158, 408n9, cf. 108–9. In any case, there is no ancient evidence whatsoever for sacred prostitution at Ephesus, even though a (secular) brothel has been excavated there; cf. Otto Meinardus, "The Alleged Advertisement for the Ephesian Lupanar," *Wiener Studien* 7 (1973): 244–48.

105. Also: "When Fl(avius) Perigenes was *prytanis*, Vedia Papiane was priestess of Athena for life, T. Fl(avius) Julianus was secretary of the people, when the fullers and whiteners of the goddess Artemis were in charge, (the following) boys and girls (παῖδες καὶ παρθένοι) presented the adornment (τὸν κόσμον) to the goddess" (there follows a list naming eight boys, no girls) (Neue Inschriften IX, 142–43). Cf. F. Sokolowski, "A New Testimony on the Cult of Artemis of Ephesus," *Harvard Theological Review* 58 (1965): 427–31.

106. "Panathenaia," in *Kl. Pauly* and *OCD*.

107. Kroeger and Kroeger, *I Suffer Not a Woman*, 70.

108. I.e., the "eponymous" office. See the series: Robert K. Sherk, "Eponymous Officials of Greek Cities, I–V," *ZPE* 83 (1990): 249–88; 84 (1990): 231–95; 88 (1991): 225–60; 93 (1992): 223–72; 96 (1993): 267–95. On the Greek prytany, see "Prytanen," *Kl. Pauly* ("erscheinen P. als Höchstmagistrate vieler Städte an der W.-Küste Kleinasiens"; 4.1206); "Prytaneis" in *OCD*; A. H. M. Jones, *The Greek City* (Oxford: Clarendon, 1940), 178–79.

109. The main witnesses of women who served as *prytaneis* come from the annual lists of *kouretes* dated by the eponymous *prytaneis* inscribed in the *prytaneion*. The *prytaneis* are collated in Knibbe, *Kureteninschriften*, 162–64; and his "Neue Kuretenliste," 125–27. There are fifty-four men and twelve women *prytaneis* from the first to third centuries AD, but only two women are from the first century AD. No women are attested as *prytaneis* on earlier inscriptions.

110. Symbolized in Greek mythology when Prometheus tricked Zeus by clandestinely giving fire to men and raising them above the brutes. In wrathful response, Zeus created a "beautiful, evil" (καλὸν κακόν) woman (Pandora) (Hesiod, *Theogonia* 562–612). Hestia herself was represented as "immortal flame" and "ever-maiden" (ἀειπάρθενος) (*IvE* 1063–64) and corresponds to the Roman Vesta. Cf. Oster, "Ephesus as a Religious Center," 1688–91.

111. Reinhold Merkelbach, "Der Kult der Hestia im Prytaneion der Griechischen Städte," *ZPE* 37 (1980): 77–92; quote from 79; cf. Knibbe, *Kureteninschriften*, 101–5.

112. Cf. Merkelbach, "Kult der Hestia," 80. One epigraphical example reads: "[Broken—see editors' note for reconstruction from *IvE* 987] . . . (a female) performed the public sacrifices and likewise made the distributions [to the council] and to the *gerousia* from the sacrifices and to the temple household and to the sacred victors of games for Artemis, [expended?] her private d[enarii?] on account of the generosity (τὰς φιλοδοξίας) of her father for the prytany and [gymnasi]archy and all the other phil[anthropic . . .]" (Neue Inschriften XII, no. 21). This girl-*prytanis* and *gymnasiarch* may never have set foot in a gymnasium; cf. Waldo E. Sweet, *Sport and Recreation in Ancient Greece* (New York: Oxford University Press, 1987), 134–44. In *IvE* 650, a mother "undertook the prytany on behalf of her son from her funds"; the *prytanis* was either dead or too young to serve himself (cf. *IvE* 4339).

113. Translated with brief comments by A. L. Connolly, in *New Docs*, 4:106–7.

114. The regulations of *IvE* 10 put the *prytanis's* activities under the oversight of a hierophant, who ensured that all was done according to "ancestral custom" (πάτριος νόμος). (He received "the head, tongue, and hide" from sacrificial animals as his due portion.) The inscription specified a fine for the negligent *prytanis;* "the *kouretes* and the hierophant are to make exaction for failure to attend to each particular point as specified."

115. Furthermore, the prytany was no longer always the eponymous office at Ephesus outside the *kouretes* inscriptions; many in the Christian era are dated by the terms of office of the provincial proconsul or the secretary of the people. For example: "[To Artemis

Ephesia] and to the Emperor Caesar Augustus and to the *neocorate* people of the Ephesians, when P. Calvisius Ruso was proconsul. Erected by Claudia Trophime daughter of Philippos and Melissa, priestess and *prytanis*, when Tib. Cl(audius) Aristio the *asiarch* was secretary (of the people), restored when J[ul]ius Titian[us] was secretary of the people" (*IvE* 508; AD 92–93). Kearsley mistakenly says that the female *prytanis* here is "the official by whose term the erection of a statue in a public place is dated" (*New Docs*, 6:26). Claudia Trophime is the donor of the statue (of Domitia or Domitian?); the eponymous officers are the proconsul and *grammateus*.

116. In *IvE* 1064, the *prytanis* Tullia spent her own funds lavishly. Similarly, an imperial freedman under Augustus, C. Julius Nicephorus, contributed heavily to games and sacrifices at Ephesus. His generosity probably explains how someone of former servile status could become a *"prytanis* for life" (*IvE* 859, 859A).

117. For example: "Especially in Asia Minor did women display public activity . . . and several of them obtained the highest priesthood of Asia—perhaps the greatest honor that could be paid to anyone" (James Donaldson, quoted in *Women in the Earliest Churches*, by Ben Witherington III [Cambridge: Cambridge University Press, 1988], 14; and in Kroeger and Kroeger, *I Suffer Not a Woman*, 93). The ranking of priesthoods implied by Donaldson's phrase "highest priesthood of Asia" is misleading. There were no other priesthoods of the provincial imperial cult, and these priests had no ex officio role in other cults.

118. S. R. F. Price, *Rituals and Power: The Roman Imperial Cult in Asia Minor* (Cambridge: Cambridge University Press, 1984); and S. Friesen, *Twice Neokoros*; cf. H. Engelmann, "Zum Kaiserkult in Ephesos," *ZPE* 97 (1993): 279–89.

119. For instance, Queen Laodice III, wife of Antiochus III, received a cult in gratitude for her establishment of dowries for the daughters of poor citizens of Iasos (ca. 196 BC). The cult was served by an unmarried "priestess of Aphrodite Laodice" and included "a procession on the queen's birthday and sacrifices by all the brides and bridegrooms to the queen" (in Price, *Rituals and Power*, 30).

120. For example, see *IvE* 9 for a name list of about thirty Ephesian priests of Roma from ca. 51–17 BC. State cults for individual Romans are also known. For instance, see a dedication for Titus Peducaeus Canax from Nero's reign (*IvE* 702). Among his other offices, Canax was "priest of Rome and of Publius Servilius Isauricus." The cult of Isauricus, who was an exceptionally beneficent provincial governor (46–44 BC), extended into the second century AD at Ephesus.

The title "high priest (of Roma and Augustus)" came into use at the beginning of the first century, and "high priest of Asia" a few decades later. See the lists of high priests, high priestesses, and *asiarchs* in Friesen, *Twice Neokoros*, 172–208; and Margarete Rossner, "Asiarchen und Archiereis Asia," *Studii Clasice* 16 (1974): 112–42.

121. For instance, these brothers and young sister (?) served the imperial family at Ephesus in the reign of Tiberius: "So then the following are priests for life with double shares (of sacrificial meat) and exception from duties: [Servilius] Bassus himself [priest] of Artemis; Servilia Secunda (priestess) of the Augustan Demeter Karpophoros; and (Servilius) Proclus (priest) of the sons of Drusus Caesar the new Dioscuri" (*IvE* 4337). (Livia Augusta, wife of Augustus and mother of Tiberius, is given divine rank by association with Demeter, although her official divinization was not decreed until the reign of Claudius; cf. Price, *Rituals and Power*, 63–64. And the Dioscuri were Castor and Polydeuces, mythological twins of Zeus. Twins were born to Drusus, son of Tiberius, and Livilla about AD 19 [Tacitus, *Annales* 2.84]).

122. See Friesen, *Twice Neokoros*, 85–88.

123. Vedia Marcia (*IvE* 1017; see above) and Julia Lydia Laterane, wife of "the princeps of the Ephesians" (Pliny, *Epistulae* 6.31) and high priest of Asia, Tib. Claudius Aristio (*IvE* 424A et al.). Friesen lists six high priestesses for the first century AD throughout the

province (compared to dozens of high priests). His total is twenty-nine high priestesses covering roughly a 150-year span compared with well over one hundred high priests (and an equally high number of *asiarchs*); see *Twice Neokoros*, 172–208.

124. Dating 1 Timothy to the second half of Nero's reign; cf. D. Carson, D. Moo, and L. Morris, *An Introduction to the New Testament* (Grand Rapids: Zondervan, 1992), 372–73.

125. Cf. Friesen, *Twice Neokoros*, 81–89.

126. As an example for high priests: "The council [and people] honored T. Flavi[us Montanus,] . . . high [priest of Asia of the temple i]n Ephesus of the *koinon* of Asia. . . . He completed the theater and dedicated (it) during his high priesthood, he sponsored (gladiatorial) single combats and hunts, he also sp[onsored] a banquet for the citizens and gave 3 den(arii) to each" (*IvE* 2061; ca. AD 102–116). The high priests and priestesses had ceremonial privileges at the cult events, of course—something like the grand marshal of a modern parade. Cf. Price, *Ritual and Power*, 101–32, 188–91, 207–33, et passim.

127. The punctuation here is probably correct: the honorary inscription, not the high priesthood itself, was given to Claudia because of the benefactions. See also Tata of Aphrodisias "who, as priestess of the imperial cult a second time, twice supplied oil for athletes in hand-bottles" (trans. in Kraemer, *Maenads*, 216).

128. See Jürgen Deininger, *Die Provinziallandtage der Römischen Kaiserzeit* (Munich: Beck, 1965), 18; and Friesen, *Twice Neokoros*, 89–92. One important duty of the provincial delegates was to send deputations to Rome to bring charges of misgovernment against proconsuls; cf. P. A. Brunt, "Charges of Provincial Maladministration under the Early Principate," *Hist.* 10 (1961): 189–227.

129. Cf. 1 Tim. 2:9, 15; Titus 2:4–5. Ammia's inscription is given in Kearsley, in *New Docs*, 6:26–27; but her conclusion from this evidence is a bit odd: "Some women stepped beyond the conventions of social anonymity and domestic fidelity [*sic*]."

130. Richard D. Sullivan, "Priesthoods of the Eastern Dynastic Aristocracy," in *Studien zur Religion und Kultur Kleinasiens*, 2:914–39.

131. For example, the fact that both men and women occasionally refer to their ancestry from priestesses as a sign of noble descent is a sign of the priesthood's honorary value (e.g., *IvE* 810, 933, 994, and 4336).

132. "We should not be too quick to equate service to ancient deities with power and authority. . . . Women's service as priestesses and other cult functionaries in classical Greece, particularly in the service of goddesses who themselves functioned as paradigms for proper women, provides one example. There is little evidence that such priesthoods extended the scope of women's public activities beyond the specific cultic context to the larger political, economic, and social spheres, even when we acknowledge that the very delineation of the religious from other spheres of human activity is a modern conception" (Ross Kraemer, *Her Share of the Blessings: Women's Religions among Pagans, Jews, and Christians in the Greco-Roman World* [New York: Oxford University Press, 1992], 90).

133. Craig S. Keener, *Paul, Women and Wives: Marriage and Women's Ministry in the Letters of Paul* (Peabody, MA: Hendrickson, 1992), 83 (on 1 Cor. 14:34–35); see 107–13 for similar reasoning for 1 Tim. 2.

134. Ephesus shook with "a chorus of rhetoricians and their noisy applause," according to Tacitus (*Dialogus de oratoribus* 15.3).

135. To say that the women were disqualified from teaching in the Christian church merely because they did not attend specialized schools in rhetoric or philosophy claims too much. Paul specifically rejected the devices of the sophists and rhetoricians as the essential component of his own preaching (1 Cor. 1:17; 2:1–2; etc.), and no such qualifications were expected for male teachers and elders (1 Tim. 3:1–7; Titus 1:5–9).

136. They are "T(ib.) Claudius Flavianus Dionysius rhetor" (*IvE* 426; 3047; Philostratus, *Vit. soph.* 1.22); T. Flavius Damianus (*IvE* 672a–b, 676a, 678a, 735, 811, 2100, 3029,

3051, 3080–81), "a most illustrious man," prominent building donor, and city councilor (Philostratus, *Vit. soph.* 2.23); Hadrianus of Tyre, "the sophist" (*IvE* 1539); P. Hordeonius Lollianus (*IvE* 20), the sophist who "was the first to be appointed to the chair of rhetoric at Athens" (Philostratus, *Vit. soph.* 1.23), whose daughter was a priestess of Artemis (*IvE* 984); Ofellius Laetus, a Platonic philosopher (*IvE* 3901); (?)ius Secundinus of Tralles, "the Platonic philosopher" (*IvE* 4340); L. Vevius Severus, "the teacher" (*IvE* 611); Soterus of Athens, known by his disciples as the "chief sophist" (*IvE* 1548), but as a mere "plaything of the Greeks" in Philostratus's opinion (Philostratus, *Vit. soph.* 2.23). Note that the list of μαθηταί of Soterus are all males (*IvE* 1548). See Neue Inschriften VIII, 149–50, for an inscribed philosophical diatribe originating from an Ephesian school; ibid., 136–40, discusses sophists' tax exemptions. Cf. G. W. Bowersock, *Greek Sophists in the Roman Empire* (Oxford: Clarendon, 1969), and Broughton, RAM, 853–55.

All doctors named on Ephesian stones are male; for instance, Tib. Claudius Demostratus Caelianus, *asiarch, grammateus, prytanis,* and priest of Asclepius (*IvE* 278, 643, 719, et al.); cf. *IvE* 1162, 2304, and 4101A; and Broughton, RAM, 851–53.

137. Obviously, the feminist Ephesus construct falters again at this point.

138. See H. I. Marrou, *A History of Education in Antiquity,* trans. George Lamb (1956; repr., New York: New American Library, 1964), 76. Contrast, for example, Keener, *Paul, Women and Wives,* 97n66.

139. "The private house seems to have been the most popular place for philosophers and sophists to hold their classes" (Stanley Stowers, "Social Status, Public Speaking and Private Teaching: The Circumstances of Paul's Preaching Activity," *Novum Testamentum* 26 [1984]: 66). A wall painting of Socrates in a first-century Ephesian home may mark the house as a lecture salon. The mural appears on the cover of a Penguin volume of Plato (*Early Socratic Dialogues,* ed. T. Saunders [Harmondsworth, Eng.: Penguin, 1987]). There was also an "auditorium" at Ephesus for public lectures (*IvE* 3009); cf. C. J. Hemer, "Audeitorion," *TynBul* 24 (1973): 128. For the "school of Tyrannus" of Acts 19:9, see Baugh, "Paul and Ephesus," 120–25.

140. See William V. Harris, *Ancient Literacy* (Cambridge, MA: Harvard University Press, 1989), 252; cf. Susan Guettel Cole, "Could Greek Women Read and Write?" in *Reflections of Women in Antiquity,* ed. H. Foley (New York: Gordon & Breach Science, 1981), 219–45.

141. For example, Telesilla of Argos (Plutarch, *Mor.* 245C–F); cf. women poets in Lefkowitz and Fant, *Women's Life,* 4–10. Samuel Dill's classic work is still helpful for Roman women here: *Roman Society from Nero to Marcus Aurelius* (London: Macmillan, 1905), 79–80.

142. We possess the thanksgiving dedication from the girl-*prytanis* Aurelia Juliane (*IvE* 1066; see above), though we can only suppose that it was actually written by her. It is not particularly inspired and follows standard lines. We also have two dedicatory prayers of the *prytanis* Tullia (see below), which are metrical with distinctly poetic vocabulary (*IvE* 1063–64). See Dill (*Roman Society,* 80) for a reference to "Balbilla, a friend of the wife of Hadrian," who wrote Greek verses on the Colossus of Memnon. This is Julia Balbilla, the Ephesian (?) granddaughter of Tib. Claudius Balbillus, an Ephesian who served as prefect of Egypt and was probably Nero's court astrologer (Suetonius, *Nero* 36; *IvE* 3041–42), founding the Balbilleia games at Ephesus; cf. PWSup 5:59–60.

143. In light of Acts 19:19, these *litterae* may have included works on magic and spells.

144. See J. J. Pollitt in *The Oxford History of Classical Art,* ed. J. Boardman (Oxford: Oxford University Press, 1993), 247, no. 242. See photos no. 89, 92, 94–95, 116A, 126, 130, 132, et al. for Greek women shown on coins, vases, and statuary, and plate xxii, no. 325A, for a gold hair ornament with sapphires and pearls from a later period. Cf. "Haartracht. Haarschmuck," *Kl. Pauly.*

145. For example, a portrait of Livia (with a somewhat elaborate hairstyle) was found in a private dwelling in Ephesus; see Maria Aurenhammer, "Römische Porträts aus Ephesos: Neue Funde aus dem Hanghaus 2," *JÖAI* 54 (1983): Beiblatt, 105–12 (photos 1–3). See also Jale Inan and Elisabeth Rosenbaum, *Roman and Early Byzantine Portrait Sculpture in Asia Minor* (London: British Academy, 1966) for Asian portraits of Livia (plate VII), Octavia (plate VIII—very elaborate coiffure), and Agrippina the elder and the younger (plates XI–XII).

146. For instance, the portrait of an Ephesian woman mirrors the hairstyle of Octavia and Livia (cf. Inan and Rosenbaum, *Roman and Early Byzantine Portrait Sculpture*, plate LXXXI, no. 140, and plates VII–VIII, nos. 11–12, and the remarks on p. 123). See plate LXIV, no. 109, for another provincial woman with the same style.

147. For men, Paul's equivalent exhortation was to avoid obsession with "body-sculpting" in gymnasia in place of piety (1 Tim. 4:8).

148. "Elaborate hairdressing and makeup were part of the self-presentation for the better-class whores" (i.e., "loose-living society ladies" as described by Juvenal [*Satire* 6]) (Gardner, *Women in Roman Law*, 251).

149. Cf. D. W. J. Gill, "Corinth: A Roman Colony in Achaea," *BZ* 37 (1993): 259–64.

150. Sharon Hodgin Gritz, "The Role of Women in the Church," in *The People of God: Essays on the Believers' Church*, ed. P. Basden and D. S. Dockery (Nashville: Broadman, 1991), 308.

151. See, for example, the varied and challenging responsibilities outlined for a fourteen-year-old Greek bride (Xenophon, *Oeconomicus*, book 7). See also the many areas of expertise of the homemaker in Prov. 31.

152. Laura Ingalls Wilder, *The Long Winter* (1940; repr., New York: HarperCollins, 1971), 4; emphasis added.

153. See esp. David Cohen, "Seclusion, Separation, and the Status of Women in Classical Athens," *G&R* 36 (1989): 3–15.

154. Gerd Theissen's seminal conclusions on the varied social strata represented in the Corinthian church can be maintained for Ephesus also. This was one of the main conclusions of my "Paul and Ephesus" (e.g., p. 202). See Theissen, "Soziale Schichtung in der korinthischen Gemeinde," *ZNW* 65 (1974): 232–72; translated as "Social Stratification in the Corinthian Community," in *The Social Setting of Pauline Christianity* (Philadelphia: Fortress, 1982), 69–119. Cf. Alan Padgett, "Wealthy Women at Ephesus: 1 Timothy 2:8–15 in Social Context," *Interpretation* 41 (1987): 19–31 (although I cannot agree with his exegesis of the target passage).

155. The "slope house" (*Hanghaus*) complex of Ephesus is a distinctly rich archaeological find. Originating in the first century AD, the connected, multistoried private dwellings measure as much as 3,000 square feet each, and contain rich frescoes and other works of art, peristyle courtyards, and indoor plumbing. Cf. Elliger, *Ephesos*, 71–78.

156. Was the tomb inherited or the office of *kosmeteira?*

157. From book 4 of Joannes Stobaeus's anthology, accessed through the *Thesaurus Linguae Graecae* of University of California, Irvine.

Chapter 2: An Important Word

1. Al Wolters, "A Semantic Study of Αὐθέντης and Its Derivatives," *Journal of Greco-Roman Christianity and Judaism* 1 (2000): 145–75.

2. David Huttar, "ΑΥΘΕΝΤΕΙΝ in the Aeschylus Scholium," *JETS* 44 (2001): 615–25.

3. It is indeed discouraging that, after the scholarly advances in our knowledge during the last decade, apparently well-intentioned and certainly well-trained scholars such as Richard Kroeger and Catherine Kroeger still cling to incongruous and unsupported definitions of αὐθεντέω. For a recent example, see Richard Kroeger and Catherine Kroeger,

"Unit 6: Now for the Hard One," in *Women Elders: Called by God?* Online at http:// first presby.org/womenelders.htm#Unit6 (accessed March 1, 2005). Somewhat earlier, L. L. Belleville evidenced no knowledge of the gains in our understanding that have been achieved subsequent to works thoroughly critiqued in the first edition of this article. See *Women Leaders and the Church: 3 Crucial Questions* (Grand Rapids: Baker, 2000) and the nearly identical arguments in James R. Beck and Craig L. Blomberg, eds., *Two Views on Women in the Ministry* (Grand Rapids: Zondervan, 2001), 120–30.

4. C. C. Kroeger, "Ancient Heresies and a Strange Greek Verb," *Reformed Journal* 29 (1979): 12–15.

5. Carroll Osburn, "ΑΥΘΕΝΤΕΩ (1 Timothy 2:12)," *Restoration Quarterly* 25 (1982): 1–12. See also A. J. Panning, "ΑΥΘΕΝΤΕΙΝ—A Word Study," *Wisconsin Lutheran Quarterly* 78 (1981): 185–91, who also takes issue with Kroeger's *Reformed Journal* article.

6. G. W. Knight III, "ΑΥΘΕΝΤΕΩ in Reference to Women in 1 Timothy 2.12," *NTS* 30 (1984): 143–57.

7. L. E. Wilshire, "The TLG Computer and Further Reference to ΑΥΘΕΝΤΕΩ in 1 Timothy 2.12," *NTS* 34 (1988): 120–34.

8. Ibid., 131.

9. His whole series of questions about 1 Timothy 2, ending with the question "Does not the extended passage in 1 Timothy argue that the concept of 'authority' is under consideration?" gives evidence of this. See ibid., 130–31.

10. L. E. Wilshire, "1 Timothy 2:12 Revisited: A Reply to Paul W. Barnett and Timothy J. Harris," *EQ* 65 (1993): 53.

11. R. C. Kroeger and C. C. Kroeger, *I Suffer Not a Woman: Rethinking 1 Timothy 2:11–15 in Light of Ancient Evidence* (Grand Rapids: Baker, 1992), 84–104, 185–88.

12. The specialist is directed to appendix 2 of the first edition of this volume for a complete citation of each instance in Greek along with translations.

13. The reverse side was also acknowledged by Saussure: While any individual speaker has his or her immediate and intended use of the language, there is an overall pattern of how language is used in sum or aggregate. The personal use of language Saussure calls *la parole* and the widespread pattern he titles *la langue*. *La langue* must exist or no one could ever communicate with another and society would lapse into linguistic solipsism. One *can* talk about what "English speakers" say, not merely what "an English speaker" says.

14. Rudolf Carnap, *The Logical Syntax of Language* (London: Kegan, 1937), 2.

15. "The combinative aspect of speech is, of course, of capital importance, for it implies that speech is constituted by the recurrence of identical signs: it is because the signs are repeated in successive discourses [with different speakers] and within one and the same discourse (although they are combined in accordance with the diversity of various people's speech) that each sign becomes an element of the language; and it is because speech is essentially a combinative activity that it corresponds to an individual act and not to pure creation." See Roland Barthes, *Elements of Semiology*, trans. A. Lavers and C. Smith (New York: Hill & Wang, 1968), 15.

16. The same must be said where a word appears in different places with distinct meanings. If one well-attested meaning is seemingly appropriate to the context under investigation, and the other rare meaning(s) strange or bizarre, the entire burden of proof is on the exegete to show why the apparently appropriate meaning should not be adopted.

17. Compare λογίζομαι/λόγος, δύναμαι/δύναμις, παρακαλέω/παράκλητος, ἐπιστατέω/ ἐπιστάτης, δεσποτέω/δεσπότης.

18. By ignoring this important caveat, Belleville is not the first exegete to get stuck in a lexical quagmire. After attempting to synthesize the meanings of the noun, the adjective, and the verb found in the Greek Bible, she can only pessimistically agree with Philip

Payne that "it is precarious to deny women anything on the basis of the uncertain meaning of a verb that occurs nowhere else in the Bible. It is even more precarious to assume the meaning is 'to have authority over'" (*Women Leaders*, 175). Eventually, she concludes with "suggestions" as to what the verb might mean, even asserting that "to instigate violence" is the "most widely found meaning of this word group" (ibid., 176). In fact, not a single case can be found of the *verb* ever meaning this. A careful review of the separate histories of the cognate nouns, adjective, and verb will provide adequate clarification. The excellent chart of Wolters ("Semantic Study," 171) will remove the doubts of all but the most ardent skeptics.

19. Hesychius of Alexandria (fifth century AD) noted in his lexicon:

αὐθεντεῖν· ἐξουσιάζειν
αὐθέντης· ἐξουσιαστής. αὐτόχειρ, φονεύς

Or, to render this into English,

αὐθεντεῖν = to exercise authority
αὐθέντης = person in authority, doer of a thing, murderer

Hesychius is only known to us in a fifteenth-century AD manuscript, and the work is known to have suffered redaction in many places. Therefore, it is not useful as a primary resource for our purposes. However, it at least corroborates the important distinction between verb and noun that I have attempted to underscore here. See entries A8259–60 of *Hesychii Alexandrini Lexicon*, vol. 1, ed. Kurt Latte (Hauniae, Den.: Munksgaard, 1953), 279.

20. The Greek corpus includes at a minimum some 60 million words of text (*Thesaurus Linguae Graecae Newsletter* 20 [May 1992]: 3) when the known edited papyri are included. The verb αὐθεντέω appears about 110 times, including its use in various citations of 1 Tim. 2.

21. Compare the number of citations found in other lexicographers: Lampe (30), BDAG (14+), Sophocles (11), and LSJ (4), including citations of 1 Tim. 2:12.

22. See, for example, Belleville, who argues that because Paul did not use the more frequent word ἐξουσιάζειν, there must be some esoteric meaning for αὐθεντεῖν unique to the Ephesian situation (*Women Leaders*, 175). This is surely belied by the use of αὐθεντεῖν in BGU 1208, which is an ordinary, private correspondence from one brother to another about "happenings down on the farm" dated to 27 BC. It was certainly written by a literate individual, but it could hardly be a more mundane, ordinary piece from among the papyri of Egypt. It uses our verb with the sense "I used my authority to insist he do what was right and just to do."

23. I have made two exceptions to this. Among the church fathers, we find direct quotation of 1 Tim. 2:12 appearing more than twenty times. Obviously, such quotation offers little lexical help in understanding the meaning of αὐθεντέω and therefore has not been considered. There are also ten uses of the verbal αὐθεντέω in four separate recensions of the *Alexander Romance*. While this "history" of Alexander the Great is believed to have been written by a certain Pseudo-Callisthenes around AD 300, it is not at all clear to what century we should date the texts at hand. Michael Grant (*Greek and Latin Authors* [New York: Wilson, 1980], 81) asserts that the "work is only available in editions of the later Roman Empire." But the citations in question are Middle Greek and appear to come from the late Byzantine MSS mentioned by A. P. Kazhdan, *The Oxford Dictionary of Byzantium*, vol. 1 (Oxford: Oxford University Press, 1991), 58. Thus, they lie beyond the period of consideration for this study.

24. At the same time, we note that there is a practical limitation to our approach. Because of the relatively smaller number of references to the verb αὐθεντέω in Greek

literature, at one or two smaller points our results do lack the level of clarity we would desire. Hence, other approaches with a greater reliance on word origins and the history of its usage have proved useful in providing further insights. A comparison with the history of the cognate nouns can offer explanation for the occasional wayward datum that appears to fall outside the clear and predictable boundaries. The results of the best of such studies are included in forming our conclusions in this second edition.

25. This is an increase of three from the previous edition. I am indebted to Wolters ("Semantic Study," 157) for identifying that not only is there a use of αὐθεντέω in the tenth-century *Scholia Graeca in Homeri Iliadem*, which I cited, but the origin of that scholium is from the first-century BC to first-century AD writer Aristonicus Alexandrinus, *De signis Iliadis*, 9.694. Thus, this latter citation provides an attestation of my meaning number 4 in table 2.2 much nearer to the time of the New Testament than I had recognized. A second addition, also found by Wolters (ibid., 159) is from A. S. Hunt and E. J. Goodspeed, *The Tebtunis Papyri: Part 2* (London: Frowde, 1907), P.Tebt. 276.28, found on page 31. If the textual reconstruction is correct, it is an instance of the future tense of αὐθεντέω with the meaning "will rule." The third addition is a scholium that Huttar believes to be the origin of a subsequent late-Byzantine scholium. (This late-Byzantine scholium is cited in my first edition with the meaning "murder." It is found in this form in Manuscript T [Naples, Biblioteca Nazionale, cod. II.F.31)], dated to around AD 1325.) The earlier scholium is now included as an independent occurrence (number 85). According to Huttar ("ΑΥΘΕΝΤΕΙΝ," 624), this participial usage of αὐθεντέω has the sense "the one having just initiated this thing," my meaning number 4, below. The text in which this additional instance occurs is found in the Medicean Manuscript in Florence (Florence, R. Biblioteca Medicea Laurenziana, cod. 32, 9), dated to around AD 1000, which contains Aeschylus's play *Eumenides*. The scholium is upon the word στάζοντα at line 42.

26. This material was originally gathered by computer searches of two CD-ROMs: (1) *Greek Documentary* (CD-ROM 6) and (2) *Thesaurus Linguae Graecae* (CD-ROM D). The first-named resource includes documentary papyri (as well as ostraca) prepared by Duke University, with the help of the University of Michigan, and Greek inscriptions prepared at Cornell University, Ohio State University, and the Institute for Advanced Study (Princeton, NJ). CD-ROM 6 contains more than 130 editions of papyri, including major collections such as BGU, POxy, PLond, PFamTebt, etc. The *Greek Documentary* CD-ROM is published by the Packard Humanities Institute, Los Altos, CA. The second-named resource, CD-ROM D of *Thesaurus Linguae Graecae*, was prepared by the University of California, Irvine. The current edition of *Thesaurus Linguae Graecae*, CD-ROM E, can be searched using any Pentium PC and a wide range of software, including the *TLG Workplace 9.0* from Silver Mountain Software (info@silvermnt.com). Searches were conducted to find all occurrences of αὐθεντέω (αὐθεντ-, ηὐθεντ-). The results of these searches were then collated with the results of manual searches of published lexicographers, ancient and modern, including those listed in table 2.1.

27. In the first edition of this chapter, I proposed a fifth meaning for αὐθεντεῖν, that is, "to murder," based on a single datum found in a reputed ninth-century AD scholium at line 40 of the play *Eumenides* by Aeschylus (see note 25, above). I found this datum odd since it fell completely outside the trajectory of the other eighty-one instances of the verb. Yet, having no better way to evaluate it at the time, I included it as a separate meaning. I am deeply indebted to David Huttar and his insightful article, "ΑΥΘΕΝ-ΤΕΙΝ," for bringing scholarly light to bear on the matter. Actually, the supposed meaning "murder" is attested in a form of the scholium found in two MSS. It is, according to Huttar, even much later than I had believed—probably as late as the fourteenth century AD—and its meaning "murder" is most likely due to a *misunderstanding* of the text

and late etymologizing of the scholiast that "created" this meaning for the verb. In his independent analysis, Wolters comes to a similar conclusion about the origins of this supposed meaning: "It is best to take this unusual usage to be an Atticistic hypercorrection on the part of a Byzantine scholar" ("Semantic Study," 169). According to Huttar, the other form of the scholium is much earlier, perhaps ultimately finding its origins in the first or second century AD. He sees no reason why the meaning there should not be the same as my number 4 above. I believe Huttar has convincingly shown that the meaning "to murder" does not exist for the verb. This judgment is further supported on etymological grounds following on Wolters's conclusion: "By the first century AD, αὐθέντης in the living language meant 'master,' and the meaning 'murderer' was largely forgotten"; and "the cognates of αὐθέντης . . . are all based on αὐθέντης in the meaning 'master'" ("Semantic Study," 153).

28. This should not be confused with "domineer." The distinction between "domineer" and "dominate" becomes an important one in the exegesis of 1 Timothy 2. Therefore, the two terms should not be taken as interchangeable. For "to dominate," a transitive verb, *The Compact Oxford Dictionary of the English Language* (Oxford: Oxford University Press, 1971), ad loc., gives the meaning as "to bear rule over, to have a commanding influence on, to master." In the context of some human relationships, this could have a negative connotation, but it is not intrinsically so. In contrast, "domineer" is defined as an intransitive verb meaning "to rule or govern arbitrarily or despotically . . . to exercise authority in an overbearing manner." Therefore, dominate and domineer are not synonyms unless it is shown that the domination is considered improper. Belleville appears to have fallen prey to this confusion and in all cases has certainly confused the noun for the verb when she says, "Second-century astronomists [*sic*] talk about the '*dominance* of Saturn over Mercury and the moon'" (*Women Leaders*, 175). The reference is to Ptolemy, *Tetrabiblos* 3.13. In fact, Ptolemy uses the verb at this point. F. E. Robbins in the Loeb Classical Library series translates the fuller passage this way (italics added to indicate the verb): "If Saturn alone is ruler of the soul and *dominates* Mercury and the moon, if he has a dignified position with reference to the universe and angels, he makes his subjects lovers of the body." Robbins clearly does not mean anything pejorative like "domineer" here. For confirmation, see E. A. Sophocles, *Greek Lexicon of the Roman and Byzantine Periods* (New York: Scribner's, 1887), 276, who lists this same instance under the meaning "be in power over, to have authority over."

29. The *Lexicon* of Hesychius agrees with this assessment. Under the entry for ἡγεῖτο, the imperfect of ἡγέομαι (I lead), Hesychius defines this with "ηὐθέντει, ἦρχεν," from αὐθεντέω and ἄρχω, respectively. See Hesychius, entry H49.

30. Origen (died ca. AD 253), in what may be the earliest extant commentary on 1 Tim. 2:12, cites the verse and then appears to go on to define αὐθεντεῖν with the words ἡγεμόνα γίνεσθαι τῷ [τοῦ ἀνδρός], "be a ruler [over a man] in speaking." See p. 42 of the text quoted in C. Jenkins, "Documents: Origen on I Corinthians," *Journal of Theological Studies* 10 (1909): 29–51.

31. Parker's choice of "despot" illustrates a closely related phenomenon in English: "despot" denotes "sole ruler." Through repeated hyperbole it has come to connote something like "tyrant." Therefore, I do find it somewhat disappointing that I. H. Marshall and P. H. Towner, in their otherwise magisterial and lucid commentary (*The Pastoral Epistles*, International Critical Commentary [Edinburgh: Clark, 1999], 454–71), do not seem to have fully appreciated my point here—though I must confess that in the first edition I did not make my case as clearly as it should have been made. As noted under meaning 2a, "to compel, to influence," when Chrysostom seeks to use the word αὐθεντέω in a pejorative sense in his *Sermons in Genesis*, he finds it necessary to add the

word "wrongly." Thus, when we turn to Chrysostom's *Homilies on Colossians* (the sole supporting datum for meaning 2c), we are on firm ground in assuming he is using the word there *hyperbolically*, to mean "play the tyrant." And as we noted above, hyperbole is an exaggerated use of language, beyond its normal meaning, for rhetorical effect. We further note that the passage from *Homilies on Colossians* is found in a highly rhetorical context. Therefore, the burden of proof is squarely on the exegete if he or she wishes to claim meaning 2c at 1 Tim. 2:12, for this would be precisely *contrary* to normal usage. I fear Marshall and Towner have not successfully borne the burden of that proof for a number of reasons:

(1) In their analysis of αὐθεντέω in 1 Tim. 2:12, after acknowledging that the definitions I presented in the first edition of this chapter were "broadly convincing" (*Pastoral Epistles*, 456), they go on to build their exegesis on what is a priori the *least* probable definition for the word, claiming the word has "the nuance of exercising autocratic power which is present in several examples. This meaning fits best into the context, which is characterized by argumentation and dogmatic intimidation" (ibid., 458). But is this so? The character and texture of Chrysostom's *Homilies on Colossians* is compassionate and tender, and particularly in the section concerned, it is aimed to tug on the emotional heart strings of his hearers. About Chrysostom and these transcripts of his oral preaching, John A. Broadus writes, "You very soon find he is profoundly in earnest, and all alive. Christianity is with him a living reality. . . . We may discern what seem to us grave errors of doctrinal opinion, but we feel the quickening pulses of genuine Christian love and zeal. And how he fully sympathizes with his hearers! He thoroughly knows them, ardently loves them, has a like temperament, shares not a little in the faults of his age and race, as must always be the case with a truly inspiring orator or poet. Even when severely rebuking, when blazing with indignation, he never seems alien, never stands aloof, but throws himself among them, in a very transport of desire to check, and rescue, and save" ("Saint Chrysostom as a Homilist," in *The Nicene and Post-Nicene Fathers*, ed. Philip Schaff, 1st series [repr., Grand Rapids: Eerdmans, 1979], 13:v–vii). Is 1 Timothy cast in the same rhetorical mold as these works of Chrysostom? It does not seem so. Rather, what we have throughout all of 1 Tim. 2 seems to be far more dispassionate in tone. In 1 Tim. 2, what we find structurally is a command followed by the theological basis for that command. Marshall and Towner themselves superbly show how the instruction for prayer in 1 Tim. 2:1 (with its digression in v. 2) is predicated on the character of God the Savior, who desires all to be saved (vv. 3ff). The analogous structure exists in vv. 11 and 12, where commands are predicated on the theological principles of vv. 13 and 14. There is no shift in tone from the well-reasoned, almost dispassionate arguments of vv. 1–7 to rhetorical passion or "dogmatic intimidation" (*Pastoral Epistles*, 458) in vv. 8–15.

(2) Noting that for both George W. Knight III and me "the essential motif that unites the various uses of the verb is the exercise of authority" (*Pastoral Epistles*, 456), Marshall and Towner go on to controvert that position: "The conclusion that this is the basic meaning or normal sense has rightly been questioned" (ibid., 457). After the recent work by Wolters, Huttar, and this second edition, it is hard to imagine how such skepticism will be tenable in the future. First, each of the questioners cited (ibid.) was addressing Knight's older work, not mine, for they were all prior to the first complete study of the verb ever undertaken, that is, this essay in the first edition of this work. Second, it is difficult to see how any impartial reader of the data of appendix 2 of the first edition would conclude, after reading the eighty-two extant usages from the ancient world found there, that the "purely neutral sense" is not the basic and normal sense of the word αὐθεντέω. The most basic sense is the positive exercise of authority. There are two denotations that are "morally negative," the hyperbolic 2c ("to play the tyrant"

[intransitive]), which appears once, and 3c ("to flout the authority of" [transitive]), which appears three times. Definition 3b ("to exercise one's own jurisdiction"), while appearing about five times in contexts that are negative, is not of itself negative, for in the other eight instances or so the meaning must be positive or is "neutral." (That a word with a positive definition can be used in a negative context without acquiring a negative definition is discussed below.) Eighty-one of eighty-five known examples would appear to be adequate to prove the point: "exercise authority" is the basic sense of the word.

(3) Marshall and Towner argue that "so unusual a word (only four instances before the Christian era) [actually, only three instances, as Wolters ("Semantic Study," 171) and I would reckon it] is used here is surely significant" (*Pastoral Epistles*, 458), and they believe that this fact therefore lends additional credence to finding a negative meaning in 1 Tim. 2. This argument can be made to stand on its head. As Wolters observes, "Although it is possible to identify isolated cases of the pejorative use of both αὐθεντέω and αὐθεντία, these are not found before the fourth century AD" ("Semantic Study," 171). Further, if one wishes to cite BGU 1208 as controversion to this, the discussion of this passage offered below (see note 50) and the verdict both of Wolters ("Semantic Study," 157) and the LSJ lexicon about the passage appear to be sufficient to call for, at the minimum, a judgment of "undecided." All current evidence suggests that negative denotations with regard to authority arise after the New Testament era.

(4) It seems infelicitous to state, as Marshall and Towner do, that "the verb characterizes the nature of the teaching rather than the role of the women in church leadership in general" (*Pastoral Epistles*, 460). From a lexical standpoint, this appears to be untenable. Not a single example can be evidenced from anywhere that αὐθεντέω is ever used of anything other than the exercise of authority (whether rightly or, in a few cases, wrongly), certainly not of teaching. Further, if indeed the exegete feels compelled by the case at hand to find that a negative denotation is required in 1 Tim. 2:12 (which, we argue, the grammar would not allow—see chapter 3 of this volume), then the only transitive option would be "flout the authority of men." This in turn would yield a meaning such as "Let a woman learn in silence, in all submissiveness. I do not allow a woman to teach a man or to flout the authority of a man." It does not seem that this would be vastly different from the traditional interpretation, when all entailments are considered.

(5) A final consideration involving context, rather than lexical matters, should be noted. Marshall and Towner state, "In the context the fact that Eve was deceived is cited as a parallel, and this strongly suggests the conclusion that behind the present prohibition lies some particular false teaching by some women" (*Pastoral Epistles*, 458). With due respect, this borders on being an error of fact. The prohibition is paralleled *most nearly* by a positive parallel, "for Adam was formed first." This is clearly a pre-fall event and therefore a sinless and positive thing in Paul's reckoning. Secondarily, and more remotely, the prohibition is paralleled with Eve's deception. This is not just an oversight on the part of Marshall and Towner, for this same lapse is seen in the introduction to the section containing vv. 8–15 (ibid., 437).

32. This investigation employs many sources from the church of the early centuries AD, where the concept of "independence" is one that would not have found wholehearted acceptance. Submission to authority, not independence, was one of the driving values of the early church. So several of the examples given are in a context where the author undoubtedly intends the context to have negative connotations.

33. Hesychius provides a confirming note here in his definition of αὐτοδικεῖ (see entry A8049). He says, αὐτοδικεῖ = αὐθεντεῖ ὅταν αὐτὸς λέγῃ. That is, "he has independent jurisdiction = αὐθεντεῖ, when he speaks himself/on his own authority."

34. Victor Antiochenus, *Catenae in Evangelia S. Matthaei et S. Marci ad fidem Codd. MSS.*, vol. 1 of *Catenae Graecorum Patrium in Novum Testamentum*, ed. J. A. Cramer (Oxford, 1840; repr., Hildesheim: Olms, 1967), 292–329.

35. Wolters, "Semantic Study," 160. Wolters (ibid., 157n69) was correct in questioning my translation of the Scholia Vetera on Homer's *Iliad*. There, under this meaning, I translated the present participle "the one originating [the writing]." This is clearly confusing and should be rendered, as he does, "the one doing [(as Huttar has it) the speech]."

36. Eusebius, *Vita Constantini*, in F. Winkelman, ed., *Eusebius Werke*, Band 1.1: *Über das Leben des Kaisers Konstantin* (Berlin: Academie-Verlag, 1975), 2.48.1.8. Though Lampe has this listed under "instigate; authorize," it is not clear from the context if God is the one simply "doing" judgment or "instigating" it.

37. As explained above (note 25), the same scholium is found in two locations: Aristonicus Alexandrinus, *De signis Iliadis*, in *Aristonici περὶ σημείων Ἰλιάδος reliquae emendatiores*, ed. L. Friedländer (Göttingen: Dieterich, 1853), 9.694; and H. Erbse, ed., *Scholia Graeca in Homeri Iliadem*, vol. 2 (Berlin: de Gruyter, 1971), book 10, entry 694.

38. Pope Leo I, *Epistle 30* (To Pulcheria), 54.788A.

39. Nicolao (Sebatian) Coleti, ed. *Sacrosancta Concilia ad Regium additionem exacta*, vol. 8 (Venice, 1728–33), 721D.

40. In these texts, "doing" and "instigating" are clearly distinguished. In both cases the reference is to "not instigating" sin. The ones "not instigating" still did sin, and ecclesial action may be taken, but judgment of a different kind is required because those who sinned were swept along with the crowd and were not the ringleaders.

41. A. Adler, ed., *Svidae Lexicon*, part 1 (repr., Stuttgart: Tübner, 1971), A4426.

42. Kroeger and Kroeger, *I Suffer Not a Woman*, chap. 9.

43. See BDAG, ad loc.

44. A similar parallel of προΐστημι and αὐθεντέω is found in Hesychius at the entry for αὐτάντας. There we read ὁ προεστώς τινος πράγματος, καὶ αὐθεντῶν, "the one who is in charge and in command of some matter." See entry A8367.

45. See note 27.

46. Huttar, "ΑΥΘΕΝΤΕΙΝ," 625.

47. This is what we will go on to argue is the case in 1 Tim. 2:12. The meaning "to exercise authority over, to control" is not negative, but the whole phrase "a woman to exercise authority over a man" is seen as something undesirable by Paul.

48. The present tense of θεραπεύω recalls the content of the Pharisees' direct speech. Maximilian Zerwick and Mary Grosvenor, *A Grammatical Analysis of the Greek New Testament*, 4th ed. (Rome: Pontifical Biblical Institute, 1996), 194.

49. Perhaps a more apt English analog to αὐθεντέω would be the word "beat," which has both positive and negative denotations. But surely it would be a mistake to take a context such as "the father beat his son at basketball before an audience of the boy's peers" as warrant for a denotation for "beat" such as "to humiliate in sporting competition." The caution required in separating transferable meaning from the context is the flip side of D. A. Carson's "illegitimate totality transfer." See D. A. Carson, *Exegetical Fallacies*, 2nd ed. (Grand Rapids: Baker, 1996), 60–61.

50. This important point is emphasized by Wolters ("Semantic Study," 170–71). Belleville's assertion that "the one meaning that does not seem to be in evidence during this period is the simple exercise of authority" is highly problematic (Belleville, *Women Leaders*, 175). Apart from the uncertainty of what is meant by "simple exercise of authority," the translations of the texts she cites are quite unsatisfactory. The actual texts in which the verb appears are these: Philodemus (first century BC), BGU 1208 (27 BC), and Aristonicus (ca. first century BC–first century AD). The texts and translational issues are as follows:

Source	Text	Translation
Philodemus, *Rhetorica*, 133.14[a]	Ἀλλὰ εἰ δεῖ ταληθῆ κα[ὶ γι]νόμενα [λέγειν, οἱ ῥ[ήτ]ορες καὶ μ[εγάλα] βλάπτ[ουσι] πολλοὺς [καὶ μαγάλους καὶ περὶ τῶν ["δεινοῖς ἔρωσι το[ξ]ευομένων" πρὸς τοὺς ἐπιθαν[εστάτους ἑκάστοτε διαμάχονται καὶ "σὺν αὐθεντ[οῦσιν ἄν[αξιν]" ὑπὲρ τῶν ὁμοίων ὡσαύτως.[b]	To tell the truth the rhetors do a great deal of harm to many people, and incur the enmity of powerful rulers, whereas philosophers gain the friendship of public men by helping them out of their trouble. Ought we not to consider that men who incur the enmity of <u>the ones in authority</u> are villains, and hated by both gods and men?[c]
BGU 1208, line 38[d]	καὶ ἐμοῦ <u>αὐθεντηκότος</u> πρὸς αὐτὸν περιποιῆσαι Καλατύτει τῷ ναυτικῷ ἐπὶ τῷ αὐτῷ φόρῳ ἐν τῇ ὥραι ἐπεχώρησεν. τὴν δὲ μετὰ ταῦτα ἐξηκολουθηκυῖαν ὕβριν μεταπε[μ]φθεὶς ὑπ' ἐμ]οῦ[e] ὁ [Καλατ]ύτις ἐξηγή[σατό μ]οι ἀκεραίως.[f]	And <u>when I compelled</u> him [prob. Antilochus] to lay by funds for Calatytis the boatman upon the same payment at that time, he acquiesced. But Calatytis, when he was summoned by me, showed to me pure hubris which followed after these things.[g]
Aristonicus Alexandrinus, *De signis Iliadis*, 9.694	ὅτι ἐκ ἄλλων τόπων ἐστὶν ὁ στίχος· νῦν γὰρ οὐξ ἁρμόζει· τότε γὰρ εἴωθεν ἐπιφωνεῖσθαι, ὅταν ὁ αὐθεντῶν τοῦ λόγου καταπληκτικά τινα προενέγκηται.[h]	This line is from another place. For now it does not fit properly. For then it was wont to be mentioned when <u>the one doing</u> the speech had set forth something astounding.[i]

a. This text is taken from a serious treatise in seven books concerning the nature and effect of rhetoric. This particular section of Philodemus deals with the negative effects of rhetors and their rhetoric. The use of our verb (participle) here is clearly positive, "those exercising authority" (i.e., people in proper leadership positions). Though the text is the reconstruction of Sudhaus, C. J. Vooys (*Lexicon Philodemeum*, Pars Prior [Purmerend, Neth.: Muusses, 1934], 53) accepts Sudhaus's reconstruction and gives the Latin equivalent for our Greek verb as *dominor*, "to be lord and master." Similarly, *DGE* lists this passage with the meaning "ejercer la autoridad" (= "exercise authority over").

b. S. Sudhaus, ed., *Philodemi: Volumina Rhetorica*, vol. 3 (Leipzig: Teubner, 1896), 133.

c. H. H. Hubbell, "The Rhetorica of Philodemus," *Transactions of the Connecticut Academy of Arts and Sciences* 23 (1920): 306.

d. This is a letter from a certain Tryphon, a farmer/landowner along the Nile, to his brother. In the letter Tryphon acknowledges receipt of a letter from his brother in which his brother inquired about the "deceit" of a certain Calatytis, who we find out later is a sailor/boatman. Tryphon's response to this deceit was to appeal to the magistrate, presumably against Calatytis. There is some discussion of contracts, then line 29 says the worst of the whole debacle was the ferryman's fee for

"the contract [presumably, for the transportation] for the sheep." The key element of our interest is the perfect genitive participle of αὐθεντέω. As an adverbial participle, it should be "when I had exercised authority" (over), but it is granted that this is the sole known instance of πρός following αὐθεντέω. It may well be that "compel" is too strong here. Tryphon is simply ordering somebody to make payment to the boatman—a legitimate act of his authority as landowner—and for his trouble this Calatytis fellow gave him a hard time, cheating him in some way. This necessitated recourse to the magistrate. It is important to note that in previous translations of this passage Tryphon's actions were seen as compelling an unwilling boatman to do something. It is now evident that this is not the case. Tryphon is compelling (i.e., exercising his authority over) someone to make a payment from Tryphon's own funds for services rendered by Calatytis. This payment should have been adequate, but when Calatytis insults and acts scandalously, Tryphon feels justified to seek out the magistrate.

e. I have emended the uncertain text from οω to εμ here. As given by the editors, it is μεταπε[μ]φθεὶς ὑπὸ ὡοῦ, which makes little sense.

f. F. Schubart et al., eds., BGU (1912), 4:351.

g. The translation is mine.

h. L. Friedländer, ed., *Aristonici περὶ σημείων Ἰλιάδος reliquae emendatiores*, 9.694.

i. The translation is mine.

51. With affirmation from William D. Mounce, *Pastoral Epistles*, Word Biblical Commentary 46 (Nashville: Nelson, 2000), 128.

52. Further, the grammatical structure, as will be shown in the next chapter, also makes this impermissible.

Chapter 3: A Complex Sentence

1. This final element (ἀλλά + infinitive) may not always be found in the examples selected for comparison.

2. P. B. Payne, "Οὐδέ in 1 Timothy 2:12" (paper presented at the annual meeting of the Evangelical Theological Society, November 1986), 10.

3. D. J. Moo, "What Does It Mean Not to Teach or Have Authority over Men? 1 Timothy 2:11–15," in *Recovering Biblical Manhood and Womanhood: A Response to Evangelical Feminism*, ed. J. Piper and W. Grudem (Wheaton: Crossway, 1991), 187.

4. Ibid.

5. Preliminary studies of οὐδέ linking nouns yielded results similar to those in the present study of οὐδέ linking verbs. The imprecision of Payne's work is also characteristic of the study by R. C. Kroeger and C. C. Kroeger, *I Suffer Not a Woman: Rethinking 1 Timothy 2:11–15 in Light of Ancient Evidence* (Grand Rapids: Baker, 1991), 83–84, 189–92, whose examples are either passages in which οὐδέ joins two nouns or in which the word is not οὐδέ but οὐδέν. The Kroegers' suggestion that αὐθεντεῖν in 1 Tim. 2:12 may be an "infinitive of indirect discourse" must be rejected since they do not provide a single example of an infinitive of indirect discourse following οὐδέ in the New Testament or elsewhere.

6. A few constraints should be noted. Although the subject of this chapter is *syntactical* background studies, the conclusions drawn from the syntax as found in 1 Tim. 2:12 will involve *semantic* judgments (especially in the two patterns of the usage of οὐδέ that will be identified). There are also other syntactical (as well as semantic) issues raised by 1 Tim. 2:12 that will not be dealt with in this study, such as the question of whether or not ἀνδρός should be read with both διδάσκειν and αὐθεντεῖν or exactly how the ἀλλά clause at the end of verse 12 relates to the preceding clause and which verb should be supplied there. Even the aspect or tense of the verbs involved will not be dealt with at this stage of the investigation, since, as will become evident, the major thesis of this essay is not materially affected by the aspect or tense of the verbs.

7. This syntactical pattern is not necessarily always found in this particular sequence. For example, in 1 Tim. 2:12, the first infinitive precedes the negated finite verb so that the order there is (2), (1), (3), and (4). A study of preceding infinitives in the Pauline literature, however, indicates that it is hard to find any consistent significance in preceding rather than following infinitives. Cf. the nineteen instances of preceding infinitives in the Pauline writings: Rom. 7:18; 8:8; 1 Cor. 7:36; 14:35; 15:50; 2 Cor. 8:10; 11:30; 12:1; Gal. 4:9, 17; Phil. 1:12; 2 Thess. 1:3; 1 Tim. 2:12; 3:5; 5:11, 25; 6:7, 16; 2 Tim. 2:13. Either way, the central thesis of this essay is not affected by whether the first infinitive precedes or follows the negated finite verb. Likewise, the presence or absence of element 4 does not substantially affect the thesis of this essay.

8. This is one major reason why, after screening less-close syntactical parallels, this study will proceed to search extrabiblical Greek literature for more exact parallels involving, as in 1 Tim. 2:12, two infinitives governed by a negated finite verb. The fact that, strictly speaking, there is only one close syntactical parallel to 1 Tim. 2:12 in the New Testament does not mean that New Testament passages in which a negated finite verb governs two verb forms other than infinitives are without value for identifying general patterns of the usage of οὐδέ. Rather, the New Testament allows one to identify a basic pattern of the usage of οὐδέ that can then be tested and refined by resorting to extrabiblical Greek literature. This is the approach followed in the present study.

9. Contrast the use of ἑτεροδιδάσκαλειν in 1 Tim. 1:3–4 and 6:3, on which see further discussion below.

10. Cf. Kroeger and Kroeger, *I Suffer Not a Woman*, 81. See also Payne ("Οὐδέ," 6–8), who argues that teaching is an activity viewed positively in and of itself in the New Testament and in Paul.

11. Cf. Kroeger and Kroeger, *I Suffer Not a Woman*, 81.

12. Translations for texts 1, 2, and 5 are taken from Bruce M. Metzger, *The Apocrypha of the Old Testament* (New York: Oxford University Press, 1977); translations for texts 3, 4, 6, and 7 are my own; and translations for texts 8–48 are taken from the Loeb Classical Library series.

13. Note that "to take part in public affairs" is not as neutral as this translation might suggest. Cf. LSJ, 1442: πολυπραγματέω: "mostly in bad sense, to be a meddlesome, inquisitive busybody; esp. meddle in state affairs, intrigue."

14. The primary thesis that this chapter seeks to establish is that the two concepts connected by οὐδέ are both viewed either positively or negatively. The following subcategories of this basic pattern may be identified: (1) synonymous concepts: Matt. 7:18; Mark 8:17; John 14:27; Acts 2:27; 1 Cor. 15:50; Gal. 4:14; Phil. 2:16; 2 Thess. 2:2; 1 Tim. 6:16; Heb. 10:8; 12:5; 13:5; 1 Pet. 3:14; (2) conceptual parallels: Matt. 6:28 = Luke 12:27; Matt. 7:6; 10:14 = Mark 6:11; Matt. 12:19; Luke 3:14; 6:44; 18:4; John 14:17; Acts 4:18; 17:24–25; Rom. 9:16; 2 Cor. 4:2; Col. 2:21; 2 Thess. 3:7–8; 1 Pet. 2:22; 1 John 3:6; Rev. 12:8; (3) complementary concepts: Acts 9:9; Rom. 14:21; 2 Cor. 7:12; Rev. 7:16; (4) sequential concepts: Matt. 6:20, 26 = Luke 12:24; Matt. 13:13; Mark 13:15; Luke 12:33; 17:23; John 4:15; Rom. 9:11; (5) ascensive concepts: Matt. 22:46; 23:13; Acts 16:21; (6) specific to general or general to specific: (a) specific to general: Acts 21:21; 1 Tim. 2:12; (b) general to specific: Gal. 1:16–17; 1 Tim. 1:3–4; 6:17. Note that there may be some overlap among these categories so that they should not be understood to be totally mutually exclusive but rather as indicating the most likely emphasis on the relationship between the two concepts linked by οὐδέ.

15. *Southern Cross Newspaper* (September 1996), published by Anglican Media in Sydney, Australia.

16. *Jahrbuch für evangelikale Theologie* 6 (1996): 421–25.

17. Alan G. Padgett, "The Scholarship of Patriarchy (on 1 Timothy 2:8–15): A Response to *Women in the Church*," *Priscilla Papers* 11, no. 1 (Winter 1997): 24.

18. *JETS* 41, no. 3 (1998): 513–16. In a perceptive comment that anticipates Craig Blomberg's 2001 essay (see below), Keener suspects that this reading would represent a challenge for "the more moderate complementarian view that allows women to teach men provided they [the women] are under male authority."

19. *The Pastoral Epistles*, International Critical Commentary (Edinburgh: Clark, 1999), 454–60, esp. 458–60.

20. Such as, "I do not permit the women to continue their false teaching." See Craig L. Blomberg, "Neither Hierarchicalist nor Egalitarian," in *Two Views on Women in Ministry*, ed. James R. Beck and Craig L. Blomberg (Grand Rapids: Zondervan, 2001), 361n137.

21. Ibid., 359, noting that this is conceded by the egalitarian Walter Liefeld in "Response," in *Women, Authority and the Bible*, ed. Alvera Mickelsen (Downers Grove, IL: InterVarsity, 1986), 220.

22. See pp. 62–63 above.

23. See further the objection dealt with and answered by Wayne Grudem discussed below.

24. *The Pastoral Epistles*, Word Biblical Commentary 46 (Nashville: Nelson, 2000), 120–30, esp. 124–26 and 128–30.

25. Ibid., 125, 129.

26. Ibid., 128.

27. Ibid., 130.

28. Kevin Giles, "A Critique of the 'Novel' Contemporary Interpretation of 1 Timothy 2:9–15 Given in the Book, *Women in the Church*: Parts I and II," *EQ* 72, no. 2 (2000): 151–67; 72, no. 3 (2000): 195–215. See my response, *"Women in the Church*: A Response to Kevin Giles," *EQ* 73 (2001): 205–24.

29. Giles, "Critique," 153.

30. Ibid., 212.

31. There is no need here to reproduce my interaction with Belleville in *JETS* 44, no. 2 (2001): 344–46. While my tone was perhaps a bit forceful, I continue to believe that my critique was essentially sound.

32. Linda Belleville, *Women Leaders and the Church: Three Crucial Questions* (Grand Rapids: Baker, 2000), 173 (the same assertion is made on 175).

33. See note 14, above.

34. Hence, the critique of Payne in the original essay also applies to Belleville.

35. Belleville, "Women in Ministry," in *Two Views on Women in Ministry*, ed. J. R. Beck and C. L. Blomberg (Grand Rapids: Zondervan, 2001), 135–36. But see esp. the reviews by Andreas J. Köstenberger (cited above) and Thomas R. Schreiner in the *Journal for Biblical Manhood and Womanhood* 6, no. 2 (Fall 2001): 24–30.

36. *Greek Grammar beyond the Basics* (Grand Rapids: Zondervan, 1996), 598–99, and 599n29.

37. See further the interaction with Belleville's subsequent critique below.

38. Blomberg, "Neither Hierarchicalist nor Egalitarian: Gender Roles in Paul," in *Two Views on Women in Ministry*, 363.

39. Ibid.

40. Ibid., 364.

41. Ibid.

42. It is not entirely clear to me how this conclusion renders Blomberg "neither hierarchicalist nor egalitarian," as he suggests in the title of his essay. I see how he wants to avoid some of the negative connotations associated with the term "hierarchicalist" and how he is more open to women in leadership than strict nonegalitarians, but he clearly shares with the latter their central tenet and thus hardly occupies a true middle position between those who believe in women holding positions of ultimate authority in the church and those who do not. Also, in his title he erects somewhat of a straw man by positing "hierarchicalist" as one of the two polar opposites. This is accomplished only by stereotyping his fellow-complementarians. Is Blomberg implying that Thomas Schreiner or Ann Bowman, for example, the authors of the two nonegalitarian essays in the same volume, are "hierarchicalists"? Blomberg appears able to occupy the center in the debate only by pushing further to the right others with whom he shares their central tenet.

43. On issues of application, see Dorothy Patterson's chapter in the present volume.

44. William J. Webb, *Slaves, Women & Homosexuals: Exploring the Hermeneutics of Cultural Analysis* (Downers Grove, IL: InterVarsity, 2001), 35. It is beyond the scope of this chapter to respond to Webb's categorization of the first edition of the present work as "patriarchal" (282 et passim), other than to note that the label is tendentious, inflammatory, and inaccurate.

45. Ibid., 225.

46. Ibid., 244n3.

47. Esther Yue L. Ng, *Reconstructing Christian Origins? The Feminist Theology of Elisabeth Schüssler Fiorenza: An Evaluation* (Carlisle, Eng.: Paternoster, 2002), 285n170.

48. Ibid., 287n184.

49. Studies in Biblical Literature 38 (New York: Peter Lang, 2001), 261–82. The reprinted essay is "Syntactical Background Studies to 1 Tim 2.12 in the New Testament and Extrabiblical Greek Literature," in *Discourse Analysis and Other Topics in Biblical Greek*, ed. Stanley E. Porter and D. A. Carson, JSNTSup 113 (Sheffield: Sheffield Academic Press, 1995), 156–79 (a slightly modified version of the essay that appeared in the first edition of the present work). Hartenstein's review can be accessed at http://www.bookreviews .org/pdf/1587_814.pdf.

50. See Tom Schreiner's comment in chapter 4 of the present volume that "those scholars who embrace the feminist position, such as Paul Jewett, but argue that Paul was wrong or inconsistent in 1 Timothy 2, are exegetically more straightforward and intellectually more convincing than those who contend that Paul did not actually intend to restrict women teaching men in 1 Timothy 2."

51. "Teaching and Usurping Authority: 1 Timothy 2:11–15," in *Discovering Biblical Equality: Complementarity without Hierarchy*, ed. R. W. Pierce and R. M. Groothuis (Downers Grove, IL: InterVarsity, 2004), 205, with reference to the first edition of the present work, 11–12.

52. Belleville, "Teaching and Usurping Authority," 217 (emphasis added).

53. Ibid.

54. This includes her argument that αὐθεντεῖν is rendered negatively throughout the history of translation and that only recent English translations have rendered the term positively (209–10; though she notes that both Martin Luther and William Tyndale translated the term positively as "des Mannes Herr sei" and "to have authoritie over a man" respectively). However, even if this argument were true, this would no more prove the accuracy of such a rendering than the abundance of Greek New Testament manuscripts supporting the Majority Text proves the superiority of the Byzantine text tradition. Nor can this argument overturn the demonstrable rules of Greek grammar and syntax with regard to 1 Tim. 2:12. What is more, Belleville's argument that the positive renderings of αὐθεντεῖν in 1 Tim. 2:12 in virtually all the major recent and current English translations is "partly to blame" for a "hierarchical, noninclusive understanding of leadership" is open to debate as well.

55. (Sisters, OR: Multnomah, 2004), 314–16.

56. Ibid., 315n111, with reference to Sarah Sumner, *Men and Women in the Church: Building Consensus on Christian Leadership* (Downers Grove, IL: InterVarsity, 2003), 253n21, who in turn cites Padgett, "Scholarship of Patriarchy," 24. See also Tom Schreiner's similar critique of Sumner in his essay in the present volume.

57. Ibid., 316, with reference to Marshall, *Pastoral Epistles*, 458. See also Tom Schreiner's critique of Marshall in his essay in the present volume and Grudem's interaction with the views of Blomberg and Belleville on the syntax of 1 Tim. 2:12 (Wayne Grudem, *Evangelical Feminism & Biblical Truth: An Analysis of More Than 100 Disputed Questions* [Sisters, OR: Multnomah, 2004], 316–19).

58. For detailed interaction with Marshall, see the earlier discussion above.

59. As discussed, Blomberg himself, while concurring with the overall thrust of the present study, takes its implications in a somewhat different direction than seems warranted.

Chapter 4: An Interpretation of 1 Timothy 2:9–15

1. I make a distinction between a call to the ministry and a call to be a pastor/overseer/ elder. Women attend seminary because they are called to the former, but some misinterpret their call in terms of being called to the latter.

2. I follow the convention today in identifying the position that sees no ministry limitations for women as the egalitarian view, and the view that women should not serve as

pastors as the complementarian view. Note the language of Robert W. Wall, who labels the traditional view as "fundamentalist": "1 Timothy 2:9–15 Reconsidered (Again)," *Bulletin for Biblical Research* 14 (2004): 81n1.

3. Some defenders of the complementarian view have said that my emotions and desires should conform to God's will on the role of women, and thus I should not wish that the situation were different from God's intention. This is probably correct. But I am telling my story here, which includes desires that have not always been in accord with God's will.

4. I am *not* saying that all those who hold a position different from mine are unfamiliar with the biblical text. Obviously, many fine scholars disagree with the complementarian position on exegetical grounds. My point is that many who have a shallow understanding of the biblical text are departing from the complementarian view for reasons other than exegetical ones.

5. Sarah Sumner's basic thesis in her work is that we are unsure what 1 Timothy means, that we cannot take it at face value, and that the simplest interpretation leads to conclusions that are clearly unbiblical. See her *Men and Women in the Church: Building Consensus on Christian Leadership* (Downers Grove, IL: InterVarsity, 2003), 210, 212, 227, 248, 251, 256, 257. Certainly there are difficulties in the text, but Sumner exaggerates them and seems to conclude that we cannot grasp what the verses mean. Her hermeneutical despair should not be embraced, for debates exist over the meaning of many verses in the New Testament (e.g., debates about justification have continued since the Reformation), and yet we still believe that the Scriptures can be understood. Her four claims on p. 212 can be taken as an example. She says that if we understand the text at face value, then (1) v. 15 teaches that women are saved by bearing children instead of by the death of Christ; (2) women should receive teaching without evaluating it; (3) women cannot wear wedding rings, but men can; and (4) men are to raise hands when they pray, but women cannot. The following observations apply to Sumner's claims: (1) she fails to distinguish between cultural practices and principles (see the remainder of this essay for the discussion); (2) most of her examples contain non sequiturs, as the following points will show; (3) the wording of v. 15 can be taken seriously without compromising the atoning death of Christ as the basis of salvation (see the exegesis of v. 15); (4) when v. 11 speaks of women receiving teaching quietly, it scarcely follows logically that discernment and evaluation of such teaching is precluded; (5) a similar logical error appears in her view of raising hands. It does not follow simply because men are exhorted to raise their hands that women are forbidden to do so.

6. In this essay, I interact mainly with "biblical" egalitarians instead of "radical" feminists, for the latter tend to agree with my exegesis of 1 Tim. 2:11–15 but regard it as patriarchal. For the most notable contribution from the radical feminist position, see Elizabeth Schüssler Fiorenza, *In Memory of Her: A Feminist Theological Reconstruction of Christian Origins* (New York: Crossroad, 1983). I am grateful to Philip H. Towner for allowing me to see his helpful unpublished essay ("Feminist Approaches to the New Testament: 1 Timothy 2:8–15 as a Test Case") in which he has briefly surveyed and analyzed the views of radical and biblical feminists on the interpretation of 1 Tim. 2:8–15.

7. Paul K. Jewett, *Man as Male and Female* (Grand Rapids: Eerdmans, 1975), 112–13, 119. Cf. also Luke Timothy Johnson, *The First and Second Letters to Timothy: A New Translation with Introduction and Commentary*, Anchor Bible (New York: Doubleday, 2001), 208, 210; Raymond F. Collins, *1 and 2 Timothy and Titus: A Commentary*, New Testament Library (Louisville: Westminster John Knox, 2002), 74–75. In a similar vein, Jouette Bassler does not regard what is said here as authoritative for today. See her "Adam, Eve, and the Pastor: The Use of Genesis 2–3 in the Pastoral Epistles," in *Genesis 1–3 in the History of Exegesis: Intrigue in the Garden*, ed. G. A. Robbins, Studies in Women

and Religion 27 (Lewiston, NY: Mellen, 1988), 43–65. Interestingly, Bassler also rejects the modern attempt to ameliorate what Paul says in order to make it fit with women in leadership in today's world. She remarks, "This, however, involves reading twentieth-century sensibilities into the text, for a comprehensive prohibition of any leadership office seems clearly indicated by the words" (48–49). Surprisingly, Clarence Boomsma (*Male and Female, One in Christ: New Testament Teaching on Women in Office* [Grand Rapids: Baker, 1993], 53–82) argues that even though Paul's exegesis of the Genesis text in 1 Timothy 2 is flawed because it does not represent the intended meaning of the text of Genesis, it was appropriate for the particular situation addressed in 1 Timothy. Thus, he claims (58) that even though Paul's "argument from Genesis 2 is without support in the text," one should not conclude that Paul was in error or uninspired. He "rightly" misinterpreted (!) the text of Genesis in order to correct an abuse by the women addressed in 1 Timothy 2. Boomsma concludes, therefore, that 1 Tim. 2:11–15 rightly interpreted does not prohibit women from serving in church office today. It is hard to imagine how Paul's argumentation in 1 Timothy 2 has any integrity if Boomsma is correct. Boomsma's exegesis is a creative (but hardly convincing) attempt to circumvent the meaning of the text. His exegesis is illustrative of the lengths to which scholars will go to sustain their presuppositions. In a brilliant and kind review, Albert Wolters (*Calvin Theological Journal* 29 [1994]: 278–85) dismantles Boomsma's thesis, showing that it squares neither with the text of 1 Tim. 2:11–15 nor with logic.

8. For a history of interpretation of the text examined in this essay, see Daniel Doriani, "Appendix 1: A History of Interpretation of 1 Timothy 2," in *Women in the Church: A Fresh Analysis of 1 Timothy 2:9–15*, ed. A. J. Köstenberger, T. R. Schreiner, and H. S. Baldwin (Grand Rapids: Baker, 1995), 213–67. Johnson surveys the contribution of commentators on 1–2 Timothy, paying special attention to their view of 1 Tim. 2:9–15 (*First and Second Timothy*, 20–54).

9. See, e.g., Stephen B. Clark, *Man and Woman in Christ* (Ann Arbor: Servant, 1980), 192.

10. This view is commonplace now. See, e.g., William D. Mounce, *Pastoral Epistles*, Word Biblical Commentary (Nashville: Nelson, 2000), passim; Gordon D. Fee, *1 and 2 Timothy, Titus*, New International Biblical Commentary (Peabody, MA: Hendrickson, 1988), 1–31; idem, *Gospel and Spirit* (Peabody, MA: Hendrickson, 1991), 54–55; Philip H. Towner, *The Goal of Our Instruction*, JSNTSup 34 (Sheffield: JSOT Press, 1989), 21–45; Sharon Hodgin Gritz, *Paul, Women Teachers, and the Mother Goddess at Ephesus* (Lanham, MD: University Press of America, 1991), 31–49, 105–16; Richard Clark Kroeger and Catherine Clark Kroeger, *I Suffer Not a Woman: Rethinking 1 Timothy 2:11–15 in Light of Ancient Evidence* (Grand Rapids: Baker, 1992), passim; Ben Witherington III, *Women in the Earliest Churches*, SNTSMS 58 (Cambridge: Cambridge University Press, 1988), 118.

11. So Fee, *1 Timothy*, 60–61.

12. Wall argues that the evidence is insufficient to support the conclusion that the writer responds to women who were a problem in the church ("1 Timothy 2:9–15 Reconsidered," 83n4).

13. For further comments on this matter, see Andreas Köstenberger, "1 and 2 Timothy and Titus," in *The Expositor's Bible Commentary*, 2nd ed. (Grand Rapids: Zondervan, 2005). Mounce maintains that Paul's remarks are directed to Ephesus, but they are normative wherever the church worships (*Pastoral Epistles*, 107, 111–12). See also the essay that appeared in the first edition of the present work, T. David Gordon, "A Certain Kind of Letter: The Genre of 1 Timothy," in *Women in the Church*, 53–63.

14. Sumner seems to embrace this reasoning (*Men and Women in the Church*, 258).

15. Contra Susan T. Foh, *Women and the Word of God* (Grand Rapids: Baker, 1979), 122–23.

16. Kroeger and Kroeger, *I Suffer Not a Woman*, esp. 42–43, 50–52, 59–66, 70–74, 105–13. Cf. also Mark D. Roberts, "Woman Shall Be Saved: A Closer Look at 1 Timothy 2:15," *TSF Bulletin* 5 (1981): 5; Ronald W. Pierce, "Evangelicals and Gender Roles in the 1990s: 1 Tim. 2:8–15: A Test Case," *JETS* 36 (1993): 347–48, 353.

17. Sumner similarly goes beyond the evidence in suggesting that v. 14 indicates that women may have been teaching the heresy, that they maintained that Eve was created first, that she was enlightened, and that there was worship of the goddess in the church (*Men and Women in the Church*, 258, 260).

18. For a thorough analysis and refutation of the view that Ephesus was influenced by an early form of feminism, see S. M. Baugh's essay in this volume.

19. Bruce Barron ("Putting Women in Their Place: 1 Timothy 2 and Evangelical Views of Women in Church Leadership," *JETS* 33 [1990]: 451–59) makes the same mistake of reconstructing the heresy on the basis of second-century Gnosticism. To read into the text (454) that Eve was the heroine for the false teachers can only be substantiated by appealing to second-century writings. That this was a plank of the adversaries' teaching is scarcely clear from 1 Timothy itself. Even if one sees the opponents as gnostic in some sense, Werner G. Kümmel (*Introduction to the New Testament*, 17th ed. [Nashville: Abingdon, 1975], 379) rightly remarks, "There is then not the slightest occasion, just because the false teachers who are being opposed are Gnostics, to link them up with the great Gnostic systems of the second century." Collins maintains there is no evidence that we have a response to liberated or charismatic women (*1 and 2 Timothy and Titus*, 70).

20. For three devastating reviews of the Kroegers' work, see Robert W. Yarbrough, "I Suffer Not a Woman: A Review Essay," *Presbyterion* 18 (1992): 25–33; Albert Wolters, "Review: *I Suffer Not a Woman*," *Calvin Theological Journal* 28 (1993): 208–13; and S. M. Baugh, "The Apostle among the Amazons," *WTJ* 56 (1994): 153–71.

21. See, e.g., John M. G. Barclay, "Mirror-Reading a Polemical Letter: Galatians as a Test Case," *Journal for the Study of the New Testament* 31 (1987): 73–93; Jerry L. Sumney, *Identifying Paul's Opponents: The Question of Method in 2 Corinthians*, JSNTSup 40 (Sheffield: Sheffield Academic Press, 1990).

22. Gritz, *Mother Goddess*, 11–49, 105–16; cf. also Philip B. Payne, "Libertarian Women in Ephesus: A Response to Douglas J. Moo's Article, '1 Timothy 2:11–15: Meaning and Significance,' " *Trinity Journal* 2 (1981): 182; Linda L. Belleville, "Women in Ministry," in *Two Views on Women in Ministry*, ed. J. R. Beck and C. L. Blomberg (Grand Rapids: Zondervan, 2001), 128; R. T. France, *Women in the Church's Ministry: A Test-Case for Biblical Hermeneutics* (Carlisle, Eng.: Paternoster, 1995), 63.

23. Baugh in his essay in this volume indicates the evidence is lacking that Artemis was identified as a mother goddess. If she was identified as such, this occurred about a millennium before the New Testament was written, and it was forgotten by Paul's day.

24. Gritz, *Mother Goddess*, 114–16.

25. For a sensible and cautious description of the opponents, see I. H. Marshall and Philip H. Towner, *A Critical and Exegetical Commentary on the Pastoral Epistles*, International Critical Commentary (Edinburgh: Clark, 1999), 140–52; cf. also Mounce, *Pastoral Epistles*, lxix–lxxxvi.

26. So Douglas J. Moo, "What Does It Mean Not to Teach or Have Authority over Men? 1 Timothy 2:11–15," in *Recovering Biblical Manhood and Womanhood*, ed. J. Piper and W. Grudem (Wheaton: Crossway, 1991), 180–81.

27. Robert J. Karris, "The Background and Significance of the Polemic of the Pastoral Epistles," *Journal of Biblical Literature* 92 (1973): 550.

28. Ibid., 562. Incidentally, I do not find persuasive Karris's own suggestion that the author used the typical polemic of the philosophers against the sophists.

29. Towner, *Goal of Our Instruction*, 21–45.

30. See Anthony C. Thiselton, "Realized Eschatology at Corinth," *NTS* 24 (1978): 510–26.

31. For a similar suggestion, see William L. Lane, "1 Tim. iv.1–3: An Early Instance of Over-realized Eschatology?" *NTS* 11 (1965): 164–67.

32. Supporting the notion that marriage was being denigrated is Collins, *1 and 2 Timothy and Titus*, 65.

33. Depending on later evidence also mars J. Massyngberde Ford's suggestion that the heresy was an early form of Montanism; see "A Note on Proto-Montanism in the Pastoral Epistles," *NTS* 17 (1970–71): 338–46.

34. Contra Fee, *Gospel and Spirit*, 55; Witherington, *Women in the Earliest Churches*, 118; Linda L. Belleville, *Women Leaders and the Church: Three Crucial Questions* (Grand Rapids: Baker, 2000), 167. Rightly Mounce, *Pastoral Epistles*, 125. Nor does the description of the heresy as "profane and old-womanish myths" (1 Tim. 4:7, Roberts's translation) imply that the false teachers were women; contra Roberts, "Woman Shall Be Saved," 5.

35. The Greek word used is λαλέω, not διδάσκω.

36. Cf. Towner, *Goal of Our Instruction*, 26, 39–40.

37. Ibid., 39–40.

38. Cf. Philip H. Towner, *1–2 Timothy and Titus*, IVP New Testament Commentary Series (Downers Grove, IL: InterVarsity, 1994), 75–76.

39. Contra J. M. Holmes, *Text in a Whirlwind: A Critique of Four Exegetical Devices at 1 Timothy 2.9–15*, JSNTSup 196 (Sheffield: Sheffield Academic Press, 2000), 117–39.

40. The contrast between ἄνδρας in v. 8 and γυναῖκες in v. 9 shows that the former refers to males, not females.

41. Cf. Alan Padgett, "Wealthy Women at Ephesus: I Timothy 2:8–15 in Social Context," *Interpretation* 41 (1987): 22.

42. So Donald Guthrie, *The Pastoral Epistles*, Tyndale New Testament Commentaries (Grand Rapids: Eerdmans, 1957), 73–74; J. N. D. Kelly, *A Commentary on the Pastoral Epistles* (Grand Rapids: Baker, 1963), 65; Ceslas Spicq, *Saint Paul: Les Épîtres pastorales*, 2 vols., 4th ed., Études bibliques (Paris: Gabalda, 1969), 371–72; Norbert Brox, *Die Pastoralbriefe*, 4th ed., Regensburger Neues Testament (Regensburg: Pustet, 1969), 130; Martin Dibelius and Hans Conzelmann, *The Pastoral Epistles*, Hermeneia (Philadelphia: Fortress, 1972), 75; Jürgen Roloff, *Der erste Brief an Timotheus*, Evangelisch-katholischer Kommentar zum Neuen Testament (Zürich: Benziger, 1988), 130; George W. Knight III, *The Pastoral Epistles*, New International Greek Testament Commentary (Grand Rapids: Eerdmans, 1992), 128; Gottlob Schrenk, *TDNT*, 1:632.

43. Everett Ferguson, "Τόπῳ in 1 Timothy 2:8," *Restoration Quarterly* 33 (1991): 65–73; Fee, *1 and 2 Timothy*, 70; Knight, *Pastoral Epistles*, 128; Padgett, "Wealthy Women," 22; Douglas J. Moo, "I Timothy 2:11–15: Meaning and Significance," *Trinity Journal*, n.s., 1 (1980): 62; Witherington, *Women in the Earliest Churches*, 119.

44. C. K. Barrett, *The Pastoral Epistles*, New Clarendon Bible (Oxford: Clarendon, 1963), 54; Robert D. Culver, "A Traditional View: Let Your Women Keep Silence," in *Women in Ministry: Four Views*, ed. B. Clouse and R. G. Clouse (Downers Grove, IL: InterVarsity, 1989), 34.

45. Walter Lock, *A Critical and Exegetical Commentary on the Pastoral Epistles*, International Critical Commentary (Edinburgh: Clark, 1936), 30; Craig S. Keener, *Paul, Women and Wives: Marriage and Women's Ministry in the Letters of Paul* (Peabody, MA: Hendrickson, 1992), 123n19; Towner, *Goal of Our Instruction*, 205–6; Paul W. Barnett, "Wives and Women's Ministry (1 Timothy 2:11–15)," *EQ* 61 (1989): 225, 236; Steve Motyer, "Expounding 1 Timothy 2:8–15," *Vox evangelica* 24 (1994): 92.

46. Marshall, however, thinks the wording should not be limited to house churches (*Pastoral Epistles*, 444–50). Cf. also Collins, *1 and 2 Timothy and Titus*, 65–66.

47. Knight, *Pastoral Epistles*, 130–31; cf. also B. Ward Powers, *The Ministry of Women in the Church: Which Way Forward? The Case for the "Middle Ground" Interpretation of the New Testament* (Adelaide, Australia: SPCK, 1996), 35–38, 42–53.

48. J. M. Holmes argues that a congregational context is not in view since many features of the text in 1 Timothy 2 cannot be restricted to a congregational context. For example, prayers for all (vv. 1–2), the prohibition against anger (v. 8), and the call for proper dress and good works (vv. 9–10) cannot be limited to congregational meetings (*Text in a Whirlwind*, 36–72). The explanation offered by Holmes is unpersuasive. Verses 1–7 can be dismissed from the discussion, for it is unnecessary to argue that *all* of 1 Timothy is addressed to gathered meetings. In vv. 8–15 congregational meetings are primarily in view, but what is said extends beyond such meetings. Hence, the instructions regarding anger and adornment were prompted by actions that occurred when the church gathered but are naturally not limited to such. Paul goes on to encourage women to engage in good works, and the latter is obviously not limited to church meetings.

Finally, it is also possible that vv. 11–14 address congregational meetings and vv. 8–10 do not. Paul may move fluidly between what happens in gathered meetings and life outside a congregational context. What is most damaging to Holmes's thesis is the reference to learning and teaching in vv. 11–12. Teaching in the Pastoral Epistles refers to the transmission of tradition in congregational contexts, not to informal sharing (rightly Mounce, *Pastoral Epistles*, 224–26; Marshall, *Pastoral Epistles*, 455; cf. also criticisms of Holmes's view in the book review by Andreas Köstenberger, online at http://www.bookreviews.org/pdf/974_506.pdf). Holmes sustains her case from vv. 11–12 by saying that a congregational context is unnecessary, not required, and not demanded (see pp. 74–75, 84–85, 87). But the question is not whether a congregational context is "required," "demanded," or "necessary." The issue is whether such a context is most likely when Paul refers to learning and teaching. We can be quite confident that teaching occurred when the church gathered. Hence, one of the fundamental planks of Holmes's view of the text is shown to be unpersuasive.

49. Cf. Gritz, *Mother Goddess*, 126; Keener, *Women's Ministry*, 103; Kelly, *Pastoral Epistles*, 66; Moo, "1 Timothy 2:11–15," 63; Roloff, *Timotheus*, 132.

50. Barrett, *Pastoral Epistles*, 55; Mary Evans, *Woman in the Bible* (Downers Grove, IL: InterVarsity, 1983), 101; Gritz, *Mother Goddess*, 126; Gottfried Holtz, *Die Pastoralbriefe*, Theologischer Handkommentar zum Neuen Testament (Berlin: Evangelische Verlagsanstalt, 1972), 65–66; Keener, *Women's Ministry*, 102; David M. Scholer, "1 Timothy 2:9–15 and the Place of Women in the Church's Ministry," in *Women, Authority and the Bible*, ed. A. Mickelsen (Downers Grove, IL: InterVarsity, 1986), 200–201; Barnett, "1 Timothy 2:11–15," 227–28; Witherington, *Women in the Earliest Churches*, 263n203.

51. So Foh, *Women and the Word of God*, 122; Knight, *Pastoral Epistles*, 132; Moo, "1 Timothy 2:11–15," 63; Roloff, *Timotheus*, 126; Towner, *Goal of Our Instruction*, 207; Brox, *Pastoralbriefe*, 132; Bassler, "Adam, Eve, and the Pastor," 48.

52. Contra Culver, "Traditional View," 35; and Clark, *Man and Woman*, 194, respectively.

53. Rightly Towner, *Goal of Our Instruction*, 207–8; so also Walter L. Liefeld, *1 and 2 Timothy, Titus*, NIV Application Commentary (Grand Rapids: Zondervan, 1999), 95.

54. Gordon P. Hugenberger, "Women in Church Office: Hermeneutics or Exegesis? A Survey of Approaches to 1 Tim. 2:8–15," *JETS* 35 (1992): 341–60. For a similar view, see Gritz, *Mother Goddess*, 125, 131, 133, 135, 136, 140; N. J. Hommes, "Let Women Be Silent in Church," *Calvin Theological Journal* 4 (1969): 13–14, 19–20; cf. Barnett, "1 Timothy 2:11–15," 232–33; Powers, *Ministry of Women in the Church*, 33–35. Jerome D. Quinn and William C. Wacker maintain that in vv. 9–10 the reference is to all women, but beginning

in v. 11 it shifts to wives (*The First and Second Letters to Timothy: A New Translation with Notes and Commentary* [Grand Rapids: Eerdmans, 2000], 218, 221). Collins argues that husbands are in view in v. 12 but does not comment on the identity of men and women in earlier verses (*1 and 2 Timothy and Titus*, 69). Bruce W. Winter assumes that wives are in view in these verses but does not present evidence from the text of 1 Tim. 2:9–15 for his interpretation. The substance of Winter's article is not affected in my judgment by whether Paul refers to women or wives ("The 'New' Roman Wife and 1 Timothy 2:9–15: The Search for a *Sitz im Leben*," *TynBul* 51 [2000]: 285–94).

55. Hugenberger, "Women in Church Office," 355.

56. So Timothy J. Harris, "Why Did Paul Mention Eve's Deception? A Critique of P. W. Barnett's Interpretation of 1 Timothy 2," *EQ* 62 (1990): 336.

57. I could cite more examples from most of these texts but have provided only one example from each so as not to prolong the point unduly. Greek is cited only insofar as it is necessary to make the point.

58. But the reference to women in 1 Cor. 14:34 is not just to wives. See D. A. Carson, "'Silent in the Churches': On the Role of Women in 1 Corinthians 14:33b–36," in *Recovering Biblical Manhood and Womanhood*, ed. J. Piper and W. Grudem (Wheaton: Crossway, 1991), 151.

59. Hugenberger ("Women in Church Office," 353) is correct, strictly speaking, in saying that the Greek article or possessive pronoun is not necessary for a reference to husbands and wives. Even though an article or possessive pronoun is not demanded, the lack of such and the generality of the context have persuaded most scholars that Paul is speaking of men and women in general. What Hugenberger fails to appreciate is that Paul provides no determinative clues (as he does in all the texts referring to husbands and wives) that husbands and wives are intended.

60. So Ben Wiebe, "Two Texts on Women (1 Tim 2:11–15; Gal 3:26–29): A Test of Interpretation," *Horizons in Biblical Theology* 16 (1994): 57; cf. also Mounce, *Pastoral Epistles*, 107, 111–12; Marshall, *Pastoral Epistles*, 444, 452.

61. And Hugenberger's thesis is improbable if "in every place" (v. 8) refers to public meetings, and thus he cites parallel texts to question the worship context here. But what makes a public worship context likely is not only the words "in every place," but also the activity occurring there: prayer (v. 8) and teaching (vv. 11–12).

62. If Paul wanted to discuss the relationship between husbands and wives, he probably would have linked it with his advice to slaves in 1 Tim. 6:1–2 (cf. Eph. 5:22–6:9; Col. 3:18–4:1).

63. In addition, Hugenberger's evidence is not decisive. First Cor. 1:2 probably refers to public Christian meetings (see Gordon D. Fee, *The First Epistle to the Corinthians*, New International Commentary on the New Testament [Grand Rapids: Eerdmans, 1987], 34), while 1 Thess. 1:8 and 2 Cor. 2:14 have a wider reference. The context is decisive for the particular interpretation of the phrase.

64. E.g., Ronald Y. K. Fung, "Ministry in the New Testament," in *The Church in the Bible and in the World*, ed. D. A. Carson (Grand Rapids: Baker, 1987), 200–201; Moo, "1 Timothy 2:11–15," 63–64; Towner, *Goal of Our Instruction*, 212; Witherington, *Women in the Earliest Churches*, 119; Belleville, *Women Leaders*, 169.

65. Alvera Mickelsen, "An Egalitarian View: There Is Neither Male nor Female in Christ," in *Women in Ministry: Four Views*, ed. B. Clouse and R. G. Clouse (Downers Grove, IL: InterVarsity, 1989), 201.

66. David Scholler [*sic*], "Women's Adornment: Some Historical and Hermeneutical Observations on the New Testament Passages," *Daughters of Sarah* 6 (1980): 3–6; idem, "1 Timothy 2:9–15," 200–202; cf. Fee, *Gospel and Spirit*, 57–58, 61; Keener, *Women's Ministry*, 103–7; Clark, *Man and Woman*, 194; Moo, "What Does It Mean?" 181–82.

67. So also Payne, "Libertarian Women," 189–90; Gordon D. Fee, "Reflections on Church Order in the Pastoral Epistles, with Further Reflection on the Hermeneutics of *Ad Hoc* Documents," *JETS* 28 (1985): 150.

68. For Scholer's interpretation of the text as a whole, see "1 Timothy 2:9–15," 193–219.

69. So Dibelius and Conzelmann, *Pastoral Epistles*, 45–46; Gritz, *Mother Goddess*, 126; Guthrie, *Pastoral Epistles*, 74; Knight, *Pastoral Epistles*, 133; Moo, "1 Timothy 2:11–15," 63; Collins, *1 and 2 Timothy and Titus*, 66; contra Lock (*Pastoral Epistles*, 31), who sees only a reference to dress.

70. Johnson remarks, "It is, indeed, unfortunate that the negative reactions by readers to the verses that follow also tends to color everything in this chapter, for Paul's statements here have important implications not only for a Christian appreciation of simplicity in the face of cultures that define and value in terms of appearance (above all, in the case of women!), but also for a way of addressing the issues of economic and ecological oppression implicit (both then and now) in the production of luxurious clothing and adornment" (*First and Second Timothy*, 204).

71. The Kroegers' suggestion (*I Suffer Not a Woman*, 74–75)—based on a fresco in Pompeii of Dionysian worshipers disrobing—that the women in Ephesus may have been disrobing during worship is an example of mirror-reading and parallelomania at its worst.

72. So Barnett, "1 Timothy 2:9–15," 226, 228; Clark, *Man and Woman*, 194; Culver, "Traditional View," 35; Susan T. Foh, "A Male Leadership View: The Head of the Woman Is the Man," in *Women in Ministry: Four Views*, ed. B. Clouse and R. G. Clouse (Downers Grove, IL: InterVarsity, 1989), 80; Gritz, *Mother Goddess*, 127; Guthrie, *Pastoral Epistles*, 75; Keener, *Women's Ministry*, 103; Knight, *Pastoral Epistles*, 135; Moo, "What Does It Mean?" 182; Thomas C. Oden, *First and Second Timothy and Titus* (Louisville: John Knox, 1989), 94; Padgett, "Wealthy Women," 23; Scholer, "1 Timothy 2:9–15," 201–2; Witherington, *Women in the Earliest Churches*, 119–20.

73. James B. Hurley, *Man and Woman in Biblical Perspective* (Grand Rapids: Zondervan, 1981), 199.

74. So Keener, *Women's Ministry*, 105; cf. Knight, *Pastoral Epistles*, 135; Collins, *1 and 2 Timothy and Titus*, 67–68.

75. Hence, Quinn and Wacker rightly remark that the sentiments expressed here were a commonplace in the Greco-Roman world (*First and Second Timothy*, 219).

76. See Keener, *Women's Ministry*, 103–4.

77. Motyer ("Expounding 1 Timothy," 94) suggests Paul speaks against the self-assertiveness of women.

78. Marshall, *Pastoral Epistles*, 449–50; Mounce, *Pastoral Epistles*, 114–15; Keener, *Women's Ministry*, 103–6; Knight, *Pastoral Epistles*, 135–36; Moo, "What Does It Mean?" 182; Scholer, "1 Timothy 2:9–15," 201–2; idem, "Women's Adornment," 6; Oden, *First Timothy*, 95; Towner, *Goal of Our Instruction*, 208; Witherington, *Women in the Earliest Churches*, 119–20; Gritz, *Mother Goddess*, 126–27. Gritz, without warrant, takes this as evidence of the influence of the Artemis cult.

79. Some scholars limit the proscription to extravagance and see no indictment of sensuality. So Holmes, *Text in a Whirlwind*, 65, 69; Johnson, *First and Second Timothy*, 200, 204. But see the evidence and argumentation from Winter in support of a reference to sensuality ("The 'New' Roman Wife," 285–94). Wall maintains that σωφροσύνη is rendered best by the word "modesty" ("1 Timothy 2:9–15 Reconsidered," 86n11).

80. For citations from Greco-Roman literature, see Scholer, "Women's Adornment," 4–5.

81. Pierce ("Gender Roles," 352) strays from the text in suggesting that humility is enjoined here. His view that humility is the "primary focus" of not only this text but all the

texts relating to leadership in 1 Timothy is mistaken. Although the women in Ephesus may have been conducting themselves in inappropriate ways because of pride, 1 Tim. 2:9–15 does not specifically pinpoint lack of humility as the problem. Nor does the passage on the appointment of elders and deacons (1 Tim. 3:1–13) highlight pride as the central issue for leaders. I am not denying that pride may have been an issue for leaders in 1 Timothy, but Pierce has not established that it is the *primary* one, nor has he provided any evidence that it was particularly a problem for women.

82. Scholer, "Women's Adornment," 3–6.

83. Cf. ibid., 4–5.

84. I am not denying that submission was expected by these authors. I am only questioning whether this submission was regularly associated with adornment.

85. We will see in our discussion of v. 15 below that a similar phenomenon is present.

86. Barnett, "1 Timothy 2:11–15," 229; Foh, *Women and the Word of God*, 124; Gritz, *Mother Goddess*, 128; Hurley, *Man and Woman*, 200; Oden, *First Timothy*, 96; Ben Witherington III, *Women in the Ministry of Jesus*, SNTSMS 51 (Cambridge: Cambridge University Press, 1984), 6–10; Towner, *Goal of Our Instruction*, 313–14n78. As Towner points out, this calls into question Jewett's view that Paul's instructions here simply reflect a rabbinic worldview (see note 7). On the other hand, Hugenberger ("Women in Church Office," 349) wisely warns against overly simplistic versions of what the rabbis taught. On this last point, see also Marshall, *Pastoral Epistles*, 452; Quinn and Wacker, *First and Second Timothy*, 215; Craig L. Blomberg, "Neither Hierarchicalist nor Egalitarian: Gender Roles in Paul," in *Two Views on Women in Ministry*, ed. J. R. Beck and C. L. Blomberg (Grand Rapids: Zondervan, 2001), 332–33.

87. Philip B. Payne, "Part II: The Interpretation of 1 Timothy 2:11–15: A Surrejoinder," in "What Does the Scripture Teach about the Ordination of Women?" (unpublished paper, Minneapolis, 1986), 96.

88. Gilbert Bilezikian, *Beyond Sex Roles* (Grand Rapids: Baker, 1985), 179; Evans, *Woman in the Bible*, 101; Keener, *Women's Ministry*, 107–8, 112; Padgett, "Wealthy Women," 24; Payne, "Surrejoinder," 97, 99; Aída D. B. Spencer, "Eve at Ephesus," *JETS* 17 (1974): 218–19.

89. So Hurley, *Man and Woman*, 201; Moo, "1 Timothy 2:11–15," 64; "What Does It Mean?" 183; Witherington, *Women in the Earliest Churches*, 263n207; Mounce, *Pastoral Epistles*, 119; Marshall, *Pastoral Epistles*, 453.

90. Rightly Mounce, *Pastoral Epistles*, 118.

91. Cf. Moo, "What Does It Mean?" 184.

92. Barnett, "1 Timothy 2:11–15," 229; Clark, *Man and Woman*, 195; Evans, *Woman in the Bible*, 101; Fee, *1 Timothy*, 84; Gritz, *Mother Goddess*, 129; Holtz, *Die Pastoralbriefe*, 69; Keener, *Women's Ministry*, 108; Payne, "Libertarian Women," 169–70; Witherington, *Women in the Earliest Churches*, 120; Wiebe, "Two Texts on Women," 58; Motyer, "Expounding 1 Timothy," 93–95; Quinn and Wacker, *First and Second Timothy*, 222; Mounce, *Pastoral Epistles*, 118–19; Holmes, *Text in a Whirlwind*, 76–77.

93. So Fung, "Ministry," 197–98; Knight, *Pastoral Epistles*, 139; Moo, "1 Timothy 2:11–15," 64; idem, "The Interpretation of 1 Timothy 2:11–15: A Rejoinder," *Trinity Journal* 2 (1981): 199; idem, "What Does It Mean?" 183; Towner, *Goal of Our Instruction*, 212–13.

94. In the first edition I argued that Paul had silence in mind, but it now seems to me that quietness is preferable.

95. Roloff, *Timotheus*, 135n125. Johnson rightly remarks that submission relates not only to attitude but to "a structural placement of one person below another" (*First and Second Timothy*, 201).

96. Oden, *First Timothy*, 97.

97. Evans, *Woman in the Bible*, 101.

98. Gritz, *Mother Goddess*, 130; Andrew C. Perriman, "What Eve Did, What Women Shouldn't Do: The Meaning of ΑΥΘΕΝΤΕΩ in 1 Timothy 2:12," *TynBul* 44 (1993): 131.

99. Towner, *Goal of Our Instruction*, 214.

100. Padgett, "Wealthy Women," 24.

101. So Barnett, "1 Timothy 2:11–15," 230; Dibelius and Conzelmann, *Pastoral Epistles*, 47; Fung, "Ministry," 198; Knight, *Pastoral Epistles*, 139; Moo, "1 Timothy 2:11–15," 64; idem, "What Does It Mean?" 183; Roloff, *Timotheus*, 135; Mounce, *Pastoral Epistles*, 120; Marshall, *Pastoral Epistles*, 454.

102. Spencer's view ("Eve at Ephesus," 219) that the δέ is a signal to the church that the prohibition in v. 12 is temporary since it contradicts v. 11 is quite arbitrary; rightly Evans, *Woman in the Bible*, 102.

103. Cf. Fung, "Ministry," 336n186; Moo, "1 Timothy 2:11–15," 64; Barnett, "1 Timothy 2:11–15," 228–29; Harris, "Eve's Deception," 340; Witherington, *Women in the Earliest Churches*, 120. I question whether there is a chiasm here, because then the idea of exercising authority should have preceded teaching. Instead, the two verses are closely related, with an inclusio binding them together. Another problem with seeing a chiasm is that the scholars cited above do not agree on the chiastic arrangement.

104. Roloff (*Timotheus*, 138) observes that learning silently with all submissiveness (v. 11) is opposed to teaching in v. 12.

105. Perriman, "What Eve Did," 129–30, 139–40. Perriman says that the shift from the imperative μανθανέτω to the indicative ἐπιτρέπω indicates the parenthetic nature of v. 12. His argument falters because he fails to see that an indicative may introduce a command. Nor is there any evidence that Perriman has considered the close relationship between vv. 11 and 12 (see note 103, above) in his study. For a rejection of Perriman's view, see also Mounce, *Pastoral Epistles*, 121.

106. Bilezikian, *Beyond Sex Roles*, 180; Fee, *1 Timothy*, 72; Kroeger and Kroeger, *I Suffer Not a Woman*, 83; Oden, *First Timothy*, 97–98; Padgett, "Wealthy Women," 25; Payne, "Libertarian Women," 170–72; idem, "Surrejoinder," 97, 100–101; Roberts, "Woman Shall Be Saved," 5; Witherington, *Women in the Earliest Churches*, 120–21; Wiebe, "Two Texts on Women," 59; Liefeld, *1 and 2 Timothy, Titus*, 109; Belleville, *Women Leaders*, 172.

107. Rightly Mounce, *Pastoral Epistles*, 106, 122–23; cf. also Marshall, *Pastoral Epistles*, 443, 454.

108. See Daniel B. Wallace, *Greek Grammar beyond the Basics: An Exegetical Syntax of the New Testament* (Grand Rapids: Zondervan, 1996), 525–26; Mounce, *Pastoral Epistles*, 122–23; Blomberg, "Gender Roles in Paul," 361; Moo, "1 Timothy 2:11–15," 65; idem, "Rejoinder," 199–200; idem, "What Does It Mean?" 185.

109. Most of the examples cited have the aorist tense, while 1 Tim. 2:12 has the present tense (cf. 1 Cor. 14:34). Too much weight should not be assigned to this fact, though, for the aorist tense has too often been said to refer to once-for-all action.

110. Rightly Scholer, "1 Timothy 2:9–15," 203n28.

111. Holmes reads the aspect of the present infinitives to say that women cannot continuously teach or continuously exercise authority. Hence, women are allowed to teach, but they cannot teach too frequently or go on and on in their teaching (*Text in a Whirlwind*, 92–96). This understanding of the aspect of the infinitive is flawed, and it is surprising that Holmes fails to take into account other evidence in her analysis. Two examples of infinitives that follow the indicative παρακαλῶ illustrate the point. When Paul exhorts the Romans to watch out for (σκοπεῖν) those causing dissension (Rom. 16:17), he hardly means, "Watch out frequently but not all the time for those creating such problems." Paul exhorts Euodia and Syntyche to be in harmony (φρονεῖν) in the Lord (Phil. 4:2). This can scarcely mean that they should frequently but not always be in

harmony. Other examples of the present infinitive that should not be defined in the way Holmes argues could be examined (e.g., Phil. 1:12; 1 Tim. 2:1; Titus 3:8; 1 Pet. 2:11). It is possible, of course, that what is enjoined in the infinitive is limited in its application. But such a limitation is gleaned from the context, not the aspect of the infinitive. Holmes (30) cites Silva, who advises against making one's interpretation "depend" on the aspect of a verbal form. Holmes proceeds to ignore that advice, and the faulty conclusions she draws demonstrate that she should have heeded it.

112. Contra Perriman, "What Eve Did," 130.

113. Contra Witherington, *Women in the Earliest Churches*, 121. Rightly Fung, "Ministry," 198; H. Greeven, "Propheten, Lehrer, Vorsteher bei Paulus," *ZNW* 44 (1952–53): 19–23; Clark, *Man and Woman*, 196; Moo, "1 Timothy 2:11–15," 65–66; idem, "What Does It Mean?" 185–86; Towner, *Goal of Our Instruction*, 215; Robert L. Saucy, "Women's Prohibition to Teach Men: An Investigation into Its Meaning and Contemporary Application," *JETS* 37 (1994): 86–91; Mounce, *Pastoral Epistles*, 124–26; Blomberg, "Gender Roles in Paul," 338. Hommes ("Let Women Be Silent," 7–13) misunderstands the nature of teaching by comparing it to mutual discussion. Pierce ("Gender Roles," 349) argues that New Testament teaching was more authoritative, involving a master-discipleship role not practiced today. He observes that teaching today is understood as the imparting of information. This last observation reveals the weakness of much modern biblical teaching. More than the impartation of information should be occurring, since mind and heart should not be so rigidly separated. Pierce overplays the master-disciple dimension of the elder/overseer, but in any case Paul believed that such elders and overseers were *necessary* for the life of the churches in his day (cf. Acts 14:23; 20:17, 28; Phil. 1:1; 1 Tim. 3:1–7; 5:17, 19; Titus 1:5–9). Elders as leaders in local churches were apparently common during New Testament times (Acts 15:2, 4, 6, 22, 23; 16:14; 21:18; James 5:14; 1 Pet. 5:1, 5). I see no reason not to have the same pattern today.

114. Rightly Foh, *Women and the Word of God*, 125; idem, "Male Headship," 81; Fung, "Ministry," 198; Knight, *Pastoral Epistles*, 140; Moo, "Rejoinder," 201; Saucy, "Women's Prohibition," 79–97. Holtz (*Pastoralbriefe*, 69) correctly observes that the object "man" shows that not all teaching or exercise of authority is prohibited. Thus, Harris's ("Eve's Deception," 342) claim that this text gives no qualifications regarding women teaching is mistaken. The context also shows that public meetings are in view, and it is legitimate to consult (although not impose) other texts to construct the boundaries of the commands given here. Of course, how to apply this instruction in practical situations is not always easy. See Saucy, "Women's Prohibition," 79–97.

115. Ἀνδρός is the object of both infinitives (Mounce, *Pastoral Epistles*, 123; Knight, *Pastoral Epistles*, 142; Moo, "Rejoinder," 202; idem, "What Does It Mean?" 186; contra Payne, "Libertarian Women," 175; Fung, "Ministry," 198–99). The singular ἀνδρός scarcely shows that a single man is in view (Perriman, "What Eve Did," 142; Payne, "Surrejoinder," 104). The word is used generically, just as γυνή is.

116. Mounce raises the possibility that women are prohibited only from teaching men who were overseers. But he proceeds to itemize a number of devastating objections against this notion: (1) the object specified in v. 12 is not "overseer" but "man"; (2) the object of submission in v. 11 does not require that ἀνδρός in v. 12 is equivalent; (3) verses 13–14 address the relationship between males and females, not females and overseers (*Pastoral Epistles*, 124). It should also be added that v. 11 does not even name men specifically, and hence one should not restrict the meaning of ἀνδρός in v. 12 from its implied use in v. 11.

117. Bilezikian, *Beyond Sex Roles*, 176–78; Payne, "Libertarian Women," 173–74; idem, "Surrejoinder," 102–4; Scholer, "1 Timothy 2:9–15," 206–7; Belleville, "Women in Ministry," 99.

118. Sumner fails to attend to the meaning of the verse in context, and so she objects that if we apply the verse today, women could not teach piano lessons to men, speak on the radio, or write books (*Men and Women in the Church*, 227, 241). The context, however, addresses the issue of the gathered church, *not* every conceivable interaction between men and women.

119. Barnett, "1 Timothy 2:11–15," 230–31; Clark, *Man and Woman*, 199; Foh, "Male Headship," 81; Brox, *Pastoralbriefe*, 134; Moo, "Rejoinder," 212. Contra Fee, *Gospel and Spirit*, 63; Harris, "Eve's Deception," 341. Harris correctly says that the prohibition involves function, not merely office. Nonetheless, 1 Tim. 3:2 and Titus 1:9 suggest that all elders had to have the ability to teach, although some invested more time in teaching (1 Tim. 5:17). Padgett ("Wealthy Women," 25) argues that deacons functioned as teachers. Contra Padgett, the evidence that those appointed in Acts 6 were deacons is uncertain. Even if they were, the text does not establish that teaching was a requirement for deacons. It is telling that being apt to teach, which is required for elders (1 Tim. 3:2; 5:17; Titus 1:9), is not mentioned with respect to deacons.

120. Knight, *Pastoral Epistles*, 141–42. So also, Craig S. Keener, "Women in Ministry," in *Two Views on Women in Ministry*, ed. J. R. Beck and C. L. Blomberg (Grand Rapids: Zondervan, 2001), 40–41, 53. Keener, however, thinks that this point demonstrates the weakness of the complementarian view. For discussion regarding practical application for today, see Saucy, "Women's Prohibition," 79–97. The comments made here would be contested by Walter Liefeld ("Women and the Nature of Ministry," *JETS* 30 [1987]: 49–61; idem, "A Plural Ministry View: Your Sons and Your Daughters Shall Prophesy," in *Women in Ministry: Four Views*, ed. A. Mickelsen [Downers Grove, IL: InterVarsity, 1989], 127–53), for apparently he does not think that any authoritative offices should be present in the church. I cannot discuss this issue here, but it seems plain from Acts 11:30; 14:23; 15:2, 4, 6, 22–23; 16:4; 20:17, 28; 21:18; Phil. 1:1; 1 Tim. 3:1–13; 5:17, 19; Titus 1:5–9; James 5:14; 1 Pet. 5:1–5 that the offices of elder/overseer and deacon existed in the early church. For critiques of Liefeld, see Culver ("Traditional View," 154–59) and Foh ("Male Leadership View," 162) in *Women in Ministry: Four Views*. For a recent defense of the importance of church office, see T. David Gordon, " 'Equipping' Ministry in Ephesians 4?" *JETS* 37 (1994): 69–78.

121. Fee, *Gospel and Spirit*, 63; Gritz, *Mother Goddess*, 132; Payne, "Libertarian Women," 184; idem, "Surrejoinder," 102; Scholer, "1 Timothy 2:9–15," 207; James G. Sigountos and Myron Shank, "Public Roles for Women in the Pauline Church: A Reappraisal of the Evidence," *JETS* 26 (1983): 285–86; Belleville, *Women Leaders*, 173–74.

122. Wayne Grudem, "Prophecy—Yes, but Teaching—No: Paul's Consistent Advocacy of Women's Participation without Governing Authority," *JETS* 30 (1987): 11–23.

123. I previously endorsed Grudem's view. See Thomas R. Schreiner, "The Valuable Ministries of Women in the Context of Male Leadership," in *Recovering Biblical Manhood and Womanhood*, ed. J. Piper and W. Grudem (Wheaton: Crossway, 1991), 217.

124. Cf. Barnett, "1 Timothy 2:11–15," 233; Moo, "1 Timothy 2:11–15," 75; idem, "Rejoinder," 206–7; Gerhard Friedrich, *TDNT*, 6:854; Karl H. Rengstorf, *TDNT*, 2:158; Greeven, "Propheten," 29–30; Towner, *Goal of Our Instruction*, 215. Sigountos and Shank ("Public Roles," 285–86) disagree with this distinction, even though some of the evidence they adduce actually supports it (289–90). Their contention that teaching was disallowed in the Greco-Roman world for cultural reasons while prophecy was permissible is unpersuasive.

125. See my "Head Coverings, Prophecies and the Trinity: 1 Corinthians 11:2–16," in *Recovering Biblical Manhood and Womanhood*, ed. J. Piper and W. Grudem (Wheaton: Crossway, 1991), 124–39. Keener (*Women's Ministry*, 244–45) misunderstood my discussion on the nature of the Old Testament prophecy practiced by Deborah, Huldah, and other women. I argued not that their prophecies were less authoritative but that they exercised

their prophetic gift in such a way that they did not subvert male leadership ("Ministries of Women," 216–17).

126. Blomberg thinks that prophecy includes preaching, so that women can preach as long as they are under male authority ("Gender Roles in Paul," 344–45). I understand 1 Tim. 2:12 to prohibit women from preaching or from functioning in any regular way as the teacher of men. Prophecy involves the reception and communication of spontaneous revelations from God (1 Cor. 14:29–32), but preaching exposits what has been divinely preserved in Scripture. Kevin Giles maintains that the gift of prophecy exercised by women shows that the complementarian view is incorrect. See his "Women in the Church: A Rejoinder to Andreas Köstenberger," EQ 73 (2001): 230–31. For Giles's review of the first edition of this book, see "A Critique of the 'Novel' Contemporary Interpretation of 1 Timothy 2:9–15 Given in the Book, Women in the Church: Parts I and II," EQ 72 (2000): 151–67, 195–215; idem, "Women in the Church: A Rejoinder to Andreas Köstenberger," 225–43. For a convincing response to Giles, see Andreas J. Köstenberger, "Women in the Church: A Response to Kevin Giles," EQ 73 (2001): 205–24.

127. Henry Scott Baldwin's article in this volume; George W. Knight III, "ΑΥΘΕΝΤΕΩ in Reference to Women in 1 Timothy 2.12," NTS 30 (1984): 143–57; Leland E. Wilshire, "The TLG Computer and Further Reference to ΑΥΘΕΝΤΕΩ in 1 Timothy 2.12," NTS 34 (1988): 120–34; A. J. Panning, "ΑΥΘΕΝΤΕΙΝ—A Word Study," Wisconsin Lutheran Quarterly 78 (1981): 185–91; Mounce, Pastoral Epistles, 128; Moo, "1 Timothy 2:11–15," 66–67; Gritz, Mother Goddess, 134; Barnett, "1 Timothy 2:11–15," 231–32; Padgett, "Wealthy Women," 25; Fung, "Ministry," 198.

128. See his essay in this volume. Cf. also David Huttar, "ΑΥΘΕΝΤΕΙΝ in the Aeschylus Scholium," JETS 44 (2001): 615–25; Al Wolters, "A Semantic Study of Αὐθέντης and Its Derivatives," Journal of Greco-Roman Christianity and Judaism 1 (2000): 145–75. Online at http://divinity.mcmaster.ca/pages/jgrchj/JGRChJ1-8_Wolters.pdf (accessed November 10, 2004). See also Wolters, "Review of I Suffer Not," 211; Yarbrough, "Review," 28.

129. Knight, "ΑΥΘΕΝΤΕΩ," 152.

130. Catherine C. Kroeger, "Ancient Heresies and a Strange Greek Verb," Reformed Journal 29 (1979): 12–15.

131. Cf. Gritz, Mother Goddess, 134; Moo, "1 Timothy 2:11–15," 67; Carroll D. Osburn, "ΑΥΘΕΝΤΕΩ (1 Timothy 2:12)," Restoration Quarterly 25 (1982): 1–8; Panning, "ΑΥΘΕΝ-ΤΕΙΝ," 185–91.

132. Kroeger and Kroeger, I Suffer Not a Woman, 103. Linda Belleville proposes a reading that is similar to the Kroegers' in some respects ("Women in Ministry," 127–28; cf. idem, Women Leaders, 177), but her own analysis of the grammar is mistaken. She says that the two infinitives "teach" and "exercise authority" function as nouns, but she does not point out that they function as complementary infinitives to the verb phrase "I do not permit." Further, she argues that the verb "teach" modifies the noun "woman," but actually the noun "woman" functions as part of the object clause of the verb "permit" and as the subject of both infinitives in the object clause. Belleville ends up with two unusual proposals for the meaning of the verse: (1) "I do not permit a woman to teach in order to gain mastery over a man," and (2) "I do not permit a woman to teach with a view to dominating a man" ("Women in Ministry," 127). She understands the Greek word οὐδέ to designate in the correlative clause a related purpose or goal. Such a reading is grammatically problematic and misunderstands the word οὐδέ, for introducing any notion of purpose here misconstrues the force of the correlative. Since Belleville demonstrates a misunderstanding of the syntax of 1 Tim. 2:12, her attempt to define the word αὐθεντεῖν ("exercise authority") must be judged as unconvincing. The substance of this footnote derives from my "Review of Two Views on Women in Ministry," Journal for Biblical Manhood and Womanhood 6 (2001): 27.

133. For criticisms, see Perriman, "What Eve Did," 132–34; Leland E. Wilshire, "1 Timothy 2:12 Revisited: A Reply to Paul W. Barnett and Timothy J. Harris," *EQ* 65 (1993): 54; Wolters, "Review of *I Suffer Not*," 210–11. Payne ("Surrejoinder," 108–10) lists five different possible meanings for the verb, but the very variety of his proposals suggests the implausibility of his suggestions. In addition, most of his proposals assign a negative meaning to the infinitive "to teach," which I argue below is mistaken.

134. Wilshire, "ΑΥΘΕΝΤΕΩ," 120–34.

135. Wilshire, "Reply," 44.

136. For scholars who interpreted Wilshire thus, see Barnett, "1 Timothy 2:11–15," 231–32; Moo, "What Does It Mean?" 497n18; Wolters, "Review of *I Suffer Not*," 211. Perriman ("What Eve Did," 134–35) rightly observes that the meaning "exercise authority" was the drift of Wilshire's essay despite his protests. In his later article, Wilshire ("Reply," 50) says that αὐθεντεῖν meant "authority" only in the second and third centuries. But in his previous article (Wilshire, "ΑΥΘΕΝΤΕΩ," 130) he said, "There are, however, a series of citations immediately *before, during,* and after the time of Paul where some sort of meaning connected with 'authority' is found for the word αὐθεντέω" (italics mine). After I had written the above comments, Paul W. Barnett ("*Authentein* Once More: A Response to L. E. Wilshire," *EQ* 66 [1994]: 159–62) published an article in which he justifies his interpretation of the first Wilshire article along lines similar to what I have argued here.

137. Wilshire, "Reply," 43–55.

138. So Perriman, "What Eve Did," 136; Barnett, "Response," 161–62.

139. Perriman's own suggestion ("What Eve Did," 136–41) is that αὐθεντεῖν means the "active wielding of influence," so that the emphasis is on the taking of authority. He compares this to Eve's actions influencing Adam with the result that he transgressed. So, too, women teachers who are uneducated should not take authoritative action because they will lead men into sin. The problems with Perriman's analysis are numerous. His interpretation depends on v. 12 being parenthetical, which is dubious. The nuance he assigns to αὐθεντεῖν is not justified contextually, for he does not adequately explain the correlation between "teach" and "exercise authority." Moreover, Köstenberger (see his essay in this volume and my discussion below) has shown that both infinitives are to be construed positively in this context. Perriman imports into this text the idea that women were prohibited from teaching because of ignorance or lack of education, but these are not stated or implied.

140. Perriman, "What Eve Did," 135; Kroeger and Kroeger, *I Suffer Not a Woman*, 84; Mickelsen, "Egalitarian View," 202; Scholer, "1 Timothy 2:9–15," 205; Towner, *Goal of Our Instruction*, 216; Wiebe, "Two Texts on Women," 59–60; Marshall, *Pastoral Epistles*, 458; Belleville, "Women in Ministry," 124–25.

141. So Moo, "What Does It Mean?" 186; cf. also Blomberg, "Gender Roles in Paul," 362.

142. Liefeld fails to consider this data in his commentary (*1 and 2 Timothy, Titus,* 99).

143. Andreas J. Köstenberger ("Gender Passages in the NT: Hermeneutical Fallacies Critiqued," *WTJ* 56 [1994]: 264–67) observes that scholars on both sides have attempted to assign exclusive meanings to words, in the case of αὐθεντεῖν either positive or negative, on the basis of extrabiblical literature. Köstenberger correctly comments that these studies are helpful in establishing the semantic range of a word, but they cannot definitively establish the meaning of a term in a specific context.

144. In favor of "domineer," see Fee, *1 Timothy,* 73; Harris, "Eve's Deception," 42; Keener, *Women's Ministry,* 109; Osburn, "ΑΥΘΕΝΤΕΩ," 1–12; Payne, "Libertarian Women," 175; Towner, *Goal of Our Instruction,* 215–16; Witherington, *Women in the Earliest Churches,* 121–22; Boomsma, *Male and Female,* 71–72; Motyer, "Expounding 1 Timothy," 95–96.

145. Payne, "Surrejoinder," 104–8; cf. Boomsma, *Male and Female*, 72–73; Motyer, "Expounding 1 Timothy," 96; Belleville, *Women Leaders*, 173. Even though Hurley (*Man and Woman*, 201) and Saucy ("Women's Prohibition," 90) differ on the interpretation of the text, they affirm that there are not two distinct commands here.

146. See his chapter in this volume.

147. So also Gritz, *Mother Goddess*, 131; Moo, "1 Timothy 2:11–15," 68; Fung, "Ministry," 199. Fung's suggestion is not persuasive that "nor is she to exercise authority over men" is parenthetical. The Kroegers' suggestion (*I Suffer Not a Woman*, 37–38, 79–80, 189–92), which they ultimately back away from, that οὐδέ and the words that follow may introduce the object of the infinitive διδάσκειν is baseless. On this question, they did not pay heed to remarks of Walter L. Liefeld (in his response to Catherine Kroeger in *Women, Authority and the Bible*, ed. A. Mickelsen [Downers Grove, IL: InterVarsity, 1986], 246).

148. Geer cites Köstenberger but misunderstands his essay and actually argues contrary to what Köstenberger says. See Thomas C. Geer Jr., "Admonitions to Women in 1 Tim. 2:8–15," in *Essays on Women in Earliest Christianity*, ed. C. D. Osburn, vol. 1 (2nd printing, corrected, Joplin, MO: College Press, 1995), 294.

149. So also Gritz, *Mother Goddess*, 134–35; Mounce, *Pastoral Epistles*, 128–30; Keener, "Women in Ministry," 41.

150. Sumner, appealing to a book review by Padgett, maintains that 1 Tim. 6:3 and Titus 1:11 demonstrate the weakness of Köstenberger's view (*Men and Women in the Church*, 253n21). But her note fails to acknowledge nor does it show any awareness of the fact that Köstenberger demonstrated in his essay why these texts do not violate his thesis.

151. Marshall agrees with Köstenberger that οὐδέ refers to two activities that should be interpreted either positively or negatively, but he concludes that both infinitives should be interpreted negatively. Women are not to teach men falsely or domineer over them. He maintains that context reveals that improper teaching is in view, and that if the author had said that women could not teach falsely, then it would imply that the men could teach false doctrine (*Pastoral Epistles*, 458–60). Contrary to Marshall, the context does not provide any clues that false teaching is in view. The verb διδάσκω, as pointed out earlier, has a positive meaning elsewhere in the Pastoral Epistles. Marshall commits a non sequitur when he says that if the text stated that women could not teach false doctrine, then it would imply men could. But if I say, "Students must not drink poison," we should hardly conclude that nonstudents are permitted to ingest poison. Marshall's attempt to interpret both of the infinitives negatively fails, and hence it follows that both infinitives refer to positive activities in and of themselves, as Köstenberger argues. For additional criticisms of Marshall's view of the verb αὐθεντεῖν, see the essay by Baldwin in the present volume.

152. Contra Kroeger and Kroeger, *I Suffer Not a Woman*, 60, 81; rightly Wolters, "Review of *I Suffer Not*," 210. It is surprising that they still maintain this view even though Liefeld (*Women*, 245), in his response to Catherine Kroeger, rightly protested that διδάσκειν does not mean "to teach error."

153. J. L. Houlden (*The Pastoral Epistles: I and II Timothy, Titus*, TPI New Testament Commentaries [Philadelphia: Trinity, 1976], 71) is mistaken, therefore, in saying that 1 Tim. 2:13 represents contemporary Jewish exegesis of Gen. 3:16–19. Genesis 3 is appealed to in v. 14, not v. 13.

154. So Barnett, "1 Timothy 2:11–15," 234; Barrett, *Pastoral Epistles*, 56; Clark, *Man and Woman*, 191; Culver, "Traditional View," 36; Foh, *Women and the Word of God*, 127; idem, "Male Headship," 82; Fung, "Ministry," 201; Hurley, *Man and Woman*, 205; Joachim Jeremias, *Die Briefe an Timotheus und Titus*, Das Neue Testament Deutsch (Göttingen: Vandenhoeck & Ruprecht, 1968), 19; Knight, *Pastoral Epistles*, 142–43; Moo, "1 Timothy 2:11–15," 68; idem, "Rejoinder," 203; idem, "What Does It Mean?" 190–91; Roloff,

Timotheus, 138; Mounce, *Pastoral Epistles,* 131–32; Quinn and Wacker, *First and Second Timothy,* 226.

155. Fee, *Gospel and Spirit*, 61–62.

156. Gritz, *Mother Goddess*, 136; Mickelsen, "Egalitarian View," 203; Padgett, "Wealthy Women," 25; Payne, "Libertarian Women," 176; idem, "Surrejoinder," 111; Scholer, "1 Timothy 2:9–15," 208; Witherington, *Women in the Earliest Churches*, 122.

157. See esp. the evidence Moo ("Rejoinder," 202–3) has marshalled in support of this thesis.

158. Contra Fee (*1 Timothy*, 73), evidence is lacking that the reasons provided in vv. 13–14 support vv. 9–10 as well as vv. 11–12.

159. Padgett, "Wealthy Women," 26–27; cf. Perriman, "What Eve Did," 140. For a more restrained use of typology, see Wiebe, "Two Texts on Women," 60–61.

160. Rightly Collins, *1 and 2 Timothy and Titus*, 70–71. Holmes's interpretation of 1 Tim. 2:13–15 is quite strained (*Text in a Whirlwind*, 250–99). She posits that vv. 13–15 represent Jewish tradition, seeing them as the faithful saying of 3:1. She also maintains that the γάρ in v. 13 is redundant. What Paul says about women in the previous verses, according to Holmes, reminds him of the faithful saying that is transmitted in vv. 13–15. Against Holmes, it is unclear that vv. 13–15 contain the faithful saying. It is much more natural to see v. 13 as providing a reason for the injunction in v. 12, instead of seeing a redundant γάρ. Rightly Blomberg, who describes Holmes's view as "tortuous" ("Gender Roles in Paul," 365n151; cf. also the remarks of Köstenberger in his online review, note 48 above).

161. Quinn and Wacker remark that the brevity of the words in v. 13 demonstrates that the truth presented here was both familiar and intelligible (*First and Second Timothy*, 227).

162. E.g., Bilezikian, *Beyond Sex Roles*, 258–59; Keener, *Women's Ministry*, 116; Kroeger and Kroeger, *I Suffer Not a Woman*, 18.

163. On 1 Cor. 11:8–9, see my comments in "Head Coverings," 133–34.

164. Contra Robert Falconer, "1 Timothy 2:14–15: Interpretive Notes," *Journal of Biblical Literature* 60 (1941): 375; A. T. Hanson, *The Pastoral Epistles*, New Century Bible Commentary (Grand Rapids: Eerdmans, 1982), 73; Brox, *Pastoralbriefe*, 134–35; Spicq, *Epîtres pastorales*, 380; Holtz, *Pastoralbriefe*, 70; Houlden, *Pastoral Epistles*, 65; Kelly, *Pastoral Epistles*, 68.

165. For further discussion on this point, see Schreiner, "Head Coverings," 128–30.

166. Evans, *Woman in the Bible*, 104.

167. Fee, *Gospel and Spirit*, 58.

168. Harris, "Eve's Deception," 343.

169. Keener, *Women's Ministry*, 116.

170. Scholer, "1 Timothy 2:9–15," 208–13.

171. Motyer, "Expounding 1 Timothy," 97–98. He finally resolves the issue (100) by accepting the Kroegers' understanding of v. 13.

172. Marshall suggests that the author may be responding to myths and genealogies claiming that women were equal to or dominant over men in the new age inaugurated by the resurrection. In response, the author cites the text of Genesis (*Pastoral Epistles*, 463). Unfortunately, we have no evidence that women were making such claims, and Marshall, like many commentators, comes to the end of v. 13 without providing a convincing explanation of its function in the text.

173. Cf., e.g., Jewett, *Man as Male and Female*, 126–27; Belleville, *Women Leaders*, 179.

174. Hurley, *Man and Woman*, 207–8.

175. William J. Webb, *Slaves, Women and Homosexuals: Exploring the Hermeneutics of Cultural Analysis* (Downers Grove, IL: InterVarsity, 2001), 135–45.

176. Webb, *Slaves, Women and Homosexuals*, 142–43.

177. For further criticisms of Webb's approach, see Thomas R. Schreiner, "William J. Webb's *Slaves, Women and Homosexuals*: A Review Article," *Southern Baptist Journal of Theology* 6 (2002): 46–64; Wayne Grudem, "Should We Move beyond the New Testament to a Better Ethic? An Analysis of William J. Webb, *Slaves, Women and Homosexuals: Exploring the Hermeneutics of Cultural Analysis*," *JETS* 47 (2004): 299–346. William Webb has responded to my review in "The Limits of a Redemptive-Movement Hermeneutic: A Focused Response to T. R. Schreiner," *EQ* 75 (2003): 327–42. Grudem rightly points out the flaw in Webb's response: "But the way Webb thinks the NT is our final revelation is just that it proves his system to be correct. He says, 'I would argue that the NT expresses an ultimate ethic in its underlying redemptive spirit (redemptive-movement meaning) but not in all of its concrete "frozen in time" particulars.' . . . He says the NT *revelation* is not final in its *realization* of ethical standards; it expresses 'an incremental or developing (not ultimate) ethic in certain concrete particulars.' . . . This is anything but the Reformation principle of *sola Scriptura*, in which the teachings and moral commands of the NT are themselves our final and ultimate authority" ("An Analysis of Webb," 307n6). In other words, Webb's response to my review does not advance the discussion substantively but merely repeats what is already stated in his book.

178. Moo, "What Does It Mean?" 498n32.

179. Hanson, *Pastoral Epistles*, 72; Jewett, *Male and Female*, 116, 126; Krijn A. van der Jagt, "Women Are Saved through Bearing Children (1 Timothy 2.11–15)," *Bible Translator* 39 (1988): 205.

180. Barron, "Women in Their Place," 455; Bilezikian, *Beyond Sex Roles*, 180–81; Gritz, *Mother Goddess*, 137–38; Kroeger and Kroeger, *I Suffer Not a Woman*, 113, 117, 120–25; Mickelsen, "Egalitarian View," 204; Payne, "Libertarian Women," 176, 185–91; idem, "Surrejoinder," 96; Scholer, "1 Timothy 2:9–15," 218.

181. Rightly Moo, "Rejoinder," 203; idem, "What Does It Mean?" 193; Mounce, *Pastoral Epistles*, 134.

182. Royce Gordon Gruenler ("The Mission-Setting of 1 Tim. 2:8–15," *JETS* 41 [1998]: 215–38; cf. also Liefeld, *1 and 2 Timothy, Titus*, 114) and Wall ("1 Timothy 2:9–15 Reconsidered," 83, 101) argue that the subordination of women can be traced to the missionary situation in 1 Timothy. But they do not really engage in an intensive exegesis of the text, nor do they persuasively demonstrate that the prohibition is due to mission. Once again, Paul could have easily communicated such an idea, but he says nothing about the prohibition being due to the mission of the church. Köstenberger remarks that such an interpretation wrongly imports Titus 2:4–10 and 1 Cor. 9:20 into the present context ("1 and 2 Timothy and Titus," ad loc.).

183. Towner (*Goal of Our Instruction*, 39, 216) cautions that the evidence is insufficient to prove that women were teaching the heresy.

184. Rightly Moo, "Rejoinder," 203.

185. Carson, "Silent in the Churches," 147.

186. Towner, *Goal of Our Instruction*, 219, 221. For an argument that is similar in some respects, see Wiebe, "Two Texts on Women," 71–79.

187. Richard N. Longenecker, *New Testament Social Ethics for Today* (Grand Rapids: Eerdmans, 1984), 70–93.

188. Fee, *1 Timothy*, 77; idem, *Gospel and Spirit*, 59–61; Scholer, "1 Timothy 2:9–15," 214; France, *Women in Ministry*, 71–72.

189. Bruce K. Waltke, "1 Timothy 2:8–15: Unique or Normative?" *Crux* 28 (1992): 26.

190. Pierce, "Gender Roles," 350.

191. Ibid., 350–51.

192. Indeed, Pierce is actually the one who falls prey to Western logic, for his whole thesis depends on the view that Gal. 3:28 sits awkwardly with the restrictions in 1 Tim. 2:11–15. He finds this difficult because he has imbibed the Western view of equality, which perceives any differences in function as a threat to equality. This is remarkably different from the biblical worldview, in which equality of personhood did not rule out differences in role and function. Once we grasp how dissimilar the Western view of equality is from the conception of equality in the Scriptures, then we can understand why this issue is so pressing in our time and was not as troubling for people in previous centuries.

193. John Stott argues that submission to authority is transcultural but teaching is a cultural expression of the principle that does not apply the same way in our culture (*Guard the Truth: The Message of 1 Timothy and Titus* [Downers Grove, IL: InterVarsity, 1996], 78–80). Köstenberger rightly responds that "v. 13 provides the rationale for vv. 11–12 in their entirety rather than only the submission-authority principle. Moreover, teaching and ruling functions are inseparable from submission-authority, as is made clear in the immediately following context when it is said that the overseer must be 'husband of one wife' (i.e., by implication male; 3:2) as well as 'able to teach' (3:2)" ("1 and 2 Timothy and Titus," ad loc.).

194. So Moo, "What Does It Mean?" 191; Köstenberger, "Gender Passages," 270.

195. Note, for example, how Fee (*1 Timothy*, 74; *Gospel and Spirit*, 58) says that Paul's real purpose in citing the Genesis narrative emerges here (cf. Witherington, *Women in the Earliest Churches*, 123; Evans, *Woman in the Bible*, 104). One wonders, then, why he bothered appealing to the order of creation at all. Fung ("Ministry," 338n204) observes that if v. 13 is merely an introduction to the substantial argument, it could have easily been jettisoned.

196. Towner, *Goal of Our Instruction*, 217; Barron, "Women in Their Place," 455.

197. Barron, "Women in Their Place," 455.

198. Bilezikian, *Beyond Sex Roles*, 180, 259; Perriman, "What Eve Did," 139; Evans, *Woman in the Bible*, 105; Gritz, *Mother Goddess*, 140; Harris, "Eve's Deception," 345, 347–50; Keener, *Women's Ministry*, 117; Kroeger and Kroeger, *I Suffer Not a Woman*, 237–42; Payne, "Libertarian Women," 177, 182; 112; Scholer, "1 Timothy 2:9–15," 195–200, 210–11; Spencer, "Eve at Ephesus," 219–20; Marshall, *Pastoral Epistles*, 458, 466–67; Belleville, "Women in Ministry," 136–37. Of course, not every scholar here describes the situation in precisely the same way, but the common elements in their reconstruction are striking.

199. Sumner wrongly implies that v. 14 more naturally supports the egalitarian view, but she does not interact with the problems I raised in the earlier edition of this book against such a claim (*Men and Women in the Church*, 256–57).

200. Rightly Hugenberger, "Women in Church Office," 349–50; Moo, "Rejoinder," 217; idem, "What Does It Mean?" 189–90.

201. The prepositional prefix could indicate that Eve was completely deceived (ἐξαπα-τάω), whereas the verb used in reference to Adam is simply ἀπατάω. More likely, though, the shift to ἐξαπατάω is stylistic and no significance should be ascribed to the change (cf. Knight, *Pastoral Epistles*, 144; Moo, "1 Timothy 2:11–15," 69). In support of this latter conclusion, Gen. 3:13 LXX uses the verb ἀπατάω.

202. Mounce says that Eve could not have deceived Adam because Adam was with her during the temptation according to Gen. 3:6 (*Pastoral Epistles*, 141).

203. Rightly ibid., 134, 139.

204. Webb argues that the traditional view that women were deceived is correct, but it does not apply in the same way today because women were deceived due "to a combination of factors such as upbringing . . . age, experience, intelligence, education, development of critical thinking, economic conditions, and personality" (*Slaves, Women and Homosexuals*, 230). Webb's view does not explain convincingly how such factors

could apply to Eve in the garden. He also wrongly concludes that deceit is due to lack of education, but in Scripture deception is tied to human sin (cf. Rom. 7:11; 16:18; 1 Cor. 3:18; 2 Cor. 11:3; Eph. 5:6; James 1:26). Webb strays from what Paul actually says and, to explain the meaning of v. 14, resorts to a multitude of explanations that are not mentioned or implied by Paul.

205. Dibelius and Conzelmann, *Pastoral Epistles*, 48; Houlden, *Pastoral Epistles*, 71–72; Holtz, *Pastoralbriefe*, 70; Anthony Tyrell Hanson, "Eve's Transgression: I Timothy 2.13–15," in *Studies in the Pastoral Epistles* (London: SPCK, 1968), 65–77; Hanson, *Pastoral Epistles*, 73; Roloff, *Timotheus*, 139; cf. Falconer, "Interpretive Notes," 376.

206. Towner, *Goal of Our Instruction*, 313–14, n. 78; cf. Gritz, *Mother Goddess*, 139; Witherington, *Women in the Earliest Churches*, 123; Mounce, *Pastoral Epistles*, 142; Quinn and Wacker, *First and Second Timothy*, 228.

207. Gritz, *Mother Goddess*, 139; Guthrie, *Pastoral Epistles*, 77; Knight, *Pastoral Epistles*, 143–44; Moo, "Rejoinder," 204.

208. Cf. Fung, "Ministry," 201–2.

209. An exception here is Clark, *Man and Woman*, 202–4.

210. Jewett, *Male and Female*, 61; Clark, *Man and Woman*, 203–4; Culver, "Traditional View," 36–37; Hanson, *Pastoral Epistles*, 73 (but he says that this proves the letter is not Pauline); Holtz, *Pastoralbriefe*, 71–72; Kelly, *Pastoral Epistles*, 68; Moo, "1 Timothy 2:11–15," 70 (but he changed his mind on this point; see "Rejoinder," 204). Johnson, *First and Second Timothy*, 208; Collins, *1 and 2 Timothy and Titus*, 71–72. Doriani argues a variant of this view, maintaining that God made the sexes differently, so that men and women have different strengths and weaknesses. Men are more inclined to doctrinal formulations, and women to nurturing relationships ("History of Interpretation," 256–67). I accepted Doriani's view in the first edition of this book (145–46). But it seems that this view also strays from the text, even if one agrees that such differences exist between men and women. If Paul argued that women were deceived because of innate dispositions, the goodness of God's creative work is called into question. For criticism of the view espoused by Doriani, see Marshall, *Pastoral Epistles*, 466; Blomberg, "Gender Roles in Paul," 366n156.

211. For arguments against the idea that women are more prone to deception, see Barnett, "1 Timothy 2:11–15," 234; Evans, *Woman in the Bible*, 104–5; Foh, *Women and the Word of God*, 127; Fung, "Ministry," 201–2; Harris, "Eve's Deception," 346; Hurley, *Man and Woman*, 215; Moo, "What Does It Mean?" 190; Payne, "Libertarian Women," 175–77.

212. Barnett, "1 Timothy 2:11–15," 234; cf. also Ann L. Bowman, "Women in Ministry: An Exegetical Study of 1 Timothy 2:11–15," *Bibliotheca sacra* 149 (1992): 206.

213. Harris, "Eve's Deception," 346.

214. Craig L. Blomberg intriguingly suggests that v. 14 should be read with v. 15 instead of functioning as a second reason for the injunction in v. 12. On this reading, Paul says that the woman will be saved even though Eve was initially deceived ("Not beyond What Is Written: A Review of Aída Spencer's *Beyond the Curse: Women Called to Ministry*," *Criswell Theological Review* 2 (1988): 414. There are at least three weaknesses with this view (cf. Mounce, *Pastoral Epistles*, 142). (1) The καί in v. 14 naturally links v. 14 with v. 13. (2) The structure of v. 13 nicely matches v. 14, for both verses compare and contrast Adam and Eve in an A-B-A'-B' pattern. (3) Blomberg's view does not account well for the reference to Adam in v. 14. Any reference to Adam is superfluous if the concern is only the salvation of women. But the reference to both Adam and Eve fits with the specific argument in v. 12 that women are not to teach men. In my view, Blomberg does not answer these objections convincingly in his "Gender Roles in Paul," 367.

215. Fee, *1 Timothy*, 74; idem, *Gospel and Spirit*, 59; cf. Moo, "1 Timothy 2:11–15," 69. I realize Fee would not agree with the conclusions I draw from his observation.

216. Rightly Scholer, "1 Timothy 2:9–15," 210; Mounce, *Pastoral Epistles*, 125, 131, 141; cf. also Köstenberger, "1 and 2 Timothy and Titus," ad loc.

217. Oden remarks (*First Timothy*, 100) that the rabbis believed that the fall also included a reversal of the creation order, in that Eve took the leadership over Adam.

218. For a similar suggestion in some respects, see Fung, "Ministry," 202; Hurley, *Man and Woman*, 214–16; Moo, "Rejoinder," 204.

219. Wall maintains that Eve functions typologically, so that she illustrates the experience of women who move from sin to salvation. Women who are freed from their sin are no longer deceived or slaves of sin. Now such women can live modestly, and since they are freed from sin, they are qualified to teach ("1 Timothy 2:9–15 Reconsidered," 81–103). Wall's exegesis fails to convince. He mistakenly (see below) understands v. 15 as the climax of the paragraph (94). Moreover, it is quite unlikely that the subject of σωθή-σεται in v. 15 is Eve (94). Paul would not use the future tense if Eve were the subject. The text focuses not on Eve but on the Christian women in Ephesus. Most important, even if we accept Wall's view that Eve is particularly in view (which is quite doubtful), the notion that v. 15 ends up trumping the admonition in v. 12 is scarcely clear. We have no evidence in the text that the salvation and modesty of women relativize the command in v. 12. Wall ultimately appeals to the rest of the canon to support his view, but he mistakenly thinks that the private instruction given to Apollos by Priscilla and Aquila (Acts 18:26) and the encouragement of women to prophesy (1 Cor. 11:5) contradict the complementarian interpretation of 1 Timothy 2 (99–100). He fails to see that 1 Tim. 2:12 refers to public and official teaching, and that prophecy and teaching are distinct gifts. In any case, the women who prophesy in 1 Cor. 11:2–16 are to do so in a manner that reflects submission to male headship. Wall's exegesis is creative, but his creativity is the problem, for it is difficult to believe that the original readers could have understood the text in the way he suggests.

220. Cf. Moo, "What Does It Mean?" 190.

221. Foh, *Women and the Word of God*, 128.

222. Keener, *Women's Ministry*, 118; Scholer, "1 Timothy 2:9–15," 196; France, *Women in Ministry*, 60; Wall, "1 Timothy 2:9–15," 11.

223. Rightly Mounce, *Pastoral Epistles*, 143.

224. Cf. Clark, *Man and Woman*, 207; Gritz, *Mother Goddess*, 141; Stanley E. Porter, "What Does It Mean to Be 'Saved by Childbirth' (1 Timothy 2.15)?" *Journal for the Study of the New Testament* 49 (1993): 93.

225. Of course, the verse is difficult and debated. One should not conclude that the interpretation of v. 15 proposed below is necessary for the understanding of vv. 11–14 that has been argued for in this chapter.

226. NASB; Barrett, *Pastoral Epistles*, 56–57; Barron, "Women in Their Place," 457; Jewett, *Male and Female*, 60; Keener, *Women's Ministry*, 118–19.

227. Keener, *Women's Ministry*, 118–19.

228. Cf. Evans, *Woman in the Bible*, 106; Gritz, *Mother Goddess*, 141; Hilde Huizenga, "Women, Salvation, and the Birth of Christ: A Reexamination of 1 Timothy 2:15," *Studia Biblica et theologica* 12 (1982): 21; Oden, *First Timothy*, 100.

229. So Gritz, *Mother Goddess*, 141; Fung, "Ministry," 203; Houlden, *Pastoral Epistles*, 72; David R. Kimberly, "1 Timothy 2:15: A Possible Understanding of a Difficult Text," *JETS* 35 (1992): 481–82; Krijn van der Jagt, "Women Are Saved through Bearing Children: A Sociological Approach to the Interpretation of 1 Timothy 2.15," in *Issues in Bible Translation*, ed. Philip C. Stine, UBS Monograph Series 3 (New York: United Bible Societies, 1988), 293; Lock, *Pastoral Epistles*, 31; Moo, "1 Timothy 2:11–15," 71; idem, "What Does It Mean?" 192; Payne, "Libertarian Women," 178; Porter, "Saved by Childbirth," 93–94; Mounce, *Pastoral Epistles*, 144–45; Marshall, *Pastoral Epistles*, 467.

230. So S. Jebb, "A Suggested Interpretation of 1 Ti 2.15," *Expository Times* 81 (1970): 221–22; Hurley, *Man and Woman*, 222. Against this interpretation, see Fee, *1 Timothy*, 75; Hanson, *Pastoral Epistles*, 74; Kimberly, "1 Tim. 2:15," 482; Porter, "Saved by Childbirth," 95; Roloff, *Timotheus*, 141.

231. The same error is committed by Roberts ("Woman Shall Be Saved," 6–7) who adopts a nonsoteriological definition for σώζω. Roberts's interpretation is even more arbitrary. He says that by giving birth to the Messiah (and continuing in the faith) women will be saved from their subordinate role and thus can be restored to teaching men. There is no evidence, however, that Paul contemplated that the "saving" in v. 15 involved liberation from the injunctions in vv. 11–12!

232. Andreas J. Köstenberger suggests that the verb σώζω refers to spiritual preservation in this particular text (cf. also NASB here and in 1 Tim. 4:16), and not spiritual salvation. He argues that Paul has in mind protection from Satan and the deception he engenders. He cites a number of other texts in the Pastoral Epistles where protection from Satan is in view ("Ascertaining Women's God-Ordained Roles: An Interpretation of 1 Timothy 2:15," *Bulletin for Biblical Research* 7 [1997]: 107–44). It is possible that σώζω refers to spiritual preservation, but in my judgment it is not very likely. Σώζω elsewhere in Paul signifies eschatological salvation, not merely preservation (Rom. 5:9, 10; 8:24; 9:27; 10:9, 13; 11:14, 26; 1 Cor. 1:18, 21; 3:15; 5:5; 7:16 [2x]; 9:22; 10:33; 15:2; 2 Cor. 2:15; Eph. 2:5, 8; 1 Thess. 2:16; 2 Thess. 2:10). One could object that the way the term is used elsewhere does not determine its usage in a particular context. Such an observation is, of course, true. Still, the normal way Paul uses a term is the way we should understand it unless there are good contextual reasons to understand it differently. When we examine the Pastorals, it is clear that Paul uses the term σώζω to designate spiritual salvation (1 Tim. 1:15; 2:4; 2 Tim. 1:9; 4:18). Indeed, in the Pastorals Paul often uses the nouns σωτήρ (1 Tim. 1:1; 2:3; 4:10; 2 Tim. 1:10; Titus 1:3, 4; 2:10, 13; 3:4, 6) and σωτηρία (2 Tim. 2:10; 3:15) to refer to spiritual salvation. Some scholars think that σώζω does not refer to spiritual salvation in 1 Tim. 2:15 and 4:16. I would argue that their primary objection is not lexical but theological, for in every other instance in Paul the reference is to spiritual salvation, and in the Pastorals he emphasizes spiritual salvation with the nouns "Savior" and "salvation." These scholars worry that assigning such a definition in 1 Tim. 2:15 and 4:16 would contradict salvation by faith alone. But understanding spiritual salvation as eschatological fits with the future tense elsewhere in Paul (e.g., Rom 5:9, 10; 2 Tim. 4:18). Nor is there any reason to think that what Paul says here contradicts what he says about salvation being by faith alone (cf. Thomas R. Schreiner and Ardel B. Caneday, *The Race Set before Us: A Biblical Theology of Perseverance and Assurance* [Downers Grove, IL: InterVarsity, 2001]). We could still retain a part of Köstenberger's view by saying that Paul has eschatological salvation in mind, and those duped by Satan will not be saved on the last day (cf. 1 Cor. 5:5; 1 Tim. 1:20; see also Eph. 6:11; 2 Tim. 2:26). But even this point is not clearly supported in the text, for Satan is not named explicitly in 1 Tim. 2:9-15 (though Satan is implied in v. 14), and hence it is unclear that the salvation in view in v. 15 is deliverance from Satan. It is more likely that salvation from sin in general is intended (so also Mounce, *Pastoral Epistles*, 147; Marshall, *Pastoral Epistles*, 469–70).

233. For references in the early fathers, see Porter, "Saved by Childbirth," 90n8. Recent advocates of this view include Knight, *Pastoral Epistles*, 146–47; Lock, *Pastoral Epistles*, 33; Padgett, "Wealthy Women," 29; Payne, "Libertarian Women," 177–78, 180–81; Roberts, "Woman Shall Be Saved," 6–7; Spencer, "Eve at Ephesus," 220; Oden, *First Timothy*, 101–2; Huizenga, "Birth of Christ," 17–26; Geer, "1 Tim. 2:8–15," 298–99; Liefeld, *1 and 2 Timothy, Titus*, 102.

234. Huizenga, "Birth of Christ," 22; Oden, *First Timothy*, 102; Payne, "Libertarian Women," 180–81.

235. Hanson, *Pastoral Epistles*, 74.

236. Guthrie, *Pastoral Epistles*, 78; cf. Evans, *Woman in the Bible*, 107; Fee, *1 Timothy*, 75; Foh, *Women and the Word of God*, 128; Gritz, *Mother Goddess*, 141; Hurley, *Man and Woman*, 222; Kelly, *Pastoral Epistles*, 69; Moo, "1 Timothy 2:11–15," 71; Porter, "Saved by Childbirth," 92; Marshall, *Pastoral Epistles*, 469.

237. Keener, *Women's Ministry*, 118; Porter, "Saved by Childbirth," 92; Dibelius and Conzelmann, *Pastoral Epistles*, 48; Brox, *Pastoralbriefe*, 136.

238. Cf. Fee, *1 Timothy*, 75.

239. For a lucid discussion of the article, with warnings about misuse, see D. A. Carson, *Exegetical Fallacies*, 2nd ed. (Grand Rapids: Baker, 1996), 79–84.

240. See Porter, "Saved by Childbirth," 92; Moo, "Rejoinder," 206.

241. Cf. Falconer, "Interpretive Notes," 377; Moo, "1 Timothy 2:11–15," 71–72; Brox, *Pastoralbriefe*, 136; Barrett, *Pastoral Epistles*, 56–57; Jeremias, *Timotheus*, 19; Hanson, *Pastoral Epistles*, 74; Spicq, *Epîtres pastorales*, 383–84.

242. So Holtz, *Pastoralbriefe*, 70–71; Huizenga, "Birth of Christ," 18; Kimberly, "1 Timothy 2:15," 482; Payne, "Libertarian Women," 178–79; Porter, "Saved by Childbirth," 95–96.

243. E. F. Scott, *The Pastoral Epistles* (New York: Harper & Bros., n.d.), 28.

244. Cf. Evans, *Woman in the Bible*, 107; Guthrie, *Pastoral Epistles*, 78; Moo, "1 Timothy 2:11–15," 71; Porter, "Saved by Childbirth," 96–97.

245. Cf. Falconer, "Interpretive Notes," 376; Roloff, *Timotheus*, 141–42.

246. So Porter, "Saved by Childbirth," 97.

247. So ibid., 97–98; Dibelius and Conzelmann, *Pastoral Epistles*, 48; van der Jagt, "Bearing Children," 292; Moo, "1 Timothy 2:11–15," 72.

248. See Porter, "Saved by Childbirth," 101; Dibelius and Conzelmann, *Pastoral Epistles*, 48; Brox, *Pastoralbriefe*, 137; Moo, "1 Timothy 2:11–15," 71; Collins, *1 and 2 Timothy and Titus*, 76–77.

249. But the idea that v. 15b stems from another source is unpersuasive, contra Falconer, "Interpretive Notes," 378; Hanson, *Pastoral Epistles*, 74; rightly Porter, "Saved by Childbirth," 98.

250. For a reference to children, see Houlden, *Pastoral Epistles*, 72–73; Jeremias, *Timotheus*, 19; while Brox (*Pastoralbriefe*, 137) sees a reference to husbands and wives.

251. So Barrett, *Pastoral Epistles*, 57; Fung, "Ministry," 204; Gritz, *Mother Goddess*, 144; Holtz, *Pastoralbriefe*, 72; Porter, "Saved by Childbirth," 98–99; Scholer, "1 Timothy 2:9–15," 196; Towner, *Goal of Our Instruction*, 221; Marshall, *Pastoral Epistles*, 471.

252. The same shift occurs with "men." Paul begins with ἄνδρας in v. 8 and shifts to ἀνδρός in v. 12. The latter is obviously generic.

253. Pierce ("Gender Roles," 351, 353) suggests that v. 15 promises "partial healing" for women in childbirth and gives "them hope that deliverance from the curse of male dominance is also possible." This is an unconvincing interpretation. It has already been argued that the verb σωθήσεται in the Pauline literature refers not to healing but to eschatological salvation. Thus, it does not refer to mitigating the pain of childbearing in this age. To say that the verse offers hope of deliverance from male dominance is puzzling, since nothing is said about that subject in the verse. It is certainly understandable that some would see the admonitions in these verses as having temporary validity, but one looks in vain anywhere in 1 Tim. 2:9–15 for any hint that the text is actually promising eventual deliverance from male dominance. Nowhere is male leadership *criticized*!

254. So Barron, "Women in Their Place," 457; Hanson, *Pastoral Epistles*, 74; Huizenga, "Birth of Christ," 197–98; Hurley, *Man and Woman*, 221; Knight, *Pastoral Epistles*, 145; Payne, "Libertarian Women," 179; idem, "Surrejoinder," 115; Oden, *First Timothy*, 100.

255. Many scholars have rightly seen that the reference to childbirth was precipitated by the impact of the false teachers. See Barron, "Women in Their Place," 457; Fee, *1 Timothy*, 74–75; idem, *Gospel and Spirit*, 59; Gritz, *Mother Goddess*, 143; Harris, "Eve's Deception," 350; Jeremias, *Timotheus*, 19; Kelly, *Pastoral Epistles*, 70; Kimberly, "1 Tim. 2:15," 484–86; van der Jagt, "Bearing Children," 293–94; Kroeger and Kroeger, *I Suffer Not a Woman*, 171–77; Moo, "What Does It Mean?" 192; Padgett, "Wealthy Women," 28; Scholer, "1 Timothy 2:9–15," 197–98; Bassler, "Adam, Eve, and the Pastor," 55–56; Mounce, *Pastoral Epistles*, 146. It should be noted that Barron, the Kroegers, and Kimberly unfortunately read into the text Gnosticism from the second century AD.

256. So Barnett, "1 Timothy 2:9–15," 235; Clark, *Man and Woman*, 207; Evans, *Woman in the Bible*, 107; Falconer, "Interpretive Notes," 377; Perriman, "What Eve Did," 140–41; Hurley, *Man and Woman*, 222–23; Kelly, *Pastoral Epistles*, 69; Padgett, "Wealthy Women," 28; Roloff, *Timotheus*, 141; Scholer, "1 Timothy 2:9–15," 197.

257. E.g., Scholer, "1 Timothy 2:9–15," 197.

258. Contra Huizenga, "Birth of Christ," 18.

259. Fung, "Ministry," 204.

260. For a careful analysis of the conditional clause used here, see Porter, "Saved by Childbirth," 99–101.

261. Cf. Barnett, "1 Timothy 2:11–15," 235 (although the chiasm he detects is not clear to me). Collins says it is the "epitome of feminine virtue" (*1 and 2 Timothy and Titus*, 77).

262. For an investigation of this issue in more detail, see my "Did Paul Believe in Justification by Works? Another Look at Romans 2," *Bulletin for Biblical Research* 3 (1993): 131–58.

263. So Witherington, *Women in the Earliest Churches*, 124.

264. Witherington (ibid.) also notices the parallel, and he comments that those spoken of were already Christians.

265. Again, it must be said that Christ's righteousness is the ultimate basis of salvation.

266. For how this fits with Christian assurance, see Schreiner and Caneday, *Race Set before Us;* D. A. Carson, "Reflections on Christian Assurance," *WTJ* 54 (1992): 1–29.

Chapter 5: Progressive *and* Historic

1. M. J. Erickson, *Evangelical Interpretation: Perspectives on Hermeneutical Issues* (Grand Rapids: Baker, 1993), 59, uses "signification" to refer to the meaning of a statement in its original setting. "Significance" would be the meaning it has, or should have, for some other setting, e.g., the modern situation. Erickson seeks here to refine E. D. Hirsch's terms "meaning" and "significance." Hirsch's outlook has been the subject of voluminous comment; for a brief defense, see J. F. Harris, *Against Relativism: A Philosophical Defense of Method* (LaSalle, IL: Open Court, 1992), 120–22. More broadly, see Kevin Vanhoozer, *Is There a Meaning in This Text?* (Grand Rapids: Zondervan, 1998).

2. For recent examinations of biblical understandings of family, see R. S. Hess and M. D. Carroll R., eds., *Family in the Bible* (Grand Rapids: Baker, 2003); K. M. Campbell, ed., *Marriage and Family in the Biblical World* (Downers Grove, IL: InterVarsity, 2003); A. Köstenberger with D. Jones, *God, Marriage, and Family* (Wheaton: Crossway, 2004). See also chaps. 2, 3, and 9 in D. Blankenhorn, D. Browning, and M. S. Van Leeuwen, eds., *Does Christianity Teach Male Headship? The Equal-Regard Marriage and Its Critics* (Grand Rapids: Eerdmans, 2004).

3. A contemporary parallel noted by social scientists: "Past research has revealed that women, working or not, perform more family labor (i.e., housework and childcare) than do men. Yet women often do not perceive this as unfair." See N. K. Grote, K. E. Naylor, and M. S. Clark, "Perceiving the Division of Family Work to Be Unfair: Do Social Comparisons, Enjoyment, and Competence Matter?" *Journal of Family Psychology* 16, no. 4 (2002): 510.

4. E. E. Ellis wisely stresses that Paul's pronouncements on men, women, and their interaction assume the presence of Christ in their hearts, of covenant commitment on the parts of the recipients of his counsel. Much misuse of Paul by Christians and maligning of Paul by non-Christians might be avoided if the primary horizon of Paul's admonitions were recognized. His epistles are addressed to persons "in Christ," not "in Adam" (*Pauline Theology, Ministry and Society* [Grand Rapids: Eerdmans, 1989], 12–14). Women's offices and roles in church and (Christian) family as Paul (and other biblical writers) outlines them ought not be treated by men as automatically and necessarily applicable to women in society at large. Or, as Sarah Sumner states, "our interpretations of Scripture" should "make sense within a gospel paradigm" (*Men and Women in the Church* [Downers Grove, IL: InterVarsity, 2003], 209).

5. At most points, they were not differentiated, as any number of theological pronouncements, moral commands, ethical expectations, and promises attest. For careful delineation of where they are, see D. Doriani, *Women and Ministry* (Wheaton: Crossway, 2003), esp. 101–32.

6. W. J. Webb, *Slaves, Women and Homosexuals* (Downers Grove, IL: InterVarsity, 2001).

7. Ibid., 256n3.

8. See 160n14 of the first edition of this book, which is nearly identically reproduced in note 20, below.

9. Webb, *Slaves, Women and Homosexuals*, 35n4.

10. I concede that biblical passages like 1 Tim. 2 are and have been misused. But negative effects of Christian teaching as a whole are pale when compared with its ennobling and dignifying effects, as may be witnessed by the relatively high regard for women in countries impacted by Christianity when compared with women in countries where this has not been the case.

11. Cf. Ellis, *Pauline Theology, Ministry and Society*, 73. I have not always followed Ellis's translation but have preferred my own at some points and the RSV at others. Italicized words are common expressions that suggest early tradition to Ellis.

12. In addition to the parallels above, see esp. Eph. 5:22–33. More broadly, see D. C. Jones, *Biblical Christian Ethics* (Grand Rapids: Baker, 1994), chap. 8, esp. 154 with note 2.

13. See, e.g., *The Women's Bible Commentary*, ed. C. Newsom and S. Ringe (London: SPCK; Louisville: Westminster/John Knox, 1992), 353ff.; R. R. Ruether, ed., *Gender, Ethnicity, and Religion* (Minneapolis: Fortress, 2002). This is the impression given frequently in Webb, for whom "the bulk of the data" in Scripture "appear to favor an assessment of patriarchy as culturally relative" and therefore to be abandoned today (*Slaves, Women and Homosexuals*, 248; cf. 249: "The second-creation material in the New Testament . . . appears to displace or supersede the patriarchy found in the first-creation story"). It is not surprising that he sets forth "strong" criticism of my essay that appeared in the first edition of this book (see ibid., 35n3).

14. As previous chapters have shown, and as this chapter confirms below, many interpreters who profess a high view of Scripture have done precisely this. It is one of the goals of this chapter to question the wisdom of appealing to 1 Tim. 2:9–15 for support of this move.

15. On "signification" and "significance," see note 1, above.

16. Elizabeth Achtemeier, "The Impossible Possibility: Evaluating the Feminist Approach to Bible and Theology," *Interpretation* 42 (January 1988): 51, cited in M. M. Schumacher, "Feminist Experience and Faith Experience," in *Women in Christ: Toward a New Feminism*, ed. M. M. Schumacher (Grand Rapids: Eerdmans, 2004), 177.

17. While interpretation struggles with the problem of the interpreter's limited horizon and preunderstanding, we do not agree that "radical relativity" must necessarily describe

the interpretive process. Those who insist on absolutizing their experience of reality as a normative interpretive grid are obviously free to do so; in this case the verdict of "radical relativity" is apt as a description of their interpretive philosophy and work. But the declaration of "radical relativity" for all interpretations of anything is, finally, self-refuting—by what standard can any interpreter call all others relative? This pronouncement itself presumes a standard by which to measure. Thus, *either* there is a standard after all, in which case "radical relativity" does not necessarily describe interpretation, *or* there truly is not a standard, and solipsism (the view that the self knows only its own knowing; perception and meaning are fundamentally different for every single person) is the human predicament. In the latter case, there is no need for anyone to heed anyone else's charge of "radical relativity." Such a charge would be a meaningless truism—if there could be a truism in a solipsistic world. For a philosophical refutation of "radical relativity," see Harris, *Against Relativism*. For a briefer and more accessible defense of the notion of objectivity despite the social construction of knowledge, see S. Dex, "Objective Facts in Social Science," in *Objective Knowledge*, ed. P. Helm (Leicester, Eng.: Inter-Varsity, 1987), 167–90. On theological grounds it may be noted that the Bible holds humans accountable for responsiveness to events and words addressed to them, ultimately, from outside their own experience. This invalidates the solipsistic thesis, unless God were unjust, which Scripture insists he is not. Further, the Bible portrays the human condition since the fall, not as radically relative to shifting immanent considerations, but as profoundly absolute in view of universal condemnation under God's law. The standards of a sovereign God, who is absolute, confer a substantial degree of nonrelativity on humans. This shatters the "radical relativity" thesis for those who acknowledge God's dominion over their lives—and, if they are correct, over everyone else's life too.

18. For seminal readings, see K. Mueller-Vollmer, ed., *The Hermeneutics Reader* (New York: Continuum, 1985). On hermeneutical theory, see A. C. Thiselton, *New Horizons in Hermeneutics* (Grand Rapids: Zondervan, 1992). For wide-ranging coverage of the history and theological dimensions of biblical hermeneutics, see G. Maier, *Biblical Hermeneutics*, trans. R. Yarbrough (Wheaton: Crossway, 1994). More generally, see, e.g., R. Morgan with J. Barton, *Biblical Interpretation* (Oxford: Oxford University Press, 1988); G. Osborne, *The Hermeneutical Spiral* (Downers Grove, IL: InterVarsity, 1991); W. Klein, C. Blomberg, and R. Hubbard Jr., *Introduction to Biblical Interpretation* (Dallas: Word, 1993); D. Doriani, *Getting the Message* (Phillipsburg, NJ: P&R, 1996); D. Black and D. Dockery, eds., *Interpreting the New Testament* (Nashville: Broadman & Holman, 2001); M. D. Johnson, *Making Sense of the Bible* (Grand Rapids: Eerdmans, 2002); V. G. Shillington, *Reading the Sacred Text* (London: Clark, 2002). For a de facto primer on egalitarian hermeneutics, see Sumner, *Men and Women in the Church*, though note where Sumner states her differences with other "biblical feminists" (291n16).

19. Marshall, "The Use of the New Testament in Christian Ethics," *Expository Times* 105, no. 5 (February 1994): 136. Addressing this problem are, e.g., G. O'Collins and D. Kendall, *The Bible for Theology* (New York: Paulist, 1997); D. Doriani, *Putting the Truth to Work* (Phillipsburg, NJ: P&R, 2001). On the distinct problem of the use of the Old Testament, see, e.g., E. A. Martens, "How Is the Christian to Construe Old Testament Law?" *Bulletin for Biblical Research* 12, no. 2 (2002): 199–216 (with numerous references); G. J. Wenham, *Story as Torah* (Grand Rapids: Baker, 2004).

20. In other words, this discussion will not seek to arrive at a set of discrete "principles" or interpretive rules that, when applied to 1 Tim. 2, will yield the proper understanding. Thiselton, *New Horizons*, has already performed the service of showing how much of feminist-leaning interpretation runs afoul of weighty theoretical, philosophical, and theological considerations. Due to space constraints, we cannot duplicate, or even apply in any extensive and systematic way, his insights here. We have chosen instead

to deal with key practical (rather than theoretical) issues that seem to be exerting the most influence on the interpretation and application of 1 Tim. 2 in many circles at the present time.

21. The position adopted in this chapter corresponds frequently with the category called "soft patriarchy" in Webb, *Slaves, Women and Homosexuals*, 26–27.

22. It is the argument of some in Blankenhorn, Browning, and Van Leeuwen, eds., *Does Christianity Teach Male Headship?* that New Testament writers were in the throes of Aristotle's views when it came to male-female relations. This is seen particularly in the "household code" sections (Eph. 5:21–33; Col. 3:18–25; 1 Pet. 3:1–7; see *Does Christianity Teach Male Headship?* 4–6, 133, and elsewhere). It is noteworthy that the standard compilation of New Testament allusions to extrabiblical writers contains over thirty pages, and thousands of references, to the Old Testament—but less than one-third of one page, and fewer than a dozen references, to any Greek writers whatsoever. See "Loci Citati vel Allegati," in *Novum Testamentum Graece*, ed. K. Aland et al., 27th ed. (Stuttgart: Deutsche Bibelgesellschaft, 1993), 770–806. No New Testament writer alludes explicitly or implicitly to Aristotle. Appeal to his formative influence on the New Testament writers to the extent posited in this book defies the New Testament's own primary overt historical and literary background. It also minimizes the revelatory nature of the New Testament writings by a reductionist hermeneutic. In the end, it makes a mere theory about the "household codes" the Archimedean point for Christian theological anthropology, with the sad result that Paul (who appeals to God and Scripture and Christ, not Greek philosophy) is saddled with Aristotle's error—from which egalitarian hermeneutics must be called in to rescue him. Paul had no qualms about defying Hellenistic conviction at any number of other points: the personal nature of God, God's creation of the world ex nihilo, the resurrection of the body, the necessarily close relation between religion and ethics, the superiority of God's scripturally revealed will over the unaided human intellect, and so forth. What right do we have to impute such uncritical cultural complicity to him on the issue of sexual identity and roles?

23. For a programmatic statement, see John Dewey, *Liberalism and Social Action* (1935; repr., New York: Capricorn, 1963), 2–3.

24. Ibid., 93.

25. Robert N. Bellah et al., *Habits of the Heart* (San Francisco: Harper & Row, 1986), passim.

26. Ibid., 283.

27. Dewey's *Liberalism and Social Action* (see note 23 above) was an attempt to reassert liberal values in the dark years of German fascist and Soviet Stalinist expansion of the 1930s. On the socialist nature of Nazi fascism, see G. Huntemann (*The Other Bonhoeffer*, trans. T. Huizinga [Grand Rapids: Baker, 1993]), who rightly calls Hitler's reign a "socialist dictatorship" (52). A 1935 German (5 RM) coin has embossed on its edge the words "Gemeinnutz geht vor Eigennutz" (Community use takes precedence over personal use)—the antithesis of the liberal creed.

28. M. B. Mahowald, ed., *Philosophy of Woman: An Anthology of Classic and Current Concepts*, 2nd ed. (Indianapolis: Hackett, 1983), 45.

29. E. Fox-Genovese, "Equality, Difference, and the Practical Problems of a New Feminism," in *Women in Christ: Toward a New Feminism*, ed. M. M. Schumacher, 302.

30. See William Baird, *History of New Testament Research*, vol. 2, *From Jonathan Edwards to Rudolf Bultmann* (Minneapolis: Fortress, 2003), 330–32, 335–37.

31. Newsom and Ringe, *Women's Bible Commentary*, xiv.

32. Cf. R. Groothuis, *Women Caught in the Conflict* (Grand Rapids: Baker, 1994), 103–8.

33. See, e.g., Schumacher, *Women in Christ: Toward a New Feminism*; R. E. Groenhout and M. Bower, eds., *Philosophy, Feminism, and Faith* (Bloomington: Indiana University Press, 2003).

34. E. K. Wondra, "By Whose Authority? The Status of Scripture in Contemporary Feminist Theologies," *Anglican Theological Review* 74, no. 1 (1993): 84. Feminist interpreters of color are no more likely to be subservient to the biblical text, though there are sure to be exceptions.

35. M. A. Kassian, *The Feminist Gospel* (Wheaton: Crossway, 1992), 205: "But conservative evangelical Christians are not unaffected by feminism. Many of them view the philosophy of feminism as a valid adjunct to their faith. They believe that the basic tenets of feminism are supported by the Bible and that feminism can naturally, easily, and homogeneously be combined with Christianity. . . . They believe in the Bible, but also believe in feminism."

36. In note 4 above, I state that care must be taken in transferring principles of church order into the larger social sphere. There may be important correlates and analogies, but these must be worked out with caution. In Stendahl's zeal for (post)modernity's social order, he and evangelicals who too facilely endorse such thinking commit this error in the opposite direction.

37. K. Stendahl, *The Bible and the Role of Women*, trans. E. Sander (Philadelphia: Fortress, 1966), 40–41.

38. J. A. McDougall, "Weaving Garments of Grace: En-gendering a Theology of the Call to Ordained Ministry for Women Today," *Theological Education* 39, no. 2 (2003): 162.

39. J. Q. Wilson, *The Marriage Problem: How Our Culture Has Weakened Families* (New York: HarperCollins, 2002). See also the document released by Pope John Paul II in early August 2004, though credited to Cardinal Ratzinger, titled "Letter to the Bishops of the Catholic Church on the Collaboration of Men and Women in the Church and in the World."

40. K. Giles ("A Critique of the 'Novel' Contemporary Interpretation of 1 Timothy 2:9–15 Given in the Book, *Women in the Church*: Part I," *EQ* 72, no. 2 [2000]: 157) calls this statement (from the first edition of this book) an overstatement. It is possible that I view things like divorce, marital infidelity, and child abuse (all documented by empirical research below) as particularly heinous because they were components of the (broken) home I grew up in. I cannot believe that Giles actually thinks the social ruin borne out by statistics and even nominal pastoral activity in Western nations is anything less than "disastrous."

41. My thanks to Margaret Boyd for bibliographic aid in the next few paragraphs.

42. *U.S. News & World Report*, March 28, 1994, 42–56. Quotes are from the table of contents and the cover respectively.

43. Martha N. Ozawa, ed., *Women's Life Cycle and Economic Insecurity* (New York: Praeger, 1989), 1. See also Terry Arendell, *Mothers and Divorce* (Berkeley: University of California Press, 1986).

44. W. Jeynes, *Divorce, Family Structure, and the Academic Success of Children* (New York: Haworth, 2002), 10.

45. Ozawa, *Women's Life Cycle and Economic Insecurity*, 2 (emphasis mine).

46. See, e.g., Irwin Garfinkel and Sara McLanahan, *Single Mothers and Their Children* (Washington, DC: Urban Institute, 1986); J. B. Elshtain, "Family Matters: The Plight of America's Children," *Christian Century*, July 14–21, 1993, 710–12.

47. Ozawa, *Women's Life Cycle and Economic Insecurity*, 3.

48. Ibid.

49. Quoted in Susan S. Phillips, "Caring for Our Children: Confronting the Crisis," *Radix* 22, no. 1 (1993): 4.

50. For particulars, see the Forum on Child and Family Statistics, *America's Children in Brief: Key National Indicators of Well-Being, 2004*, online at http://childstats.gov/ac2004/intro.asp (accessed November 10, 2004).

51. Angela E. Coulombis, "New Report Finds Youth Deaths by Homicide Doubled since 1985," *Christian Science Monitor*, Monday, April 25, 1994, 18, reporting on the Annie E. Casey Foundation's 1994 Kids Count Report.

52. R. A. Berk, S. B. Sorenson, D. J. Wiebe, and D. M. Upchurch, "The Legalization of Abortion and Subsequent Youth Homicide: A Time Series Analysis," *Analyses of Social Issues and Public Policy* 3, no. 1 (2003): 45–64.

53. Barbara Defoe Whitehead, "Dan Quayle Was Right," *Atlantic Monthly*, April 1993, 47–84.

54. R. Bauserman, "Child Adjustment in Joint-Custody versus Sole-Custody Arrangements: A Meta-analytic Review," *Journal of Family Psychology* 16, no. 1 (2002): 91.

55. "Children after Divorce: Wounds That Don't Heal," *New York Times Magazine*, January 22, 1989, 19ff. See also S. McLanahan and G. Sandefur, *Growing Up with a Single Parent* (Cambridge, MA: Harvard University Press, 1994).

56. See, e.g., Andrew J. Cherlin, *Marriage, Divorce, Remarriage*, rev. ed. (Cambridge, MA: Harvard University Press, 1992), 76ff. But see Jeynes, *Divorce, Family Structure, and the Academic Success of Children*, 4, who argues that Wallerstein's methods may have actually minimized divorce's deleterious effects on study participants.

57. Pat Conroy, quoted in Judith Wallerstein and Sandra Blakeslee, *Second Chances* (New York: Ticknor & Fields, 1989), xxi.

58. Ibid., xx.

59. Jeynes, *Divorce, Family Structure, and the Academic Success of Children*, 11.

60. Ibid., xix.

61. C. B. Horton and T. C. Cruise, *Child Abuse and Neglect* (New York: Guilford, 2001), 167.

62. *The Seattle Times* (December 14–17, 2003) reports that "in a dark side of the growing world of girls sports, 159 coaches have been reprimanded or fired for sexual misconduct in the past decade. And 98 continued to coach or teach."

63. The summer of 2004 saw a public campaign by Virginia's Department of Health, using billboards and other means, to stop men from engaging in sex with underage girls (C. L. Jenkins, "Stern Warning on Sex with Minors," *Washington Post*, Tuesday, June 15, 2004, A01).

64. See J. Morse, "Cops Arrest Ch[annel] 9 Reporter: Sex with Minors Charged," *Cincinnati Enquirer*, Saturday, February 28, 2004. In 2002, Chicago was rocked by news that one of the *Chicago Tribune*'s best-known advocates for victims and the underprivileged had to resign because of sexual indiscretions with subjects of his work. For an update, see P. Johnson, "Greene, a 'Lost Voice,' Awaits Renewal," *USA Today* (posted March 4, 2003; online at http://www.usatoday.com/life/columnist/mediamix/2003-03-04-mediamix_x.htm [accessed November 10, 2004]).

65. As a single example, see "Student-Teacher Sexual Relations," online at http://www.karisable.com/crsssstr.htm (accessed November 10, 2004).

66. Giles, *EQ* 72, no. 2 (2000): 156 (critiquing my essay that appears in the first edition of *Women in the Church*).

67. "Mandatory Sentences Lead to Surge of Women in Prison," *Christian Science Monitor*, Monday, November 29, 1993. The number of male inmates increased 160 percent in the same period. Four out of five women inmates are mothers; their incarceration is at the same time apt to be punitive for their children.

68. U.S. Department of Justice, Bureau of Justice Statistics, online at http://www.ojp.usdoj.gov/bjs/glance/d_jailag.htm (accessed November 10, 2004).

69. Craig Keener insists that the "progressive" reading of New Testament texts on women's and men's roles "is not, as some would argue, an agenda borrowed from the secular world" (*Paul, Women & Wives* [Peabody, MA: Hendrickson, 1992], 10). Keener attempts valiantly to be true to the biblical text rather than a secular mind-set, but his own work is studded with references to current progressive objections to historic Christian interpretation and practice. These references may not necessarily furnish him with his agenda, but they certainly suggest it. F. F. Bruce's statement may be closer to the truth: "We too are culturally conditioned; only we do not notice it. The women's liberation movement has conditioned not only our practices but our very vocabulary" ("Women in the Church: A Biblical Survey," in *A Mind for What Matters* [Grand Rapids: Eerdmans, 1990], 266).

70. "Saving Our Children in a World without Fathers," *Urban Family* (Winter 1994): 12. Cf. similar statements by comedian Bill Cosby in various forums in 2004.

71. See, e.g., Stendahl, *Bible and the Role of Women*, 41, who endorses the direction but speaks of not "being blind to" the problems.

72. Groothuis, *Women Caught in the Conflict*, 135, is willing (for somebody) to pay the price. She attempts to distinguish between social breakdown and social liberalization understood as "women's liberation," as she terms it. She denies any causal link between the two. I agree that "women's liberation" is not the sole cause of breakdown. In fact, I think that men are more to blame than women. But the reasoning on which Groothuis bases her view does not begin to deal with the widely recognized fact that recent innovations in views of gender roles are of a piece with recent demolition of the social fabric. Nor is her appeal to nineteenth-century feminism convincing: by comparison with recent feminism, the nineteenth-century version was hardly feminism at all in the fundamental philosophical sense. In particular, the earlier version tended to affirm a Christian ethos rather than militantly oppose it. (Groothuis [46] admits that "the anti-Christian element was a minority one in the nineteenth century, whereas today it characterizes the secular feminist movement.") Finally, Groothuis's belief that the disintegration "would not happen if the beliefs of today's evangelical feminists were implemented in church and society" is a moot point and a naïve confession of utopian hope. The horse is already out of the barn, in fact out of sight. How long before we can retrieve it, if we must wait for church and society to embrace evangelical feminist views?

73. Ibid., 216.

74. As quoted by his son Spencer in *Urban Family* (Winter 1994): 14.

75. W. Ramsay, *The Teaching of Paul in Terms of the Present Day*, 2nd ed. (London: Hodder & Stoughton, 1914), 212.

76. See also Susanne Fields, "Career Women Taking Aim at Housewives in the 'Mommy Wars,'" Lake County, IL, *Daily Herald*, Thursday, June 17, 2004, sec. 1, p. 14.

77. James Tooley, "Brainwashed: Correcting the Modern Miseducation of Women," *Chicago Tribune*, August 31, 2003, sec. 2, p. 1; cf. Tooley's book *The Miseducation of Women* (New York: Continuum, 2002). See also J. Gavora, *Tilting the Playing Field: Schools, Sports, Sex, and Title IX* (San Francisco: Encounter, 2002).

78. S. Baron-Cohen, *The Essential Difference: The Truth about the Male and Female Brain* (New York: Basic Books, 2003).

79. Cf. M. S. Van Leeuwen, *My Brother's Keeper: What the Social Sciences Do (and Don't) Tells Us about Masculinity* (Downers Grove, IL: InterVarsity, 2002).

80. "Reflections on Headship," in *Does Christianity Teach Male Headship?* ed. Blankenhorn, Browning, and Van Leeuwen, 120.

81. Representative of a large literature is L. Doyle, *The Surrendered Wife: A Practical Guide to Finding Intimacy, Passion, and Peace with a Man* (New York: Simon & Schuster, 1999). The orientation of the book is spiritist, not Christian (see 239–40).

82. Groothuis, *Women Caught in the Conflict*, 240–41, s.v. "For Further Reading," is an example. She cites only post-1980, evangelical feminist literature and clearly relies on it for her own exegetical conclusions. There is little or no precedent for much of this exegesis in serious exegetical discussion before the 1960s and 1970s. More recently, Kevin Giles has argued that it is not a "progressive" understanding of 1 Tim. 2 that is novel but rather the traditional reading. See his *"Women in the Church*: A Rejoinder to Andreas Köstenberger," *EQ* 73 (2001): 230–31. For Giles's review of the first edition of this book, see "A Critique of the 'Novel' Contemporary Interpretation of 1 Timothy 2:9–15 Given in the Book, *Women in the Church*: Parts I and II," 151–67, 195–215. For a convincing response to Giles, see Andreas J. Köstenberger, *"Women in the Church*: A Response to Kevin Giles," *EQ* 73 (2001): 205–24, to which Giles replied in *"Women in the Church*: A Rejoinder to Andreas Köstenberger," 225–43.

83. See, e.g., R. F. Horton, ed., *The Pastoral Epistles: Timothy and Titus* (Edinburgh: Jack, 1901), 102–3. Commenting on 1 Tim. 2:12, Horton posits a misogynist "personal element" in Paul and declares, "The question after all must be, not, Does Paul prohibit women from teaching? but Does the Spirit of God use them as teachers?" A more recent critical strategy is to relegate the Pastorals to non-Pauline status and therefore regard them as not indicative of his theology; see, e.g., M. Dibelius and H. Conzelmann, *The Pastoral Epistles*, trans. Philip Buttolph and Adela Yarbro (Philadelphia: Fortress, 1972), 49; S. Terrien, *Till the Heart Sings: A Biblical Theology of Manhood and Womanhood* (Philadelphia: Fortress, 1985), 190–91.

84. This is not to overlook the work of figures like Antoinette Brown (1825–1921) and Elizabeth Cady Stanton (1815–1902) as they combined antislavery efforts with the promotion of women's rights. It cannot be said, however, that their biblical exegesis had much direct impact on New Testament scholarship until recently and then chiefly by way of historical research into how their understanding of passages like 1 Cor. 14 or 1 Tim. 2 do or do not resemble approaches to those passages today.

85. *New Testament Abstracts* 20, no. 1 (1976): 45, commenting on J. A. Díaz, "Restricción en algunos textos paulinos de las reivindicaciones de la mujer en la Iglesia,"*Estudios eclesiásticos* 50 (1975): 77–93.

86. G. Bilezikian, review of *The IVP Women's Bible Commentary*, ed. C. C. Kroeger and M. J. Evans, *JETS* 47, no. 2 (June 2004): 350.

87. Not every article cataloged in Religion Index One was accessible to me, thus precluding my making a precise determination.

88. Similar hermeneutical approaches, and a use of Gal. 3:28 virtually unheard of in technical exegesis prior to the latter half of the twentieth century, were subsequently taken up by, e.g., P. K. Jewett, *Man as Male and Female* (Grand Rapids: Eerdmans, 1975); R. Longenecker, *New Testament Social Ethics for Today* (Grand Rapids: Eerdmans, 1984); C. Boomsma, *Male and Female, One in Christ* (Grand Rapids: Baker, 1993); S. Sumner, *Men and Women in the Church*, 128. For trenchant criticism of Longenecker, see T. Tiessen, "Toward a Hermeneutic for Discerning Universal Moral Absolutes," *JETS* 36, no. 2 (1993): 189–207, esp. 203–7. For nineteenth-century adumbrations of current views, see D. Dayton, *Discovering an Evangelical Heritage* (Peabody, MA: Hendrickson, 1976), 90–93. These earlier interpretations developed more in connection with the application of Gal. 3:28 to the slavery issue than to the theories of personhood that make Gal. 3:28 so central at present.

89. Stendahl, *Bible and the Role of Women*, 10.

90. Ibid., 11.

91. Ibid., 13.

92. Ibid.

93. Ibid., 23.

94. Ibid., 24.

95. Ibid., 26.

96. Ibid., 27.

97. Ibid., 32.

98. Cf. V. Hasler, *Die Briefe an Timotheus und Titus* (Zürich: Theologischer Verlag, 1978), 25: "In ancient thought people did not think of themselves as individuals but only as members of a community. This community was in turn a constituent element in a comprehensive order that encompassed heaven and earth. As a result, believers in their churches, synagogues, and other religious affiliations ordered their social and religious lives according to set ranks and classes. Thus Paul speaks of the baptized Christian's embeddedness in the body of Christ (1 Cor 12:27; Rom 12:5), of a God who does not promote disorder but peace (1 Cor 14:33), and even of the coiffure and proper place of the woman in the worship setting (1 Cor 11:2–16)" (my translation). Hasler's statement is too sweeping and unqualified, but it does point out how out of sympathy with biblical anthropology Stendahl seems to be—not on exegetical grounds, but because of his cultural allegiance to the social order to which he felt committed as he wrote in the mid-twentieth century.

99. G. Bilezikian, *Beyond Sex Roles*, 2nd ed. (Grand Rapids: Baker, 1989), 128, argues on this basis that "sex distinctions are irrelevant in the church. Therefore, the practice of sex discrimination in the church is sinful."

100. Stendahl, *Bible and the Role of Women*, 35, 34.

101. Ibid., 17, 35, 36.

102. Ibid., 41.

103. Ibid. One could wish that subsequent "progressive" thinkers were more honest in their historical judgments and less prone to revisionism.

104. D. Allen, "Christianity and the Creed of Postmodernism," *Christian Scholars Review* 23, no. 2 (1993): 121, calls this a "pillar of the modern mentality" and one of the key points on which postmodernism has not in any way separated from modernism.

105. This is also the underlying conviction of, e.g., Keener, *Paul, Women and Wives*, along with G. Fee and A. B. Spencer. See Doriani, *Women in Ministry*, 140–41.

106. Boucher, "Some Unexplored Parallels to 1 Cor 11,11–12 and Gal 3,28: The NT on the Role of Women," *Catholic Biblical Quarterly* 31 (1969): 57 (Boucher's emphasis). Boucher's insightful remark not only uncovers an irony, it also creates a new one. In using "inferiority" to describe women's subordination in the biblical social order, she seems to be using the same modern criteria of judgment that she cautions others not to employ.

107. Bruce, "Women in the Church: A Biblical Survey," 259.

108. "Christianity and the Creed of Postmodernism," 119.

109. Ibid.

110. Ibid. Challenging this view in a comprehensive way is Harris, *Against Relativism*.

111. Bruce, "Women in the Church," 260: "The local and temporary situation in which the message was first delivered must be appreciated if we are to discern what its permanent essence really is and learn to re-apply it in the local and temporary circumstances of our own culture."

112. Maier, *Biblical Hermeneutics*, 299–301, notes the use of this figure in Lessing, Strauss, Harnack, Dibelius, Dobschütz, and others. He points out that such separation of revelation's form from its content destroys "the Reformation foundation of *sola scriptura*" and ultimately attacks "the very foundation of being Christian itself" (301). Cf. Groothuis (*Women Caught in the Conflict*, 102), who attributes the masculine imagery of God in the Bible not to any truth about God's person or being but to God's need to "reveal himself to people in a patriarchal culture." Here the kernel of a more feminine God is removed from the husk of a paternal God required by the cultural order.

113. Bruce, "Women in the Church," 263.

114. Ibid.: "In applying the New Testament text to our own situation, we need not treat it as the scribes of our Lord's day treated the Old Testament. We should not turn what were meant as guiding lines for worshipers in one situation into laws binding for all time. . . . The freedom of the Spirit, which can be safeguarded by one set of guiding lines in a particular situation, may call for a different procedure in a new situation." Bruce's dim view of written Scripture in comparison to the living Spirit, who transcends written definition, comes to the fore repeatedly in his *Paul: Apostle of the Heart Set Free* (Grand Rapids: Eerdmans, 1977), e.g., 80, 124, 182, 186–87, 463. In explicating Paul's alleged view of the Torah, Bruce continually separates the (written) form of Scripture from its (spiritual) content. With due respect for the fact that Paul was not a legalist or even a nomist as such, Bruce's separation is more reminiscent of Semler or Gabler than of Paul. Semler and Gabler were key figures in the New Testament's gradual loss of authority in early post-Enlightenment biblical studies.

115. Bruce, "Women in the Church," 264.

116. Ibid., 262.

117. For a more recent example of this move, see R. Pierce, "Evangelicals and Gender Roles in the 1990s: 1 Tim. 2:8–15: A Test Case," *JETS*," 36, no. 3 (1993): 343–55.

118. Bruce, "Women in the Church," 263.

119. There are affinities here to the position represented by Sumner (*Men and Women in the Church*, 248), who thinks that the meaning of 1 Tim. 2 is opaque and leads to error if taken at face value. For a response to this approach, see Schreiner's essay in this volume, 208n5 above.

120. Bruce, "Women in the Church," 262.

121. Augustine, e.g., states, on the one hand: "Thus whatever evidence we have of past times in that which is called history helps us a great deal in the understanding of the sacred books [the Bible], even if we learn it outside of the Church as a part of our childhood education." Yet, on the other hand: "The truth of propositions is a matter to be discovered in the sacred books of the Church [the Bible]." See Augustine's *On Christian Doctrine*, trans. D. W. Robertson Jr. (Indianapolis: Bobbs-Merrill, 1983), 63, 68. Augustine does not disparage extrabiblical learning in principle, yet refuses to grant it parity with biblical revelation.

122. "The Biblical Case for Slavery: Can the Bible Mislead? A Case Study in Hermeneutics," *EQ* 66, no. 1 (1994): 3–17.

123. Ibid., 4, italics added.

124. Giles, "Critique of the 'Novel' Contemporary Interpretation of 1 Timothy 2:9–15 Given in the Book, *Women in the Church*: Part I," 151–67, esp. 155–58.

125. "Women in the Church: A Response to Kevin Giles," 205–24.

126. Ibid., 158, 157.

127. This is true also of Webb, *Slaves, Women and Homosexuals*, 33, 36–37, 84, 106, 186.

128. *ABD*, 6:65.

129. Webb, *Slaves, Women and Homosexuals*, 33. It is a mystery to me how Webb determines that my "static" hermeneutic mandates slavery for subsequent times. What does need to be pointed out is that slavery still exists in numerous places and forms around the globe. At this writing, the Darfur region in Sudan has seen genocide and (reportedly) enslavement, particularly of women and children. Where this is the case, the biblical counsel (particularly in the New Testament) to the affected parties and their masters retains relevance trivialized by Webb. (See the Anti-Slavery website, http://www. antislavery.org [accessed November 10, 2004]; one estimate puts the number in slavery worldwide today at 27 million.) And as many point out, mutatis mutandis this counsel

is still directly applicable to employer-employee relations. Much of the work of the International Justice Mission involves liberating persons from actual or de facto slavery in various quarters around the world (http://www.ijm.org [accessed November 10, 2004]). It is by no means a thing of the past, nor can we be assured that it ever will be. In that sense we can be grateful that biblical writers spoke into their world in such a socially and ethically timeless manner on this point.

130. Bruce, *Apostle of the Heart Set Free*, 401.

131. M. A. Dandamayev, *ABD*, 6:65.

132. Cf. W. Grudem, "Should We Move beyond the New Testament to a Better Ethic?" *JETS* 47, no. 2 (June 2004): 323: "If we take the entire NT as the very words of God for us in the new covenant today, then any claim that Gal 3:28 should overrule other texts, such as Ephesians 5 and 1 Timothy 2, should be seen as a claim that Paul the apostle contradicts himself, and therefore that the word of God contradicts itself."

133. "Biblical Case for Slavery," 4.

134. See, e.g., A. Schlatter, *Die Kirche der Griechen im Urteil des Paulus*, 2nd ed. (Stuttgart: Calwer, 1958), 91n, for detailed examples of the close ties in Paul's writings between sanctification and relations between the sexes.

135. See, e.g., Groothuis, *Women Caught in the Conflict*, 31–39, and elsewhere; Webb, *Slaves, Women and Homosexuals*.

136. "Egalitarianism and Homosexuality: Connected or Autonomous Ideologies?" *Journal for Biblical Manhood and Womanhood* 8, no. 2 (Fall 2003): 13.

137. To his credit, Webb (*Slaves, Women and Homosexuals*, 252) argues that the Bible's *"homosexual texts are in a different category than the women and slavery texts"* (his italics). So he does not foresee endorsing homosexuality as some have done using biblical themes and passages. My concern is that (especially younger) Christians who approach the Bible with Webb's assumptions and sociologically apprised hermeneutic may not be as willing to acknowledge the category difference as is someone of Webb's generation.

138. Gal. 3:28, as Stendahl and Bruce understand it, is the foundation of Groothuis, *Women Caught in the Conflict*; this verse or its context accounts for nine of only fifty-four Scripture references in a book of over two hundred pages. On the opening page, Groothuis defines "the gospel of Jesus Christ" with reference to Gal. 3:28, expanded on later with the assertion that "the biblical truth of the equality of all persons under God is entailed by the biblical message of salvation" (155). In this understanding, Gal. 3:28 essentially replaces the function of, e.g., Rom. 1:16–17 or John 3:16 in earlier understandings of the heart of the gospel. Similarly, J. W. Cooper (*A Cause for Division? Women in Office and the Unity of the Church* [Grand Rapids: Calvin Theological Seminary, 1991], 42–43) establishes "the analogy of Scripture" along a continuum stretching from "The First Word" of Gen. 1:26–28 to "The Last Word" of Rev. 22:5 with "Paul's Middle Word" being Gal. 3:28. It is no wonder that he dismisses 1 Cor. 14 and 1 Tim. 2 because "the right exegesis cannot be established with certainty" (53). See also Sumner, *Men and Women in the Church*, 248. Preset hermeneutical parameters have ruled out certain exegetical conclusions.

139. Cf. the contention by Maggie Gallagher ("Reflections on Headship," in *Does Christianity Teach Male Headship?* ed. Blankenhorn, Browning, and Van Leeuwen, 111–25) that in calling for replacement of headship with dialogic servanthood, those calling for "equal regard" marriage and egalitarianism in the church may be destroying the best hope for what they wish to see emerge. By denying, or wishing to reinvent, male nature they effectively destroy optimal conditions for male self-giving.

140. Martin Luther took Gal. 3:28 to be underscoring that only in Christ lies justification: even if the Jew does his best under the law, even if the Gentile arrives at his highest wisdom, even if the slave fulfills the highest standards set for him, even if the master performs in the most upright fashion, even if husband and wife comply fully with their duties by the

best of works—"yet are all these nothing in comparison of that righteousness which is before God" (*A Commentary on St. Paul's Epistle to the Galatians* [London: Clarke, 1953], 342). Despite fashionable polemic against Paul's understanding not only of social roles but also even of the doctrine of salvation by grace through faith itself (see T. Schreiner, *The Law and Its Fulfillment* [Grand Rapids: Baker, 1993]) as Reformers like Luther propounded it, this exegesis of Gal. 3:28 is probably a firmer basis for Christian ethics than that pioneered by Stendahl and now common currency in "progressive" circles.

141. Another might be the ancient Near Eastern head covering or veil, a convention much discussed with respect to 1 Cor. 11. See, e.g., C. Keener, *Paul, Women and Wives*, 46–47, who points out that while Paul was not "making a transcultural argument in favor of women wearing head coverings in church, we can notice some transcultural points in his argument." It is definitely not the case that if women go without head coverings now, they are also free to set aside 1 Tim. 2:11–12. See T. Schreiner, "Head Coverings, Prophecies and the Trinity: 1 Corinthians 11:2–16," in *Recovering Biblical Manhood and Womanhood* (Wheaton: Crossway, 1991), 124–39, 485–87. In many (not all) settings it is quite possible to be in full compliance with the apostolic directives of 1 Cor. 11 without wearing headgear, just as missionaries can be in full compliance with the so-called Great Commission (Matt. 28:19–20) without applying Jesus' commands about belt, bag, tunic, and staff (Matt. 10:9–11) with pedantic precision. For newer discussion on veils or head coverings, see B. W. Winter, *Roman Wives, Roman Widows: The Appearance of New Women and the Pauline Communities* (Grand Rapids: Eerdmans, 2003).

142. *Women Caught in the Conflict*, 126.

143. See, e.g., A. McGrath, *The Mystery of the Cross* (Grand Rapids: Zondervan, 1988).

144. Thiselton, *New Horizons*, 610 (Thiselton's italics).

145. See, e.g., "The Interpreter," in *Biblical Hermeneutics*, by G. Maier, 45–63; Augustine, *On Christian Doctrine*, passim; Thiselton, *New Horizons*, 609; Doriani, *Putting the Truth to Work*, 59–80.

146. Cf. A. Schlatter, "The Theology of the New Testament and Dogmatics," in *The Nature of New Testament Theology*, ed. R. Morgan (Naperville, IL: Allenson, 1973), 202, commenting on academic biblical studies generally.

147. J. G. Stackhouse Jr., "Women in Public Ministry in Twentieth-Century Canadian and American Evangelicalism: Five Models," *Studies in Religion/Sciences Religieuses* 17, no. 4 (1988): 471–85.

148. M. Maudlin, "1994 Book Awards," *Christianity Today*, April 4, 1994, 39.

149. This is not to minimize the existence of analogous miscues on the part of women. It is doubtful that they are significantly less guilty than men of failing to love God and others as they ought, though in the current climate, an air of feminine moral supremacy may occasionally be detected. But our focus here lies elsewhere.

150. It is hard to imagine, e.g., that F. F. Bruce's views were not affected by chauvinist excesses in his own conservative denomination.

151. The qualifier is important. Scripture itself portrays God's willingness to use women to serve as judges or prophets (though there are no indisputable examples of pastors) to fill a void in men's devotion or in other special circumstances. The "historic" position needs to be as open to unusual situations today as the Lord was in times past, according to Scripture. But the scriptural exception cannot be used to establish an extrascriptural rule.

152. K. Bockmühl, *The Challenge of Marxism* (Colorado Springs: Helmers & Howard, 1986).

153. Cf. R. Clapp, *Families at the Crossroads* (Downers Grove, IL: InterVarsity, 1993).

154. The strong anecdotal basis for much of Sumner, *Men and Women in the Church*, is striking.

155. Blankenhorn, Browning, and Van Leeuwen, eds., *Does Christianity Teach Male Headship?* viii.

156. See John H. Leith, *Crisis in the Church* (Louisville: Westminster John Knox, 1997), for reflections on the (unsuccessful) Presbyterian Church (U.S.A.) experiment with this approach.

157. See R. Stark, "The Role of Women in Christian Growth," in *The Rise of Christianity: A Sociologist Reconsiders History* (Princeton, NJ: Princeton University Press, 1996), chap. 5.

158. The family is under siege in developing nations just as in the West (typically as the result of the incursion of Western media and other cultural forces). Note analysis and pleas for reaffirmation of biblical teaching and behavior from Nigerian, Kenyan, and pan-global perspectives in various articles of *REC* [Reformed Ecumenical Council] *Focus* 3, no. 3 (September 2003). Online at http://community.gospelcom.net/Brix?pageID=6076 (accessed March 2, 2005).

159. Cf. Philip Jenkins, *The Next Christendom: The Coming of Global Christianity* (Oxford: Oxford University Press, 2002).

160. I do not deny that in settings where Western ideas of women's rights and male culpability have been spread, the solution of a progressive hermeneutic will find a following among some.

161. Lamin Sanneh, *Whose Religion Is Christianity? The Gospel beyond the West* (Grand Rapids: Eerdmans, 2003), 83.

Chapter 6: What Should a Woman Do in the Church?

1. Alvera Mickelsen argues that 1 Tim. 2:11–12 is a "regulation for people where they were—not a highest norm or standard in the Bible." See "An Egalitarian View: There Is Neither Male nor Female in Christ," in *Women in Ministry: Four Views*, ed. B. Clouse and R. Clouse (Downers Grove, IL: InterVarsity, 1989), 199. David M. Scholer supports this line of reasoning in his comment, "The statements of 2:11–12 are thus ad hoc instructions intended for a particular situation in Ephesus of false teaching focused on women. These statements are not to be understood as universal principles." See "1 Timothy 2:9–12 and the Place of Women in the Church's Ministry," in *Women, Authority and the Bible*, ed. Alvera Mickelsen (Downers Grove, IL: InterVarsity, 1986), 203.

2. So much is the language of heaven and home intertwined that the euphemism *heavenly home* is a common theme in Christian hymnody and poetry. To die in Christ is to go *home*. Within the church, Scripture teaches that congregants are *brothers* and *sisters* in a *family* of believers, and the church is said to be God's household (1 Tim. 3:15).

3. Dorothy K. Patterson, "The Role of Women in the Church," in *We Believe*, ed. Paige Patterson and Luis Pantoja Jr., vol. 1 (Dallas: Criswell, 1977), 163–70.

4. Dorothy Kelley Patterson, "Says Her Guidelines Are Certain," *North Carolina Biblical Recorder*, November 28, 1998.

5. See F. F. Bruce, *Commentary on Galatians*, New International Greek Testament Commentary (Grand Rapids: Eerdmans, 1982), 190. Richard Hove refutes this assertion in his book, *Equality in Christ? Galatians 3:28 and the Gender Dispute* (Wheaton: Crossway, 1999).

6. See the chapter by Henry Scott Baldwin in the present volume.

7. See the chapter by Andreas J. Köstenberger in the present volume.

8. See also note 11, below.

9. For additional discussion, see Andreas Köstenberger, "Women in the Pauline Mission," in *The Gospel to the Nations: Perspectives on Paul's Mission*, ed. Peter Bolt and Mark Thompson (Leicester, Eng.: Inter-Varsity, 2000), 221–47.

10. Many Christians gather in assembly outside official gatherings of the church. Although the spirit of the passage is important to consider in this regard, the specific mandate is not meant as a blanket for every group of men and women who gather.

11. Some biblical interpreters hold to a division among pastoral leadership, that is, pastors as distinct from elders. As a congregationalist, I do not hold that position but see the different words used as describing one office. Note 1 Peter 5:1–4, where the pastoral office is described with three Greek words: πρεσβυτέρους (elders), ποιμάνατε (shepherd; a verb), and ἐπισκοποῦντες (overseers; a participle). See also the use of these three root words in Acts 20:17, 28.

12. Eleanor Jackson, ed., *The Question of Woman: The Collected Writings of Charlotte von Kirschbaum*, trans. John Shepherd (Grand Rapids: Eerdmans, 1996), 112.

13. See also the essay by Thomas R. Schreiner in the present volume.

14. J. I. Packer, "Understanding the Differences," in *Women, Authority and the Bible*, ed. Alvera Mickelson (Downers Grove, IL: InterVarsity, 1986), 299.

15. Wendy Shalit, *A Return to Modesty: Discovering the Lost Virtue* (New York: Free Press, 1999); Dannah Gresch, *Secret Keeper: The Delicate Power of Modesty* (Chicago: Moody, 2002); Elisabeth Elliot, *Passion and Purity: Learning to Bring Your Love Life under Christ's Control* (Grand Rapids: Revell, 1984); and Jeff Pollard, *Christian Modesty and the Public Undressing of America* (San Antonio: Vision Forum, 2001).

16. Both of these words are derived from the Greek word κόσμος (world), which may lead some to believe that using cosmetics is worldly! However, for women the transliteration may be of greater interest because of the connection with uniquely feminine products and rituals.

17. See also the conclusion to S. M. Baugh's essay in the present volume.

18. Bonnie C. Harvey, "The Woman Question," *Christian History* 75 (Summer 2002): 21–22.

19. Richard Clark Kroeger and Catherine Clark Kroeger, *I Suffer Not a Woman: Rethinking 1 Timothy 2:11–15 in Light of Ancient Evidence* (Grand Rapids: Baker, 1992), 181. Kroeger's observation is worth noting because this volume is one with which I would have little in common because of the existential and experiential hermeneutic that governs its interpretation of the text. An affirmation of the importance of maternity is something on which we can agree.

20. For further discussion, see Thomas Schreiner's chapter in the present volume. See also Andreas Köstenberger, "Ascertaining Women's God-Ordained Roles: An Interpretation of 1 Timothy 2:15," *Bulletin for Biblical Research* 7 (1997): 107–44.

21. See Köstenberger, "Women in the Pauline Mission."

22. I would like to acknowledge and express appreciation to Candi Finch, a student in women's studies at Southwestern Baptist Theological Seminary and my research assistant, for her helpful research and attention to details in completing this project.

Epilogue

1. See 1 Tim. 1:10; 4:6, 13, 16; 5:17; 6:1, 3; 2 Tim. 3:10, 16; 4:3; Titus 1:9; 2:1, 7, 10. The only exception is 1 Tim. 4:1, where the teaching is described as demonic.

2. See Thomas R. Schreiner, "Women in Ministry," in *Two Views on Women in Ministry*, ed. J. R. Beck and C. L. Blomberg, Counterpoints Series (Grand Rapids: Zondervan, 2001), 177–235.

BIBLIOGRAPHY

Aland, Kurt. "The Problem of Anonymity and Pseudonymity in the Christian Literature of the First Two Centuries." *Journal of Theological Studies* 12 (1961): 39–49.

Albertz, Martin. *Die Botschaft des Neuen Testaments*. Zollikon-Zürich: Evangelischer Verlag, 1954.

———. "Die Krisis der sogenannten neutestamentlichen Theologie." *Zeichen der Zeit* 8 (1954): 371–75.

Alföldy, Géza. *The Social History of Rome*. London: Croom Helm, 1985.

Allen, Diogenes. "Christianity and the Creed of Postmodernism." *Christian Scholars Review* 23 (1993): 117–26.

Aman, Kenneth, ed. *Border Regions of Faith*. Maryknoll, NY: Orbis, 1987.

Ameling, Walter, ed. *Die Inschriften von Prusias ad Hypium*. Bonn: Habelt, 1985.

Anti-Slavery Home Page. Online at http://www.antislavery.org (accessed November 10, 2004).

Arendell, Terry. *Mothers and Divorce*. Berkeley: University of California Press, 1986.

Arnold, Clinton E. *Ephesians: Power and Magic; The Concept of Power in Ephesians in Light of Its Historical Setting*. Society for New Testament Studies Monograph Series 63. Cambridge: Cambridge University Press, 1989.

Arnold, Franz X. *Woman and Man: Their Nature and Mission*. Translated by R. Brennan. New York: Herder & Herder, 1963.

Augustine. *On Christian Doctrine*. Translated by D. W. Robertson Jr. Indianapolis: Bobbs-Merrill, 1983.

Aurenhammer, Maria. "Römische Porträts aus Ephesos: Neue Funde aus dem Hanghaus 2." *Jahreshefte des Österreichischen Archäologischen Instituts in Wien* 54 (1983): 105–12.

Baird, William. *History of New Testament Research*. Vol. 1, *From Deism to Tübingen*. Minneapolis: Fortress, 1992.

———. *History of New Testament Research*. Vol. 2, *From Jonathan Edwards to Rudolf Bultmann*. Minneapolis: Fortress, 2003.

Balch, David L. *Let Wives Be Submissive: The Domestic Code in 1 Peter*. Society of Biblical Literature Monograph Series 26. Atlanta: Scholars Press, 1981.

Bammer, Anton. *Führer durch das archäologische Museum in Selçuk-Ephesos*. Vienna: Österreichisches Archäologisches Institut, 1974.

———. *Das Heiligtum der Artemis von Ephesos*. Graz, Austria: Akademische Druck, 1984.

Barclay, John M. G. "Mirror-Reading a Polemical Letter: Galatians as a Test Case." *Journal for the Study of the New Testament* 3 (1987): 73–93.

Barnett, Paul W. "*Authentein* Once More: A Response to L. E. Wilshire." *Evangelical Quarterly* 66 (1994): 159–62.

———. "Wives and Women's Ministry (1 Timothy 2:11–15)." *Evangelical Quarterly* 61 (1989): 225–38.

Baron-Cohen, S. *The Essential Difference: The Truth about the Male and Female Brain*. New York: Basic Books, 2003.

Barrett, C. K. *The Pastoral Epistles*. Oxford: Clarendon, 1963.

Barron, Bruce. "Putting Women in Their Place: 1 Timothy 2 and Evangelical Views of Women in Church Leadership." *Journal of the Evangelical Theological Society* 33 (1990): 451–59.

Bartchy, Scott. "Power, Submission, and Sexual Identity among the Early Christians." In *Essays in New Testament Christianity*, edited by C. Robert Wetzel, 50–80. Cincinnati: Standard, 1978.

Barth, Karl. *Die kirchliche Dogmatik*. 4th ed. Zürich: Evy-Verlag, 1970.

Barthes, Roland. *Elements of Semiology*. Translated by A. Lavers and C. Smith. New York: Hill & Wang, 1968.

Bauckham, Richard. "Pseudo-Apostolic Letters." *Journal of Biblical Literature* 107 (1988): 469–94.

Baugh, Steven M. "The Apostle Paul among the Amazons." *Westminster Theological Journal* 56 (1994): 153–71.

———. "Cult Prostitution in New Testament Ephesus: A Reappraisal." *Journal of the Evangelical Theological Society* 42, no. 3 (1999): 443–60.

———. "Feminism at Ephesus: 1 Timothy 2:12 in Historical Context." *Outlook* 42 (May 1992): 7–10.

———. "Paul and Ephesus: The Apostle among His Contemporaries." Ph.D. diss., University of California, Irvine, 1990.

Bauserman, R. "Child Adjustment in Joint-Custody versus Sole-Custody Arrangements: A Meta-analytic Review." *Journal of Family Psychology* 16, no. 1 (2002).

Beck, James R., and Craig L. Blomberg, eds. *Two Views on Women in the Ministry*. Grand Rapids: Zondervan, 2001.

Beckwith, R. T. "The Office of Women in the Church to the Present Day." In *Why Not? Priesthood and Ministry of Women: A Theological Study*, edited by M. Bruce and G. E. Duffield, revised and augmented edition prepared by R. T. Beckwith, 26–39. Nashville: Abingdon, 1976.

Bellah, Robert N., et al. *Habits of the Heart*. San Francisco: Harper & Row, 1986.

Belleville, Linda L. "Women in Ministry." In *Two Views on Women in Ministry*, edited by J. R. Beck and C. L. Blomberg. Grand Rapids: Zondervan, 2001.

———. *Women Leaders and the Church: 3 Crucial Questions*. Grand Rapids: Baker, 2000.

Berdyaev, Nicolai. *Slavery and Freedom*. Translated by R. M. French. New York: Scribner's Sons, 1944.

Berk, R. A., S. B. Sorenson, D. J. Wiebe, and D. M. Upchurch. "The Legalization of Abortion and Subsequent Youth Homicide: A Time Series Analysis." *Analyses of Social Issues and Public Policy* 3, no. 1 (2003): 45–64.

Bernstein, Richard. *Beyond Objectivism and Relativism*. Philadelphia: University of Pennsylvania Press, 1983.

Betz, Hans Dieter. *Galatians: A Commentary on Paul's Letter to the Churches in Galatia*. Hermeneia. Philadelphia: Fortress, 1979.

Bilezikian, Gilbert. *Beyond Sex Roles: A Guide for the Study of Female Roles in the Bible*. 2nd ed. Grand Rapids: Baker, 1989.

———. Review of *The IVP Women's Bible Commentary*, ed. C. C. Kroeger and M. J. Evans. *Journal of the Evangelical Theological Society* 47, no. 2 (June 2004): 347–50.

Black, David Alan, and David S. Dockery, eds. *Interpreting the New Testament*. Nashville: Broadman & Holman, 2001.

———. *New Testament Criticism and Interpretation*. Grand Rapids: Zondervan, 1991.

Blankenhorn, D., D. Browning, and M. S. Van Leeuwen, eds. *Does Christianity Teach Male Headship? The Equal-Regard Marriage and Its Critics*. Grand Rapids: Eerdmans, 2004.

Blomberg, Craig L. "Neither Hierarchicalist nor Egalitarian: Gender Roles in Paul." In *Two Views on Women in Ministry*, edited by J. R. Beck and C. L. Blomberg. Grand Rapids: Zondervan, 2001.

Blum, G. G. "Das Amt der Frau im Neuen Testament." *Novum Testamentum* 7 (1965): 142–61.

Boardman, J., ed. *The Oxford History of Classical Art*. Oxford: Oxford University Press, 1993.

Bockmühl, Klaus. *The Challenge of Marxism*. Colorado Springs: Helmers & Howard, 1986.

Boomsma, Clarence. *Male and Female, One in Christ: New Testament Teaching on Women in Office*. Grand Rapids: Baker, 1993.

Booth, Catherine. *Female Ministry or Woman's Right to Preach the Gospel*. 1959. Reprint, New York: Salvation Army, 1975.

Börker, Christian. "Eine pantheistische Weihung in Ephesos." *Zeitschrift für Papyrologie und Epigraphik* 41 (1981): 181–88.

Boucher, Madeleine. "Some Unexplored Parallels to 1 Cor 11,11–12 and Gal 3,28: The NT on the Role of Women." *Catholic Biblical Quarterly* 31 (1969): 50–57.

Bowersock, G. W. *Augustus and the Greek World*. Oxford: Clarendon, 1965.

———. *Greek Sophists in the Roman Empire*. Oxford: Clarendon, 1969.

Bowman, Ann L. "Women in Ministry: An Exegetical Study of 1 Timothy 2:11–15." *Bibliotheca sacra* 149 (1992): 193–213.

Bratt, John. "The Role and Status of Women in the Writings of John Calvin." In *Renaissance, Reformation, Resurgence: Colloquium on Calvin and Calvin Studies*, edited by Peter DeKlerk, 1–17. Grand Rapids: Calvin Theological Seminary, 1976.

Brewer, David I. *Techniques and Assumptions in Jewish Exegesis before 70 CE*. Tübingen: Mohr (Siebeck), 1992.

Bristow, John Temple. *What Paul Really Said about Women: An Apostle's Liberating Views on Equality in Marriage, Leadership, and Love*. San Francisco: HarperCollins, 1991.

Broughton, T. R. S. "Roman Asia Minor." In *An Economic Survey of Ancient Rome*, edited by T. Frank, 4:499–950. Baltimore: Johns Hopkins University Press, 1938.

Brox, Norbert. *Die Pastoralbriefe*. 4th ed. Regensburger Neues Testament. Regensburg: Pustet, 1969.

Bruce, F. F. *Commentary on Galatians*. New International Greek Testament Commentary. Grand Rapids: Eerdmans, 1982.

———. *Paul: Apostle of the Heart Set Free*. Grand Rapids: Eerdmans, 1977.

———. "Women in the Church: A Biblical Survey." In *A Mind for What Matters*, 259–66, 323–25. Grand Rapids: Eerdmans, 1990.

Bruce, M., and G. E. Duffield. *Why Not? Priesthood and Ministry of Women: A Theological Study*. Edited by M. Bruce and G. E. Duffield. Revised and augmented edition prepared by R. T. Beckwith. Nashville: Abingdon, 1976.

Brueggemann, Walter. *Texts under Negotiation*. Minneapolis: Fortress, 1993.

Bultmann, Rudolf. "Das Problem einer theologischen Exegese des Neuen Testaments." In *Das Problem der Theologie des Neuen Testaments*, edited by Georg Strecker, 249–77. Darmstadt: Wissenschaftliche Buchgesellschaft, 1975.

Burkert, Walter. *Greek Religion*. Cambridge, MA: Harvard University Press, 1985.

Burnham, Frederic B., ed. *Postmodern Theology*. San Francisco: Harper & Row, 1989.

Bushnell, Katherine C. *God's Word to Women: One Hundred Bible Studies on the Place of Women in the Divine Economy*. 1919. Reprint, North Collins, NY: Munson, 1976.

Butler, Christine. "Was Paul a Male Chauvinist?" *New Blackfriars* 56 (1975): 174–79.

Bynum, Caroline. *Jesus as Mother: Studies in the Spirituality of the High Middle Ages*. Berkeley: University of California Press, 1982.

Calvin, John. *Commentary on the Epistles of Paul the Apostle to the Corinthians*. Translated by John Pringle. Edinburgh: Calvin Translation Society, 1848.

———. *Commentary on the First Epistle to Timothy*. Translated by John Pringle. Edinburgh: Calvin Translation Society, 1848.

Cameron, Averil. "Neither Male Nor Female." *Greece and Rome* 27 (1980): 60–68.

Campbell, K. M., ed. *Marriage and Family in the Biblical World*. Downers Grove, IL: InterVarsity, 2003.

Cardman, Francis. "The Medieval Question of Women and Orders." *Thomist* 42 (1978): 588–90.

Carnap, Rudolf. *The Logical Syntax of Language*. London: Kegan, 1937.

Carson, D. A. *Exegetical Fallacies*. 2nd ed. Grand Rapids: Baker, 1996.

———. "Reflections on Christian Assurance." *Westminster Theological Journal* 54 (1992): 1–29.

Carson, D. A., Douglas J. Moo, and Leon Morris. *An Introduction to the New Testament*. Grand Rapids: Zondervan, 1992.

Casarico, L. "Donne ginnasiarco." *Zeitschrift für Papyrologie und Epigraphik* 48 (1982): 117–23.

Cavanaugh, John. *Following Christ in a Consumer Society*. Maryknoll, NY: Orbis, 1989.

Cherlin, Andrew J. *Marriage, Divorce, Remarriage*. Rev. ed. Cambridge, MA: Harvard University Press, 1992.

Clapp, Rodney. *Families at the Crossroads*. Downers Grove, IL: InterVarsity, 1993.

Clark, Elizabeth, and Herbert Richardson, eds. *Women and Religion: A Feminine Sourcebook of Christian Thought*. New York: Harper & Row, 1977.

Clark, Stephen B. *Man and Woman in Christ: An Examination of the Roles of Men and Women in Light of Scripture and the Social Sciences*. Ann Arbor, MI: Servant, 1980.

Clouse, Bonnidell, and Robert G. Clouse, eds. *Women in Ministry: Four Views*. Downers Grove, IL: InterVarsity, 1989.

Clowney, Edmund P. "The Biblical Theology of the Church." In *The Church in the Bible and the World*, edited by D. A. Carson, 13–87. Grand Rapids: Baker, 1987.

Cobern, Camden M. *New Archeological Discoveries*. 2nd ed. New York: Funk & Wagnalls, 1917.

Cohen, David. "Seclusion, Separation, and the Status of Women in Classical Athens." *Greece and Rome* 36 (1989): 3–15.

Cole, Susan Guettel. "Could Greek Women Read and Write?" In *Reflections of Women in Antiquity*, edited by H. Foley, 219–45. New York: Gordon & Breach Science, 1981.

Collins, Raymond F. *1 and 2 Timothy and Titus: A Commentary*. New Testament Library. Louisville: Westminster John Knox, 2002.

Coloumbis, Angela E. "New Report Finds Youth Deaths by Homocide [*sic*] Doubled since 1985." *Christian Science Monitor*, Monday, April 25, 1994, 18.

Contarella, Eva. *Pandora's Daughters*. Baltimore: Johns Hopkins University Press, 1987.

Cooper, John W. *A Cause for Division? Women in Office and the Unity of the Church*. Grand Rapids: Calvin Theological Seminary, 1991.

Danet, A.-L. "I Timothée 2,8–15 et le ministère pastoral féminin." *Hokhma* 44 (1990): 23–44.

Daniélou, Jean. *The Ministry of Women in the Early Church*. Translated by Glen Symon. New York: Faith, 1961.

Danker, Frederick William, ed. *A Greek-English Lexicon of the New Testament and Other Early Christian Literature*. 3rd ed. Chicago: University of Chicago Press, 2000.

Dayton, Donald. *Discovering an Evangelical Heritage*. Peabody, MA: Hendrickson, 1976.

DeBoer, Willis P. "Calvin on the Role of Women." In *Exploring the Heritage of John Calvin: Essays in Honor of John H. Bratt*, edited by D. E. Holwerda, 236–72. Grand Rapids: Baker, 1976.

Deininger, Jürgen. *Die Provinziallandtage der römischen Kaiserzeit*. Munich: Beck, 1965.

Detienne, Marcel. "The Violence of Wellborn Ladies: Women in the Thesmophoria." In *The Cuisine of Sacrifice among the Greeks*, edited by Marcel Detienne and J.-P. Vernant, 129–47. Chicago: University of Chicago Press, 1989.

Dewey, John. *Liberalism and Social Action*. New York: Capricorn, 1935.

Dex, Shirley. "Objective Facts in Social Science." In *Objective Knowledge*, edited by Paul Helm, 167–90. Leicester, Eng.: Inter-Varsity, 1987.

De Yong, P., and D. R. Wilson. *Husband and Wife: The Sexes in Scripture and Society*. Grand Rapids: Zondervan, 1979.

Díaz, J. A. "Restricción en algunos textos paulinos de las reivindicaciones de la mujer en la Iglesia." *Estudios eclesiásticos* 50 (1975): 77–93.

Dibelius, Martin, and Hans Conzelmann. *The Pastoral Epistles*. Translated by Philip Buttolph and Adela Yarbro. Hermeneia. Philadelphia: Fortress, 1972.

Dill, Samuel. *Roman Society from Nero to Marcus Aurelius*. London: Macmillan, 1905.

Donfried, Karl P., and I. Howard Marshall, eds. *The Theology of the Shorter Pauline Epistles*. Cambridge: Cambridge University Press, 1993.

Doriani, Daniel. *Getting the Message*. Phillipsburg, NJ: P&R, 1996.

———. *Putting the Truth to Work*. Phillipsburg, NJ: P&R, 2001.

———. *Women and Ministry*. Wheaton: Crossway, 2003.

Doyle, L. *The Surrendered Wife: A Practical Guide to Finding Intimacy, Passion, and Peace with a Man*. New York: Simon & Schuster, 1999.

Eckenstein, Lina. *Women under Monasticism*. New York: Russell & Russell, 1896.

Edwards, David L., with a response from John Stott. *Evangelical Essentials: A Liberal-Evangelical Dialogue*. Downers Grove, IL: InterVarsity, 1988.

Elliger, W. *Ephesos: Geschichte einer antiken Weltstadt*. Stuttgart: Kohlhammer, 1985.

Elliot, Elisabeth. *Let Me Be a Woman*. London: Hodder & Stoughton, 1979.

———. *Passion and Purity: Learning to Bring Your Love Life under Christ's Control*. Grand Rapids: Revell, 1984.

Ellis, E. Earle. *Pauline Theology, Ministry and Society*. Grand Rapids: Eerdmans, 1989.

———. "Pseudonymity and Canonicity of New Testament Documents." In *Worship, Theology and Ministry in the Early Church: Essays in Honor of Ralph P. Martin*, edited by Michael J. Wilkins and Terence Paige, 212–24. Sheffield: JSOT, 1992.

Elshtain, Jean Bethke. "Family Matters: The Plight of America's Children." *Christian Century* (July 14–21, 1993): 710–12.

Engelmann, H. "Neue Inschriften aus Ephesos XIII." *Jahreshefte des Österreichischen Archäologischen Instituts in Wien* 69 (2000).

———. "Zu Inschriften aus Ephesos." *Zeitschrift für Papyrologie und Epigraphik* 26 (1977): 154–56.

———. "Zum Kaiserkult in Ephesos." *Zeitschrift für Papyrologie und Epigraphik* 97 (1993): 279–89.

Erickson, Millard J. *Evangelical Interpretation: Perspectives on Hermeneutical Issues*. Grand Rapids: Baker, 1993.

Evans, Mary. *Woman in the Bible*. Downers Grove, IL: InterVarsity, 1983.

Falconer, Robert. "1 Timothy 2:14–15: Interpretive Notes." *Journal of Biblical Literature* 60 (1941): 375–79.

Feder, T. *Great Treasures of Pompeii and Herculaneum*. New York: Abbeville, 1978.

Fee, Gordon D. *1 and 2 Timothy, Titus*. New International Biblical Commentary on the New Testament. Peabody, MA: Hendrickson, 1988.

———. *Gospel and Spirit*. Peabody, MA: Hendrickson, 1991.

———. "Issues in Evangelical Hermeneutics, Part III: The Great Watershed—Intentionality and Particularity/Eternality: 1 Timothy 2:8–15 as a Test Case." *Crux* 26 (1990): 31–37.

———. "Reflections on Church Order in the Pastoral Epistles, with Further Reflection on the Hermeneutics of *Ad Hoc* Documents." *Journal of the Evangelical Theological Society* 28 (1985): 141–51.

———. "Women in Ministry: The Meaning of 1 Timothy 2:8–15 in Light of the Purpose of 1 Timothy." *Journal of the Christian Brethren Research Fellowship* 122 (1990): 11–18.

Fee, Gordon D., and Douglas Stuart. *How to Read the Bible for All Its Worth*. Grand Rapids: Zondervan, 1982.

Ferguson, Everett. *Backgrounds of Early Christianity*. 2nd ed. Grand Rapids: Eerdmans, 1993.

Fields, Susanne. "Career Women Taking Aim at Housewives in the 'Mommy Wars.'" *Lake County, IL, Daily Herald*, Thursday, June 17, 2004, sec. 1, p. 14.

Fiorenza, Elisabeth Schüssler. *In Memory of Her: A Feminist Theological Reconstruction of Christian Origins*. New York: Crossroad, 1983.

Fleischer, Robert. *Artemis von Ephesos und verwandte Kultstatuen aus Anatolien und Syrien*. Leiden: Brill, 1973.

———. "Artemis von Ephesos und verwandte Kultstatuen aus Anatolien und Syrien Supplement." In *Studien zur Religion und Kultur Kleinasiens*, edited by S. Sahin et al., 324–31. Leiden: Brill, 1978.

Foh, Susan T. *Women and the Word of God*. Grand Rapids: Baker, 1979.

Ford, J. Massyngberde. "A Note on Proto-Montanism in the Pastoral Epistles." *New Testament Studies* 17 (1970–71): 338–46.

Forum on Child and Family Statistics. *America's Children in Brief: Key National Indicators of Well-Being, 2004*. Online at http://childstats.gov/ac2004/intro.asp (accessed November 10, 2004).

Forward, Susan, and Juan Torres. *Men Who Hate Women and the Women Who Love Them*. New York: Bantam, 1986.

France, R. T. *Women in the Church's Ministry: A Test-Case for Biblical Hermeneutics*. Carlisle: Paternoster, 1995.

Franke, Peter Robert. *Kleinasien zur Römerzeit: Griechisches Leben im Spiegel der Münzen*. Munich: Beck, 1968.

French, David. "Acts and the Roman Roads of Asia Minor." In *The Book of Acts in Its Graeco-Roman Setting*, edited by David W. J. Gill and Conrad Gempf, 55–57. The Book of Acts in Its First Century Setting 2. Grand Rapids: Eerdmans; Carlisle: Paternoster, 1994.

Friesen, Steven J. *Twice Neokoros: Ephesus, Asia, and the Cult of the Flavian Imperial Family*. Leiden: Brill, 1993.

Fung, Ronald Y. K. "Ministry in the New Testament." In *The Church in the Bible and the World*, edited by D. A. Carson, 154–212. Grand Rapids: Baker, 1987.

Funk, Robert, R. Hoover, and the Jesus Seminar. *The Five Gospels*. New York: Macmillan, 1993.

Gardner, Jane F. *Women in Roman Law and Society*. Bloomington: Indiana University Press, 1991.

Garfinkel, Irwin, and Sara McLanahan. *Single Mothers and Their Children*. Washington, DC: Urban Institute Press, 1986.

Gavora, J. *Tilting the Playing Field: Schools, Sports, Sex, and Title IX*. San Francisco: Encounter, 2002.

Geer, Thomas C., Jr. "Admonitions to Women in 1 Tim. 2:8–15." In *Essays on Women in Earliest Christianity*, edited by C. D. Osburn, vol. 1. 2nd printing, corrected, Joplin, MO: College Press, 1995.

Geivett, R. Douglas. "Is Jesus the Only Way?" In *Jesus under Fire*, edited by Michael J. Wilkins and J. P. Moreland, 177–205. Grand Rapids: Zondervan, 1995.

Gies, Frances, and Joseph Gies. *Women in the Middle Ages*. New York: Harper & Row, 1978.

Giles, Kevin. "The Biblical Case for Slavery: Can the Bible Mislead? A Case Study in Hermeneutics." *Evangelical Quarterly* 66 (1994): 3–17.

———. "A Critique of the 'Novel' Contemporary Interpretation of 1 Timothy 2:9–15 Given in the Book, *Women in the Church*: Parts I and II." *Evangelical Quarterly* 72, no. 2 (2000): 151–67; 72, no. 3 (2000): 195–215.

———. "*Women in the Church*: A Rejoinder to Andreas Köstenberger." *Evangelical Quarterly* 73 (2001): 225–43.

Gill, D. W. J. "Corinth: A Roman Colony in Achaea." *Biblische Zeitschrift* 37 (1993): 259–64.

Gordon, T. David. "'Equipping' Ministry in Ephesians 4?" *Journal of the Evangelical Theological Society* 37 (1994): 69–78.

Graf, Fritz. "An Oracle against Pestilence from a Western Anatolian Town." *Zeitschrift für Papyrologie und Epigraphik* 92 (1992): 267–79.

Grant, Michael. *Greek and Latin Authors*. New York: Wilson, 1980.

———. *A Social History of Greece and Rome*. New York: Scribner's Sons, 1992.

Grayston, Kenneth, and G. Herdan. "The Authorship of the Pastorals in the Light of Statistical Linguistics." *New Testament Studies* 6 (1959): 1–15.

Greeven, H. "Propheten, Lehrer, Vorsteher bei Paulus." *Zeitschrift für die neutestamentliche Wissenschaft* 44 (1952–53): 1–43.

Grenz, Stanley J. *Revisioning Evangelical Theology: A Fresh Agenda for the Twenty-first Century*. Downers Grove, IL: InterVarsity, 1993.

Gresch, Dannah. *Secret Keeper: The Delicate Power of Modesty*. Chicago: Moody, 2002.

Grey, M. "'Yet Women Will Be Saved through Bearing Children' (1 Tim 2.15): Motherhood and the Possibility of a Contemporary Discourse for Women." *Bijdragen* 52 (1991): 58–69.

Gritz, Sharon Hodgin. *Paul, Women Teachers, and the Mother Goddess at Ephesus: A Study of 1 Timothy 2:9–15 in Light of the Religious and Cultural Milieu of the First Century*. Lanham, MD: University Press of America, 1991.

———. "The Role of Women in the Church." In *The People of God: Essays on the Believers' Church*, edited by Paul Basden and David S. Dockery, 299–314. Nashville: Broadman, 1991.

Groenhout, R. E., and M. Bower, eds. *Philosophy, Feminism, and Faith*. Bloomington: Indiana University Press, 2003.

Groothuis, Rebecca. *Women Caught in the Conflict*. Grand Rapids: Baker, 1994.

Grote, N. K., K. E. Naylor, and M. S. Clark. "Perceiving the Division of Family Work to Be Unfair: Do Social Comparisons, Enjoyment, and Competence Matter?" *Journal of Family Psychology* 16, no. 4 (2002): 510–22.

Grudem, Wayne. "Prophecy—Yes, but Teaching—No: Paul's Consistent Advocacy of Women's Participation without Governing Authority." *Journal of the Evangelical Theological Society* 30 (1987): 11–23.

———. "Should We Move beyond the New Testament to a Better Ethic? An Analysis of William J. Webb, *Slaves, Women and Homosexuals: Exploring the Hermeneutics of Cultural Analysis*." *Journal of the Evangelical Theological Society* 47 (2004): 299–346.

Gruenler, Royce Gordon. "The Mission-Setting of 1 Tim 2:8–15." *Journal of the Evangelical Theological Society* 41 (1998): 215–38.

Gryson, Roger. *The Ministry of Women in the Early Church*. Translated by Jean Laporte and Mary Louise Hall. Collegeville, MN: Liturgical Press, 1976.

Guthrie, Donald. *New Testament Introduction*. Rev. ed. Downers Grove, IL: InterVarsity, 1990.

———. *The Pastoral Epistles*. Tyndale New Testament Commentaries. Grand Rapids: Eerdmans, 1957.

Guthrie, W. K. C. *The Greeks and Their Gods*. Boston: Beacon, 1950.

Hammond, N., and H. Scullard, eds. *The Oxford Classical Dictionary*. 2nd ed. Oxford: Clarendon, 1970.

Hanson, A. T. *The Pastoral Epistles*. New Century Bible Commentary. Grand Rapids: Eerdmans, 1982.

Hardwick, Lorna. "Ancient Amazons—Heroes, Outsiders or Women?" *Greece and Rome* 37 (1990): 14–36.

Harper, Michael. *Equal and Different: Male and Female in Church and Family*. London: Hodder & Stoughton, 1994.

Harris, James F. *Against Relativism: A Philosophical Defense of Method*. LaSalle, IL: Open Court, 1992.

Harris, Timothy J. "Why Did Paul Mention Eve's Deception? A Critique of P. W. Barnett's Interpretation of 1 Timothy 2." *Evangelical Quarterly* 62 (1990): 335–52.

Harris, William V. *Ancient Literacy*. Cambridge, MA: Harvard University Press, 1989.

Hartenstein, Judith. Review of *Studies on John and Gender*, by Andreas J. Köstenberger. *Review of Biblical Literature*. May 2004. Online at http://www.book reviews.org/pdf/1587_814.pdf (accessed May 13, 2005).

Harvey, Bonnie C. "The Woman Question." *Christian History* 75 (Summer 2002): 21–22.

Hasler, Victor. *Die Briefe an Timotheus und Titus*. Zürich: Theologischer Verlag, 1978.

Hauerwas, Stanley. *Unleashing the Scripture*. Nashville: Abingdon, 1993.

Hauke, Manfred. *Women in the Priesthood? A Systematic Analysis in Light of the Order of Creation and Redemption*. Translated by D. Kipp. San Francisco: Ignatius, 1988.

Hayter, Mary. *The New Eve in Christ: The Use and Abuse of the Bible in the Debate about Women in the Church*. Grand Rapids: Eerdmans, 1987.

Head, Barclay V. *Catalogue of the Greek Coins of Ionia*. Edited by R. S. Poole. Catalogue of the Greek Coins in the British Museum 14. 1892. Reprint, Bologna: Forni, 1964.

———. *Historia Numorum: A Manual of Greek Numismatics*. 2nd ed. Oxford: Clarendon, 1911. Reprint, Chicago: Argonaut, 1967.

Heschel, Susannah. "Jewish and Christian Feminist Theologies." In *Critical Issues in Modern Religion*, edited by Robert A. Johnson et al., 309–45. 2nd ed. Englewood Cliffs, NJ: Prentice Hall, 1990.

Hess, R. S., and M. D. Carroll R., eds. *Family in the Bible*. Grand Rapids: Baker, 2003.

Hicks, E. L., ed. *The Collection of Ancient Greek Inscriptions in the British Museum*. Part 3. Oxford: Clarendon, 1890.

Hill, A. "Ancient Art and Artemis: Toward Explaining the Polymastic Nature of the Figurine." *Journal of the Ancient Near Eastern Society of Columbia University* 21 (1992): 91–94.

Hill, David. *New Testament Prophecy*. Atlanta: John Knox, 1979.

Hölbl, Günther. *Zeugnisse ägyptischer Religionsvorstellungen für Ephesos*. Leiden: Brill, 1978.

Holmes, J. M. *Text in a Whirlwind: A Critique of Four Exegetical Devices at 1 Timothy 2.9–15*. Journal for the Study of the New Testament: Supplement Series 196. Sheffield: Sheffield Academic Press, 2000.

Holtz, Gottfried. *Die Pastoralbriefe*. Theologischer Handkommentar zum Neuen Testament. Berlin: Evangelische Verlagsanstalt, 1972.

Hommes, N. J. "Let Women Be Silent in Church." *Calvin Theological Journal* 4 (1969): 5–22.

Horsley, G. H. R. "The Inscriptions of Ephesus and the New Testament." *Novum Testamentum* 34 (1992): 105–68.

Horton, C. B., and T. C. Cruise. *Child Abuse and Neglect*. New York: Guilford, 2001.

Horton, Robert F., ed. *The Pastoral Epistles: Timothy and Titus*. Edinburgh: Jack, 1901.

Houlden, J. L. *The Pastoral Epistles: I and II Timothy, Titus*. TPI New Testament Commentaries. Philadelphia: Trinity, 1976.

House, H. Wayne. "A Biblical View of Women in the Ministry." *Bibliotheca sacra* 145 (1988): 301–18.

Hove, Richard. *Equality in Christ? Galatians 3:28 and the Gender Dispute.* Wheaton: Crossway, 1999.

Howe, E. Margaret. *Women and Church Leadership.* Grand Rapids: Zondervan, 1982.

Hugenberger, Gordon P. "Women in Church Office: Hermeneutics or Exegesis? A Survey of Approaches to 1 Tim 2:8–15." *Journal of the Evangelical Theological Society* 35 (1992): 341–60.

Huizenga, Hilde. "Women, Salvation, and the Birth of Christ: A Reexamination of 1 Timothy 2:15." *Studia Biblica et theologica* 12 (1982): 17–26.

Hull, Gretchen Gaebelein. *Equal to Serve: Women and Men in the Church and Home.* Old Tappan, NJ: Revell, 1987.

Hunt, A. S., and C. C. Edgar. *Select Papyri.* 2 vols. Loeb Classical Library. Cambridge, MA: Harvard University Press; London: Heinemann, 1932–34.

Huntemann, Georg. *The Other Bonhoeffer.* Translated by T. Huizinga. Grand Rapids: Baker, 1993.

Hurley, James B. *Man and Woman in Biblical Perspective.* Grand Rapids: Zondervan, 1981.

Huttar, David. "ΑΥΘΕΝΤΕΙΝ in the Aeschylus Scholium." *Journal of the Evangelical Theological Society* 44 (2001): 615–25.

Inan, Jale, and Elisabeth Rosenbaum. *Roman and Early Byzantine Portrait Sculpture in Asia Minor.* London: British Academy, 1966.

International Justice Mission Home Page. Online at http://www.ijm.org (accessed November 10, 2004).

Jackson, Eleanor, ed. *The Question of Woman: The Collected Writings of Charlotte von Kirschbaum.* Translated by John Shepherd. Grand Rapids: Eerdmans, 1996.

Jagt, Krijn A. van der. "Women Are Saved through Bearing Children: A Sociological Approach to the Interpretation of 1 Timothy 2.15." In *Issues in Bible Translation,* edited by Philip C. Stine, 287–95. UBS Monograph Series 3. New York: United Bible Societies, 1988.

———. "Women Are Saved through Bearing Children (1 Timothy 2.11–15)." *Bible Translator* 39 (1988): 201–8.

Jebb, S. "A Suggested Interpretation of 1 Ti 2.15." *Expository Times* 81 (1970): 221–22.

Jenkins, C. "Documents: Origen on I Corinthians." *Journal of Theological Studies* 10 (1909): 29–51.

Jenkins, C. L. "Stern Warning on Sex with Minors." *Washington Post,* Tuesday, June 15, 2004, A01.

Jenkins, Philip. *The Next Christendom: The Coming of Global Christianity.* Oxford: Oxford University Press, 2002.

Jeremias, Joachim. *Die Briefe an Timotheus und Titus*. Das Neue Testament Deutsch. Göttingen: Vandenhoeck & Ruprecht, 1968.

Jewett, Paul K. *Man as Male and Female*. Grand Rapids: Eerdmans, 1975.

Jeynes, W. *Divorce, Family Structure, and the Academic Success of Children*. New York: Haworth, 2002.

Pope John Paul II and Cardinal Joseph Ratzinger. "Letter to the Bishops of the Catholic Church on the Collaboration of Men and Women in the Church and in the World." Rome: Offices of the Congregation for the Doctrine of the Faith, May 31, 2004. Online at http://www.vatican.va/roman_curia/congrega tions/cfaith/documents/rc_con_cfaith_doc_20040731_collaboration_en.html (accessed May 5, 2005).

Johnson, Luke Timothy. *The First and Second Letters to Timothy: A New Translation with Introduction and Commentary*. Anchor Bible. New York: Doubleday, 2001.

———. *The Writings of the New Testament: An Interpretation*. Philadelphia: Fortress, 1986.

Johnson, M. D. *Making Sense of the Bible*. Grand Rapids: Eerdmans, 2002.

Johnson, P. "Greene, a 'Lost Voice,' Awaits Renewal." *USA Today*. Posted March 4, 2003. Online at http://www.usatoday.com/life/columnist/mediamix/2003-03-04-mediamix_x.htm (accessed November 10, 2004).

Johnson, P. F. "The Use of Statistics in the Analysis of the Characteristics of Pauline Writing." *New Testament Studies* 20 (1973): 92–100.

Johnson, Philip E. *Darwin on Trial*. Downers Grove, IL: InterVarsity, 1991.

Jones, A. H. *Essenes: The Elect of Israel and the Priests of Artemis*. New York: University Press of America, 1985.

Jones, A. H. M. *The Greek City from Alexander to Justinian*. Oxford: Clarendon, 1940.

Jones, D. W. "Egalitarianism and Homosexuality: Connected or Autonomous Ideologies?" *Journal for Biblical Manhood and Womanhood* 8, no. 2 (Fall 2003): 5–19.

Kampen, J. "A Reconsideration of the Name 'Essene.'" *Hebrew Union College Annual* 57 (1986): 61–81.

Karris, Robert J. "The Background and Significance of the Polemic of the Pastoral Epistles." *Journal of Biblical Literature* 92 (1973): 549–64.

Karwiese, Stefan. "Ephesos: Numismatischer Teil." *PW Supplement* 12 (1970): 297–364.

Kassian, Mary A. *The Feminist Gospel: The Movement to Unite Feminism with the Church*. Wheaton: Crossway, 1992.

———. *Women, Creation and the Fall*. Westchester, IL: Crossway, 1990.

Kearsley, R. A. "Women in Public Life." In *New Documents Illustrating Early Christianity*, edited by S. R. Llewelyn, 6:24–27. North Ryde, Australia: Ancient History Documentary Research Centre, Macquarie University, 1992.

————. "Women in Public Life in the Roman East: Iunia Theodora, Claudia Metrodora and Phoebe, Benefactress of Paul." *Tyndale Bulletin* 50, no. 2 (1999): 189–211.

Keener, Craig S. *Paul, Women and Wives: Marriage and Women's Ministry in the Letters of Paul.* Peabody, MA: Hendrickson, 1992.

————. Review of *Women in the Church. Journal of the Evangelical Theological Society* 41, no. 3 (1998): 513–16.

————. "Women in Ministry." In *Two Views on Women in Ministry,* edited by J. R. Beck and C. L. Blomberg, 27–73. Grand Rapids: Zondervan, 2001.

Kelly, J. N. D. *A Commentary on the Pastoral Epistles.* Grand Rapids: Baker, 1963.

Kern, O., ed. *Die Inschriften von Magnesia am Maeander.* Berlin: Spemann, 1900.

Kimberly, David R. "1 Timothy 2:15: A Possible Understanding of a Difficult Text." *Journal of the Evangelical Theological Society* 35 (1992): 481–86.

Klein, William W., Craig L. Blomberg, and Robert L. Hubbard Jr. *Introduction to Biblical Interpretation.* Dallas: Word, 1993.

Knibbe, Dieter. "Ephesos: Historisch-epigraphischer Teil." In *Paulys Real-Encyclopädie der classischen Altertumswissenschaft, Supplement,* edited by G. Wissowa, W. Kroll, and K. Witte, 12:248–97. Stuttgart: J. B. Metzler, 1970.

————. "Ephesos—Nicht nur die Stadt der Artemis: Die 'anderen' ephesischen Götter." In *Studien zur Religion und Kultur Kleinasiens,* edited by S. Sahin et al., 2:489–503. Leiden: Brill, 1978.

————. *Forschungen in Ephesos 9.1.1: Der Staatsmarkt; Die Inschriften des Prytaneions; Die Kureteninschriften and sonstige religiöse Texte.* Vienna: Österreichische Akademie der Wissenschaften, 1981.

————. "Eine neue Kuretenliste aus Ephesos." *Jahreshefte des Österreichischen Archäologischen Instituts in Wien* 54 (1983): 125–27.

Knibbe, Dieter, and Wilhelm Alzinger. "Ephesos vom Beginn der römischen Herrschaft in Kleinasien bis zum Ende der Principatszeit." In *Aufstieg und Niedergang der römischen Welt,* 2.7.2:748–830. Berlin: de Gruyter, 1980.

Knibbe, Dieter, H. Engelmann, and B. Iplikçioglu. "Neue Inschriften aus Ephesos XI." *Jahreshefte des Österreichischen Archäologischen Instituts in Wien* 59 (1989): 163–237.

————. "Neue Inschriften aus Ephesos XII." *Jahreshefte des Österreichischen Archäologischen Instituts in Wien* 62 (1993): 113–50.

Knibbe, Dieter, and B. Iplikçioglu. *Ephesos im Spiegel seiner Inschriften.* Vienna: Schindler, 1984.

————. "Neue Inschriften aus Ephesos VIII." *Jahreshefte des Österreichischen Archäologischen Instituts in Wien* 53 (1981–82): 87–150.

————. "Neue Inschriften aus Ephesos IX." *Jahreshefte des Österreichischen Archäologischen Instituts in Wien* 55 (1984): 107–35.

————. "Neue Inschriften aus Ephesos X." *Jahreshefte des Österreichischen Archäologischen Instituts in Wien* 55 (1984): 137–45.

Knibbe, Dieter, R. Meriç, and R. Merkelbach. "Der Grundbesitz der ephesischen Artemis im Kaystrostal." *Zeitschrift für Papyrologie und Epigraphik* 33 (1979): 139–46.

Knight, George W., III. "ΑΥΘΕΝΤΕΩ in Reference to Women in 1 Timothy 2.12." *New Testament Studies* 30 (1984): 143–57.

————. *The Pastoral Epistles.* New International Greek Testament Commentary. Grand Rapids: Eerdmans, 1992.

————. *The Role Relationship of Men and Women: New Testament Teaching.* Rev. ed. Chicago: Moody, 1985.

Koester, Helmut, ed. *Ephesos: Metropolis of Asia.* Valley Forge, PA: Trinity, 1995.

Köstenberger, Andreas J. "Ascertaining Women's God-Ordained Roles: An Interpretation of 1 Timothy 2:15." *Bulletin for Biblical Research* 7 (1997): 107–44.

————. "1 and 2 Timothy and Titus." In *The Expositor's Bible Commentary,* 2nd ed. Grand Rapids: Zondervan, 2005.

————. "Gender Passages in the New Testament: Hermeneutical Fallacies Critiqued." *Westminster Theological Journal* 56 (1994): 259–83.

————. Review of *Women Leaders and the Church: Three Crucial Questions,* by Linda L. Belleville. *Journal of the Evangelical Theological Society* 44, no. 2 (2001): 344–46.

————. "*Women in the Church*: A Response to Kevin Giles." *Evangelical Quarterly* 73 (2001): 205–24.

————. "Women in the Pauline Mission." In *The Gospel to the Nations: Perspectives on Paul's Mission,* edited by Peter Bolt and Mark Thompson, 221–47. Leicester, Eng.: Inter-Varsity, 2000.

Köstenberger, Andreas J., with David W. Jones. *God, Marriage, and Family: Rebuilding the Biblical Foundation.* Wheaton: Crossway, 2004.

Kraabel, A. Thomas. "*Hypsistos* and the Synagogue at Sardis." *Greek, Roman and Byzantine Studies* 10 (1969): 81–93.

Kraemer, Ross. *Her Share of the Blessings: Women's Religions among Pagans, Jews, and Christians in the Greco-Roman World.* New York: Oxford University Press, 1992.

Kreeft, Peter. *Christianity for Modern Pagans.* San Francisco: Ignatius, 1993.

Kroeger, Catherine Clark. "Ancient Heresies and a Strange Greek Verb." *Reformed Journal* 29 (1979): 12–15.

————. "Women in the Church: A Classicist's View of 1 Tim 2:11–15." *Journal of Biblical Equality* 1 (1989): 3–31.

Kroeger, Richard Clark, and Catherine Clark Kroeger. *I Suffer Not a Woman: Rethinking 1 Timothy 2:11–15 in Light of Ancient Evidence.* Grand Rapids: Baker, 1992.

——. *Women Elders: Called by God?* Online at http://firstpresby.org/womenelders.htm#Unit6 (accessed March 1, 2005).

Kroner, Richard. *The Primacy of Faith.* New York: Macmillan, 1943.

Kuske, D. F. "An Exegetical Brief on 1 Timothy 2:12 (*oude authentein andros*)." *Wisconsin Lutheran Quarterly* 88 (1991): 64–67.

Lacey, W. K. "Patria Potestas." In *The Family in Ancient Rome*, edited by B. Rawson, 121–44. Ithaca, NY: Cornell University Press, 1986.

Lane, William L. "1 Tim. iv.1–3: An Early Instance of Over-realized Eschatology?" *New Testament Studies* 11 (1965): 164–67.

Langley, Myrtle S. *Equal Woman: A Christian Feminist Perspective.* London: Marshall, Morgan & Scott, 1983.

Lassman, E. "1 Timothy 3:1–7 and Titus 1:5–9 and the Ordination of Women." *Concordia Theological Quarterly* 56 (1992): 291–95.

Lefkowitz, Mary. "Influential Women." In *Images of Women in Antiquity*, edited by Averil Cameron and A. Kuhrt, 49–64. Detroit: Wayne State University Press, 1983.

Lefkowitz, Mary, and Maureen Fant, eds. *Women's Life in Greece and Rome: A Source Book in Translation.* Baltimore: Johns Hopkins University Press, 1982.

Leith, John H. *Crisis in the Church.* Louisville: Westminster John Knox, 1997.

Lewis, C. S. "Priestesses in the Church?" In *God in the Dock*, edited by W. Hooper, 234–39. Grand Rapids: Eerdmans, 1970.

Libby, J. A. "A Proposed Methodology and Preliminary Data on Statistically Elucidating the Authorship of the Pastoral Epistles." M.Div. thesis, Denver Seminary, 1987.

LiDonnici, Lynn. "The Images of Artemis Ephesia and Greco-Roman Worship: A Reconsideration." *Harvard Theological Review* 85 (1992): 389–415.

Liefeld, Walter L. *1 & 2 Timothy, Titus.* NIV Application Commentary. Grand Rapids: Zondervan, 1999.

——. "Women and the Nature of Ministry." *Journal of the Evangelical Theological Society* 30 (1987): 49–61.

Lightfoot, N. "The Role of Women in Religious Services." *Restoration Quarterly* 19 (1976): 129–36.

Lips, Hermann von. "Die Haustafel als 'Topos' im Rahmen der urchristlichen Paränese." *New Testament Studies* 40 (1994): 261–80.

Lock, Walter. *A Critical and Exegetical Commentary on the Pastoral Epistles.* International Critical Commentary. Edinburgh: Clark, 1936.

Longenecker, Richard N. *New Testament Social Ethics for Today.* Grand Rapids: Eerdmans, 1984.

Luick, J. "The Ambiguity of Kantian Faith." *Scottish Journal of Theology* 36 (1983): 339–46.

Luther, Martin. *A Commentary on St. Paul's Epistle to the Galatians.* London: Clarke, 1953.

———. *Lectures on Genesis: Chapters 1–5.* Vol. 1 in *Luther's Works,* edited by Jaroslav Pelikan. St. Louis: Concordia, 1958.

MacMullen, Ramsay. "Woman in Public in the Roman Empire." *Historia* 29 (1980): 208–18.

Magie, David. *Roman Rule in Asia Minor.* 2 vols. Princeton, NJ: Princeton University Press, 1950.

Mahowald, Mary B., ed. *Philosophy of Woman: An Anthology of Classic and Current Concepts.* 2nd ed. Indianapolis: Hackett, 1983.

Maier, Gerhard. *Biblical Hermeneutics.* Translated by Robert Yarbrough. Wheaton: Crossway, 1994.

Malherbe, A., ed. *The Cynic Epistles.* Society of Biblical Literature Sources for Biblical Study 12. Atlanta: Scholars Press, 1977.

Mancha, Rita. "The Woman's Authority: Calvin to Edwards." *Journal of Christian Reconstruction* 6 (1979–80): 86–98.

Marrou, H. I. *A History of Education in Antiquity.* Translated by George Lamb. New York: Sheed & Ward, 1956. Reprint, New York: New American Library, 1964.

Marshall, I. Howard. "The Use of the New Testament in Christian Ethics." *Expository Times* 105 (1994): 131–36.

Marshall, I. Howard, and Philip H. Towner. *A Critical and Exegetical Commentary on the Pastoral Epistles.* International Critical Commentary. Edinburgh: Clark, 1999.

Martens, E. A. "How Is the Christian to Construe Old Testament Law?" *Bulletin for Biblical Research* 12, no. 2 (2002): 199–216.

Martin, Faith. *Call Me Blessed.* Grand Rapids: Eerdmans, 1988.

Martin, Hubert. "Artemis." *Anchor Bible Dictionary,* edited by David Noel Freedman, 1:464–65. New York: Doubleday, 1992.

McDougall, J. A. "Weaving Garments of Grace: En-gendering a Theology of the Call to Ordained Ministry for Women Today." *Theological Education* 39, no. 2 (2003).

McGrath, Alister. *The Mystery of the Cross.* Grand Rapids: Zondervan, 1988.

McKenzie, D. "Kant and Protestant Theology." *Encounter* 43 (1982): 157–67.

Meade, David G. *Pseudonymity and Canon: An Investigation into the Relationship of Authorship and Authority in Jewish and Earliest Christian Tradition.* Grand Rapids: Eerdmans, 1987.

Meinardus, Otto. "The Alleged Advertisement for the Ephesian Lupanar." *Wiener Studien* 7 (1973): 244–48.

Meiselman, Moshe. *Jewish Woman in Jewish Law.* New York: Ktav, 1978.

Merk, Otto. *Biblische Theologie des Neuen Testaments in ihrer Anfangszeit.* Marburg: Elwert, 1972.

Merkelbach, Reinhold. "Die ephesischen Dionysosmysten vor der Stadt." *Zeitschrift für Papyrologie und Epigraphik* 36 (1979): 151–56.

———. "Der Kult der Hestia im Prytaneion der griechischen Städte." *Zeitschrift für Papyrologie und Epigraphik* 37 (1980): 77–92.

Mickelsen, Alvera. "An Egalitarian View: There Is Neither Male nor Female in Christ." In *Women in Ministry: Four Views*, edited by B. Clouse and R. Clouse. Downers Grove, IL: InterVarsity, 1989.

———, ed. *Women, Authority and the Bible*. Downers Grove, IL: InterVarsity, 1986.

Millar, Fergus. "The World of the *Golden Ass.*" *Journal of Roman Studies* 71 (1981): 63–75.

Mitchell, Stephen. *Anatolia*. Oxford: Clarendon, 1993.

———. "Festivals, Games, and Civic Life in Roman Asia Minor." *Journal of Roman Studies* 80 (1990): 183–93.

Mollenkott, Virginia R. *Women, Men and the Bible*. Nashville: Abingdon, 1977.

Mommsen, Theodor. *The Provinces of the Roman Empire from Caesar to Diocletian*. Translated by William P. Dickson. London: Macmillan, 1909. Reprint, Chicago: Ares, 1974.

Montgomery, Hugo. "Women and Status in the Greco-Roman World." *Studia theologica* 43 (1989): 115–24.

Moo, Douglas J. "1 Timothy 2:11–15: Meaning and Significance." *Trinity Journal*, n.s., 1 (1980): 62–83.

———. "The Interpretation of 1 Timothy 2:11–15: A Rejoinder." *Trinity Journal*, n.s., 2 (1981): 198–222.

———. "What Does It Mean Not to Teach or Have Authority over Men? 1 Timothy 2:11–15." In *Recovering Biblical Manhood and Womanhood: A Response to Evangelical Feminism*, edited by John Piper and Wayne Grudem, 179–93. Wheaton: Crossway, 1991.

Morford, Mark P. O., and Robert J. Lenardon. *Classical Mythology*. 4th ed. New York: Longman, 1991.

Morgan, Robert, with John Barton. *Biblical Interpretation*. Oxford: Oxford University Press, 1988.

Morris, Joan. *The Lady Was a Bishop: The Hidden History of Women with Clerical Ordination and the Jurisdiction of Bishops*. New York: Macmillan, 1973.

Morse, J. "Cops Arrest Ch[annel] 9 Reporter: Sex with Minors Charged." *Cincinnati Enquirer*, Saturday, February 28, 2004.

Motyer, Steve. "Expounding 1 Timothy 2:8–15." *Vox evangelica* 24 (1994): 91–102.

Mounce, William D. *The Pastoral Epistles*. Word Biblical Commentary 46. Nashville: Nelson, 2000.

Mueller-Vollmer, Kurt, ed. *The Hermeneutics Reader*. New York: Continuum, 1985.

Murphy-O'Connor, Jerome. "St. Paul: Promoter of the Ministry of Women." *Priests and People* 6 (1992): 307–11.

Neuer, Werner. *Man and Woman in Christian Perspective*. Translated by Gordon J. Wenham. Wheaton: Crossway, 1991.

Newsom, Carol, and Sharon Ringe, eds. *The Women's Bible Commentary*. London: SPCK; Westminster/John Knox, 1992.

Noll, Mark A. *A History of Christianity in the United States and Canada*. Grand Rapids: Eerdmans, 1992.

Norwood, Robin. *Women Who Love Too Much*. Los Angeles: Tarcher, 1985.

Nugent, M. Rosamond. *Portrait of the Consecrated Woman in Greek Christian Literature of the First Four Centuries*. Washington, DC: Catholic University Press, 1941.

O'Brien, P. T. Review of *Women in the Church*. *Southern Cross Newspaper*, September 1996.

O'Collins, G., and D. Kendall. *The Bible for Theology*. New York: Paulist, 1997.

Oden, Thomas C. *First and Second Timothy and Titus*. Louisville: John Knox, 1989.

Osborne, Grant R. *The Hermeneutical Spiral*. Downers Grove, IL: InterVarsity, 1991.

———. "Hermeneutics and Women in the Church." *Journal of the Evangelical Theological Society* 20 (1977): 337–52.

Osburn, Carroll D. "ΑΥΘΕΝΤΕΩ (1 Timothy 2:12)." *Restoration Quarterly* 25 (1982): 1–12.

Oster, Richard E. *A Bibliography of Ancient Ephesus*. ATLA Bibliography Series 19. [Philadelphia]: American Theological Library Association; Metuchen, NJ: Scarecrow, 1987.

———. "The Ephesian Artemis as an Opponent of Early Christianity." *Jahrbuch für Antike und Christentum* 19 (1976): 24–44.

———. "Ephesus as a Religious Center under the Principate, I: Paganism before Constantine." In *Aufstieg und Niedergang der römischen Welt*, 2.18.3:1661–1728. Berlin: de Gruyter, 1990.

———. "When Men Wore Veils to Worship: The Historical Context of 1 Corinthians 11.4." *New Testament Studies* 34 (1988): 481–505.

Ozawa, Martha N. *Women's Life Cycle and Economic Insecurity*. New York: Praeger, 1989.

Packer, J. I. "Understanding the Differences." In *Women, Authority and the Bible*, edited by Alvera Mickelson. Downers Grove, IL: InterVarsity, 1986.

Padgett, Alan G. "The Scholarship of Patriarchy (on 1 Timothy 2:8–15): A Response to *Women in the Church*." *Priscilla Papers* 11, no. 1 (Winter 1997): 24–29.

———. "Wealthy Women at Ephesus: 1 Timothy 2:8–15 in Social Context." *Interpretation* 41 (1987): 19–31.

Pagels, Elaine. *The Gnostic Gospels*. New York: Random, 1979.

Panning, A. J. "ΑΥΘΕΝΤΕΙΝ—A Word Study." *Wisconsin Lutheran Quarterly* 78 (1981): 185–91.

Pantel, Pauline Schmitt, ed. *A History of Women in the West*. Vol. 1, *From Ancient Goddesses to Christian Saints*. Cambridge, MA: Harvard University Press, Belknap Press, 1992.

Patterson, Dorothy Kelley. "The Role of Women in the Church." In *We Believe*, edited by Paige Patterson and Luis Pantoja Jr., 1:163–70. Dallas: Criswell, 1977.

———. "Says Her Guidelines Are Certain." *North Carolina Biblical Recorder* November 28, 1998.

Payne, Philip B. "Libertarian Women in Ephesus: A Response to Douglas J. Moo's Article '1 Timothy 2:11–15: Meaning and Significance.'" *Trinity Journal*, n.s., 2 (1981): 169–97.

———. "Οὐδέ in 1 Timothy 2:12." Paper presented at the 1988 annual meeting of the Evangelical Theological Society.

Perriman, Andrew C. "What Eve Did, What Women Shouldn't Do: The Meaning of ΑΥΘΕΝΤΕΩ in 1 Timothy 2:12." *Tyndale Bulletin* 44 (1993): 129–42.

Phillips, Susan S. "Caring for Our Children: Confronting the Crisis." *Radix* 22 (1993): 4.

Pierce, Ronald. "Evangelicals and Gender Roles in the 1990s: 1 Tim 2:8–15: A Test Case." *Journal of the Evangelical Theological Society* 36 (1993): 343–55.

Piper, John, and Wayne Grudem, eds. *Recovering Biblical Manhood and Womanhood: A Response to Evangelical Feminism*. Wheaton: Crossway, 1991.

Pollard, Jeff. *Christian Modesty and the Public Undressing of America*. San Antonio: Vision Forum, 2001.

Porter, Stanley E. "What Does It Mean to Be 'Saved by Childbirth' (1 Timothy 2.15)?" *Journal for the Study of the New Testament* 49 (1993): 87–102.

Powers, B. Ward. *The Ministry of Women in the Church: Which Way Forward? The Case for the "Middle Ground" Interpretation of the New Testament*. Adelaide, Australia: SPCK, 1996.

Poythress, Vern. *The Church as Family*. Wheaton: Council of Biblical Manhood and Womanhood, 1990. Reprinted in *Recovering Biblical Manhood and Womanhood: A Response to Evangelical Feminism*, edited by John Piper and Wayne Grudem, 233–47. Wheaton: Crossway, 1991.

Price, S. R. F. *Rituals and Power: The Roman Imperial Cult in Asia Minor*. Cambridge: Cambridge University Press, 1984.

Pritchard, J. B., ed. *The Harper Atlas of the Bible*. New York: Harper & Row, 1987.

Quasten, Johannes. *Music and Worship in Pagan and Christian Antiquity*. Translated by B. Ramsay. Washington, DC: National Association of Pastoral Musicians, 1983.

Quinn, Jerome D., and William C. Wacker. *The First and Second Letters to Timothy: A New Translation with Notes and Commentary*. Grand Rapids: Eerdmans, 2000.

Ramsay, William. *Asianic Elements in Greek Civilisation*. 1927. Reprint, Chicago: Ares, 1976.

———. *Cities and Bishoprics of Phrygia*. Oxford: Clarendon, 1895.

———. *A Historical Commentary on St. Paul's Epistle to the Galatians*. 1900. Reprint, Grand Rapids: Baker, 1965.

———. *The Teaching of Paul in Terms of the Present Day*. 2nd ed. London: Hodder & Stoughton, 1914.

Reardon, B. P., ed. *Collected Ancient Greek Novels*. Translated by Graham Anderson et al. Berkeley: University of California Press, 1989.

Redekop, Gloria. "Let the Woman Learn: 1 Timothy 2:8–15 Reconsidered." *Studies in Religion/Sciences Religieuses* 19 (1990): 235–45.

Renié, J. *Les origines de l'humanité d'après la Bible*. Lyon: Vitte, 1950.

Riesner, R. *Apostolischer Gemeindebau: Die Herausforderung der paulinischen Gemeinden*. Giessen-Basel: Brunnen, 1978.

Ringwood, I. "Festivals of Ephesus." *American Journal of Archaeology* 76 (1972): 17–22.

Roberts, Mark D. "Woman Shall Be Saved: A Closer Look at 1 Timothy 2:15." *TSF Bulletin* 5 (1981): 4–7.

Rogers, Guy M. "The Assembly of Imperial Ephesos." *Zeitschrift für Papyrologie und Epigraphik* 94 (1992): 224–28.

———. "Constructions of Women at Ephesus." *Zeitschrift für Papyrologie und Epigraphik* 90 (1992): 215–23.

———. *The Sacred Identity of Ephesos*. London: Routledge, 1991.

Roloff, Jürgen. *Der erste Brief an Timotheus*. Evangelisch-katholischer Kommentar zum Neuen Testament. Zürich: Benziger, 1988.

Rossner, M. "Asiarchen und Archiereis Asia." *Studii Clasice* 16 (1974): 112–42.

Ruether, Rosemary R., ed. *Gender, Ethnicity, and Religion*. Minneapolis: Fortress, 2002.

———. "Misogynism and Virginal Feminism in the Fathers." In *Religion and Sexism: Images of Women in Jewish and Christian Tradition*, edited by Rosemary R. Ruether, 150–83. New York: Simon & Schuster, 1974.

———, ed. *Religion and Sexism: Images of Woman in the Jewish and Christian Traditions*. New York: Simon & Schuster, 1974.

Ryrie, Charles C. *The Role of Women in the Church*. Chicago: Moody, 1970.

Saller, R. P. *Personal Patronage under the Early Empire*. Cambridge: Cambridge University Press, 1982.

Sandnes, K. " '. . . et liv som vinner respekt.' En sentralt perspektiv på 1 Tim 2:11–15." *Tidsskrift for Teologi og Kirke* 59 (1988): 225–37.

Sanneh, Lamin. *Whose Religion Is Christianity? The Gospel beyond the West*. Grand Rapids: Eerdmans, 2003.

Saucy, Robert L. "Women's Prohibition to Teach Men: An Investigation into Its Meaning and Contemporary Application." *Journal of the Evangelical Theological Society* 37 (1994): 79–97.

Scanzoni, Letha Dawson, and Nancy A. Hardesty. *All We're Meant to Be: Biblical Feminism for Today*. 3rd ed. Grand Rapids: Eerdmans, 1992.

Schlatter, Adolf. *The Church in the New Testament Period*. Translated by Paul P. Levertoff. London: SPCK, 1955.

———. *Die Kirche der Griechen im Urteil des Paulus*. 2nd ed. Stuttgart: Calwer, 1958.

———. *Die Theologie des Neuen Testaments*. Vol. 2, *Die Theologie der Apostel*. 2nd ed. Stuttgart: Calwer, 1922.

———. "The Theology of the New Testament and Dogmatics." In *The Nature of New Testament Theology*, edited by Robert Morgan, 117–66. Naperville, IL: Allenson, 1973.

Scholder, Klaus. *The Birth of Modern Critical Theology*. Translated by John Bowden. London: SCM; Trinity, 1990.

Scholer, David M. "1 Timothy 2:9–12 and the Place of Women in the Church's Ministry." In *Women, Authority and the Bible*, edited by Alvera Mickelsen, 193–224. Downers Grove, IL: InterVarsity, 1986.

———. "Women in the Church's Ministry: Does 1 Timothy 2:9–15 Help or Hinder?" *Daughters of Sarah* 16, no. 4 (1990): 7–12.

Scholler [*sic*], David. "Women's Adornment: Some Historical and Hermeneutical Observations on the New Testament Passages." *Daughters of Sarah* 6, no. 1 (1980): 3–6.

Schreiner, Thomas R. "Did Paul Believe in Justification by Works? Another Look at Romans 2." *Bulletin for Biblical Research* 3 (1993): 131–58.

———. "Head Coverings, Prophecies and the Trinity: 1 Corinthians 11:2–16." In *Recovering Biblical Manhood and Womanhood: A Response to Evangelical Feminism*, edited by John Piper and Wayne Grudem, 124–39, 485–87. Wheaton: Crossway, 1991.

———. *Interpreting the Pauline Epistles*. Grand Rapids: Baker, 1990.

———. *The Law and Its Fulfillment*. Grand Rapids: Baker, 1993.

———. Review of *Two Views on Women in Ministry*. *Journal for Biblical Manhood and Womanhood* 6 (2001): 24–30.

———. "William J. Webb's *Slaves, Women and Homosexuals*: A Review Article." *Southern Baptist Journal of Theology* 6 (2002): 46–64.

———. "Women in Ministry." In *Two Views on Women in Ministry*, edited by J. R. Beck and C. L. Blomberg, 177–235. Grand Rapids: Zondervan, 2001.

Schreiner, Thomas R., and Ardel B. Caneday. *The Race Set before Us: A Biblical Theology of Perseverance and Assurance*. Downers Grove, IL: InterVarsity, 2001.

Schumacher, M. M. "Feminist Experience and Faith Experience." In *Women in Christ: Toward a New Feminism*, edited by M. M. Schumacher, 169–200. Grand Rapids: Eerdmans, 2004.

Shalit, Wendy. *A Return to Modesty: Discovering the Lost Virtue*. New York: Free Press, 1999.

Sherk, Robert K. "Eponymous Officials of Greek Cities I–V." *Zeitschrift für Papyrologie und Epigraphik* 83 (1990): 249–88; 84 (1990): 231–95; 88 (1991): 225–60; 93 (1992): 223–72; 96 (1993): 267–95.

Sherwin-White, A. N. *The Letters of Pliny: A Historical and Social Commentary.* Oxford: Clarendon, 1966.

Shillington, V. G. *Reading the Sacred Text.* London: Clark, 2002.

Sigountos, James G., and Mygren Shank. "Public Roles for Women in the Pauline Church: A Reappraisal of the Evidence." *Journal of the Evangelical Theological Society* 26 (1983): 283–95.

Smith, M., et al., eds. *The Holman Book of Biblical Charts, Maps, and Reconstructions.* Nashville: Broadman & Holman, 1993.

Snodgrass, Klyne R. "The Ordination of Women—Thirteen Years Later: Do We Really Value the Ministry of Women?" *Covenant Quarterly* 48, no. 3 (1990): 26–43.

Sölle, Dorothee. "Response to H. D. Betz." In *Paul's Concept of Freedom in the Context of Hellenistic Discussions about the Possibilities of Human Freedom: Protocol of the Twenty-sixth Colloquy, 9 January 1977,* edited by Hans Dieter Betz, Center for Hermeneutical Studies in Hellenistic and Modern Culture 26. Berkeley, CA: The Center, 1977.

Solokowski, F. "A New Testimony on the Cult of Artemis of Ephesus." *Harvard Theological Review* 58 (1965): 427–31.

Specht, Edith. "Kulttradition einer weiblichen Gottheit: Beispiel Ephesos." In *Maria, Abbild oder Vorbild?* edited by H. Röckelein et al., 37–47. Tübingen: Edition Diskord, 1990.

Spencer, Aída Besançon. "Eve at Ephesus: Should Women Be Ordained as Pastors according to the First Letter of Timothy 2:1–15?" *Journal of the Evangelical Theological Society* 17 (1974): 215–22.

Spicq, Ceslas. *Saint Paul: Les épitres pastorales.* 4th ed. 2 vols. Études bibliques. Paris: Gabalda, 1969.

Stackhouse, John G., Jr. "Women in Public Ministry in Twentieth-Century Canadian and American Evangelicalism: Five Models." *Studies in Religion/Sciences Religieuses* 17 (1988): 471–85.

Stadelmann, Helge. Review of *Women in the Church. Jahrbuch für evangelikale Theologie* 6 (1996): 421–25.

Stagg, Evelyn, and Frank Stagg, eds. *Women in the World of Jesus.* Edinburgh: St. Andrew, 1978.

Stark, R. "The Role of Women in Christian Growth." Chapter 5 in *The Rise of Christianity: A Sociologist Reconsiders History.* Princeton, NJ: Princeton University Press, 1996.

Stauffer, Ethelbert. *New Testament Theology.* Translated by John Marsh. London: SCM, 1955.

Stendahl, Krister. "The Apostle Paul and the Introspective Conscience of the West." *Harvard Theological Review* 56 (1963): 199–215.

———. *The Bible and the Role of Women: A Case Study in Hermeneutics.* Translated by E. Sander. Facet Books Biblical Series 15. Philadelphia: Fortress, 1966.

Stott, John R. W. *Decisive Issues Facing Christians Today.* Old Tappan, NJ: Revell, 1990.

———. *Guard the Truth: The Message of 1 Timothy and Titus.* Downers Grove, IL: InterVarsity, 1996.

Stowers, Stanley. "Social Status, Public Speaking and Private Teaching: The Circumstances of Paul's Preaching Activity." *Novum Testamentum* 26 (1984): 59–82.

Strecker, Georg. "Das Problem der Theologie des Neuen Testaments." In *Das Problem der Theologie des Neuen Testaments,* edited by Georg Strecker, 9–31. Darmstadt: Wissenschaftliche Buchgesellschaft, 1975.

"Student-Teacher Sexual Relations." Online at http://www.karisable.com/crsssstr. htm (accessed November 10, 2004).

Stuhlmacher, Peter. ". . . in verrosteten Angeln." *Zeitschrift für Theologie und Kirche* 77 (1980): 222–38.

Sullivan, Richard D. "Priesthoods of the Eastern Dynastic Aristocracy." In *Studien zur Religion und Kultur Kleinasiens,* edited by S. Sahin et al., 2:914–39. Leiden: Brill, 1978.

Sumner, Sarah. *Men and Women in the Church: Building Consensus on Christian Leadership.* Downers Grove, IL: InterVarsity, 2003.

Swartley, Willard M. *Slavery, Sabbath, War and Women.* Scottsdale, PA: Herald, 1983.

Sweet, Waldo E. *Sport and Recreation in Ancient Greece.* New York: Oxford University Press, 1987.

Taylor, Henry Osborn. *The Medieval Mind.* Cambridge, MA: Harvard University Press, 1949.

Taylor, L. R. "Artemis of Ephesus." In *The Beginnings of Christianity,* edited by F. Foakes Jackson and Kirsopp Lake, 5:251–56. London: Macmillan, 1933.

Terrien, Samuel. *Till the Heart Sings: A Biblical Theology of Manhood and Womanhood.* Philadelphia: Fortress, 1985.

Theissen, Gerd. "Soziale Schichtung in der korinthischen Gemeinde." *Zeitschrift für die neutestamentliche Wissenschaft* 65 (1974): 232–72.

Thielicke, Helmut. *The Evangelical Faith.* Vol. 1, *Prolegomena: The Relationship of Theology to Modern Thought Forms.* Translated by Geoffrey Bromiley. Grand Rapids: Eerdmans, 1974.

Thiessen, Werner. *Christen in Ephesus: Die historische und theologische Situation in vorpaulinischer und paulinischer Zeit und zur Zeit der Apostelgeschichte und der Pastoralbriefe.* Texte und Arbeiten zum neutestamentlichen Zeitalter 12. Tübingen: Francke, 1995.

Thiselton, Anthony C. *New Horizons in Hermeneutics.* Grand Rapids: Zondervan, 1992.

——. "Realized Eschatology at Corinth." *New Testament Studies* 24 (1978): 510–26.

Thomas, Rosalind. *Oral Tradition and Written Record in Classical Athens*. Cambridge: Cambridge University Press, 1989.

Tiessen, Terrance. "Toward a Hermeneutic for Discerning Moral Absolutes." *Journal of the Evangelical Theological Society* 36 (1993): 189–207.

Tooley, James. "Brainwashed: Correcting the Modern Miseducation of Women." *Chicago Tribune*, August 31, 2003, sec. 2, p. 1.

——. *The Miseducation of Women*. New York: Continuum, 2002.

Towner, Philip H. *1–2 Timothy and Titus*. IVP New Testament Commentary. Downers Grove, IL: InterVarsity, 1994.

——. *The Goal of Our Instruction*. Journal for the Study of the New Testament: Supplement Series 34. Sheffield: JSOT, 1989.

Trebilco, Paul. "Asia." In *The Book of Acts in Its Graeco-Roman Setting*, edited by David W. J. Gill and Conrad Gempf, 316–36. The Book of Acts in Its First Century Setting 2. Grand Rapids: Eerdmans; Carlisle, Eng.: Paternoster, 1994.

Tucker, Ruth A. *Women in the Maze: Questions and Answers on Biblical Equality*. Downers Grove, IL: InterVarsity, 1992.

Tucker, Ruth A., and Walter Liefeld. *Daughters of the Church: Women and Ministry from New Testament Times to the Present*. Grand Rapids: Zondervan, 1987.

U.S. Department of Justice, Bureau of Justice Statistics. Online at http://www.ojp.usdoj.gov/bjs/glance/d_jailag.htm (accessed November 10, 2004).

Vanhoozer, Kevin J. *Is There a Meaning in This Text?* Grand Rapids: Zondervan, 1998.

Van Leeuwen, Mary Stewart. *Gender and Grace*. Downers Grove, IL: InterVarsity, 1989.

——. *My Brother's Keeper: What the Social Sciences Do (and Don't) Tells Us about Masculinity*. Downers Grove, IL: InterVarsity, 2002.

Verner, David C. *The Household of God: The Social World of the Pastoral Epistles*. Society of Biblical Literature Dissertation Series 71. Chico, CA: Scholars Press, 1983.

Voegelin, Ernst. *Science, Politics, and Gnosticism*. Chicago: Regnery, 1968.

Wall, Robert W. "1 Timothy 2:9–15 Reconsidered (Again)." *Bulletin for Biblical Research* 14 (2004): 81–103.

Wallace, Daniel B. *Greek Grammar beyond the Basics: An Exegetical Syntax of the New Testament*. Grand Rapids: Zondervan, 1996.

Wallerstein, Judith S., and Sandra Blakeslee. *Second Chances*. New York: Ticknor & Fields, 1989.

Waltke, Bruce K. "1 Timothy 2:8–15: Unique or Normative?" *Crux* 28 (1992): 22–23, 26–27.

Wankel, Hermann, et al., eds. *Die Inschriften von Ephesos*. 8 vols. Bonn: Habelt, 1979–84.

Warden, Preston Duane, and Roger S. Bagnall. "The Forty Thousand Citizens of Ephesus." *Classical Philology* 83 (1988): 220–23.

Webb, William J. "The Limits of a Redemptive-Movement Hermeneutic: A Focused Response to T. R. Schreiner." *Evangelical Quarterly* 75 (2003): 327–42.

———. *Slaves, Women and Homosexuals: Exploring the Hermeneutics of Cultural Analysis.* Downers Grove, IL: InterVarsity, 2001.

Wenham, Gordon J. "The Ordination of Women: Why Is It So Divisive?" *The Churchman* 92 (1978): 310–19.

———. *Story as Torah.* Grand Rapids: Baker, 2004.

Whitehead, Barbara Defoe. "Dan Quayle Was Right." *Atlantic Monthly,* April 1993, 47–84.

Wiebe, Ben. "Two Texts on Women (1 Tim 2:11–15; Gal 3:26–29): A Test of Interpretation." *Horizons in Biblical Theology* 16 (1994): 54–85.

Willard, Frances E. *Women in the Pulpit.* Boston: Lothrop, 1888.

Wilshire, Leland E. "1 Timothy 2:12 Revisited: A Reply to Paul W. Barnett and Timothy J. Harris." *Evangelical Quarterly* 65 (1993): 43–55.

———. "The TLG Computer and Further Reference to ΑΥΘΕΝΤΕΩ in 1 Timothy 2.12." *New Testament Studies* 34 (1988): 120–34.

Wilson, J. Q. *The Marriage Problem: How Our Culture Has Weakened Families.* New York: HarperCollins, 2002.

Winter, Bruce W. "The 'New' Roman Wife and 1 Timothy 2:9–15: The Search for a *Sitz im Leben.*" *Tyndale Bulletin* 51 (2000): 285–94.

———. *Roman Wives, Roman Widows: The Appearance of New Women and the Pauline Communities.* Grand Rapids: Eerdmans, 2003.

Witherington, Ben, III. *Women and the Genesis of Christianity.* Cambridge: Cambridge University Press, 1990.

———. *Women in the Earliest Churches.* Society for New Testament Studies Monograph Series 59. Cambridge: Cambridge University Press, 1988.

———. *Women in the Ministry of Jesus.* Society for New Testament Studies Monograph Series 51. Cambridge: Cambridge University Press, 1984.

Wohlers-Scharf, Traute. *Die Forschungsgeschichte von Ephesos.* 2nd ed. Europäische Hochschulschriften 38, vol. 54. Frankfurt am Main: Lang, 1996.

Wolters, Albert. Review of *I Suffer Not a Woman,* by Richard Clark Kroeger and Catherine Clark Kroeger. *Calvin Theological Journal* 28 (1993): 208–13.

———. Review of *Male and Female, One in Christ: New Testament Teaching on Women in Office,* by Clarence Boomsma. *Calvin Theological Journal* 29 (1994): 278–85.

———. "A Semantic Study of Αὐθέντης and Its Derivatives." *Journal of Greco-Roman Christianity and Judaism* 1 (2000): 145–75. Online at http://divinity.mcmaster.ca/pages/jgrchj/JGRChJ1-8_Wolters.pdf (accessed November 10, 2004).

Wondra, E. K. "By Whose Authority? The Status of Scripture in Contemporary Feminist Theologies." *Anglican Theological Review* 74, no. 1 (1993): 83–101.

Wright, Conrad. *The Beginnings of Unitarianism in America*. Hamden, CT: Shoe String, 1976.

Wright, Robert. "Infidelity: It May Be in Our Genes." *Time,* August 15, 1994, 28–36.

Yamauchi, Edwin. "Ramsay's Views on Archeology in Asia Minor Reviewed." In *The New Testament Student and His Field,* edited by J. Skilton, 27–40. New Testament Student 5. Phillipsburg, NJ: Presbyterian & Reformed, 1982.

Yarbrough, Robert W. "*I Suffer Not a Woman*: A Review Essay." *Presbyterion* 18, no. 1 (1992): 25–33.

———. "New Light on Paul and Woman?" *Christianity Today* 37, no. 11 (October 4, 1993): 68–70.

Zaidman, Louise Bruit, and Pauline Schmitt Pantel. *Religion in the Ancient Greek City*. Translated by P. Cartledge. Cambridge: Cambridge University Press, 1992.

Zerwick, Maximilian, and Mary Grosvenor. *A Grammatical Analysis of the Greek New Testament*. 4th ed. Rome: Pontifical Biblical Institute, 1996.

Ziegler, K., and W. Sontheimer, eds. *Der Kleine Pauly*. 5 vols. Munich: Deutscher Taschenbuch, 1979.

INDEX OF SCRIPTURE

INDEX OF ANCIENT AUTHORS

INDEX OF MODERN AUTHORS

INDEX OF SUBJECTS